STAN LEE PRESENTS

A MARVEL COMICS PRODUCTION

SECRET WAR

BRIAN MICHAEL BENDIS
WRITER

**VIRTUAL CALLIGRAPHY'S
CORY PETIT**
LETTERER

**NICOLE WILEY, AUBREY SITTERSON
& MOLLY LAZER**
ASSISTANT EDITORS

ANDY SCHMIDT
EDITOR

TOM BREVOORT
CONSULTING EDITOR

MARK D. BEAZLEY
COLLECTION EDITOR

JENNIFER GRÜNWALD
ASSOCIATE EDITOR

MICHAEL SHORT
ASSISTANT EDITOR

GABRIELE DELL'OTTO
PAINTER

JEFF YOUNGQUIST
SENIOR EDITOR,
SPECIAL PROJECTS

DAVID GABRIEL
VICE PRESIDENT OF SALES

JERRY KALINOWSKI
PRODUCTION

PATRICK MCGRATH
BOOK DESIGNER

TOM MARVELLI
CREATIVE DIRECTOR

JOE QUESADA
EDITOR IN CHIEF

DAN BUCKLEY
PUBLISHER

SPECIAL THANKS TO ADAM CICHOWSKI, PATRICK MCGRATH, & OMAR OTIEKU.

SECRET WAR. Contains material originally published in magazine form as SECRET WAR #1-5 and SECRET WAR: FROM THE FILES OF NICK FURY. First printing 2005. ISBN# 0-7851-1837-3. Published by MARVEL PUBLISHING, INC., A SUBSIDIARY OF MARVEL ENTERTAINMENT, INC. OFFICE OF PUBLICATION: 417 5th Avenue, New York, NY 10016. Copyright © 2004 and 2005 Marvel Characters, Inc. All rights reserved. $29.99 per copy in the U.S. and $48.00 in Canada (GST #R127032852); Canadian Agreement #40668537. All characters featured in this issue and the distinctive names and likenesses thereof, and all related indicia are trademarks of Marvel Characters, Inc. No similarity between any of the names, characters, persons, and/or institutions in this magazine with those of any living or dead person or institution is intended, and any such similarity which may exist is purely coincidental. **Printed in the U.S.A.** AVI ARAD, Chief Creative Officer; ALAN FINE, President & CEO Of Marvel Toys and Marvel Publishing, Inc.; DAVID BOGART, VP Of Publishing Operations; DAN CARR, Director of Production; JUSTIN F. GABRIE, Managing Editor; STAN LEE, Chairman Emeritus. For information regarding advertising in Marvel Comics or on Marvel.com, please contact Joe Maimone, Advertising Director, at jmaimone@marvel.com or 212-576-8534.

SCORPION_

CAPTAIN AMERICA_

UNKNOWN_

MARY JANE WATSON-PARKER_

THING_
SCORPION_

CYCL

BY ANONYMOUS

I can't tell you who I am. I can't tell you what I do for a living. All I can say is that I am a high ranking officer in the intelligence community of the United States government, and I've known Brian Bendis since he was a toddler.

Outside of his parents, very few people can appreciate how pure Brian's dreams and goals were to become a comic book creator, and how amazing it is that all of those dreams have come true. Little did I know my true life would become fodder for Brian's additions to the legends of Marvel Comics.

When Brian became old enough to understand exactly what it was I did for a living, his curiosity was unquenchable. Every moment we had together was a game of twenty questions. I thought that Brian was going to grow up and join the ranks of the intelligence community. I thought I was talking to "one of us." What I didn't understand at the time was that seeds were being planted - an imagination was being fueled. Now that I think back, it wouldn't surprise me to find that he went back to his room and wrote everything I told him down in notebooks and saved it for years and years.

The stories I told Brian were stories I know I should not have shared. They were stories that were very much illegal to share. And now here they are in this graphic novel called *SECRET WAR*. All of it. Except the super heroes.

Yes, many of the scenes in this comic actually happened. Conversations are transcribed almost verbatim from my recollection. The conflict, danger, intrigue... all of it is true. Except the super heroes.

In fact, when telling young Brian about a debriefing with the president about our own secret war in the early eighties - and I remember calling it a secret war - Young Brian said to me: "you know there's a comic called *SECRET WARS*, but this secret war sounds cooler."

I explained that though lives were saved in our war, real people did die. Young Brian said, "Yes, but that doesn't make the story any less interesting. They should make a comic of this secret war." I said: well, when you're older, maybe you will.

And here it is. Except with super heroes.

When Brian sent me the galley of the first chapters of the book you are about to read, I sat and read them awestruck. It was like looking into a mirror world of the one I called home. And I did something I rarely do, I cried. It may have been the realization that I had made such a profound effect on a young man, or the fact that Brian was so respectful of my words and memories. Either way I was profoundly moved. I hope you will be too.

The funny thing is, one day I may just write my own book. Maybe come clean and tell the world how their lives were kept safe fighting wars they never even heard about on TV or in the paper. I'll tell my tales, and I'll put it out there for the world to see. And someone somewhere will read it, and think to themselves, "Wait, didn't I read this is in a comic book?"

Congratulations Brian and Gabriele. You made it all worthwhile for this old war horse.

Wish I had an eye patch. It's a great look.

Anonymous.
Washington DC, 2006

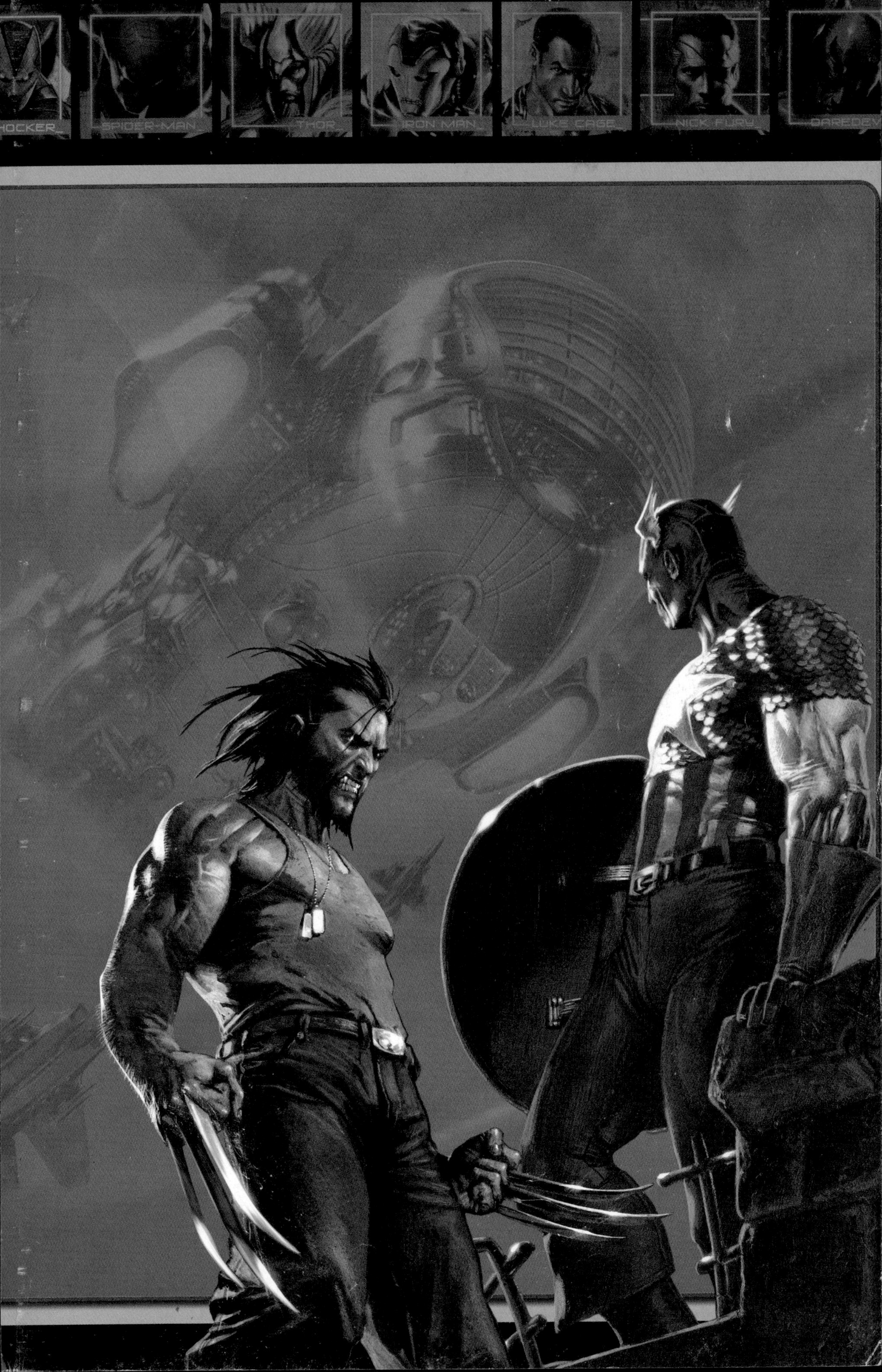

SPIDER-MAN
THOR
IRON MAN
LUKE CAGE
NICK FURY

SECRET WAR

BOOK ONE OF FIVE

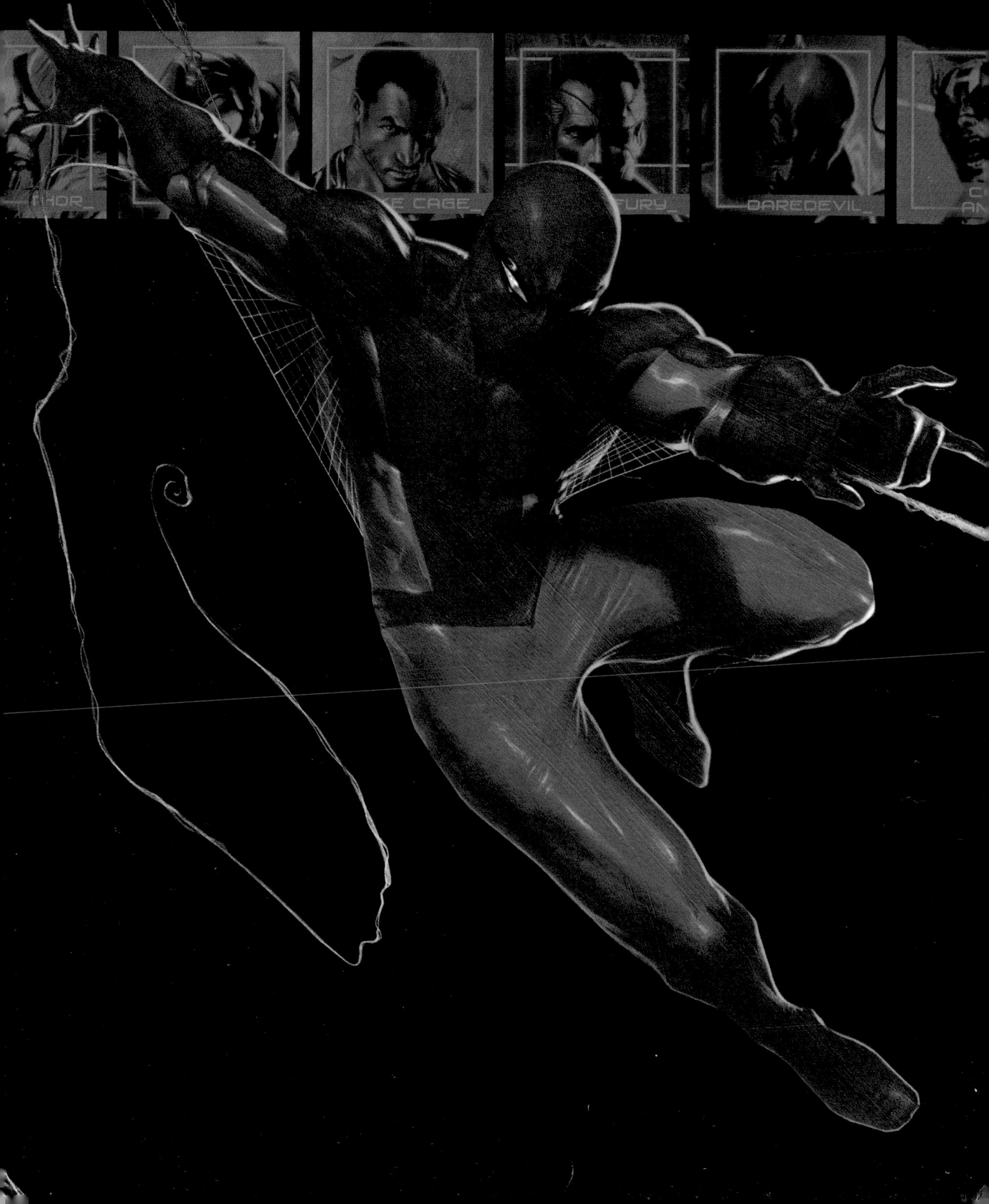
THOR_
DAREDEVIL_

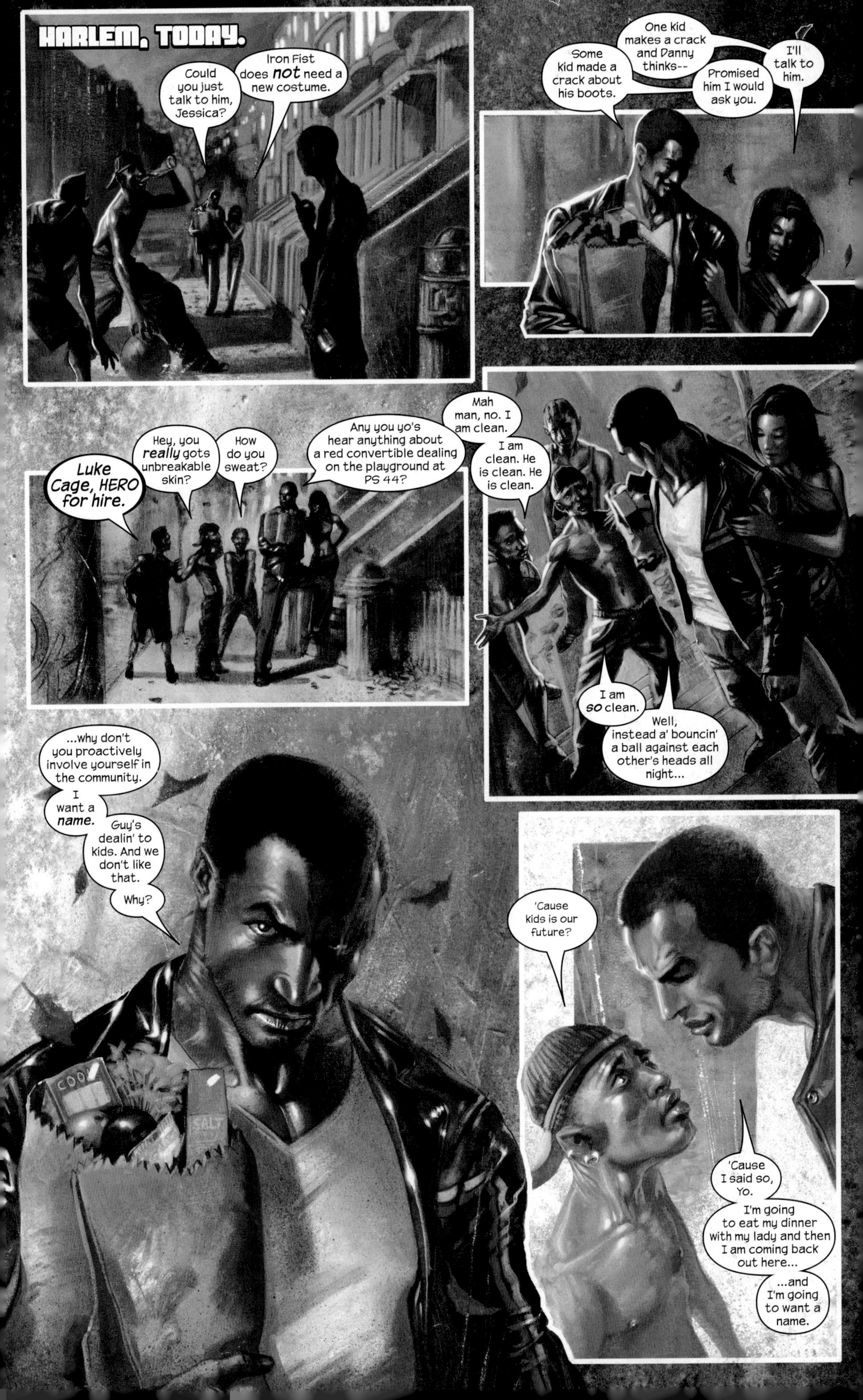
HARLEM, TODAY.
Could you just talk to him, Jessica?
Iron Fist does not need a new costume.
Some kid made a crack about his boots.
One kid makes a crack and Danny thinks--
Promised him I would ask you.
I'll talk to him.
Luke Cage, HERO for hire.
Hey, you really gots unbreakable skin?
How do you sweat?
Any you yo's hear anything about a red convertible dealing on the playground at PS 44?
Mah man, no. I am clean.
I am clean. He is clean. He is clean.
I am so clean.
Well, instead a' bouncin' a ball against each other's heads all night...
...why don't you proactively involve yourself in the community.
I want a name.
Guy's dealin' to kids. And we don't like that.
Why?
'Cause kids is our future?
'Cause I said so, Yo.
I'm going to eat my dinner with my lady and then I am coming back out here...
...and I'm going to want a name.

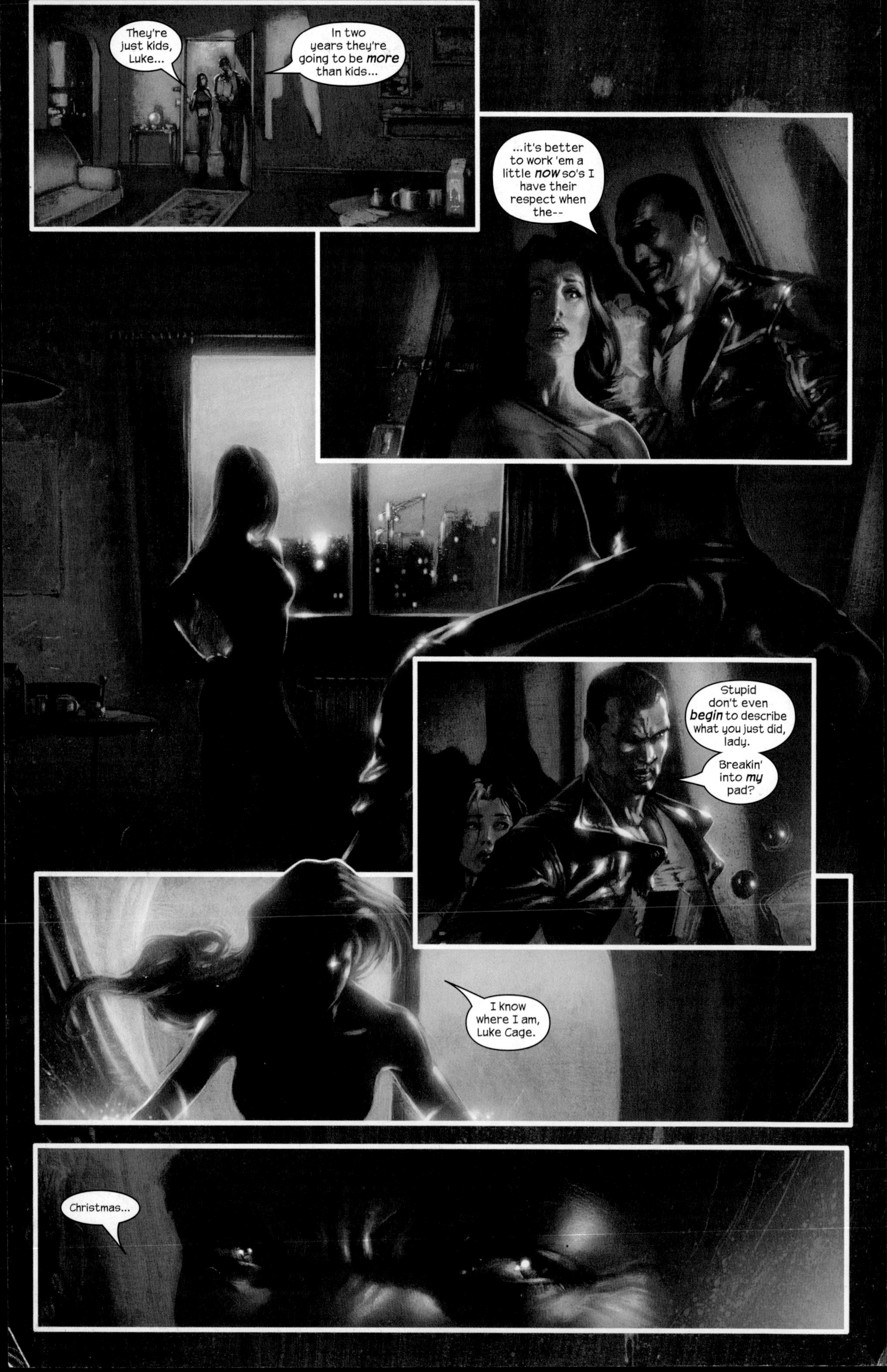
They're just kids, Luke...
In two years they're going to be more than kids...
...it's better to work 'em a little now so's I have their respect when the--
Stupid don't even begin to describe what you just did, lady.
Breakin' into my pad?
I know where I am, Luke Cage.
Christmas...

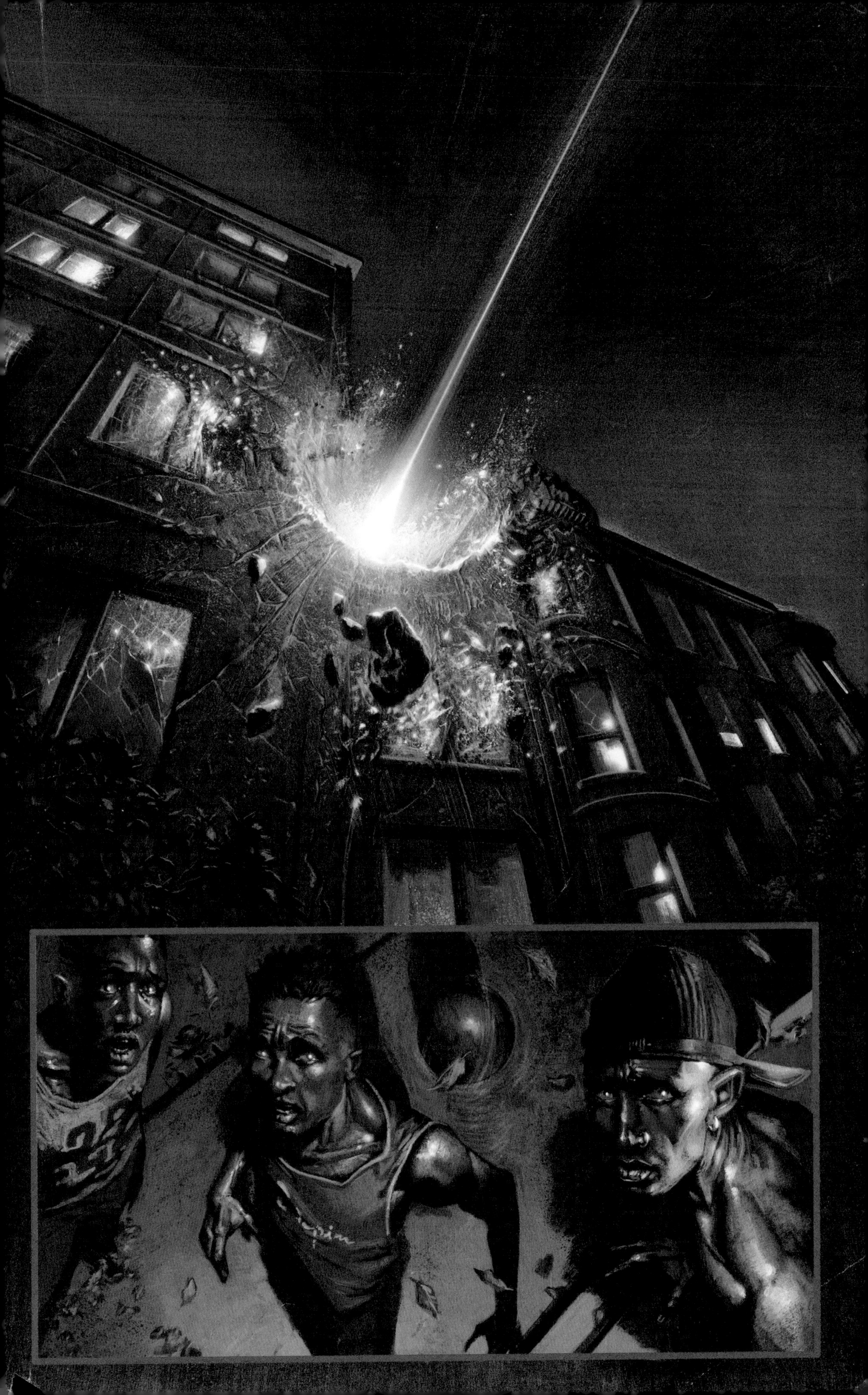

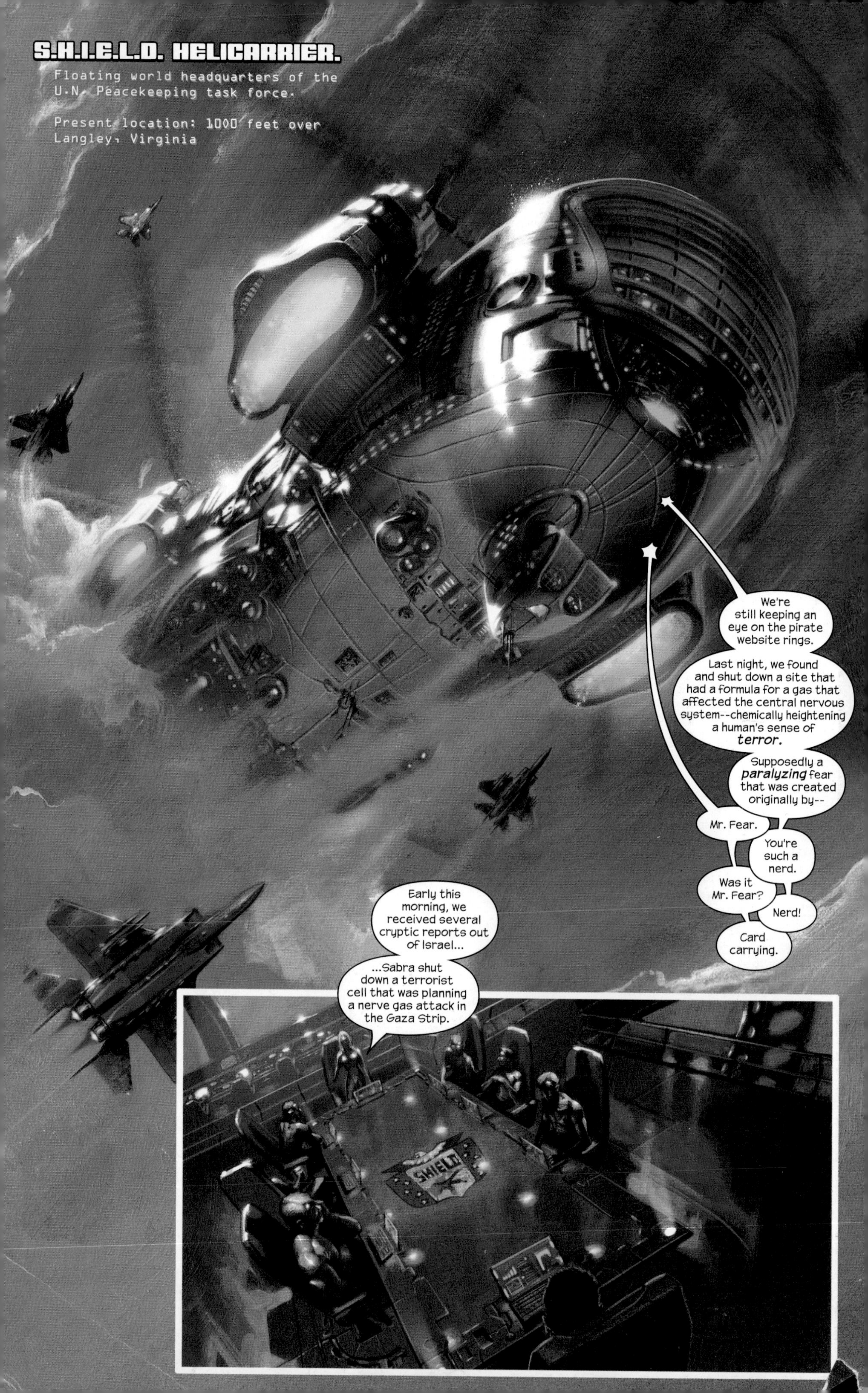
S.H.I.E.L.D. HELICARRIER.
Floating world headquarters of the U.N. Peacekeeping task force.
Present location: 1000 feet over Langley, Virginia
We're still keeping an eye on the pirate website rings.
Last night, we found and shut down a site that had a formula for a gas that affected the central nervous system--chemically heightening a human's sense of *terror.*
Supposedly a *paralyzing* fear that was created originally by--
Mr. Fear.
You're such a nerd.
Was it Mr. Fear?
Nerd!
Card carrying.
Early this morning, we received several cryptic reports out of Israel...
...Sabra shut down a terrorist cell that was planning a nerve gas attack in the Gaza Strip.
SHIELD

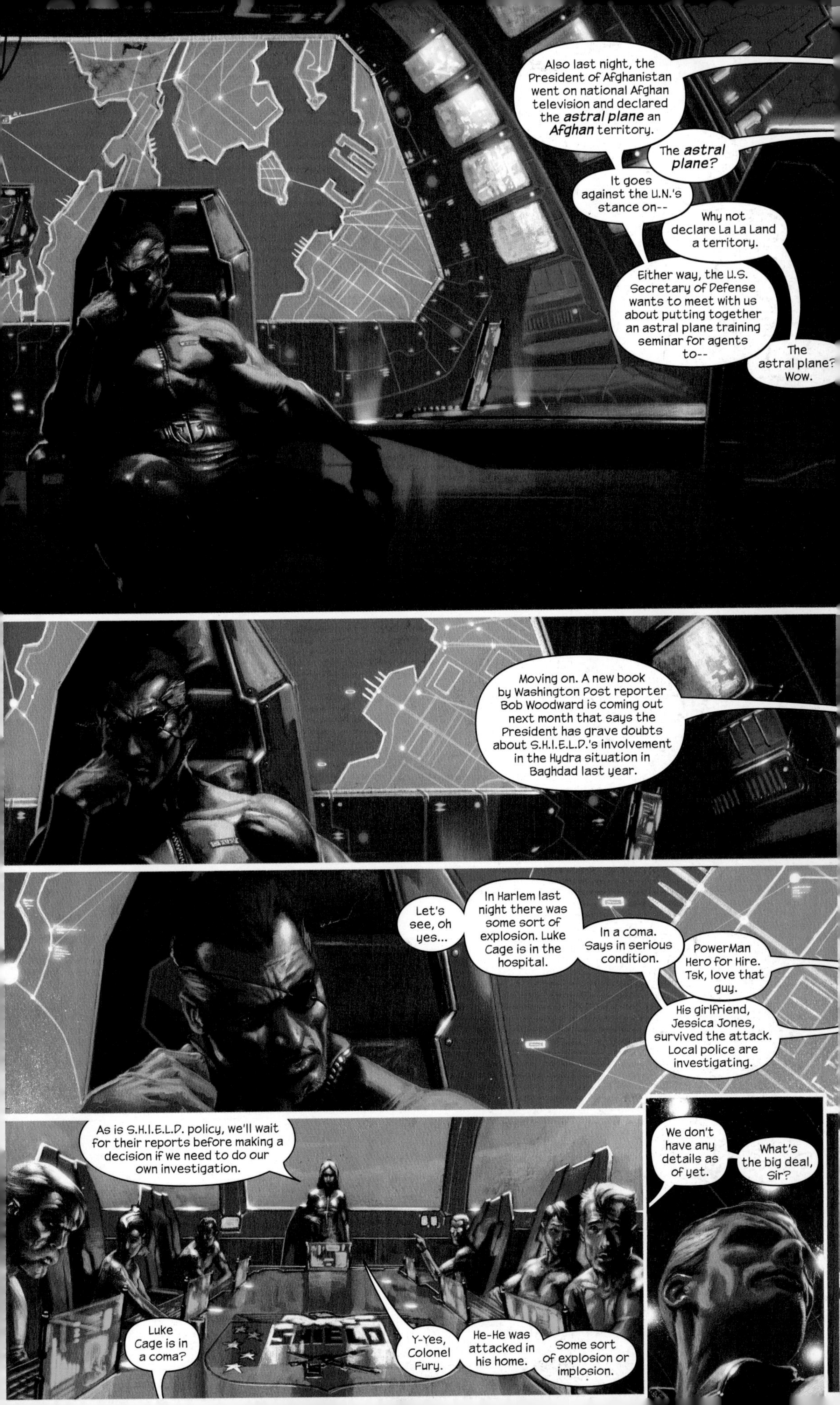

Also last night, the President of Afghanistan went on national Afghan television and declared the *astral plane* an *Afghan* territory.
The *astral plane?*
It goes against the U.N.'s stance on--
Why not declare La La Land a territory.
Either way, the U.S. Secretary of Defense wants to meet with us about putting together an astral plane training seminar for agents to--
The astral plane? Wow.
Moving on. A new book by Washington Post reporter Bob Woodward is coming out next month that says the President has grave doubts about S.H.I.E.L.D.'s involvement in the Hydra situation in Baghdad last year.
Let's see, oh yes...
In Harlem last night there was some sort of explosion. Luke Cage is in the hospital.
In a coma. Says in serious condition.
PowerMan Hero for Hire. Tsk, love that guy.
His girlfriend, Jessica Jones, survived the attack. Local police are investigating.
As is S.H.I.E.L.D. policy, we'll wait for their reports before making a decision if we need to do our own investigation.
Luke Cage is in a coma?
Y-Yes, Colonel Fury.
He-He was attacked in his home.
Some sort of explosion or implosion.
We don't have any details as of yet.
What's the big deal, Sir?

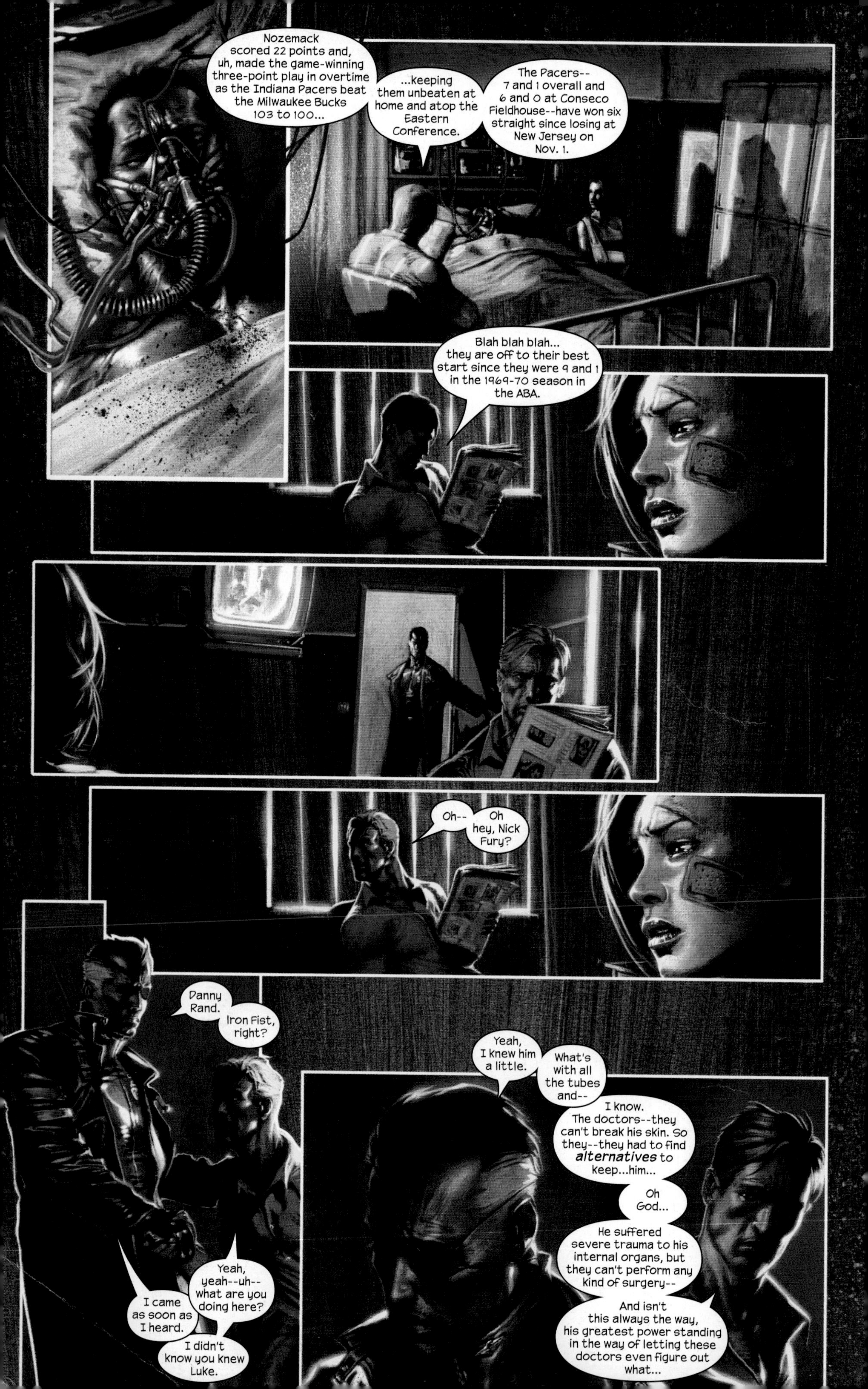
Nozemack scored 22 points and, uh, made the game-winning three-point play in overtime as the Indiana Pacers beat the Milwaukee Bucks 103 to 100...
...keeping them unbeaten at home and atop the Eastern Conference.
The Pacers-- 7 and 1 overall and 6 and 0 at Conseco Fieldhouse--have won six straight since losing at New Jersey on Nov. 1.
Blah blah blah... they are off to their best start since they were 9 and 1 in the 1969-70 season in the ABA.
Oh--
Oh hey, Nick Fury?
Danny Rand.
Iron Fist, right?
I came as soon as I heard.
Yeah, yeah--uh--what are you doing here?
I didn't know you knew Luke.
Yeah, I knew him a little.
What's with all the tubes and--
I know. The doctors--they can't break his skin. So they--they had to find *alternatives* to keep...him...
Oh God...
He suffered severe trauma to his internal organs, but they can't perform any kind of surgery--
And isn't this always the way, his greatest power standing in the way of letting these doctors even figure out what...

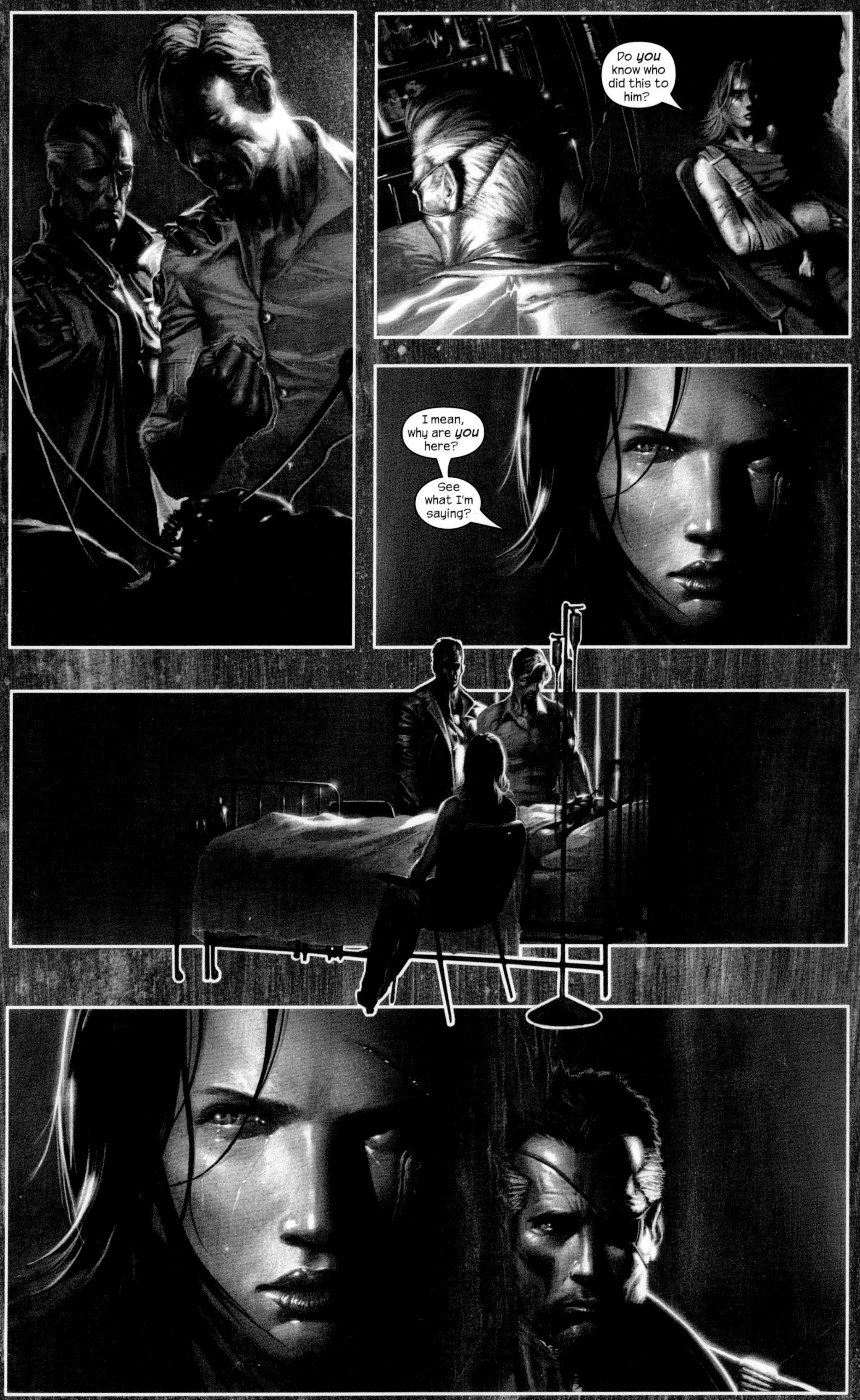
Do you know who did this to him?
I mean, why are you here?
See what I'm saying?

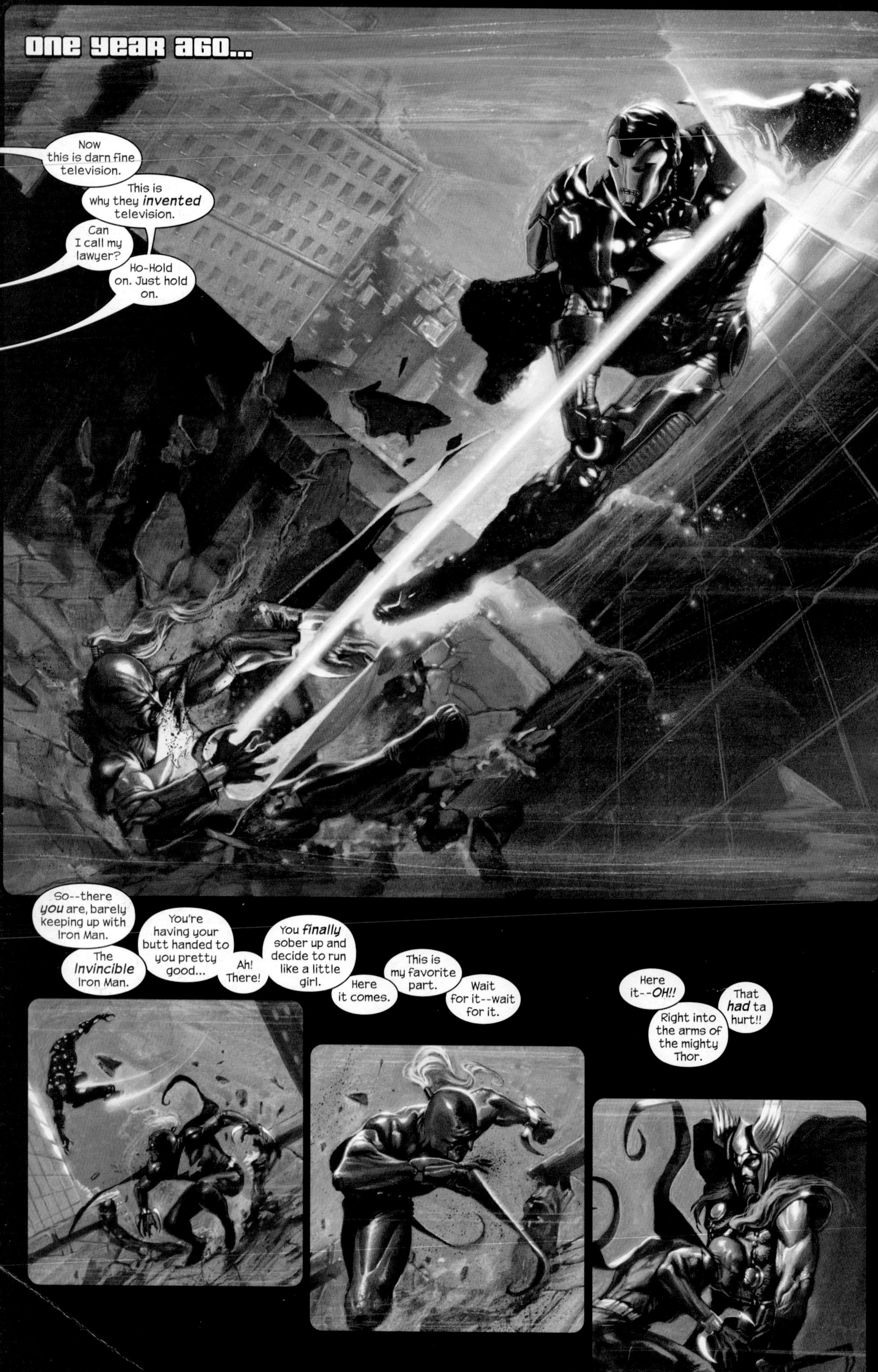
ONE YEAR AGO...
Now this is darn fine television.
This is why they *invented* television.
Can I call my lawyer?
Ho-Hold on. Just hold on.
So--there *you* are, barely keeping up with Iron Man.
The *Invincible* Iron Man.
You're having your butt handed to you pretty good...
Ah! There!
You *finally* sober up and decide to run like a little girl.
Here it comes.
This is my favorite part.
Wait for it--wait for it.
Here it--*OH!!*
Right into the arms of the mighty Thor.
That *had* ta hurt!!

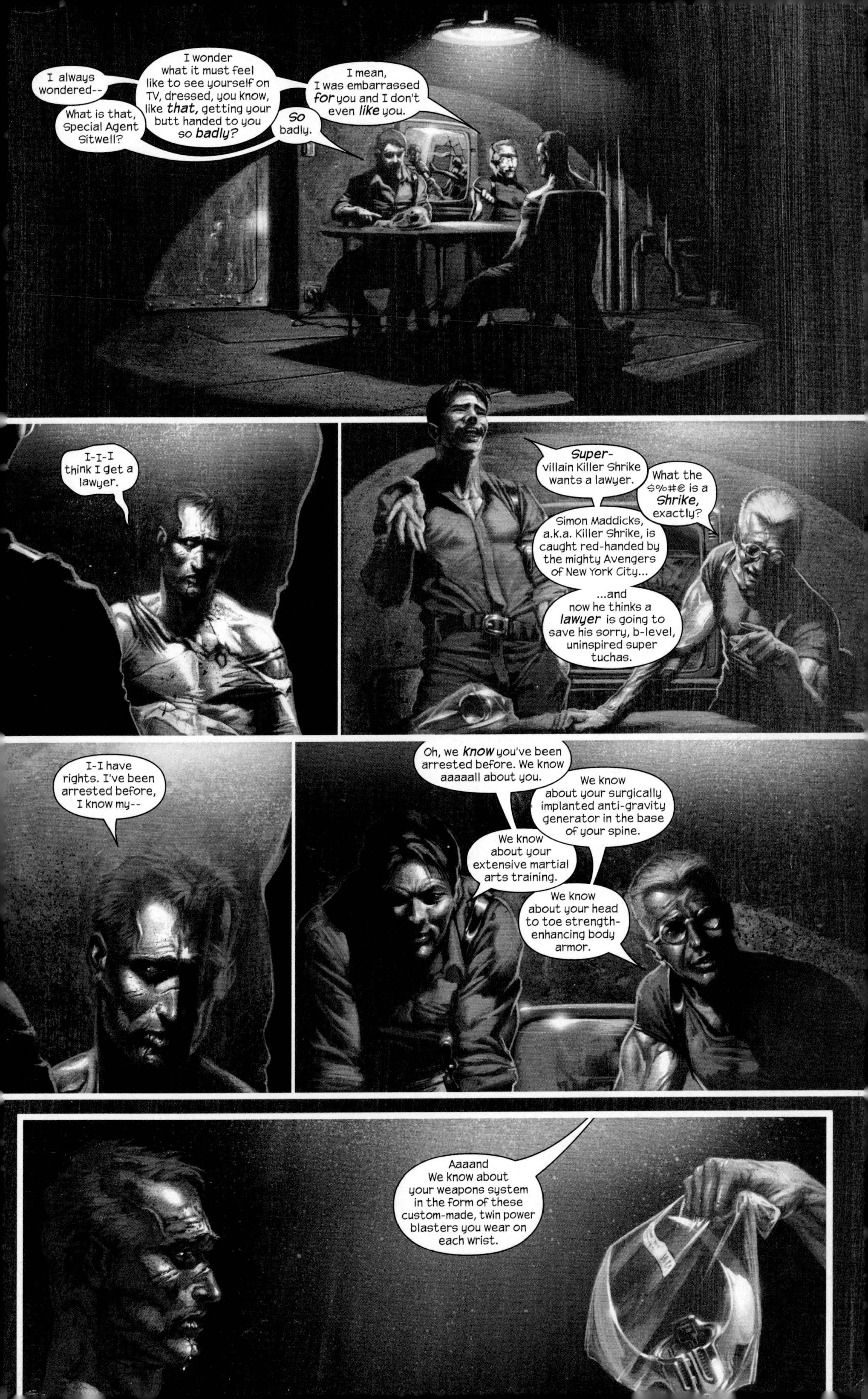
I always wondered--
I wonder what it must feel like to see yourself on TV, dressed, you know, like *that,* getting your butt handed to you so *badly?*
What is that, Special Agent Sitwell?
So badly.
I mean, I was embarrassed *for* you and I don't even *like* you.
I-I-I think I get a lawyer.
Super-villain Killer Shrike wants a lawyer.
What the $%#@ is a *Shrike,* exactly?
Simon Maddicks, a.k.a. Killer Shrike, is caught red-handed by the mighty Avengers of New York City...
...and now he thinks a *lawyer* is going to save his sorry, b-level, uninspired super tuchas.
I-I have rights. I've been arrested before, I know my--
Oh, we *know* you've been arrested before. We know aaaaall about you.
We know about your surgically implanted anti-gravity generator in the base of your spine.
We know about your extensive martial arts training.
We know about your head to toe strength-enhancing body armor.
Aaaand We know about your weapons system in the form of these custom-made, twin power blasters you wear on each wrist.

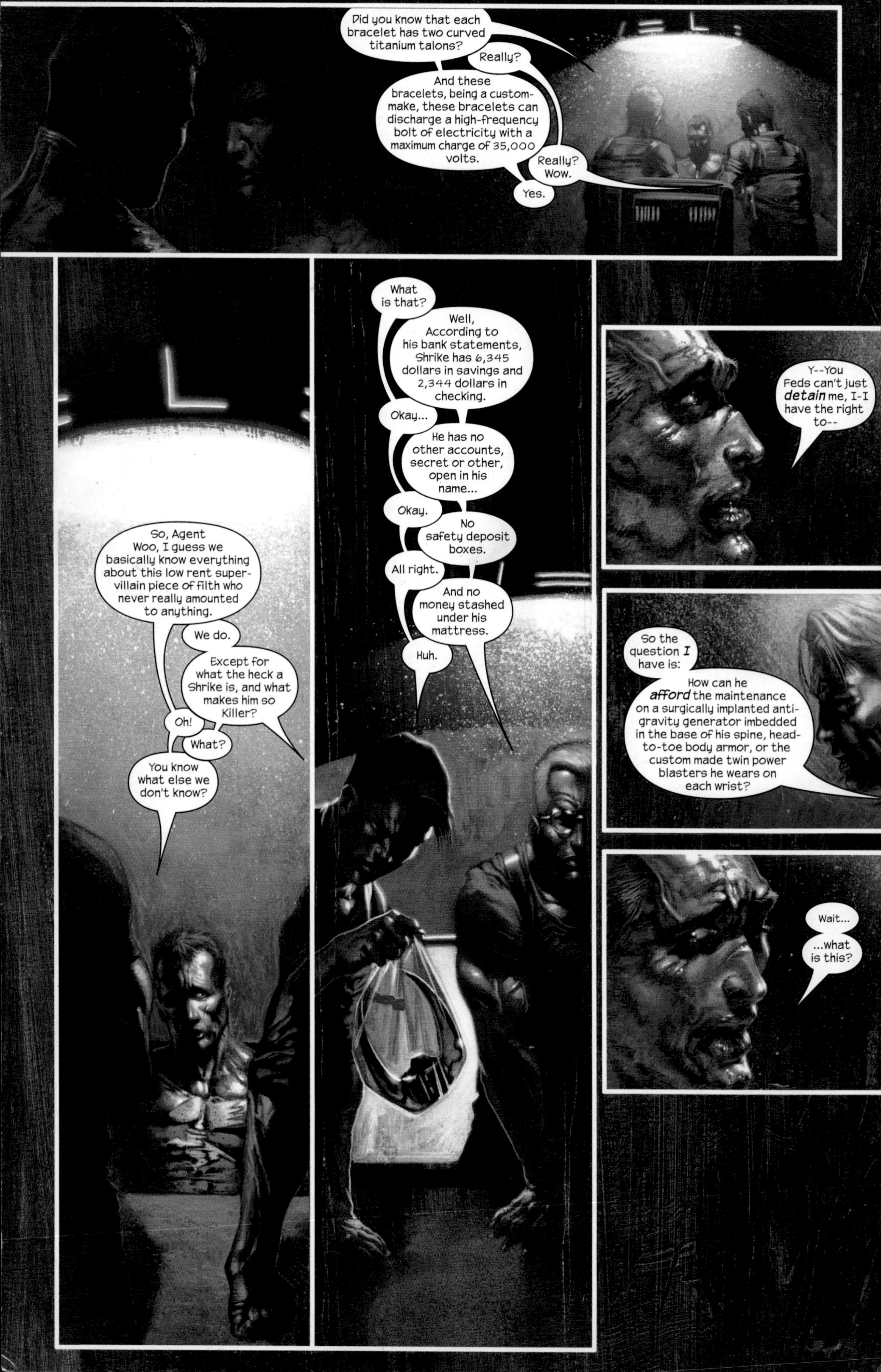
Did you know that each bracelet has two curved titanium talons?
Really?
And these bracelets, being a custom-make, these bracelets can discharge a high-frequency bolt of electricity with a maximum charge of 35,000 volts.
Really? Wow.
Yes.
So, Agent Woo, I guess we basically know everything about this low rent super-villain piece of filth who never really amounted to anything.
We do.
Except for what the heck a Shrike is, and what makes him so Killer?
Oh!
What?
You know what else we don't know?
What is that?
Well, According to his bank statements, Shrike has 6,345 dollars in savings and 2,344 dollars in checking.
Okay...
He has no other accounts, secret or other, open in his name...
Okay.
No safety deposit boxes.
All right.
And no money stashed under his mattress.
Huh.
Y--You Feds can't just *detain* me, I-I have the right to--
So the question *I* have is:
How can he *afford* the maintenance on a surgically implanted anti-gravity generator imbedded in the base of his spine, head-to-toe body armor, or the custom made twin power blasters he wears on each wrist?
Wait...
...what is this?

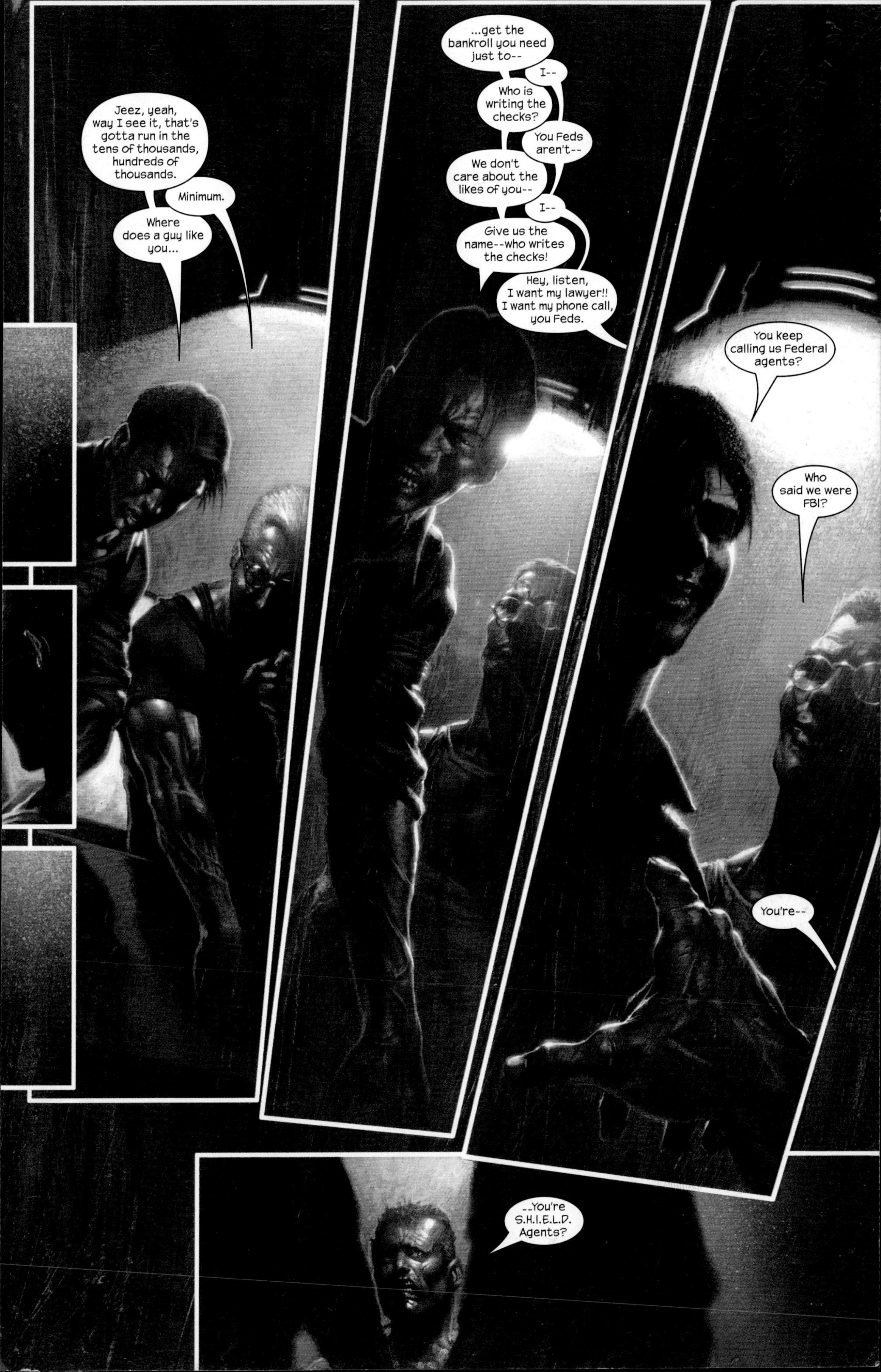
Jeez, yeah, way I see it, that's gotta run in the tens of thousands, hundreds of thousands.
Minimum.
Where does a guy like you...
...get the bankroll you need just to--
I--
Who is writing the checks?
You Feds aren't--
We don't care about the likes of you--
I--
Give us the name--who writes the checks!
Hey, listen, I want my lawyer!! I want my phone call, you Feds.
You keep calling us Federal agents?
Who said we were FBI?
You're--
--You're S.H.I.E.L.D. Agents?

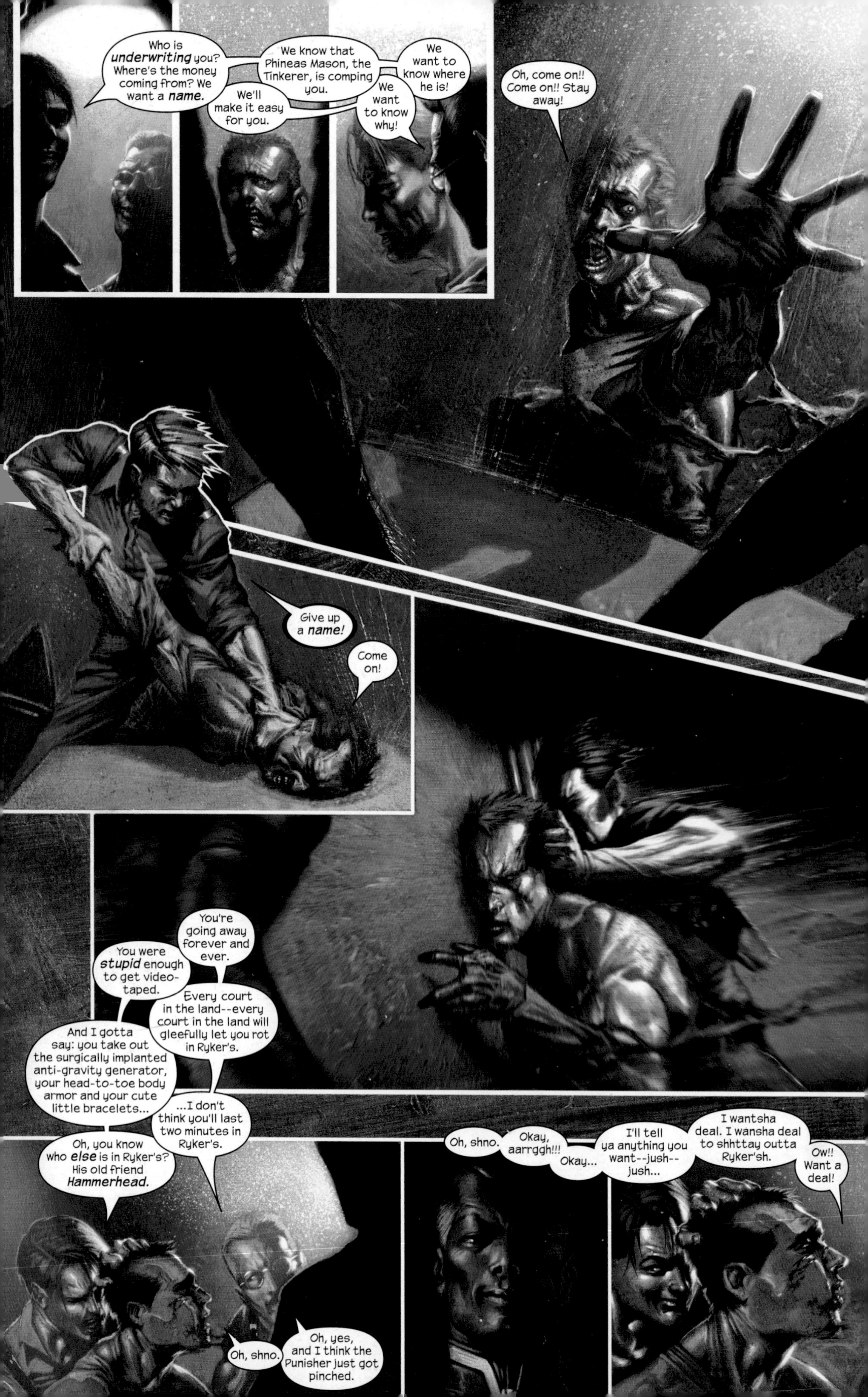
Who is *underwriting* you? Where's the money coming from? We want a *name.*
We know that Phineas Mason, the Tinkerer, is comping you.
We'll make it easy for you.
We want to know where he is!
We want to know why!
Oh, come on!! Come on!! Stay away!
Give up a *name!*
Come on!
You were *stupid* enough to get video-taped.
You're going away forever and ever.
Every court in the land--every court in the land will gleefully let you rot in Ryker's.
And I gotta say: you take out the surgically implanted anti-gravity generator, your head-to-toe body armor and your cute little bracelets...
...I don't think you'll last two minutes in Ryker's.
Oh, you know who *else* is in Ryker's? His old friend *Hammerhead.*
Oh, shno.
Oh, yes, and I think the Punisher just got pinched.
Oh, shno.
Okay, aarrggh!!!
Okay...
I'll tell ya anything you want--jush--jush...
I wantsha deal. I wansha deal to shhttay outta Ryker'sh.
Ow!! Want a deal!

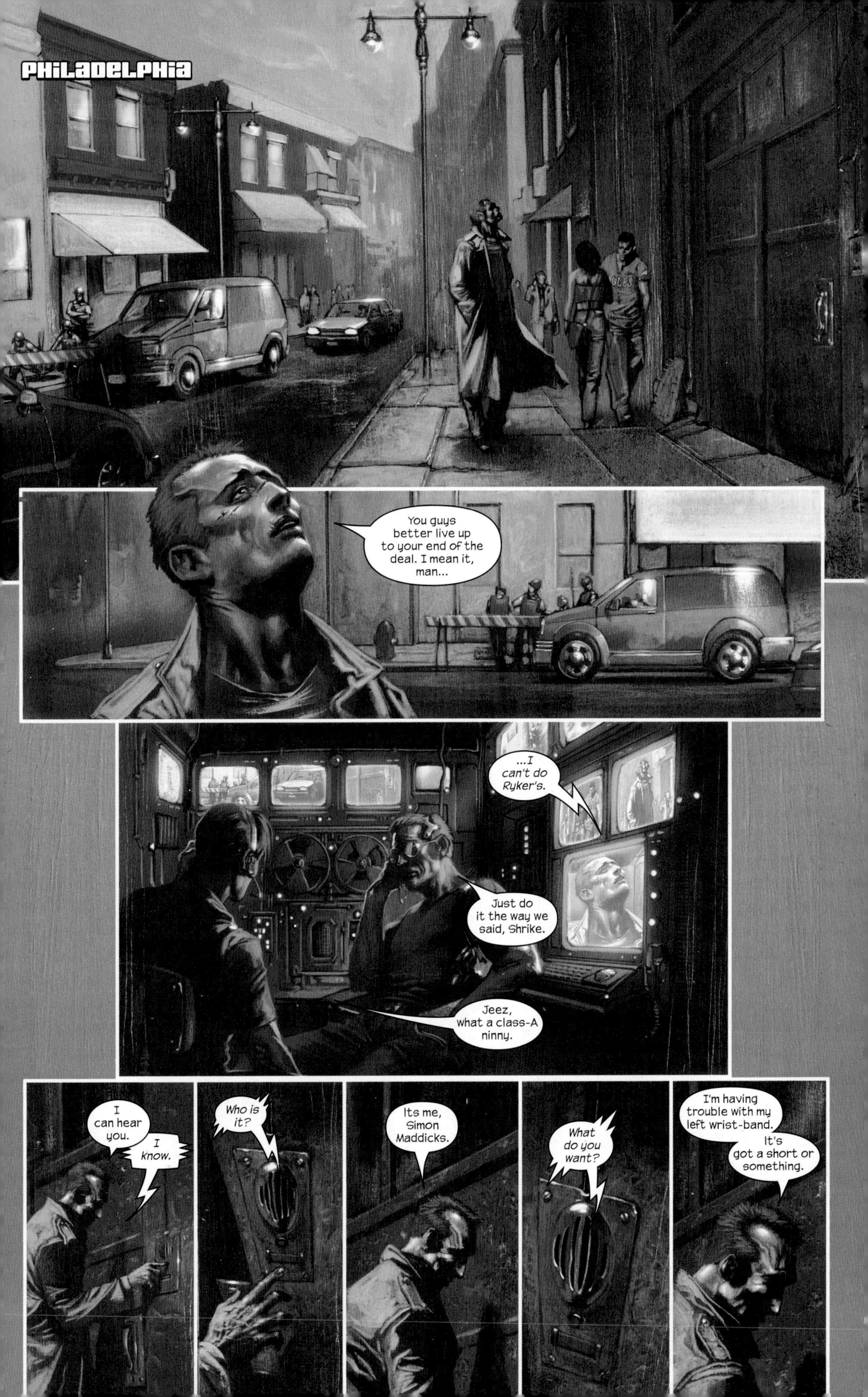
PHILADELPHIA
You guys better live up to your end of the deal. I mean it, man...
...I can't do Ryker's.
Just do it the way we said, Shrike.
Jeez, what a class-A ninny.
I can hear you.
I know.
Who is it?
Its me, Simon Maddicks.
What do you want?
I'm having trouble with my left wrist-band.
It's got a short or something.

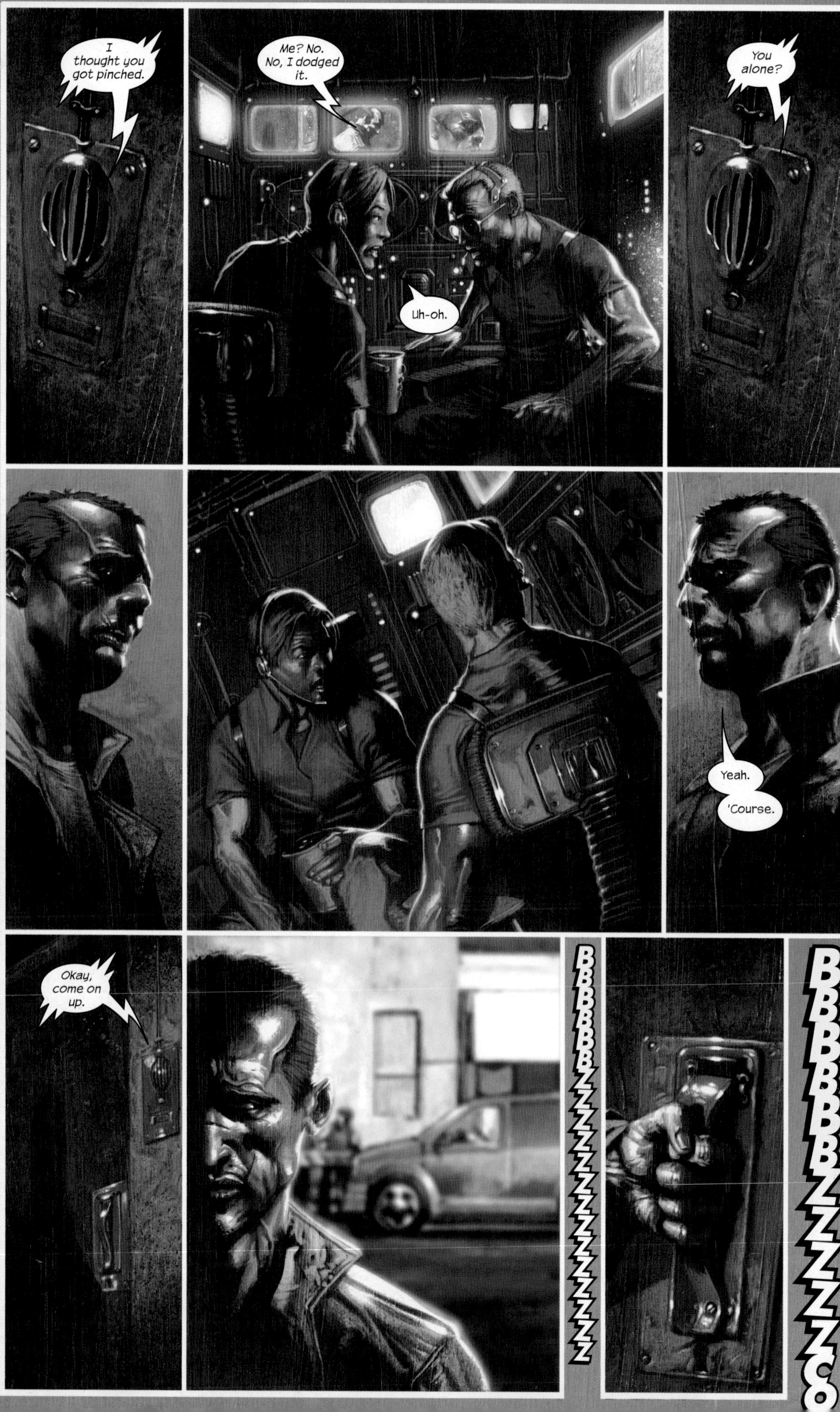
I thought you got pinched.
Me? No. No, I dodged it.
Uh-oh.
You alone?
Yeah.
'Course.
Okay, come on up.
BBBBBBZZZZZZZZZZZZZZ
BBBBBBBZZZZZZZO

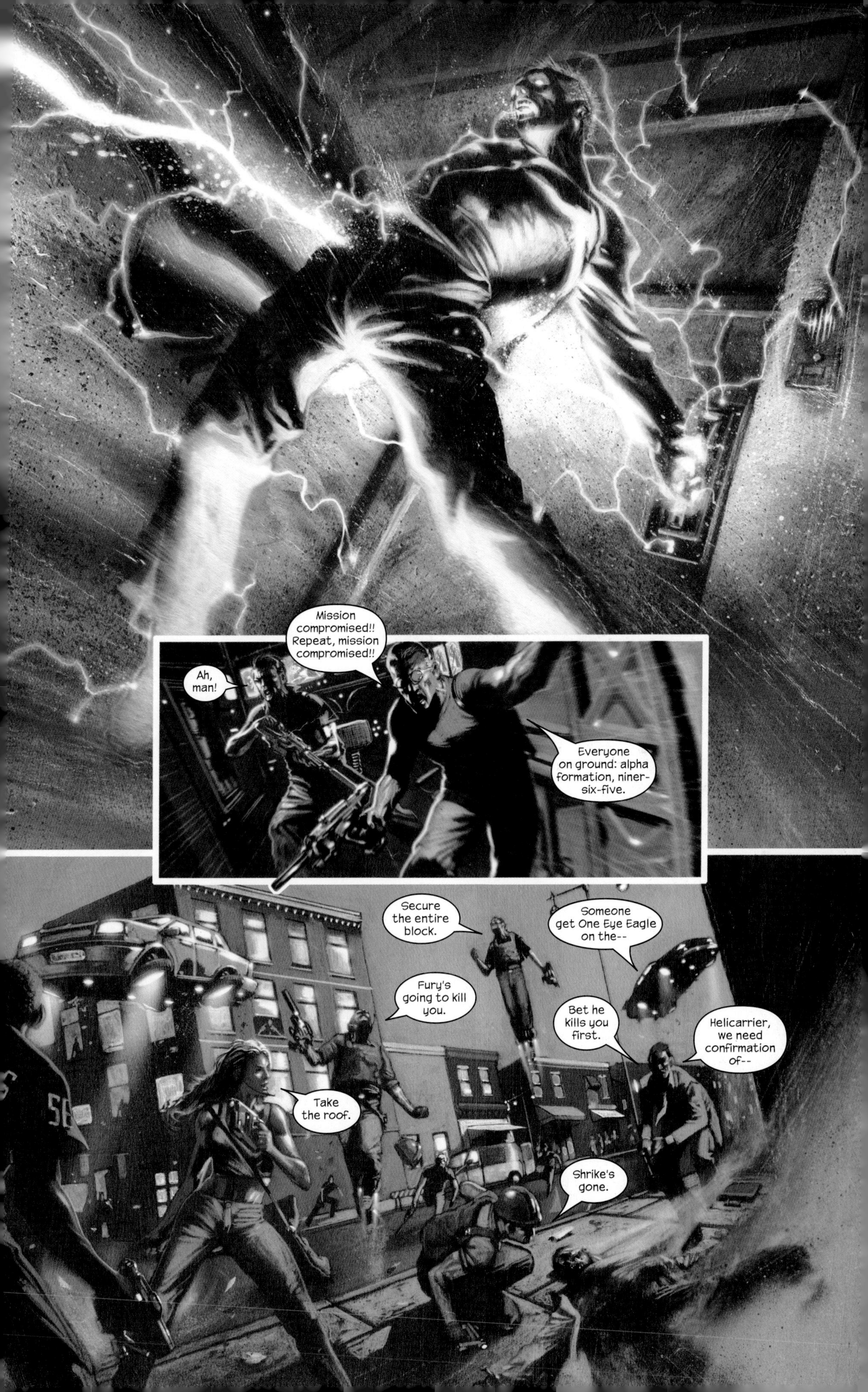
Mission compromised!! Repeat, mission compromised!!
Ah, man!
Everyone on ground: alpha formation, niner-six-five.
Secure the entire block.
Someone get One Eye Eagle on the--
Fury's going to kill you.
Bet he kills you first.
Helicarrier, we need confirmation of--
Take the roof.
Shrike's gone.

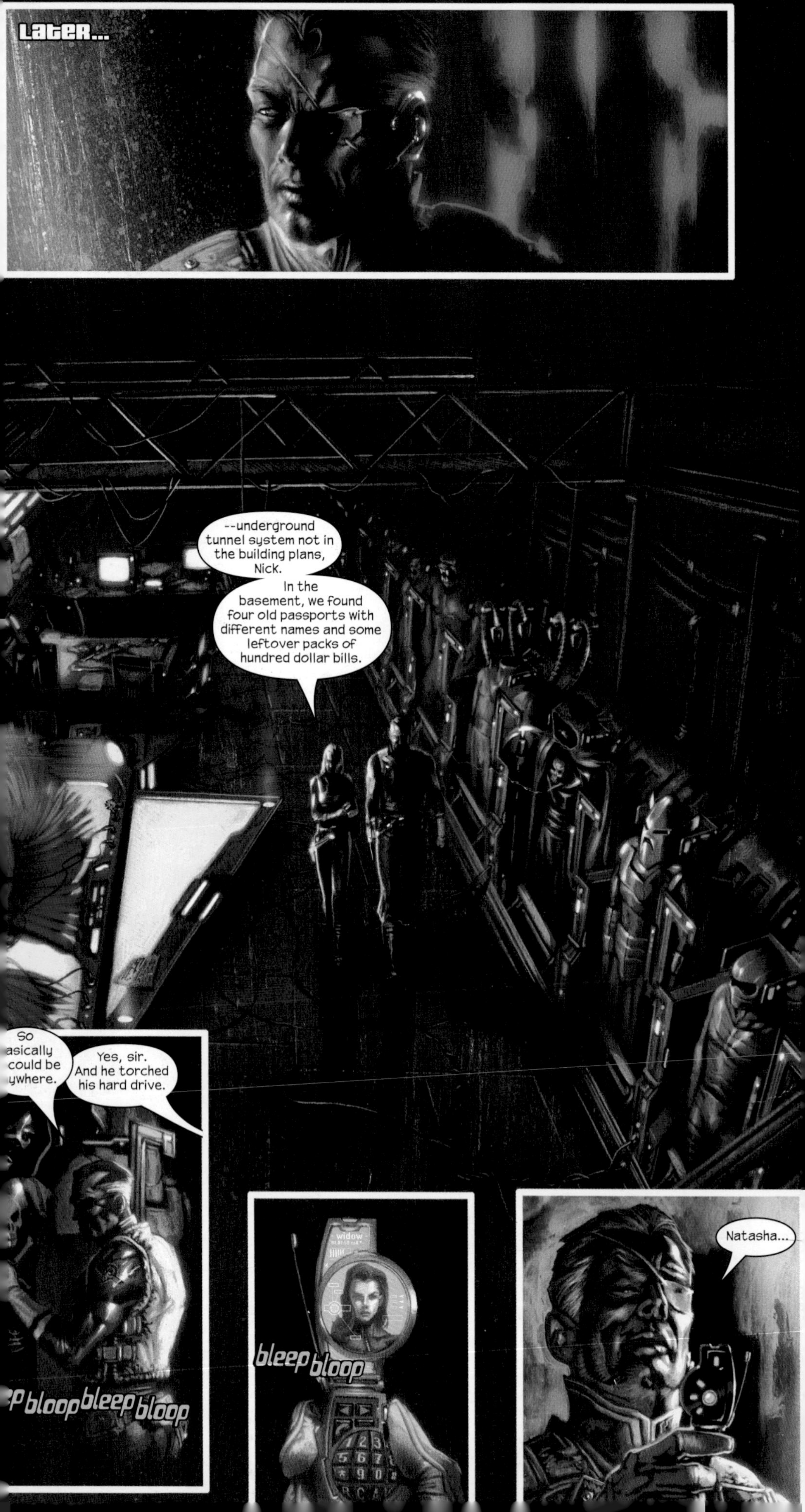
LATER...
--underground tunnel system not in the building plans, Nick.
In the basement, we found four old passports with different names and some leftover packs of hundred dollar bills.
So asically could be ywhere.
Yes, sir. And he torched his hard drive.
p bloop bleep bloop
widow
bleep bloop
Natasha...

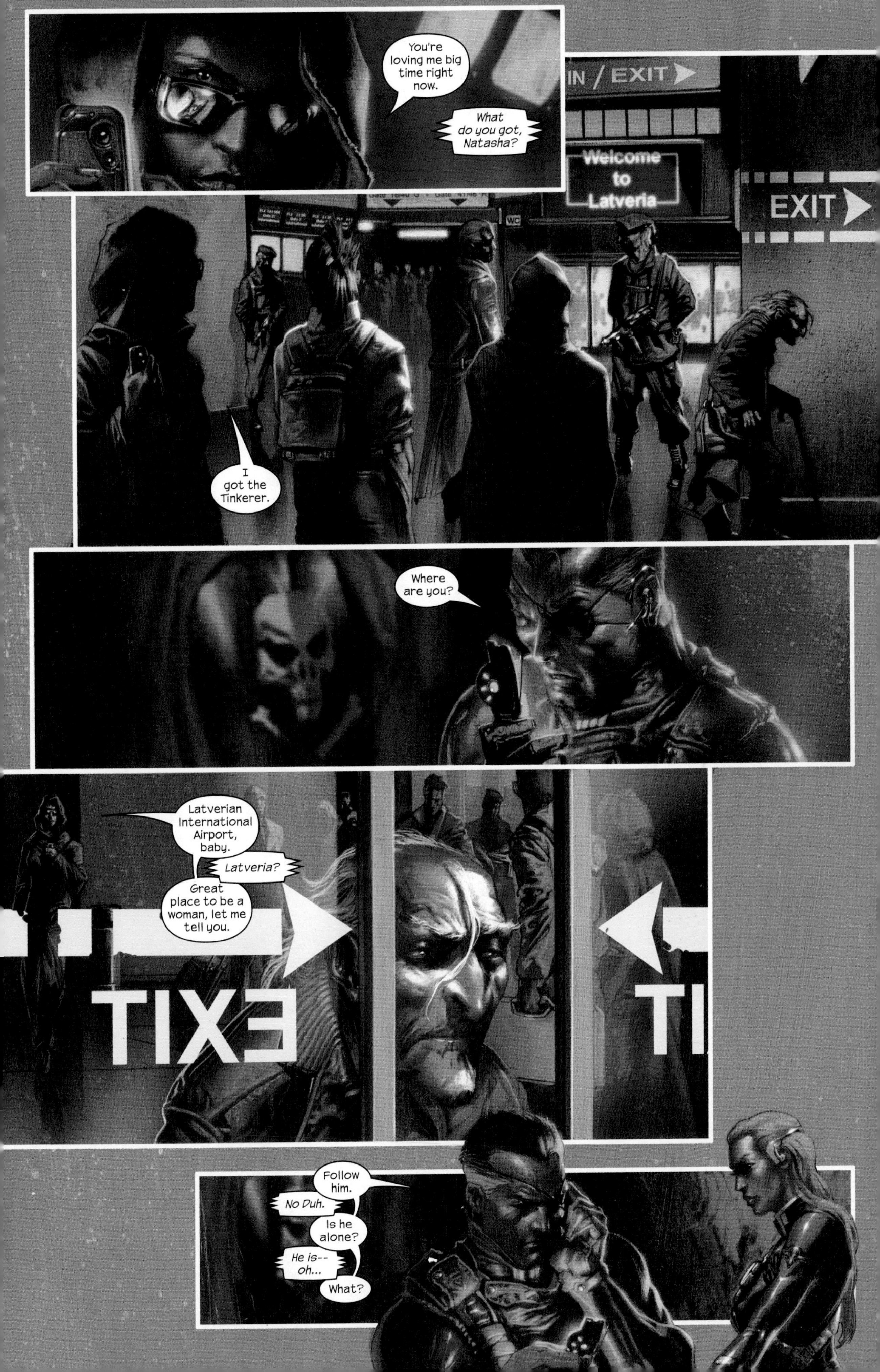

You're loving me big time right now.
What do you got, Natasha?
IN / EXIT
Welcome to Latveria
EXIT
I got the Tinkerer.
Where are you?
Latverian International Airport, baby.
Latveria?
Great place to be a woman, let me tell you.
EXIT
Follow him.
No Duh.
Is he alone?
He is-- oh...
What?

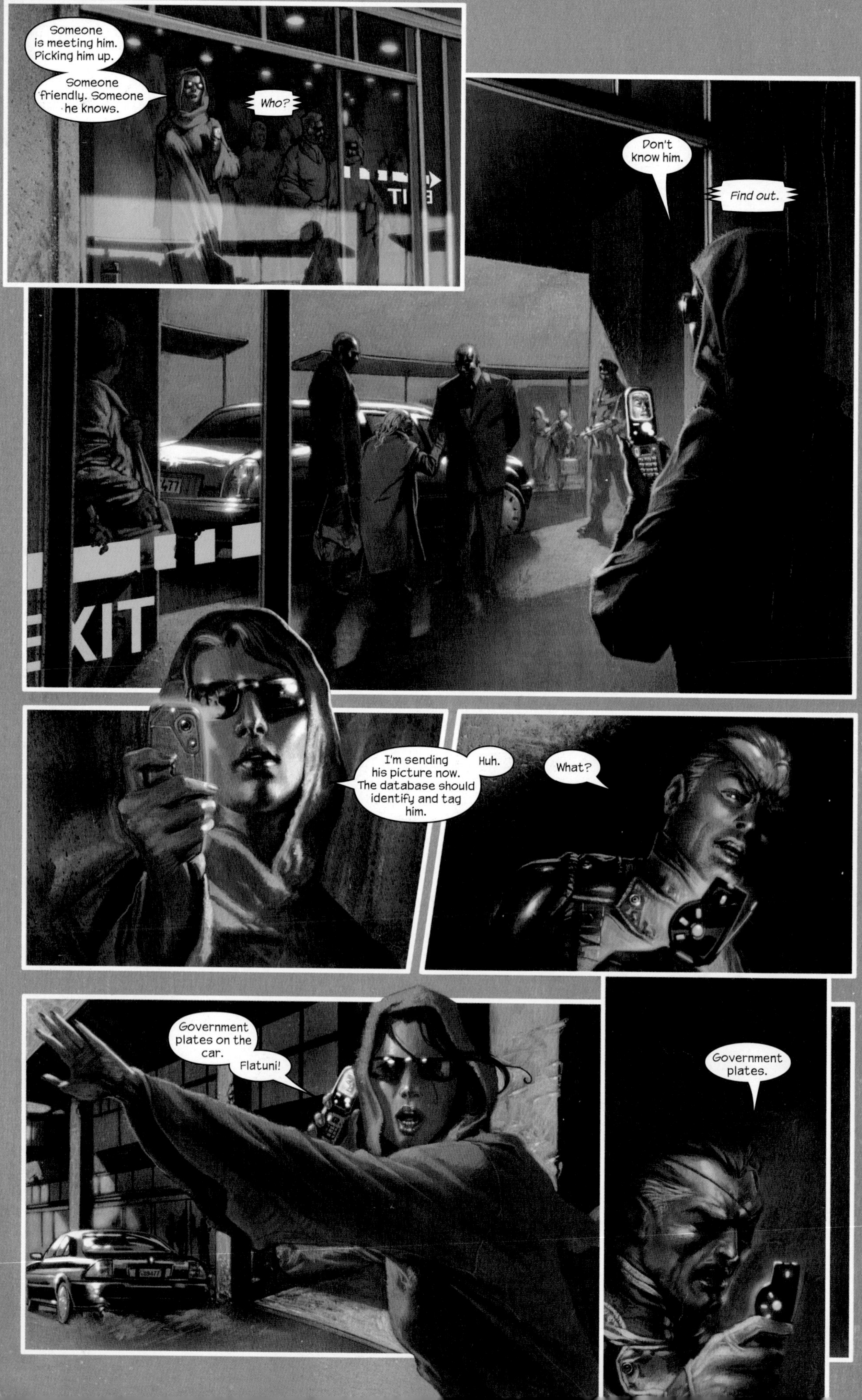
Someone is meeting him. Picking him up.
Someone friendly. Someone he knows.
Who?
Don't know him.
Find out.
EXIT
I'm sending his picture now. The database should identify and tag him.
Huh.
What?
Government plates on the car.
Flatuni!
Government plates.

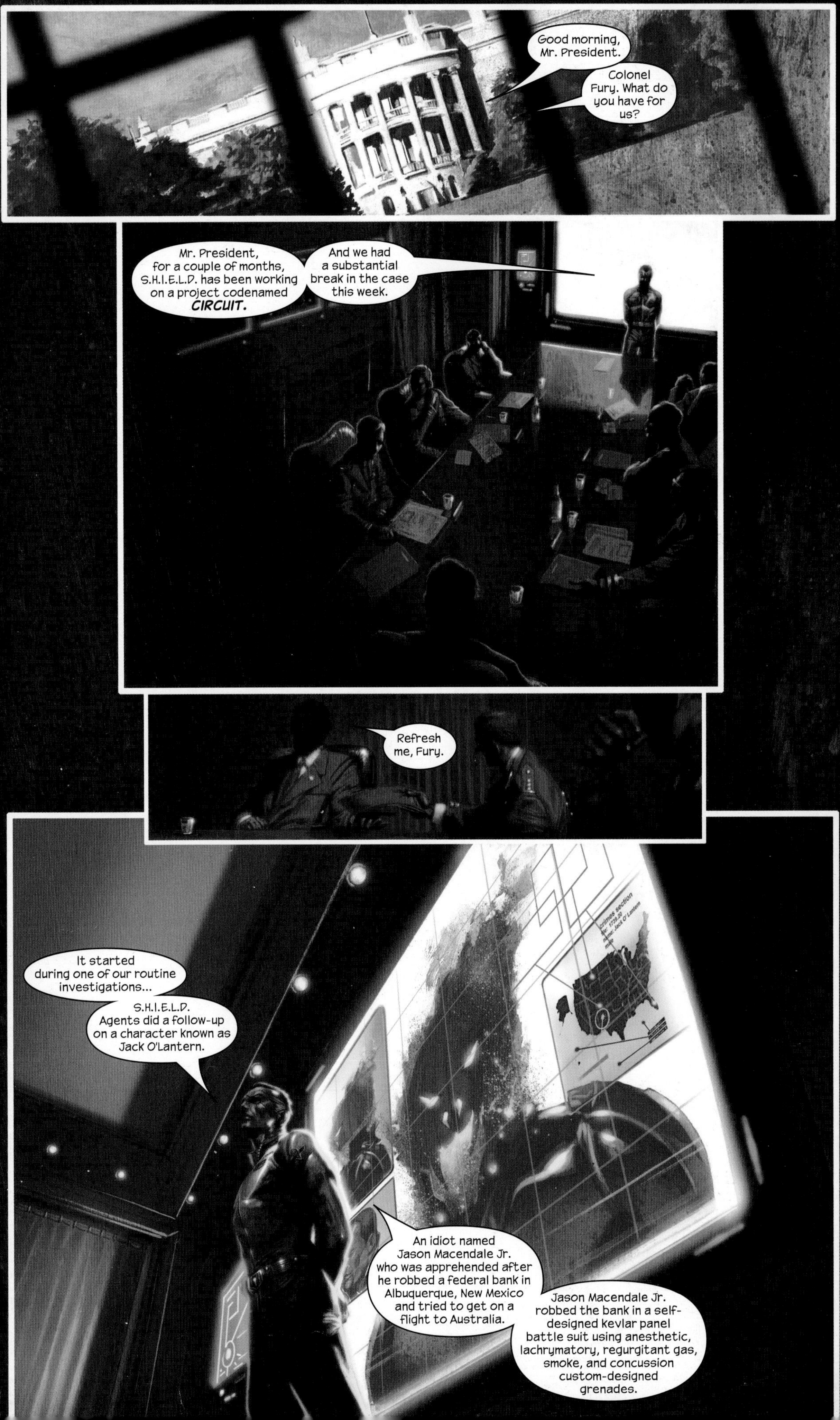
Good morning, Mr. President.
Colonel Fury. What do you have for us?
Mr. President, for a couple of months, S.H.I.E.L.D. has been working on a project codenamed CIRCUIT.
And we had a substantial break in the case this week.
Refresh me, Fury.
It started during one of our routine investigations...
S.H.I.E.L.D. Agents did a follow-up on a character known as Jack O'Lantern.
An idiot named Jason Macendale Jr. who was apprehended after he robbed a federal bank in Albuquerque, New Mexico and tried to get on a flight to Australia.
Jason Macendale Jr. robbed the bank in a self-designed kevlar panel battle suit using anesthetic, lachrymatory, regurgitant gas, smoke, and concussion custom-designed grenades.

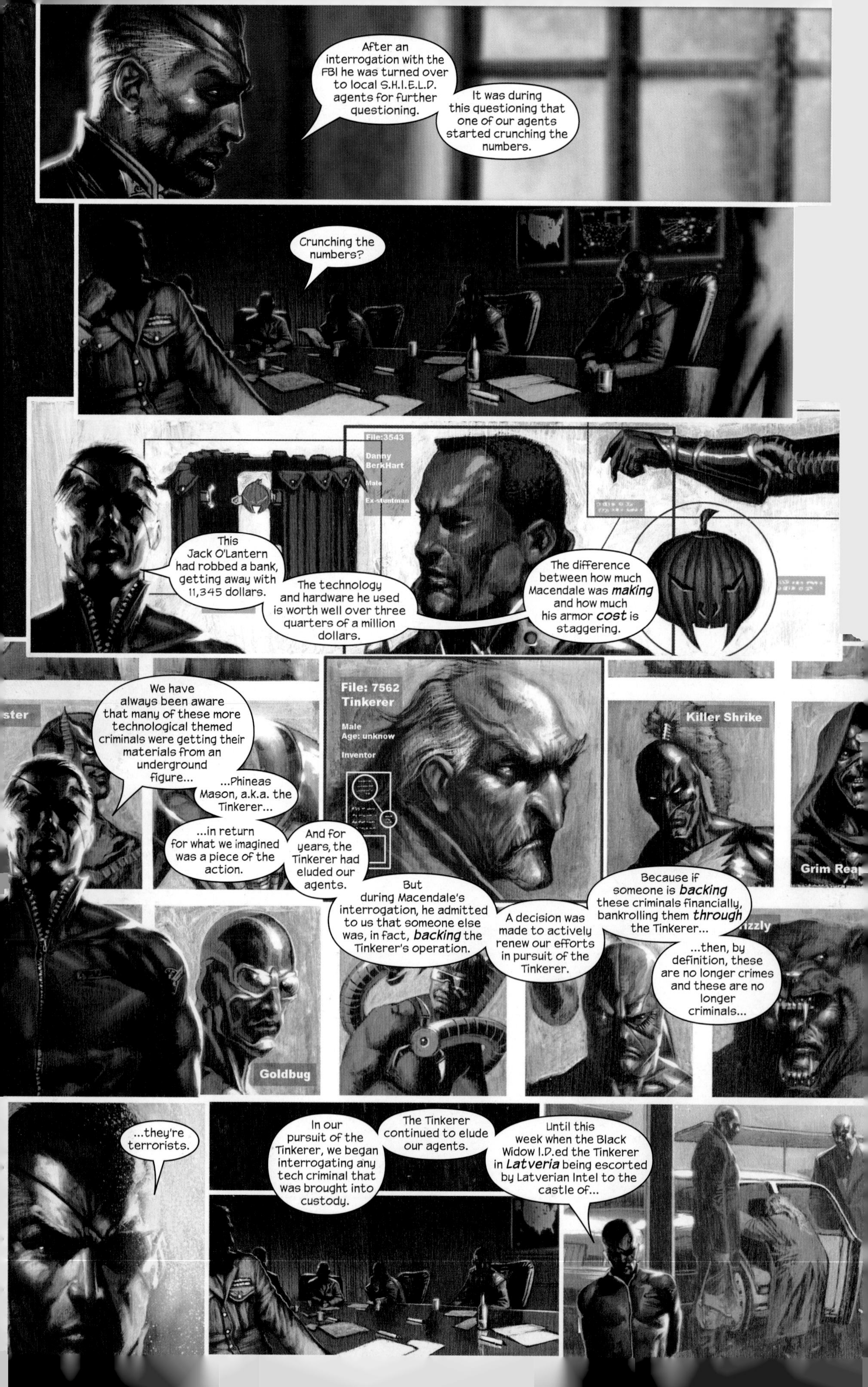
After an interrogation with the FBI he was turned over to local S.H.I.E.L.D. agents for further questioning.
It was during this questioning that one of our agents started crunching the numbers.
Crunching the numbers?
File:3543
Danny BerkHart
Male
Ex-stuntman
This Jack O'Lantern had robbed a bank, getting away with 11,345 dollars.
The technology and hardware he used is worth well over three quarters of a million dollars.
The difference between how much Macendale was *making* and how much his armor *cost* is staggering.
We have always been aware that many of these more technological themed criminals were getting their materials from an underground figure...
...Phineas Mason, a.k.a. the Tinkerer...
...in return for what we imagined was a piece of the action.
File: 7562
Tinkerer
Male
Age: unknow
Inventor
Killer Shrike
Grim Rea
And for years, the Tinkerer had eluded our agents.
But during Macendale's interrogation, he admitted to us that someone else was, in fact, *backing* the Tinkerer's operation.
A decision was made to actively renew our efforts in pursuit of the Tinkerer.
Because if someone is *backing* these criminals financially, bankrolling them *through* the Tinkerer...
...then, by definition, these are no longer crimes and these are no longer criminals...
Goldbug
...they're terrorists.
In our pursuit of the Tinkerer, we began interrogating any tech criminal that was brought into custody.
The Tinkerer continued to elude our agents.
Until this week when the Black Widow I.D.ed the Tinkerer in *Latveria* being escorted by Latverian Intel to the castle of...

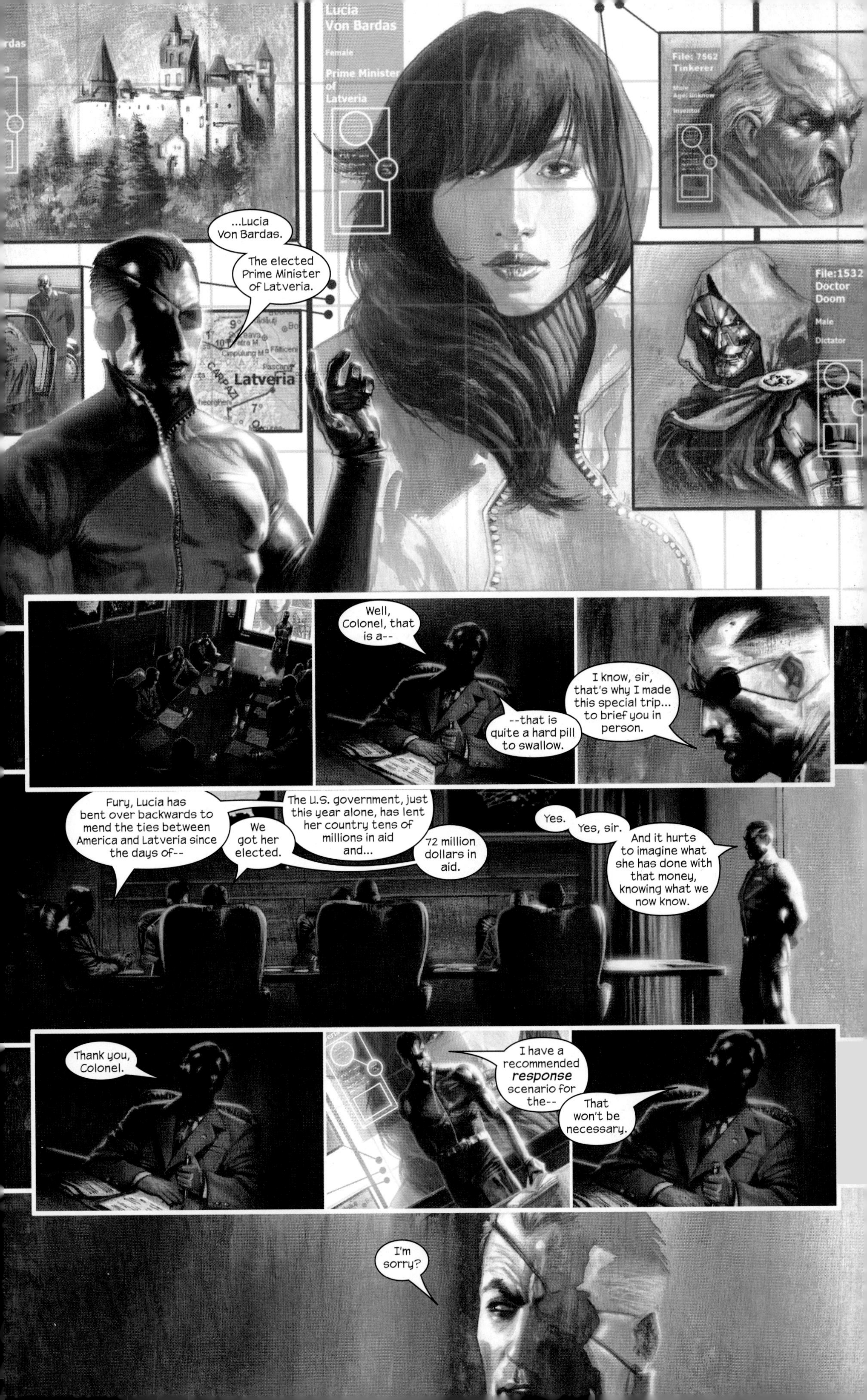
Lucia
Von Bardas
Female
Prime Minister of Latveria
File: 7562
Tinkerer
File:1532
Doctor
Doom
Male
Dictator
...Lucia Von Bardas.
The elected Prime Minister of Latveria.
Latveria
Well, Colonel, that is a--
--that is quite a hard pill to swallow.
I know, sir, that's why I made this special trip... to brief you in person.
Fury, Lucia has bent over backwards to mend the ties between America and Latveria since the days of--
We got her elected.
The U.S. government, just this year alone, has lent her country tens of millions in aid and...
72 million dollars in aid.
Yes.
Yes, sir.
And it hurts to imagine what she has done with that money, knowing what we now know.
Thank you, Colonel.
I have a recommended *response* scenario for the--
That won't be necessary.
I'm sorry?

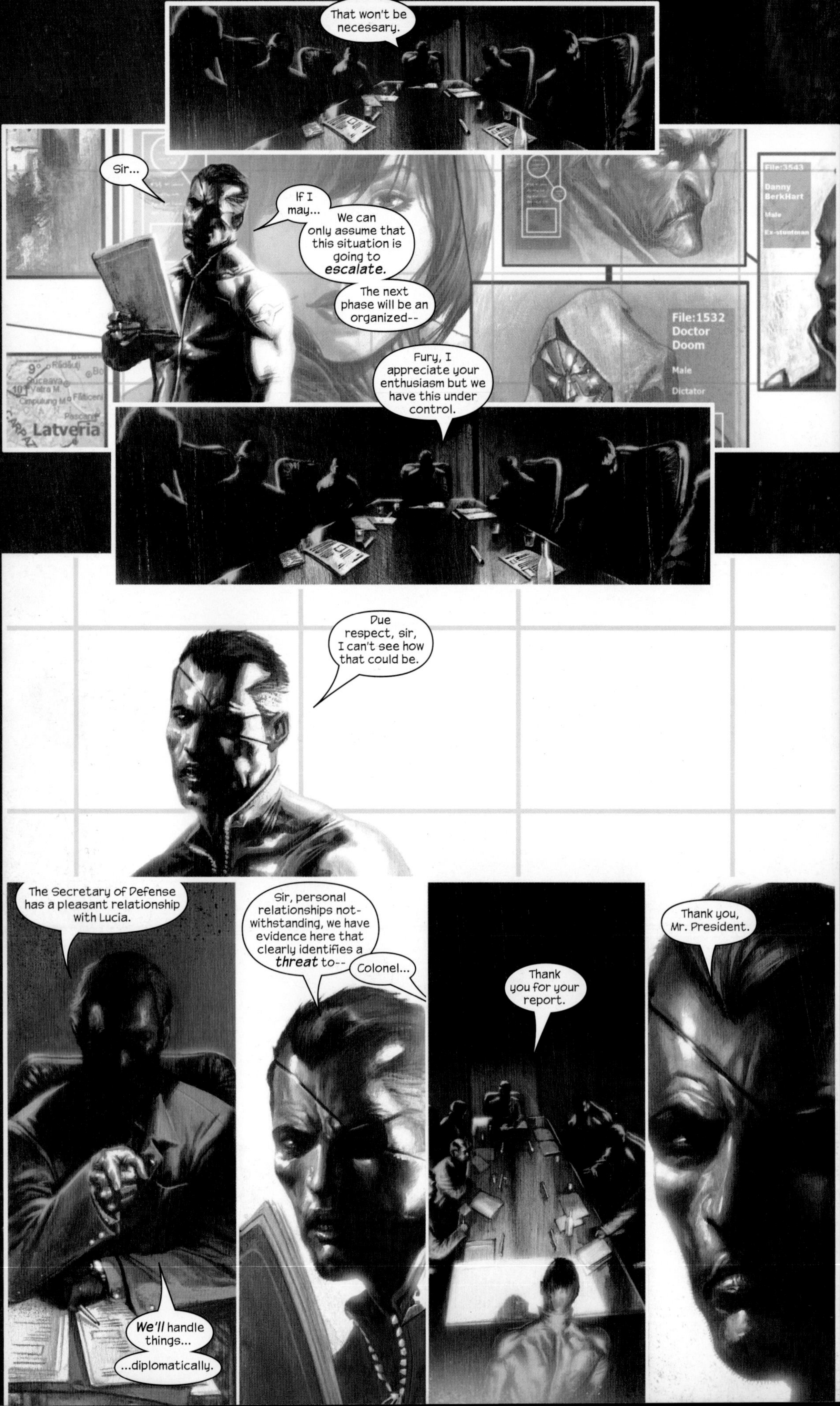
That won't be necessary.
Sir...
If I may...
We can only assume that this situation is going to escalate.
The next phase will be an organized--
File:3543
Danny BerkHart
Male
Ex-stuntman
File:1532
Doctor Doom
Male
Dictator
Latveria
Fury, I appreciate your enthusiasm but we have this under control.
Due respect, sir, I can't see how that could be.
The Secretary of Defense has a pleasant relationship with Lucia.
We'll handle things...
...diplomatically.
Sir, personal relationships notwithstanding, we have evidence here that clearly identifies a threat to--
Colonel...
Thank you for your report.
Thank you, Mr. President.

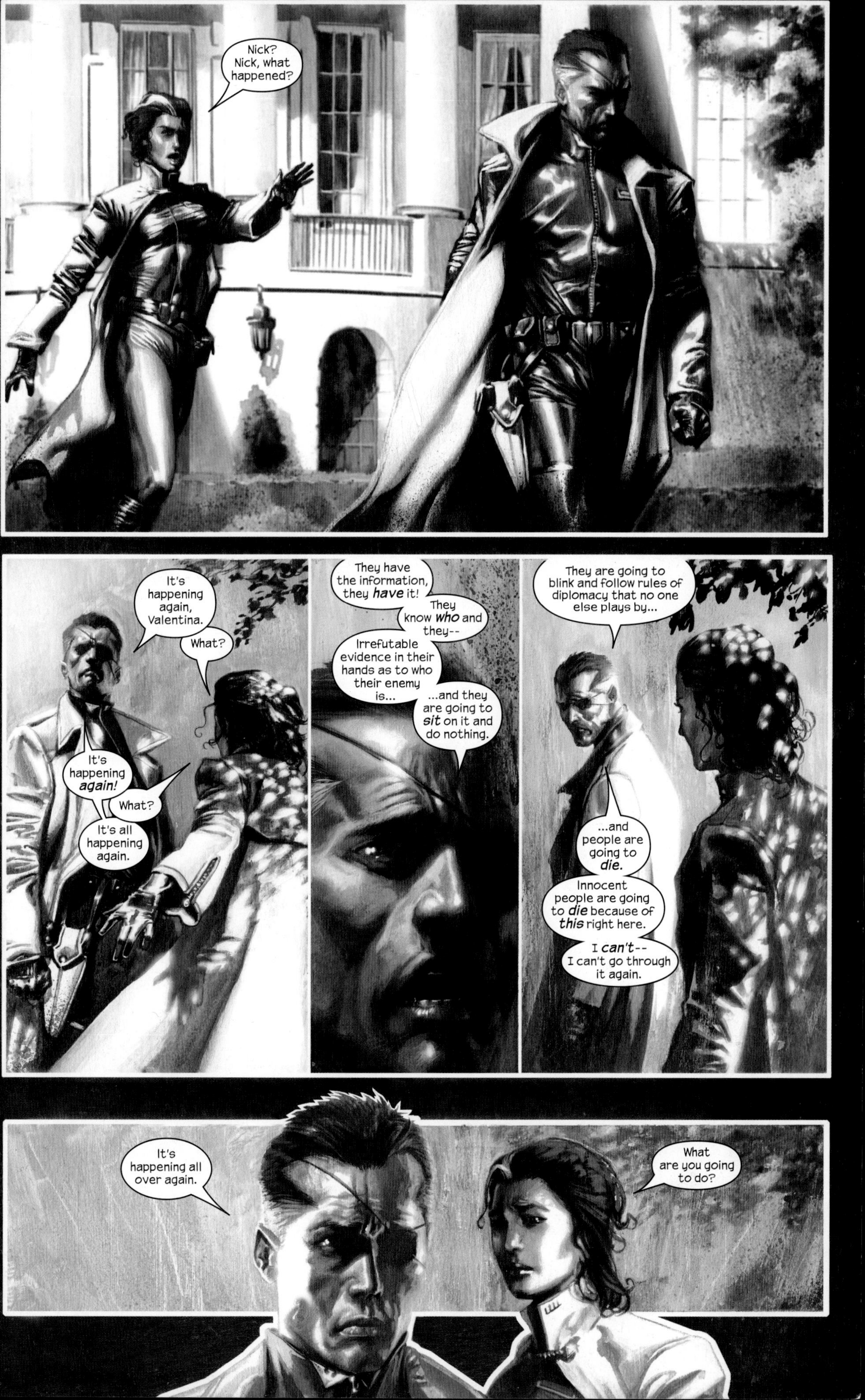
Nick? Nick, what happened?
It's happening again, Valentina.
What?
It's happening *again!*
What?
It's all happening again.
They have the information, they *have* it!
They know *who* and they--
Irrefutable evidence in their hands as to who their enemy is...
...and they are going to *sit* on it and do nothing.
They are going to blink and follow rules of diplomacy that no one else plays by...
...and people are going to *die.*
Innocent people are going to *die* because of *this* right here.
I *can't*-- I can't go through it again.
It's happening all over again.
What are you going to do?

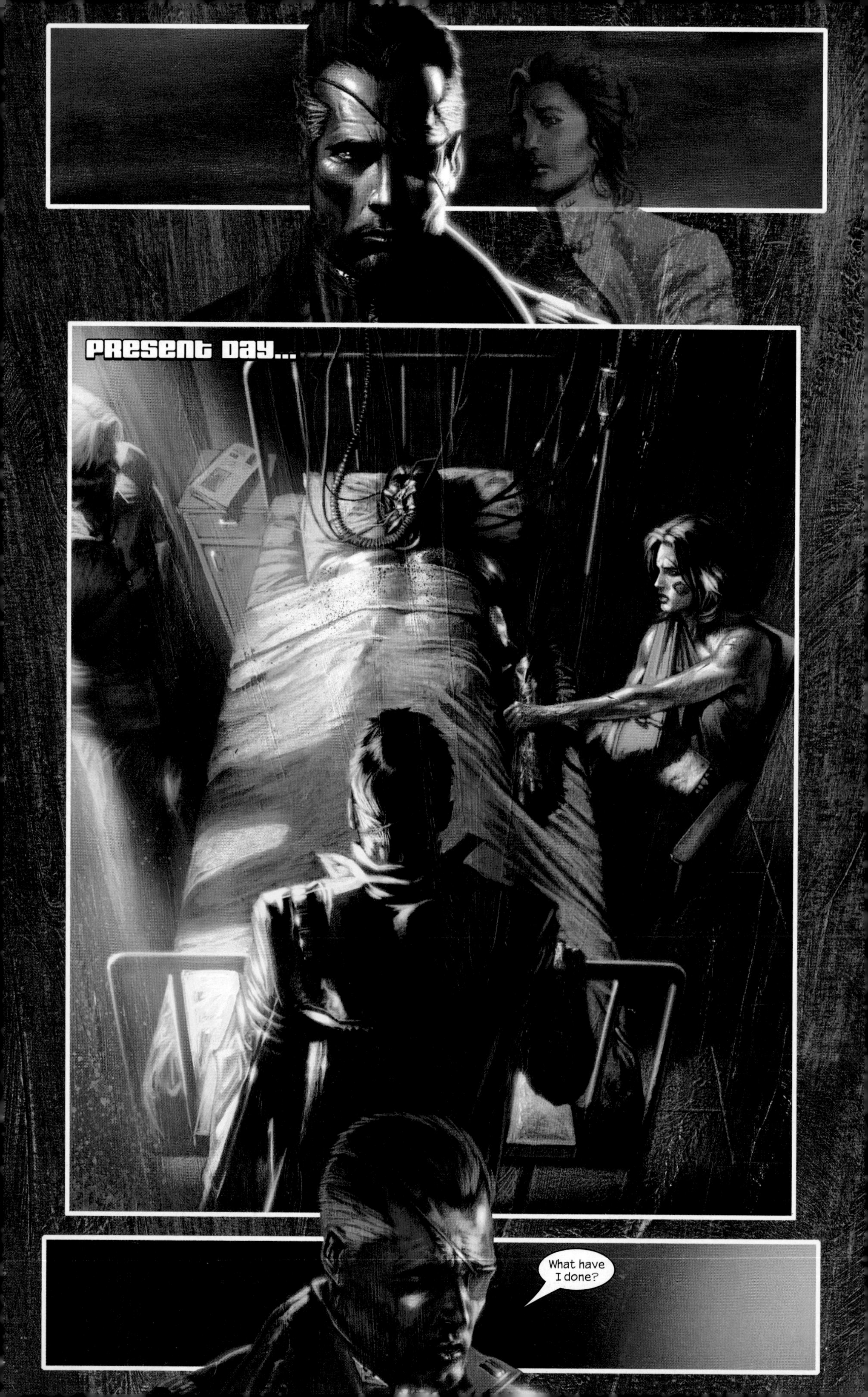
PRESENT DAY...
What have I done?

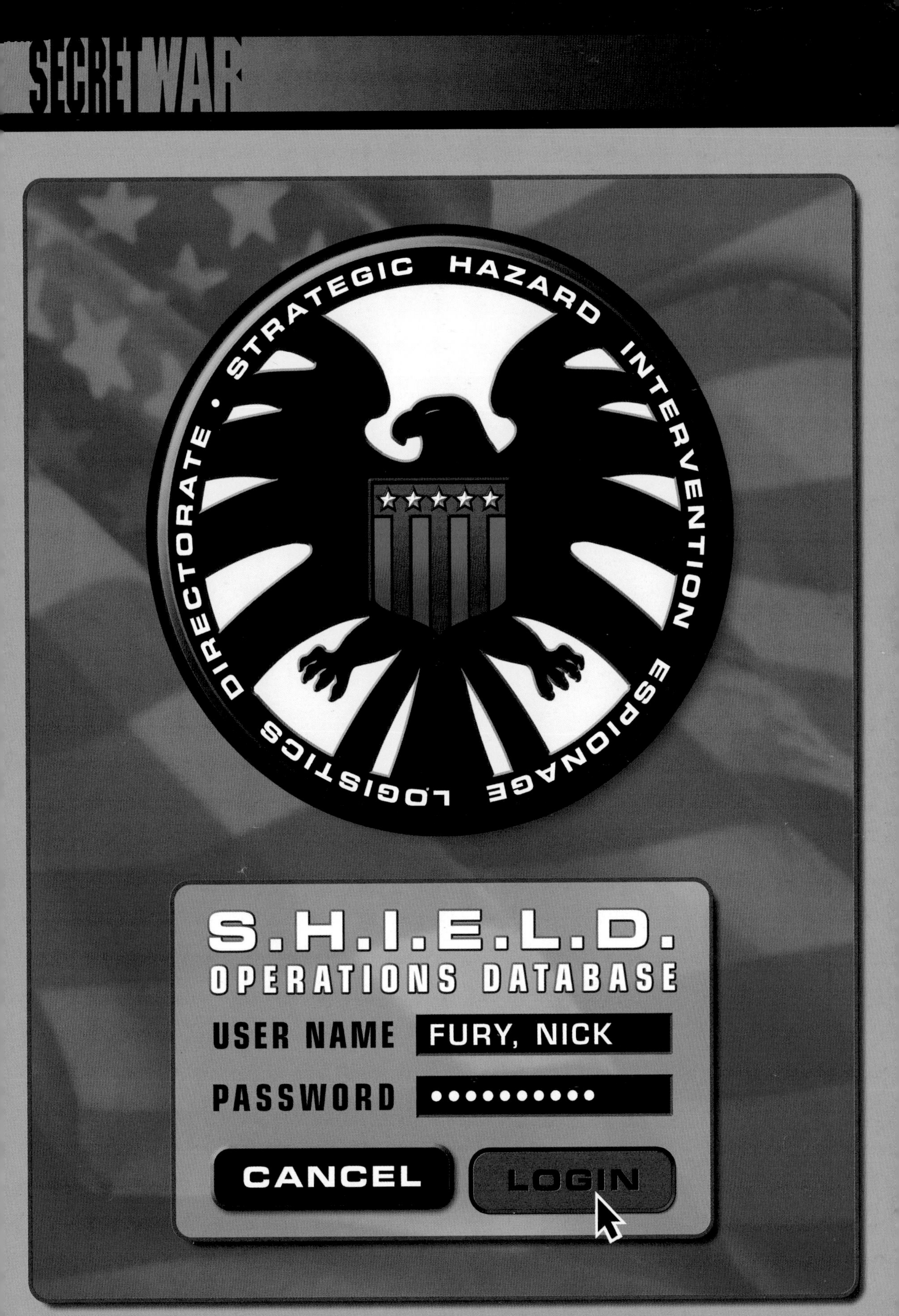
STRATEGIC HAZARD INTERVENTION ESPIONAGE LOGISTICS DIRECTORATE
S.H.I.E.L.D.
OPERATIONS DATABASE
USER NAME
FURY, NICK
PASSWORD
•••••••••••
CANCEL
LOGIN

SECRET WAR

S.H.I.E.L.D.
OPERATIONS DATABASE

HOME **ADVANCED SEARCH** **DATABASES** **LOG OUT**

AGENT **CRIMINAL** **PROJECT** **OPERATIONS ARCHIVE**

CRIMINAL PROFI

BANNER, ROBERT BRU

BERKHART, DANNY ak

BROCK, EDWARD aka

CASTLE, FRANK aka T

CREED, VICTOR aka SA

DILLON, MAX aka ELE

ESSEX, NATHANIAL ak

FISK, WILSON aka KIN

KRAVENOFF, ALEX aka

KRAVENOFF, SERGEI a

LEHNSHERR, ERIC MA

MACENDALE, JASON JR

MARKO, CAIN aka JUG

MARKO, FLINT aka SA

NATCHIOS, ELEKTRA

OCTAVIUS, OTTO aka D

OSBORN, HARRY aka (

OSBORN, NORMAN aka GREEN GOBLIN

VON DOOM, VICTOR aka DOCTOR DOOM

S.H.I.E.L.D. FILE: 3VVV1- 4457JACK
CRIMINAL DATABASE >> CRIMINAL PROFILES

REAL NAME: Jason Macendale Jr.
A.K.A.: Maguire Beck, Mad Jack, Jack O'Lantern, Hobgoblin
IDENTITY: Secret; became the second Hobgoblin until his death at the hands of the original Hobgoblin.
RELATIVES: None known.
HEIGHT: 6 ft. 1 in.
WEIGHT: 210 lbs
EYES: Brown
HAIR: Black
GROUP AFFILIATIONS: Norman Osborn, Maggia
ENEMIES: Spider-Man, Silver Sable
POWERS: Military training, hand-to-hand combat & Martial Arts
WEAPONS: Anaesthetic, lachrymal, regurgitant gas, smoke, & concussion grenades. Bulletproof helmet with telescopic infrared image intensifiers. Body armor made of metal-covered, multi-segment Kevlar panels. High-frequency electric transducers wrist blasters.
RELATED DOCUMENTS: 347631-00854 SPM, 158965-00973 SPM, 876543-00364 GGB, 904356-00094 HOB, **696369-34934 THK**

SEARCH DATABASE SEARCH

S.H.I.E.L.D. DOCUMENT 696369-34934 THK

CRIMINAL DATABASE >> OPERATIONS DOCUMENTS >> INTERROGATIONS

SECRET CODE: WHITE

Interrogation Transcript

Subject: Jason Macendale Jr.

A.K.A.: Maguire Beck, Mad Jack, Jack O'Lantern, Hobgoblin

Interrogation conducted by: S.H.I.E.L.D. Agent Jasper Sitwell -- level 5 and S.H.I.E.L.D. Agent James Woo -- level 8

Interrogation observed by Colonel Nicholas Fury -- S.H.I.E.L.D. Director -- Agent security level 10

Recording date: 4/5/2003

Place: S.H.I.E.L.D. Compound, Tulsa, Arizona

S.H.I.E.L.D. AGENT JAMES WOO
Good morning.

S.H.I.E.L.D. AGENT JASPER SITWELL
Morning, Mr. Macendale.

JASON MACENDALE
I don't know who that is.

S.H.I.E.L.D. AGENT JASPER SITWELL
That would be the name on your service record.

JASON MACENDALE
Don't know that name.

S.H.I.E.L.D. AGENT JASPER SITWELL
Well, I hope you don't expect us to address you as Jack O'Lantern

S.H.I.E.L.D. AGENT JAMES WOO
Because that ain't going to happen.

S.H.I.E.L.D. AGENT JASPER SITWELL
Yeah, let's stick to Jason Macendale.

JASON MACENDALE
I don't know who that is.

S.H.I.E.L.D. AGENT JASPER SITWELL
Well, it's a good thing we do. We only have a few questions being that you were caught red-handed during your daylight robbery.

S.H.I.E.L.D. AGENT JAMES WOO
In front of witnesses.
On videotape.

S.H.I.E.L.D. AGENT JAMES WOO
So we wanted to talk to you a little about your life as a costumed goofball.

S.H.I.E.L.D.
OPERATIONS DATABASE

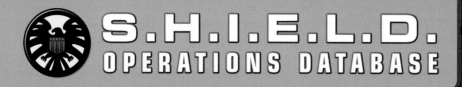

HOME ADVANCED SEARCH DATABASES LOG OUT

CRIMINAL DATABASE >> S.H.I.E.L.D. DOCUMENT 696369-34934 THK (Cont.)

S.H.I.E.L.D. AGENT JASPER SITWELL
We have your backstory.

S.H.I.E.L.D. AGENT JAMES WOO
Recruited by the C.I.A. eleven years ago...

S.H.I.E.L.D. AGENT JASPER SITWELL
Discharged four years later after a series of questionable actions during the *(OMITTED)*.

S.H.I.E.L.D. AGENT JAMES WOO
Now you use the costumed identity of Jack O'Lantern.

S.H.I.E.L.D. AGENT JASPER SITWELL
Green Goblin rip-off.

S.H.I.E.L.D. AGENT JAMES WOO
No doubt.

S.H.I.E.L.D. AGENT JASPER SITWELL
Hobgoblin wannabe.

S.H.I.E.L.D. AGENT JAMES WOO
Ha! But let's not discount the military training in hand-to-hand combat & Martial Arts...

S.H.I.E.L.D. AGENT JASPER SITWELL
I am sure the United States government is very happy with the investment they made in you.

S.H.I.E.L.D. AGENT JAMES WOO
Well, we can't win them all.

S.H.I.E.L.D. AGENT JASPER SITWELL
Their investment in me turned out okay.

S.H.I.E.L.D. AGENT JAMES WOO
You think?

S.H.I.E.L.D. AGENT JASPER SITWELL
So we were looking over your battlesuit.

S.H.I.E.L.D. AGENT JAMES WOO
Which is shockingly less impressive without the flaming head all aflame.

S.H.I.E.L.D. AGENT JASPER SITWELL
The flaming head is a statement.

S.H.I.E.L.D. AGENT JAMES WOO
It says: I'm not a Hobgoblin rip-off. My head's on fire, see?

S.H.I.E.L.D. AGENT JASPER SITWELL
So we were going through your arsenal and we were counting up your little grenades. And we had some anaesthetic, lachrymal, and regurgitant gas...

SEARCH DATABASE

SEARCH

CRIMINAL DATABASE >> S.H.I.E.L.D. DOCUMENT 696369-34934 THK (Cont.)

S.H.I.E.L.D. AGENT JAMES WOO
Regurgitant--my favorite.

S.H.I.E.L.D. AGENT JASPER SITWELL
...smoke and concussion...

S.H.I.E.L.D. AGENT JAMES WOO
We had the mono alloy wrist-blasters for each wrist...

S.H.I.E.L.D. AGENT JASPER SITWELL
And the state-of-the-art hovercraft.

S.H.I.E.L.D. AGENT JAMES WOO
State of the art hovercraft that is not available in your local stores.

S.H.I.E.L.D. AGENT JASPER SITWELL
It's not available anywhere.

S.H.I.E.L.D. AGENT JAMES WOO
Hey, what does that put you back?
(Macendale declines to answer).

S.H.I.E.L.D. AGENT JASPER SITWELL
No answer?

S.H.I.E.L.D. AGENT JAMES WOO
Well, it was a rude question.

S.H.I.E.L.D. AGENT JASPER SITWELL
I know, but still, guy has a flaming pumpkin for a head, it's hard to know what constitutes for rude and--

JASON MACENDALE
Smart mouth. That's what they teach at S.H.I.E.L.D. now?

S.H.I.E.L.D. AGENT JASPER SITWELL
Teach? No. Encourage? Yes.

S.H.I.E.L.D. AGENT JAMES WOO
Who said we were S.H.I.E.L.D.?

JASON MACENDALE
Please. I can smell Fury's cigar on you.

S.H.I.E.L.D. AGENT JAMES WOO
So you know we can detain you indefinitely without a trial.

JASON MACENDALE
I know you think you can.

S.H.I.E.L.D. AGENT JAMES WOO
Oh we can, Goblinboy.

S.H.I.E.L.D. AGENT JASPER SITWELL
And we will.

S.H.I.E.L.D.
OPERATIONS DATABASE

HOME | ADVANCED SEARCH | DATABASES | LOG OUT

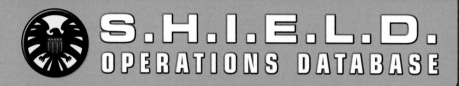

CRIMINAL DATABASE >> S.H.I.E.L.D. DOCUMENT 696369-34934 THK (Cont.)

S.H.I.E.L.D. AGENT JAMES WOO
So do yourself a favor and tell us what we want to know.

S.H.I.E.L.D. AGENT JASPER SITWELL
We want the source.

S.H.I.E.L.D. AGENT JAMES WOO
We want to know who you are getting your gear from.

S.H.I.E.L.D. AGENT JASPER SITWELL
Your tech.

S.H.I.E.L.D. AGENT JAMES WOO
Cost a pretty penny, all this high-tech flaming head gear you got.

S.H.I.E.L.D. AGENT JASPER SITWELL
More than you have.

S.H.I.E.L.D. AGENT JAMES WOO
Who's the supplier?

S.H.I.E.L.D. AGENT JASPER SITWELL
What's the deal you cooked? Percentage of the loot?

S.H.I.E.L.D. AGENT JAMES WOO
We want the name.

S.H.I.E.L.D. AGENT JASPER SITWELL
You know the deal. The name would buy you a lot.

S.H.I.E.L.D. AGENT JAMES WOO
We want the name!

JASON MACENDALE
I want my lawyer.

S.H.I.E.L.D. AGENT JAMES WOO
It's nice to want things. Give us a name or you're going to rot.

JASON MACENDALE
A name...

S.H.I.E.L.D. AGENT JAMES WOO
Yeah.

JASON MACENDALE
Threaten me all you want, I'm not scared of you. And I know you know where I get my stuff. You know. The Tinkerer hooked me up. Phineas Mason. You know who he is. But you want the guy behind the guy. That I do not know. Good luck finding him and good luck finding who's backing him.

SEARCH DATABASE SEARCH

S.H.I.E.L.D. AGENT JAMES WOO
Backing him?

JASON MACENDALE
Yeah, good luck.

S.H.I.E.L.D. AGENT JAMES WOO
What do you mean backing him?

JASON MACENDALE
I mean, the guy's in bed with who-the-hell-knows-who and all I know is I get the hookup on a handshake promise to return the favor in hourly.

S.H.I.E.L.D. AGENT JAMES WOO
What does that mean?

S.H.I.E.L.D. AGENT JASPER SITWELL
It means he gets his stuff for free in return for his pulling a job. But he doesn't know for who.

JASON MACENDALE
Or for what. But you know what? You want any more from me, you're going to have to cut me a check.

S.H.I.E.L.D. AGENT JASPER SITWELL
A check?

S.H.I.E.L.D. AGENT JAMES WOO
As in pay you?

S.H.I.E.L.D. AGENT JASPER SITWELL
You want us to pay you for what?

JASON MACENDALE
I was C.I.A. for four years. You don't think I don't know how this is played. You don't think I don't know how much you paid *(OMITTED)* **for** *(OMITTED)*.

S.H.I.E.L.D. AGENT JASPER SITWELL
We don't--

JASON MACENDALE
Or how about the *(OMITTED)* **and the** *(OMITTED)*.

S.H.I.E.L.D. AGENT JAMES WOO
Ending record.

Recording device switched off at 4:45:22.

Transcript reviewed and edited by Colonel Nick Fury for security clearance.

566-788

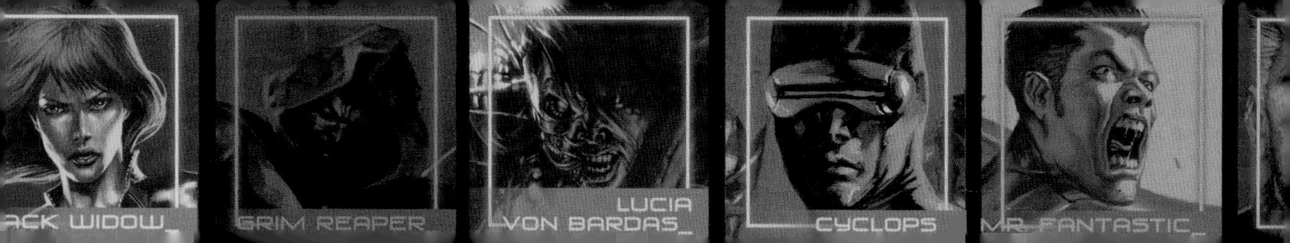
ACK WIDOW_
GRIM REAPER
LUCIA
VON BARDAS_
CYCLOPS
MR. FANTASTIC_

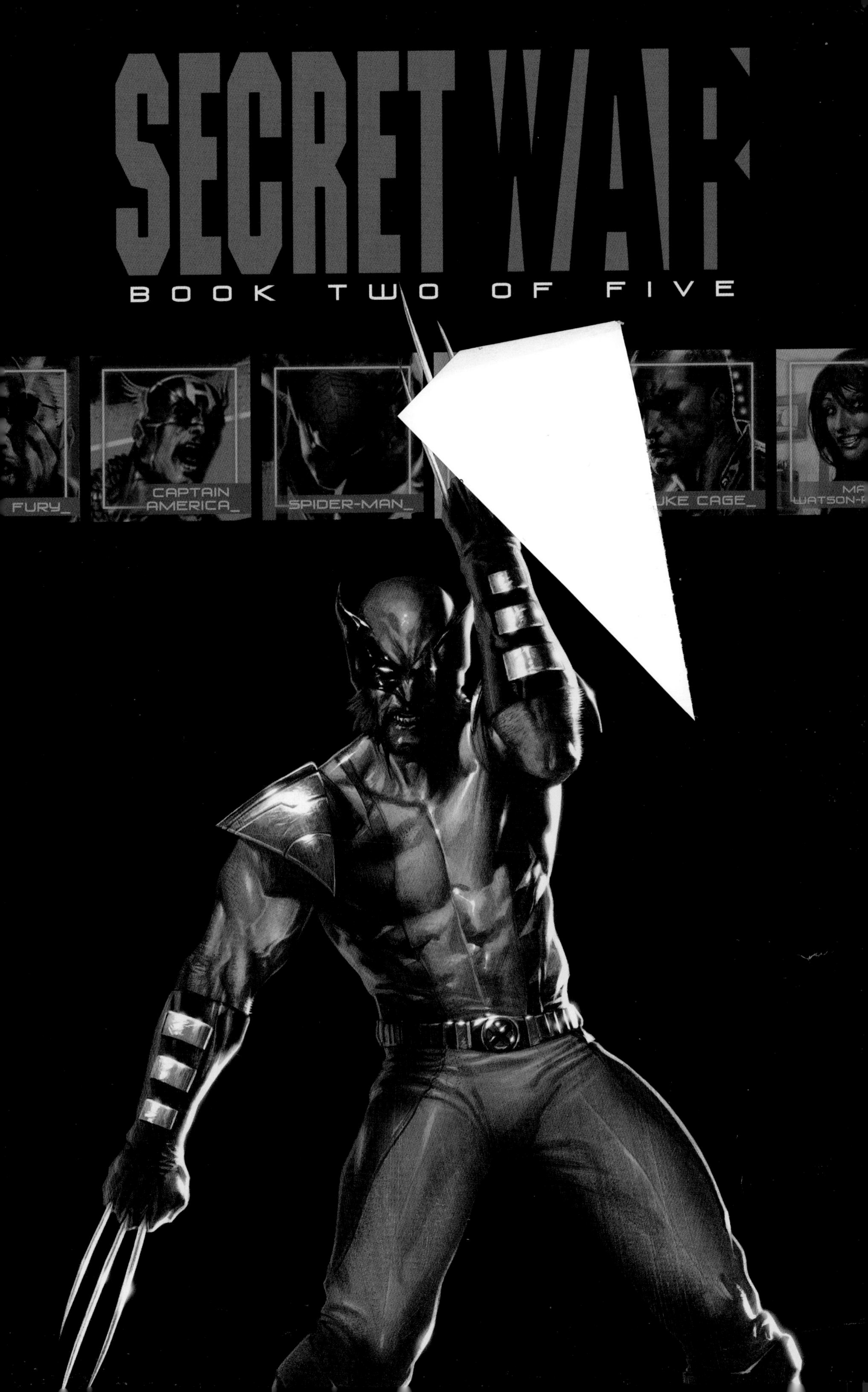
SECRET WAR
BOOK TWO OF FIVE
FURY_
CAPTAIN AMERICA_
SPIDER-MAN_

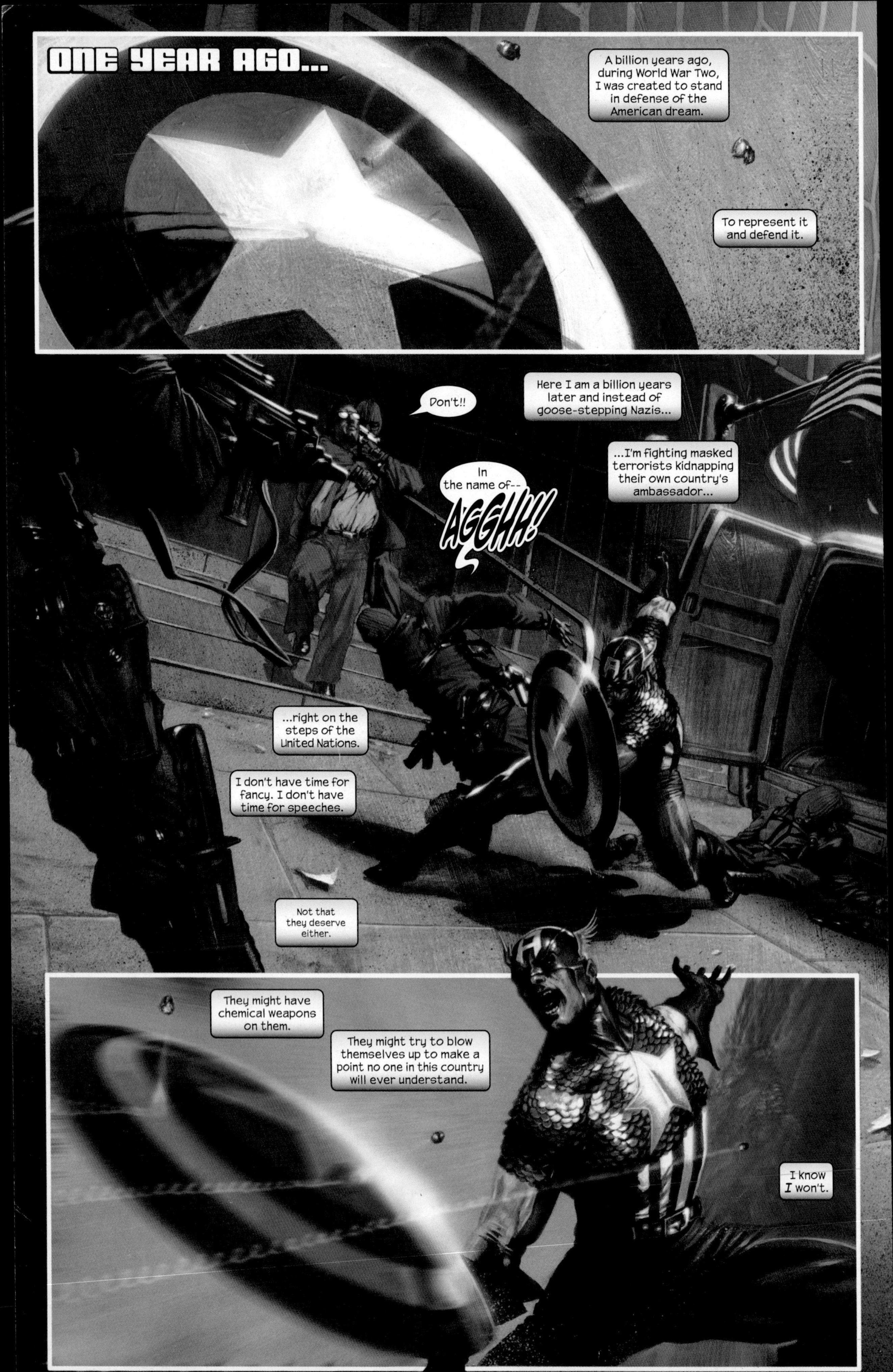
ONE YEAR AGO...
A billion years ago, during World War Two, I was created to stand in defense of the American dream.
To represent it and defend it.
Don't!!
Here I am a billion years later and instead of goose-stepping Nazis...
...I'm fighting masked terrorists kidnapping their own country's ambassador...
In the name of--
AGGHH!
...right on the steps of the United Nations.
I don't have time for fancy. I don't have time for speeches.
Not that they deserve either.
They might have chemical weapons on them.
They might try to blow themselves up to make a point no one in this country will ever understand.
I know *I* won't.

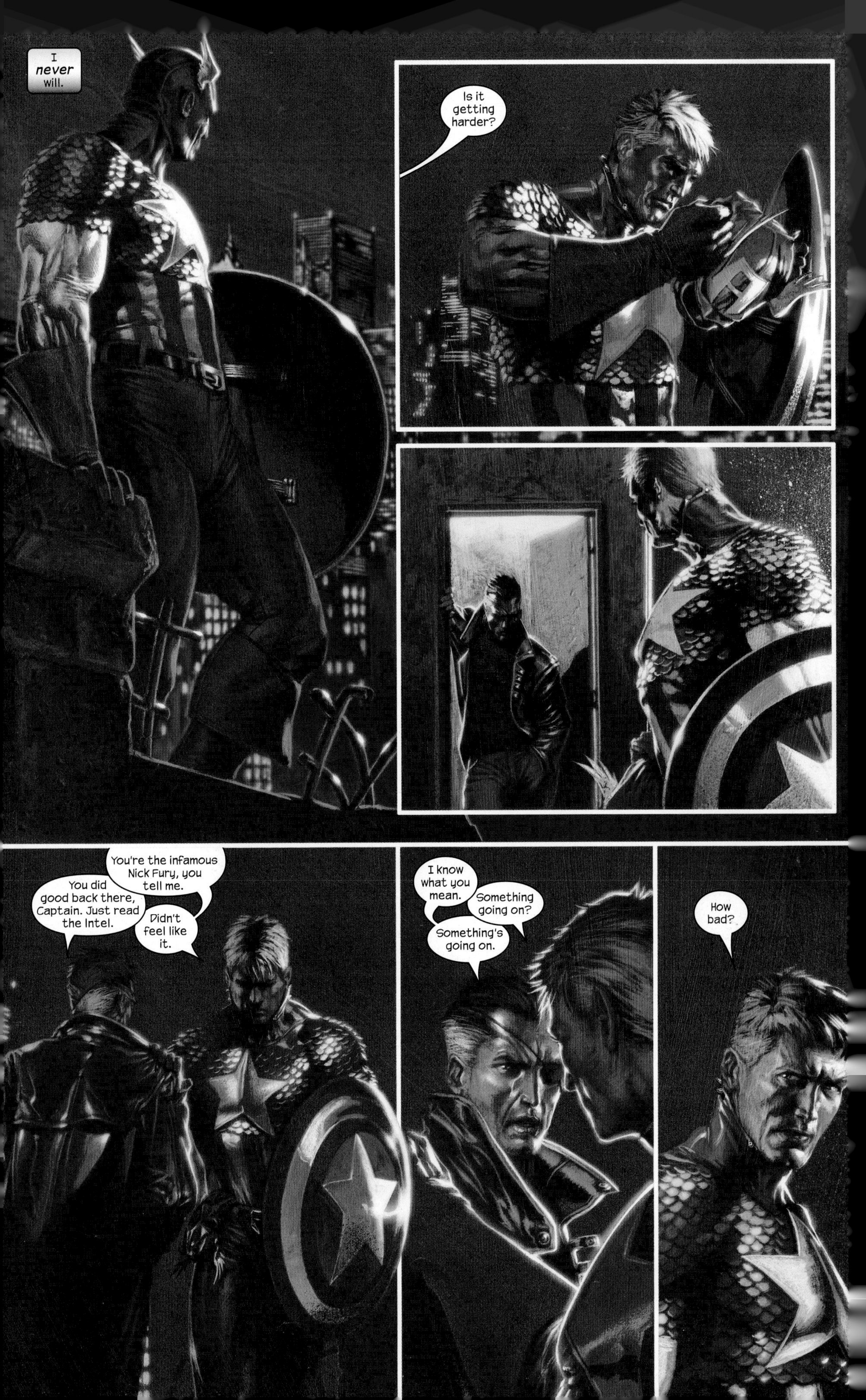
I *never* will.
Is it getting harder?
You did good back there, Captain. Just read the Intel.
You're the infamous Nick Fury, you tell me.
Didn't feel like it.
I know what you mean.
Something going on?
Something's going on.
How bad?

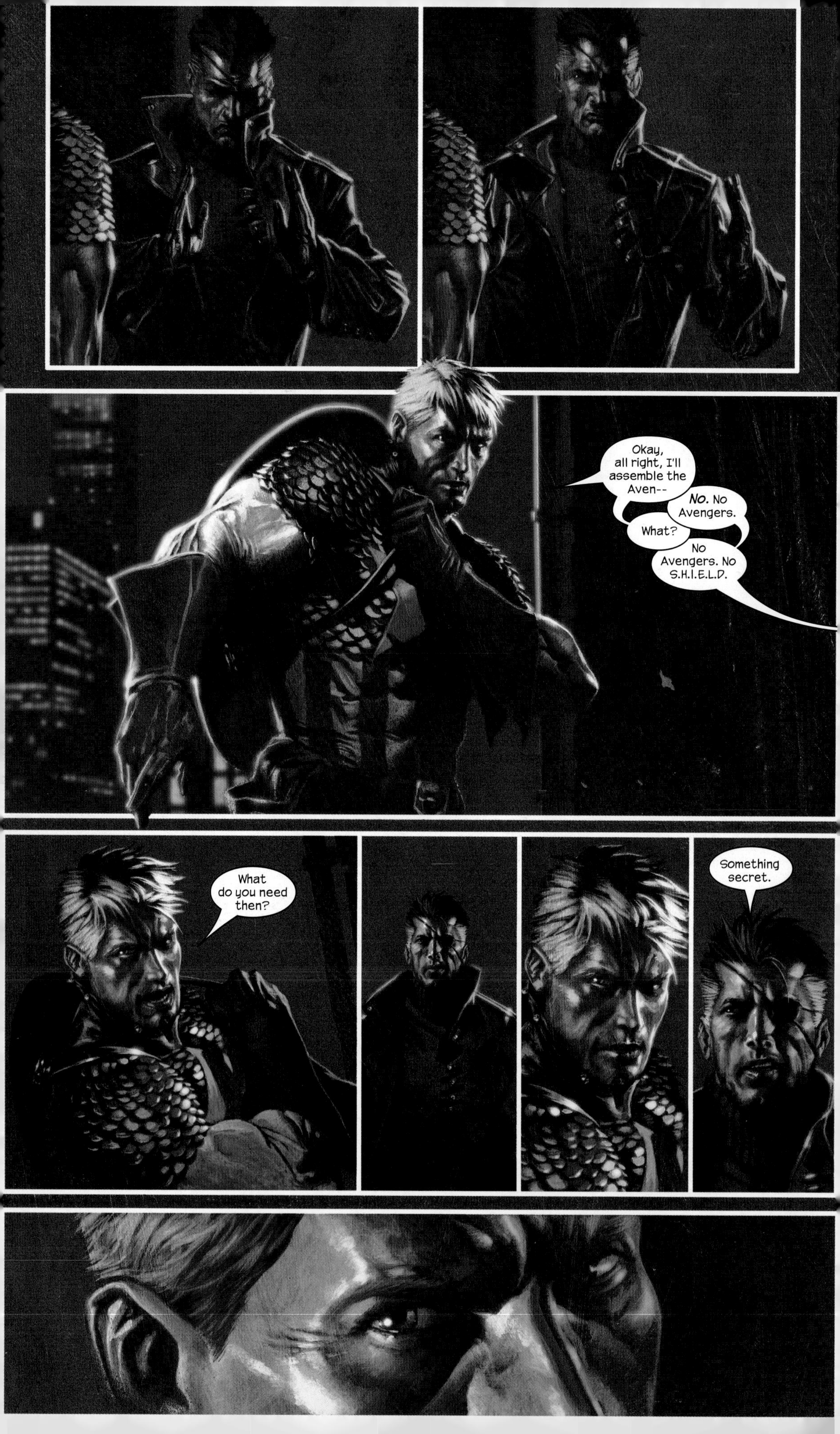
Okay, all right, I'll assemble the Aven--
NO. No Avengers.
What?
No Avengers. No S.H.I.E.L.D.
What do you need then?
Something secret.

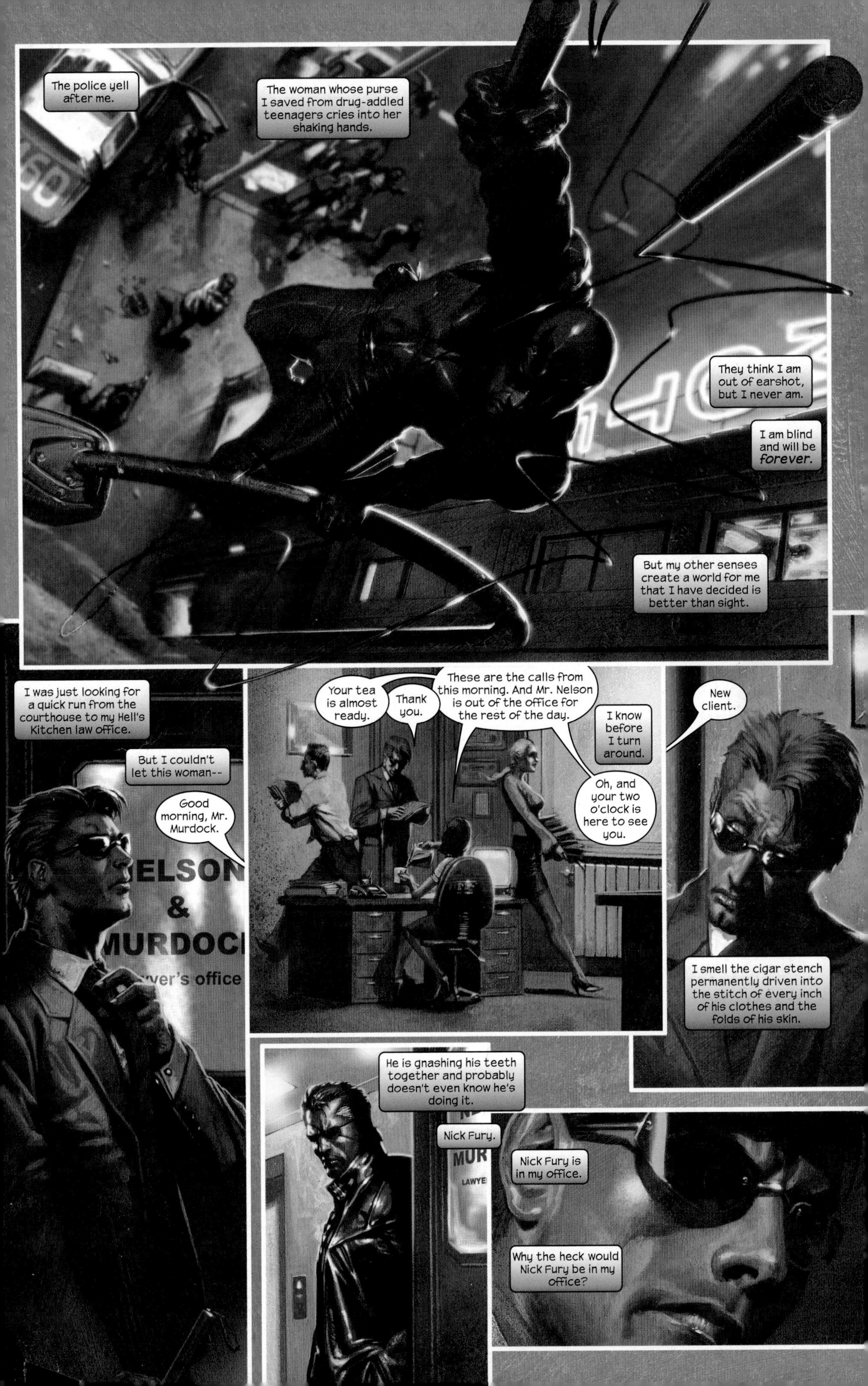
The police yell after me.
The woman whose purse I saved from drug-addled teenagers cries into her shaking hands.
They think I am out of earshot, but I never am.
I am blind and will be *forever.*
But my other senses create a world for me that I have decided is better than sight.
I was just looking for a quick run from the courthouse to my Hell's Kitchen law office.
But I couldn't let this woman--
Good morning, Mr. Murdock.
NELSON & MURDOCK lawyer's office
Your tea is almost ready.
Thank you.
These are the calls from this morning. And Mr. Nelson is out of the office for the rest of the day.
I know before I turn around.
Oh, and your two o'clock is here to see you.
New client.
I smell the cigar stench permanently driven into the stitch of every inch of his clothes and the folds of his skin.
He is gnashing his teeth together and probably doesn't even know he's doing it.
Nick Fury.
Nick Fury is in my office.
Why the heck would Nick Fury be in my office?

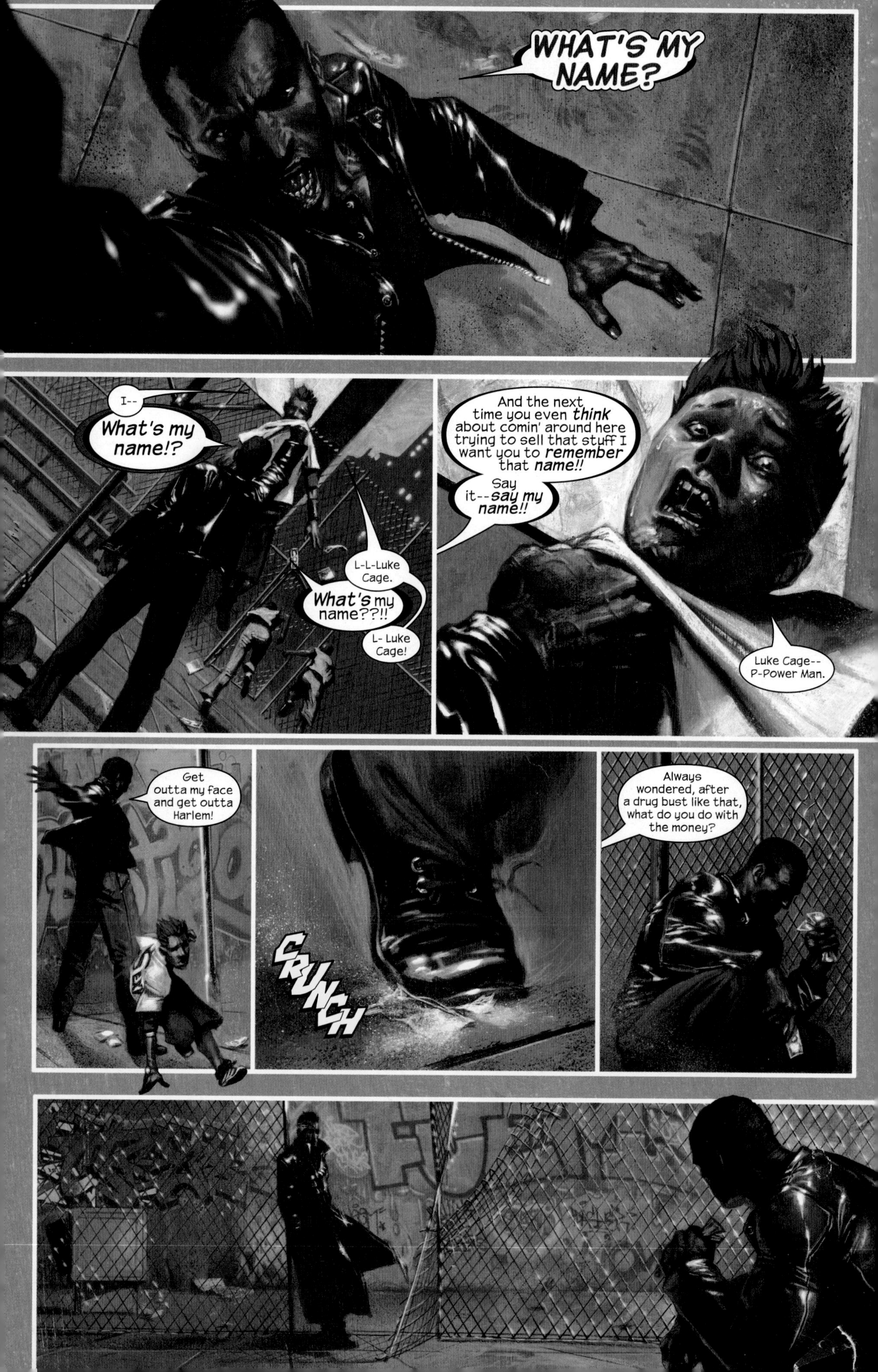
WHAT'S MY NAME?
I--
What's my name!?
L-L-Luke Cage.
What's my name??!!
L- Luke Cage!
And the next time you even think about comin' around here trying to sell that stuff I want you to remember that name!!
Say it--say my name!!
Luke Cage-- P-Power Man.
Get outta my face and get outta Harlem!
CRUNCH
Always wondered, after a drug bust like that, what do you do with the money?

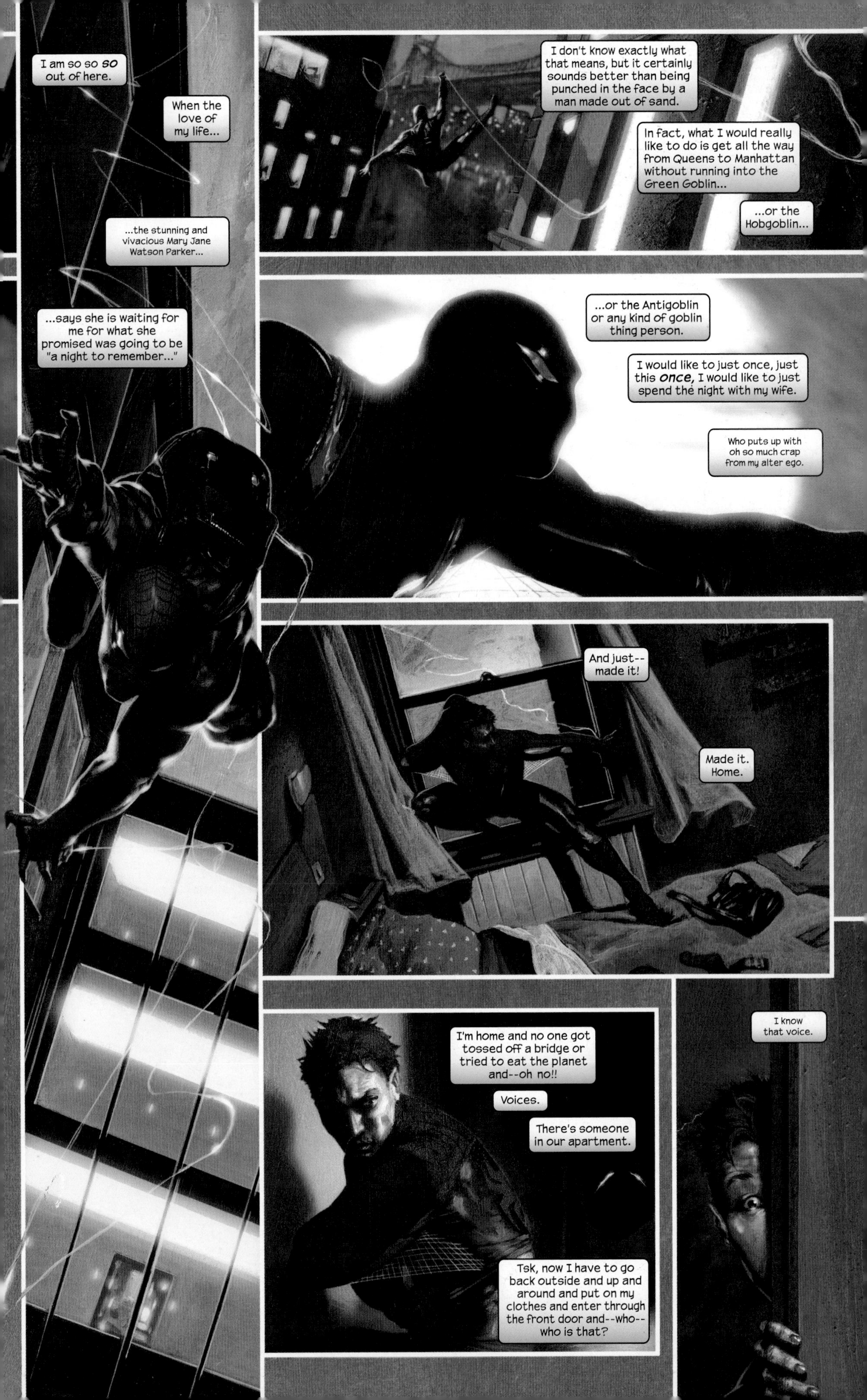

I am so so *SO* out of here.
When the love of my life...
...the stunning and vivacious Mary Jane Watson Parker...
...says she is waiting for me for what she promised was going to be "a night to remember..."
I don't know exactly what that means, but it certainly sounds better than being punched in the face by a man made out of sand.
In fact, what I would really like to do is get all the way from Queens to Manhattan without running into the Green Goblin...
...or the Hobgoblin...
...or the Antigoblin or any kind of goblin thing person.
I would like to just once, just this *once,* I would like to just spend the night with my wife.
Who puts up with oh so much crap from my alter ego.
And just--made it!
Made it. Home.
I'm home and no one got tossed off a bridge or tried to eat the planet and--oh no!!
Voices.
There's someone in our apartment.
Tsk, now I have to go back outside and up and around and put on my clothes and enter through the front door and--who--who is that?
I know that voice.

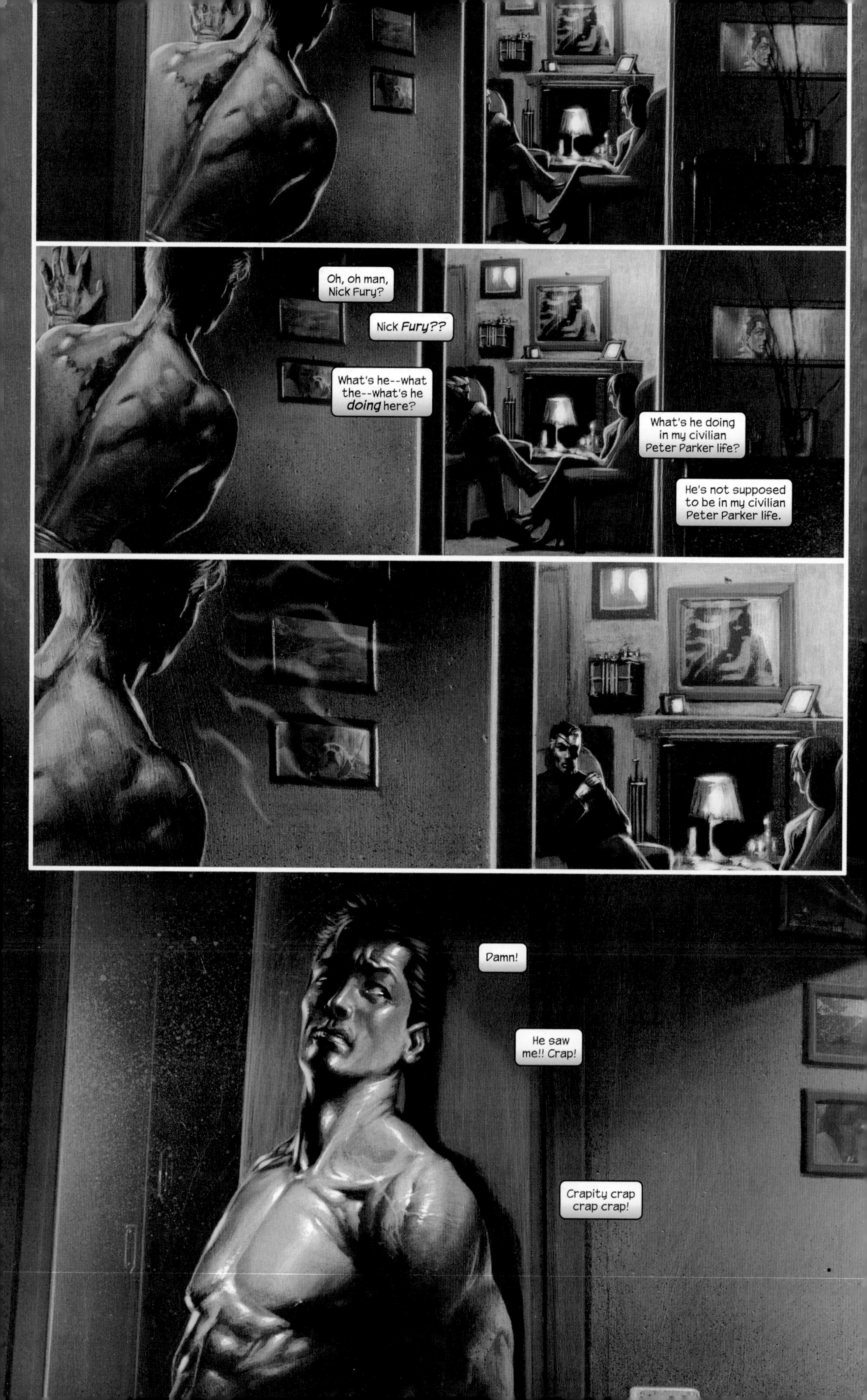

Oh, oh man, Nick Fury?
Nick Fury??
What's he--what the--what's he doing here?
What's he doing in my civilian Peter Parker life?
He's not supposed to be in my civilian Peter Parker life.
Damn!
He saw me!! Crap!
Crapity crap crap crap!

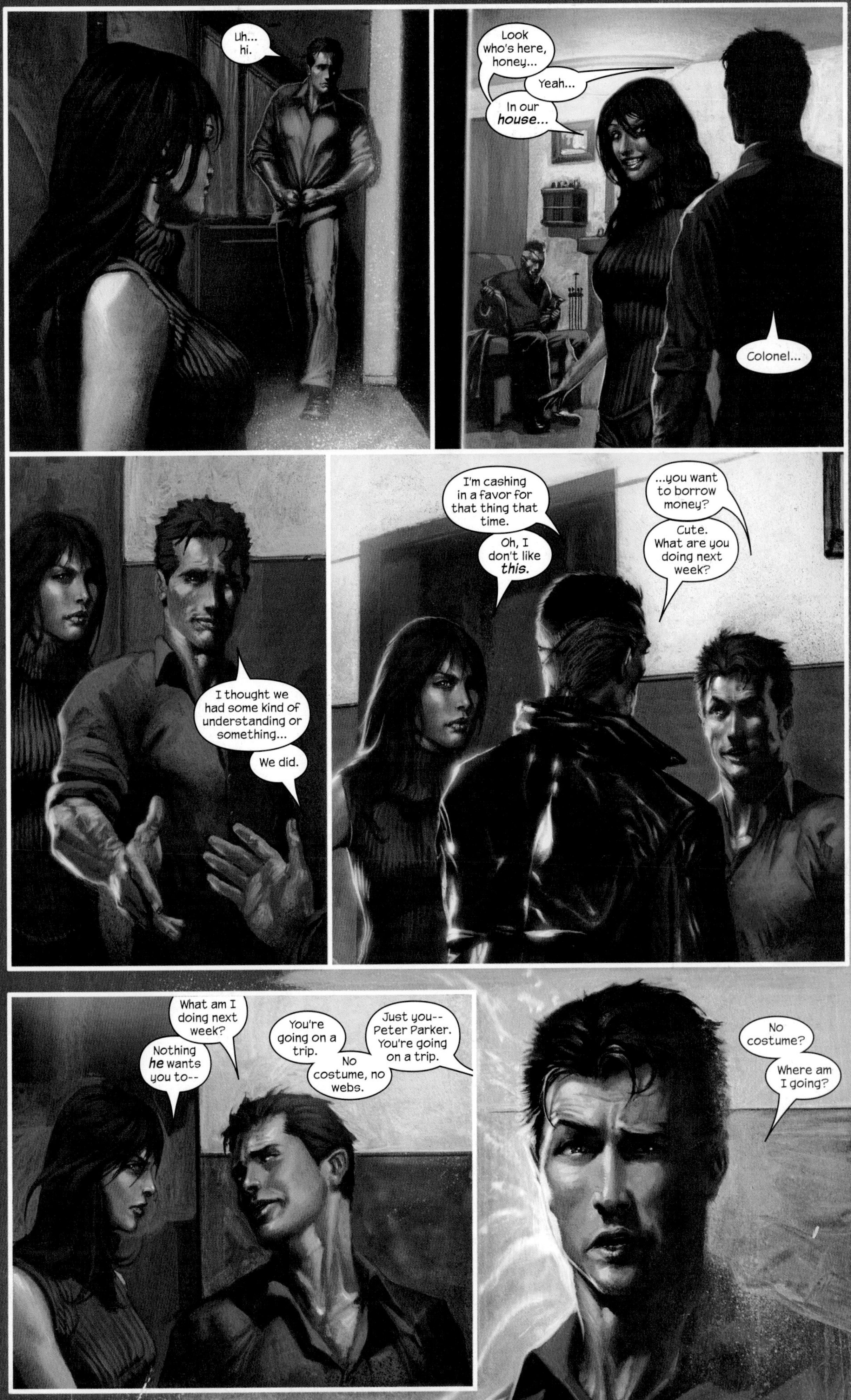
Uh... hi.
Look who's here, honey...
Yeah...
In our *house...*
Colonel...
I thought we had some kind of understanding or something...
We did.
I'm cashing in a favor for that thing that time.
Oh, I don't like *this.*
...you want to borrow money?
Cute. What are you doing next week?
What am I doing next week?
Nothing *he* wants you to--
You're going on a trip.
No costume, no webs.
Just you-- Peter Parker. You're going on a trip.
No costume?
Where am I going?

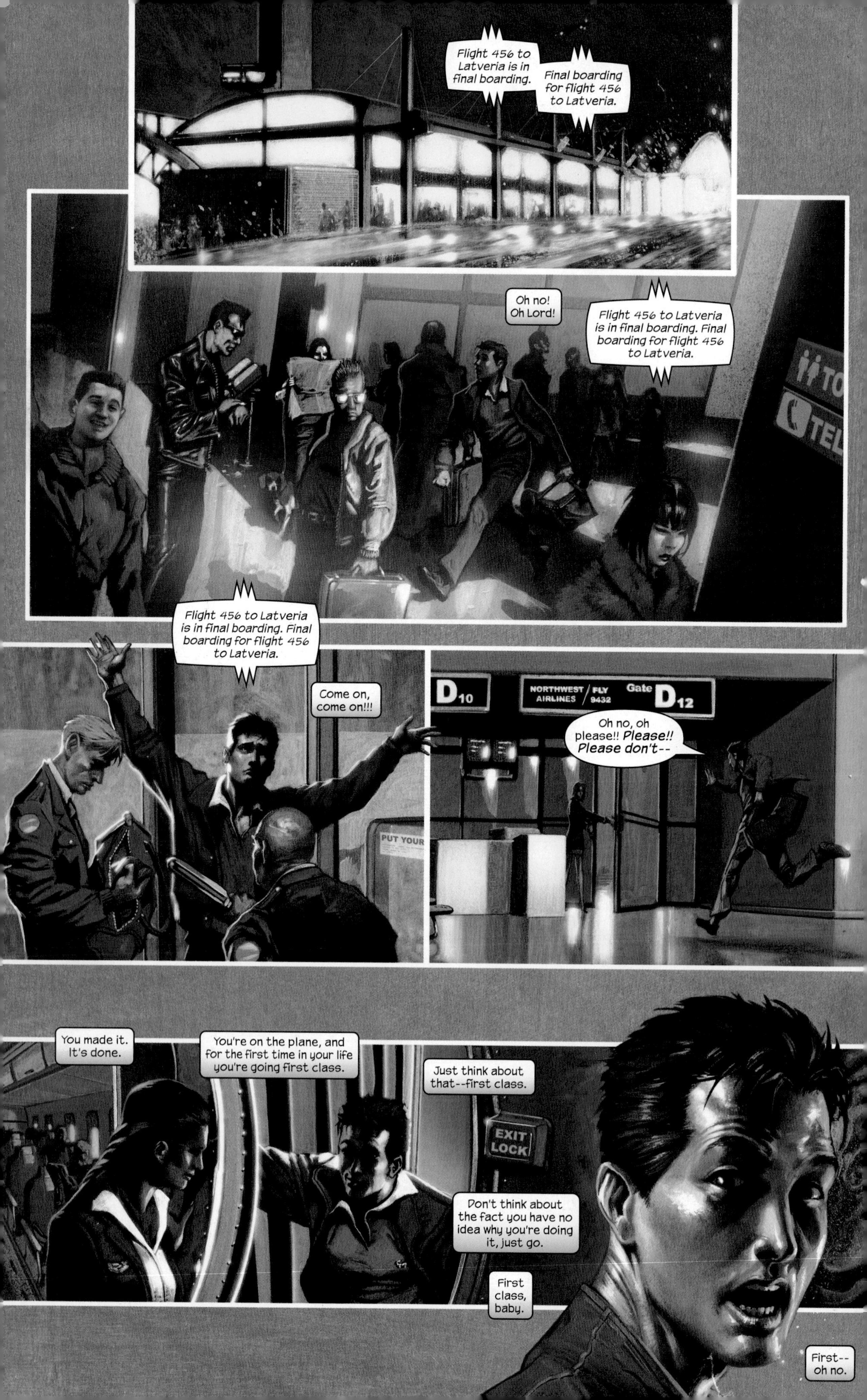
Flight 456 to Latveria is in final boarding.
Final boarding for flight 456 to Latveria.
Oh no! Oh Lord!
Flight 456 to Latveria is in final boarding. Final boarding for flight 456 to Latveria.
TO
TEL
Flight 456 to Latveria is in final boarding. Final boarding for flight 456 to Latveria.
Come on, come on!!!
PUT YOUR
D10
NORTHWEST AIRLINES / FLY 9432
Gate D12
Oh no, oh please!! *Please!! Please don't--*
You made it. It's done.
You're on the plane, and for the first time in your life you're going first class.
Just think about that--first class.
EXIT LOCK
Don't think about the fact you have no idea why you're doing it, just go.
First class, baby.
First-- oh no.

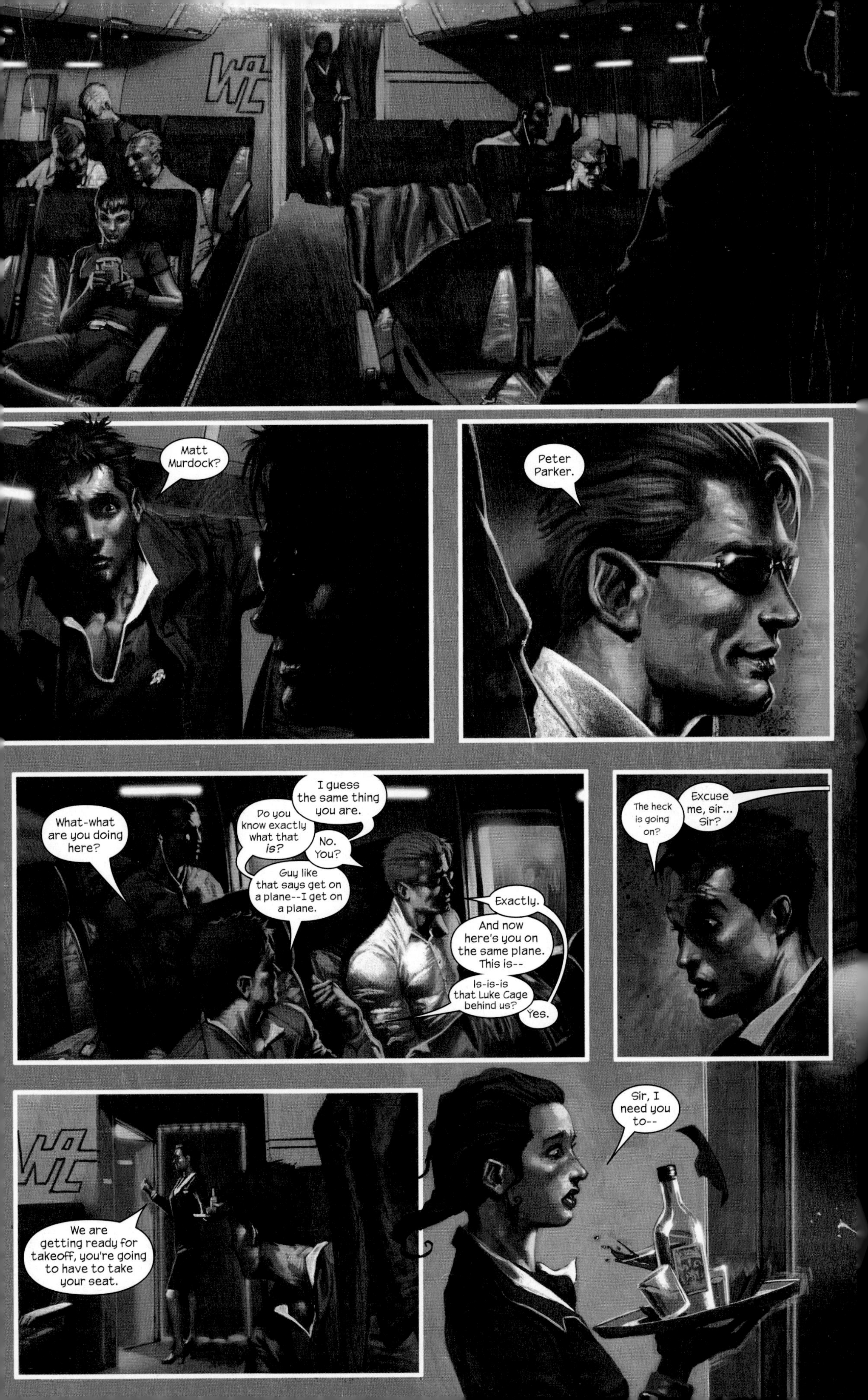
Matt Murdock?
Peter Parker.
What-what are you doing here?
I guess the same thing you are.
Do you know exactly what that *is*?
No. You?
Guy like that says get on a plane--I get on a plane.
Exactly.
And now here's you on the same plane. This is--
Is-is-is that Luke Cage behind us?
Yes.
The heck is going on?
Excuse me, sir... Sir?
We are getting ready for takeoff, you're going to have to take your seat.
Sir, I need you to--

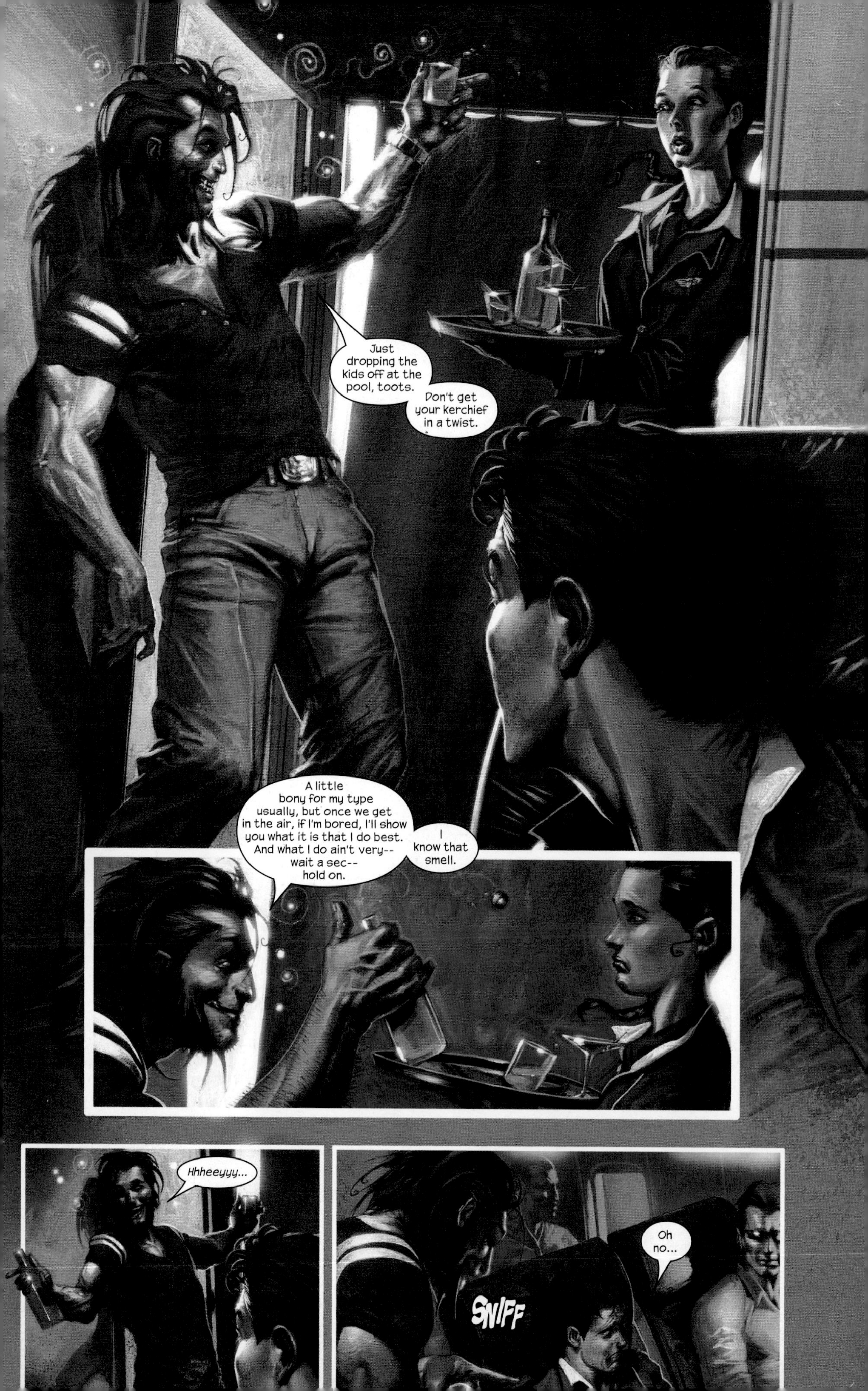
Just dropping the kids off at the pool, toots.
Don't get your kerchief in a twist.
A little bony for my type usually, but once we get in the air, if I'm bored, I'll show you what it is that I do best. And what I do ain't very-- wait a sec-- hold on.
I know that smell.
Hhheeyyy...
Oh no...
SNIFF

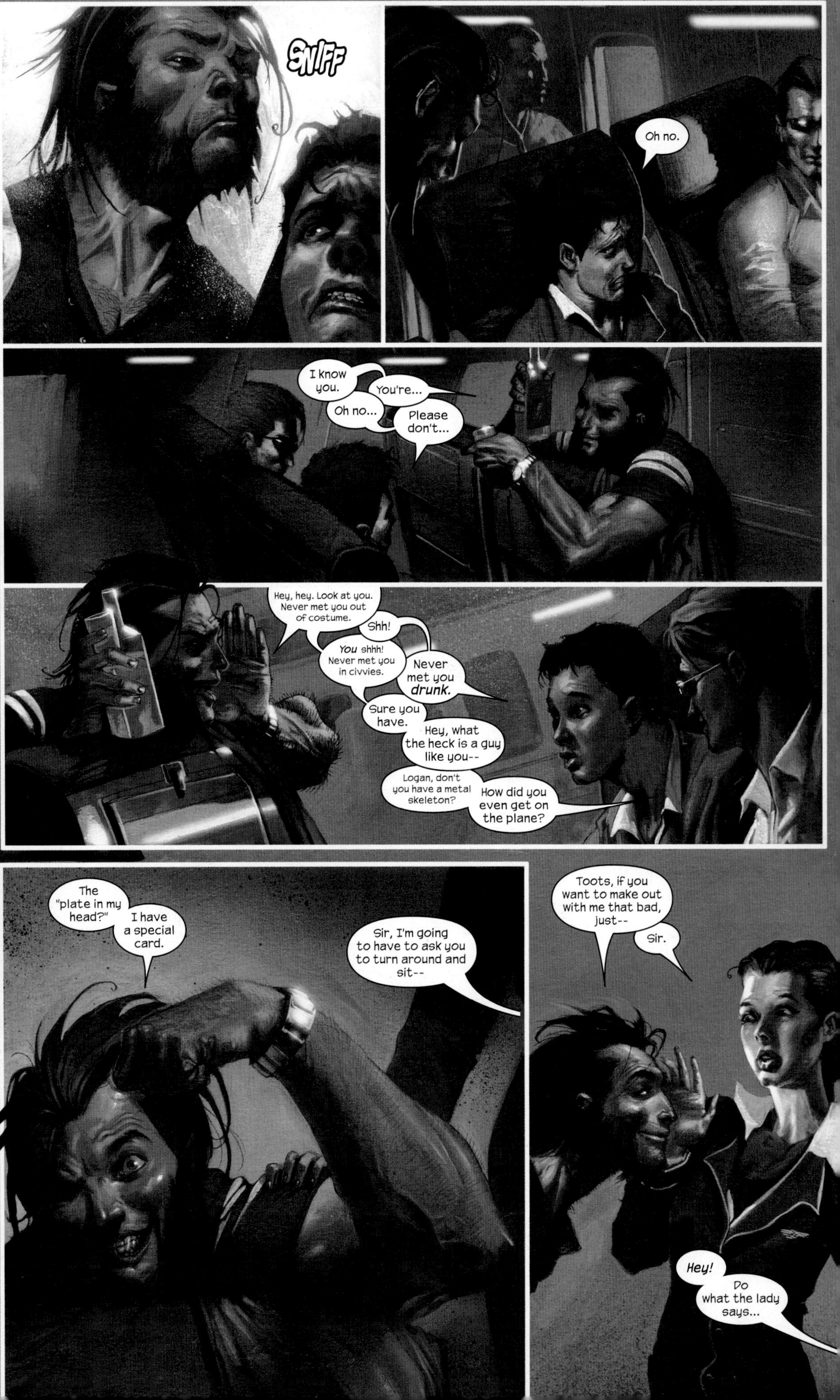
SNIFF
Oh no.
I know you.
You're...
Oh no...
Please don't...
Hey, hey. Look at you. Never met you out of costume.
Shh!
You shhh! Never met you in civvies.
Never met you *drunk.*
Sure you have.
Hey, what the heck is a guy like you--
Logan, don't you have a metal skeleton?
How did you even get on the plane?
The "plate in my head?"
I have a special card.
Sir, I'm going to have to ask you to turn around and sit--
Toots, if you want to make out with me that bad, just--
Sir.
Hey!
Do what the lady says...

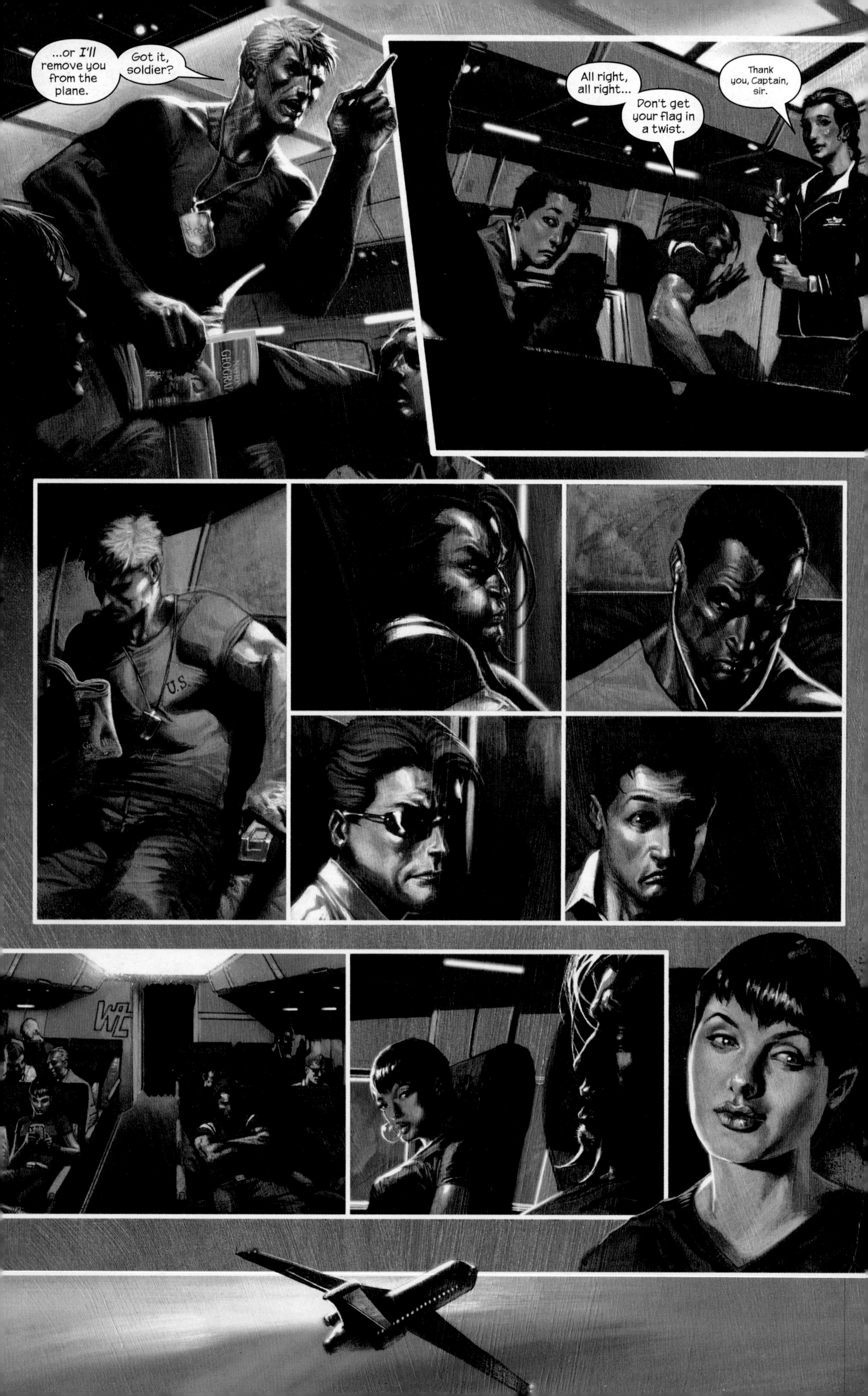
...or *I'll* remove you from the plane.
Got it, soldier?
All right, all right...
Don't get your flag in a twist.
Thank you, Captain, sir.

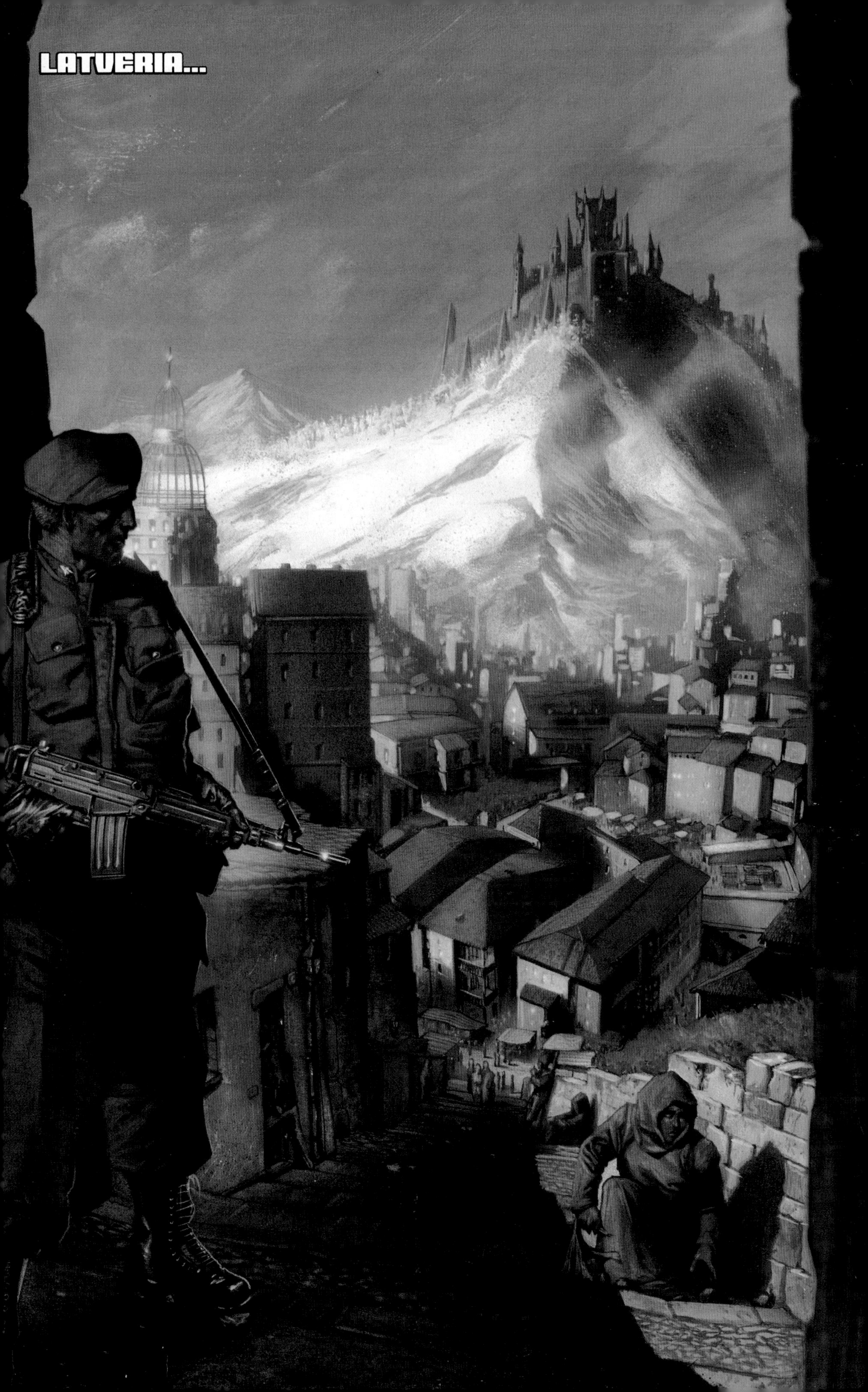
LATVERIA...

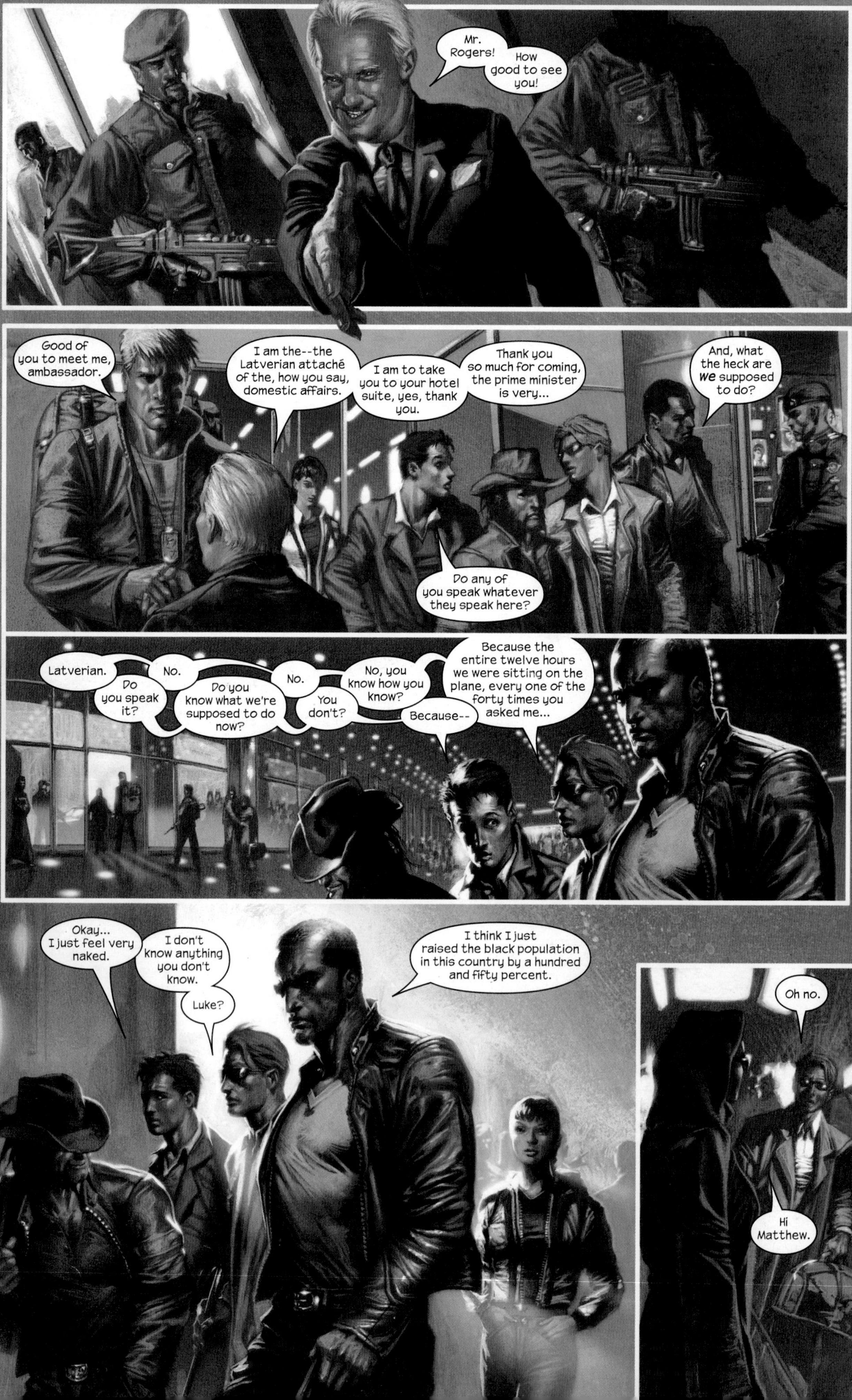
Mr. Rogers!
How good to see you!
Good of you to meet me, ambassador.
I am the--the Latverian attaché of the, how you say, domestic affairs.
I am to take you to your hotel suite, yes, thank you.
Thank you so much for coming, the prime minister is very...
And, what the heck are *we* supposed to do?
Do any of you speak whatever they speak here?
Latverian.
Do you speak it?
No.
Do you know what we're supposed to do now?
No.
You don't?
No, you know how you know?
Because--
Because the entire twelve hours we were sitting on the plane, every one of the forty times you asked me...
Okay... I just feel very naked.
I don't know anything you don't know.
Luke?
I think I just raised the black population in this country by a hundred and fifty percent.
Oh no.
Hi Matthew.

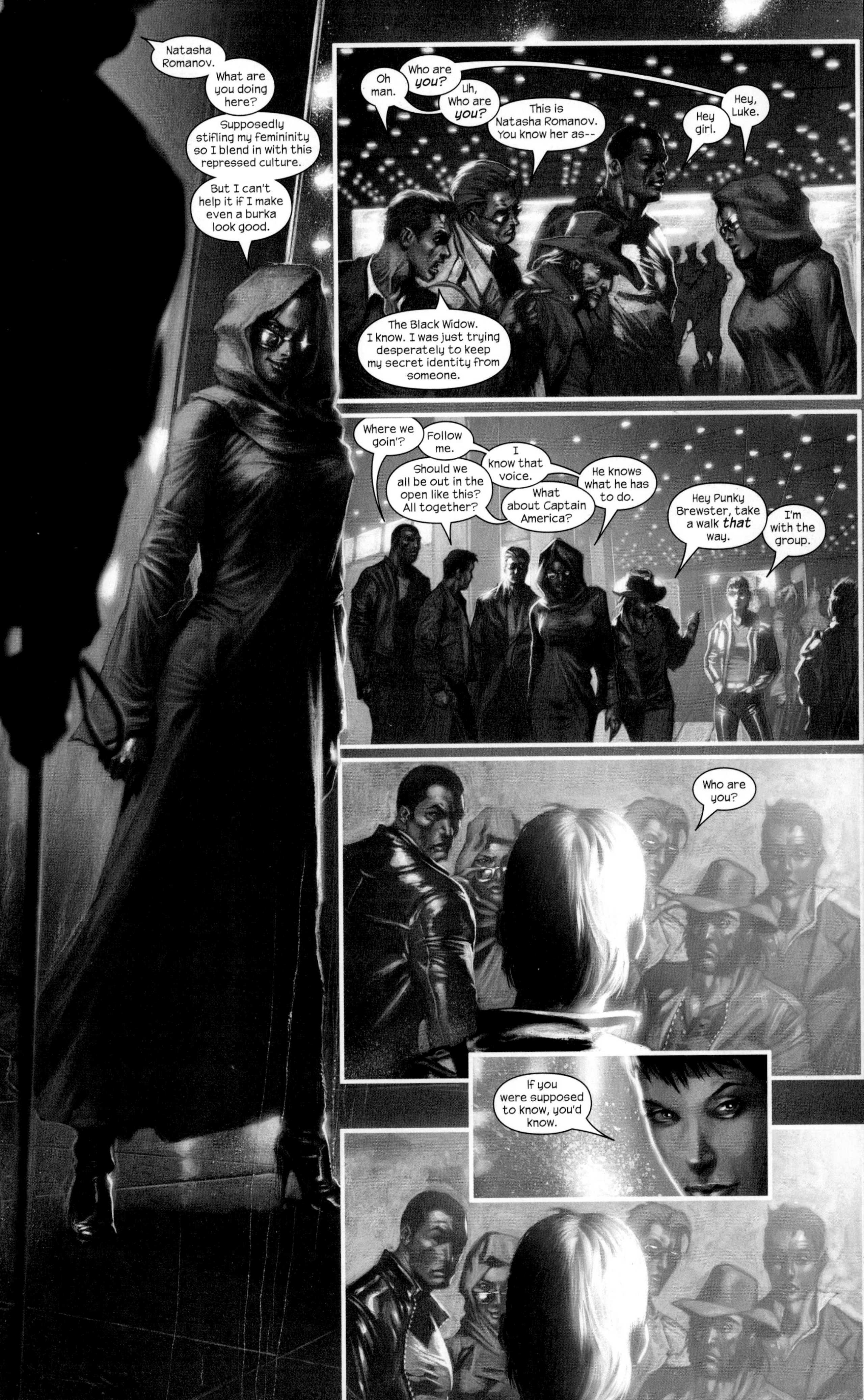
Natasha Romanov.
What are you doing here?
Supposedly stifling my femininity so I blend in with this repressed culture.
But I can't help it if I make even a burka look good.
Oh man.
Who are *you?*
Uh, Who are *you?*
This is Natasha Romanov. You know her as--
Hey girl.
Hey, Luke.
The Black Widow. I know. I was just trying desperately to keep my secret identity from someone.
Where we goin'?
Follow me.
Should we all be out in the open like this? All together?
I know that voice.
What about Captain America?
He knows what he has to do.
Hey Punky Brewster, take a walk *that* way.
I'm with the group.
Who are you?
If you were supposed to know, you'd know.

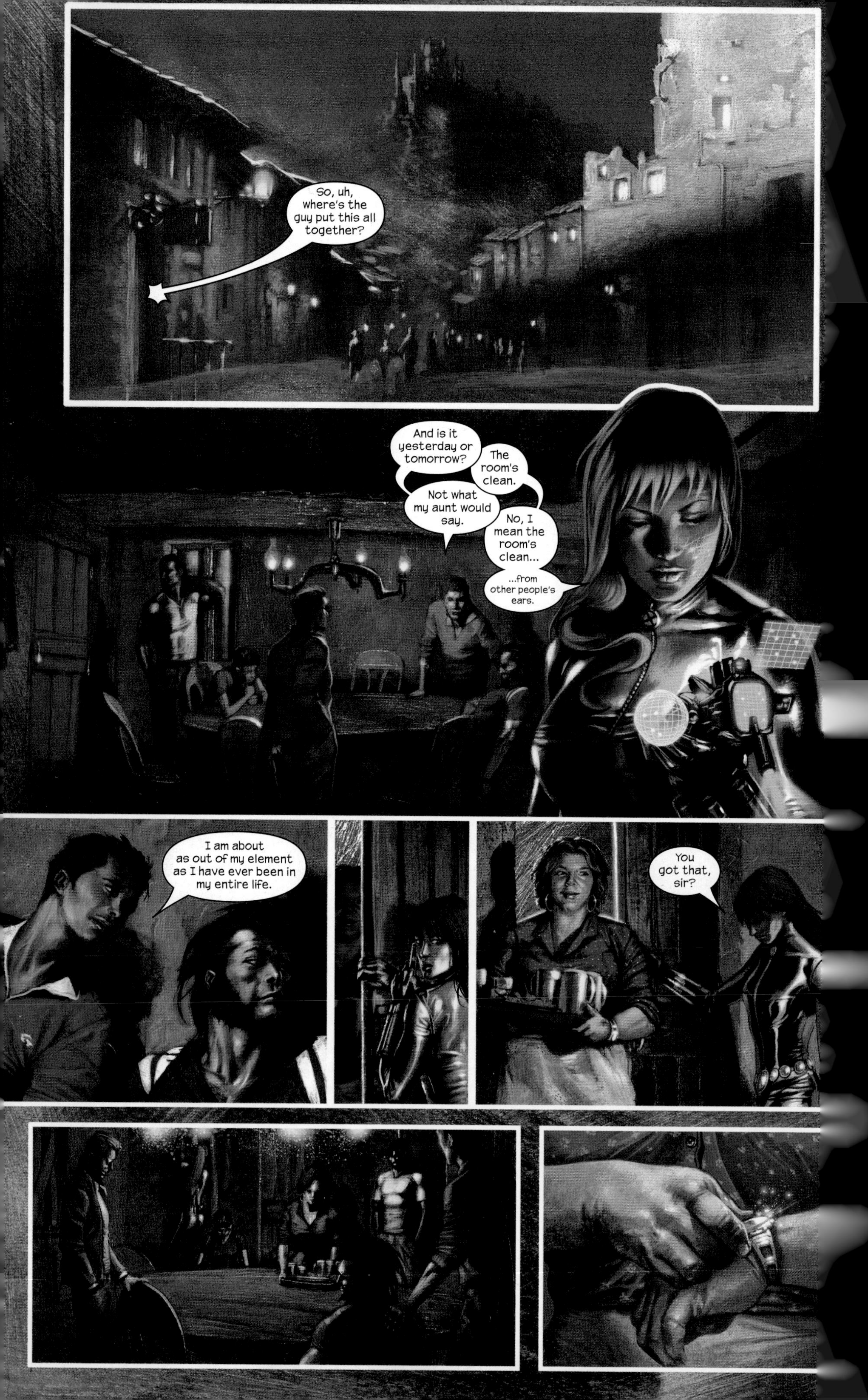
So, uh, where's the guy put this all together?
And is it yesterday or tomorrow?
The room's clean.
Not what my aunt would say.
No, I mean the room's clean...
...from other people's ears.
I am about as out of my element as I have ever been in my entire life.
You got that, sir?

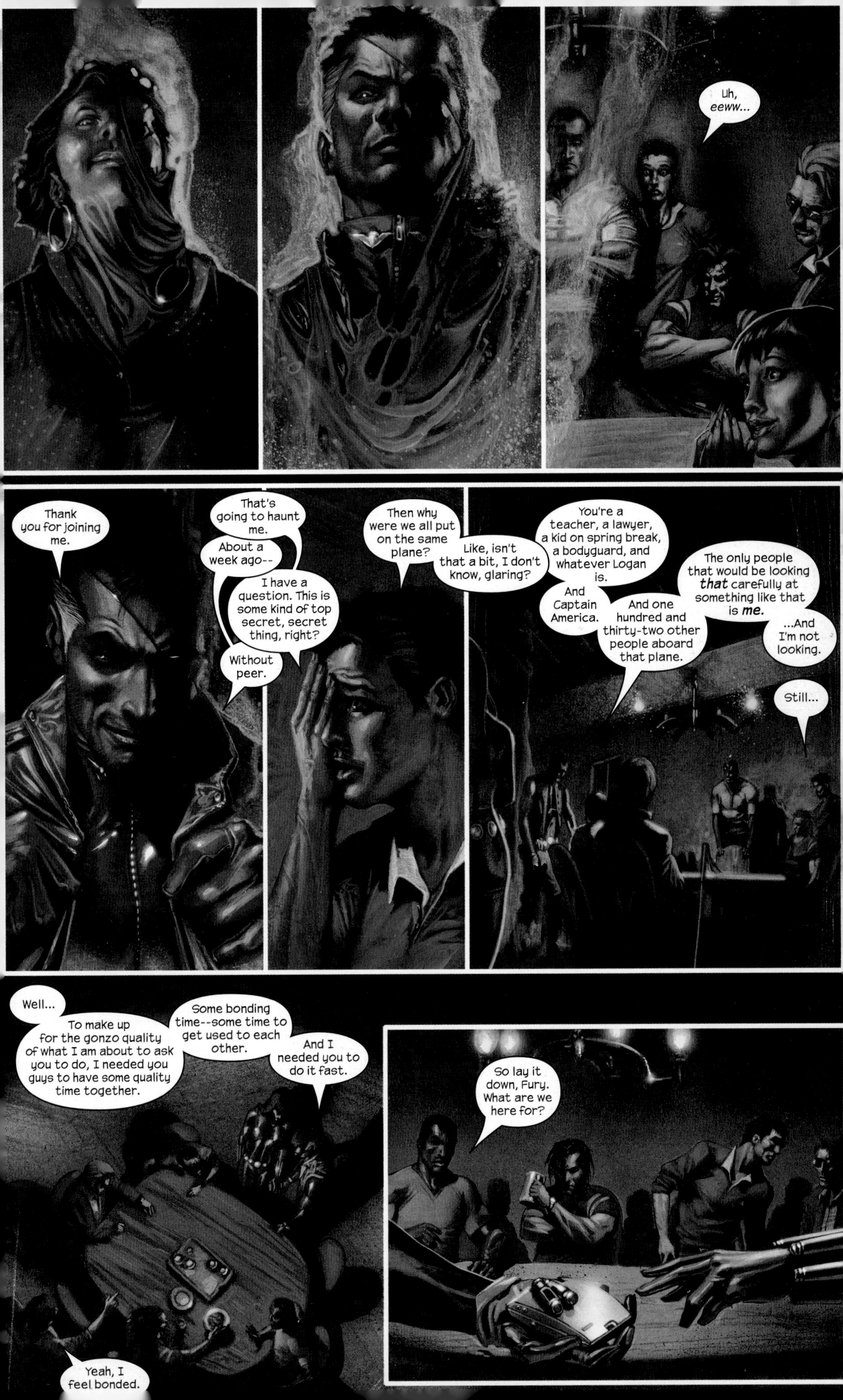
Uh, eeww...
Thank you for joining me.
That's going to haunt me.
About a week ago--
I have a question. This is some kind of top secret, secret thing, right?
Without peer.
Then why were we all put on the same plane?
Like, isn't that a bit, I don't know, glaring?
You're a teacher, a lawyer, a kid on spring break, a bodyguard, and whatever Logan is.
And Captain America.
And one hundred and thirty-two other people aboard that plane.
The only people that would be looking **that** carefully at something like that is **me.**
...And I'm not looking.
Still...
Well...
To make up for the gonzo quality of what I am about to ask you to do, I needed you guys to have some quality time together.
Some bonding time--some time to get used to each other.
And I needed you to do it fast.
Yeah, I feel bonded.
So lay it down, Fury. What are we here for?

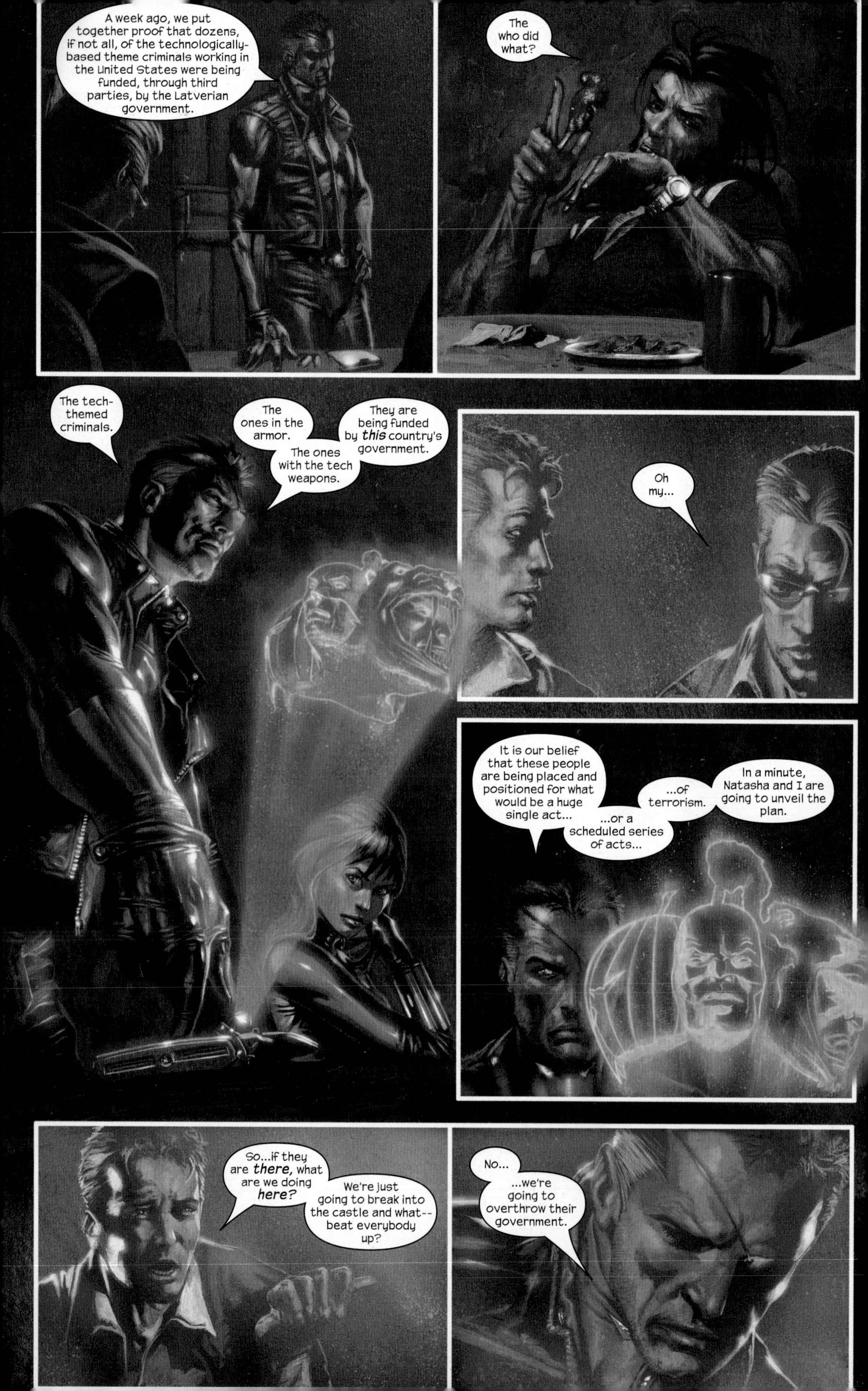

A week ago, we put together proof that dozens, if not all, of the technologically-based theme criminals working in the United States were being funded, through third parties, by the Latverian government.
The who did what?
The tech-themed criminals.
The ones in the armor.
The ones with the tech weapons.
They are being funded by *this* country's government.
Oh my...
It is our belief that these people are being placed and positioned for what would be a huge single act...
...or a scheduled series of acts...
...of terrorism.
In a minute, Natasha and I are going to unveil the plan.
So...if they are *there,* what are we doing *here?*
We're just going to break into the castle and what--beat everybody up?
No...
...we're going to overthrow their government.

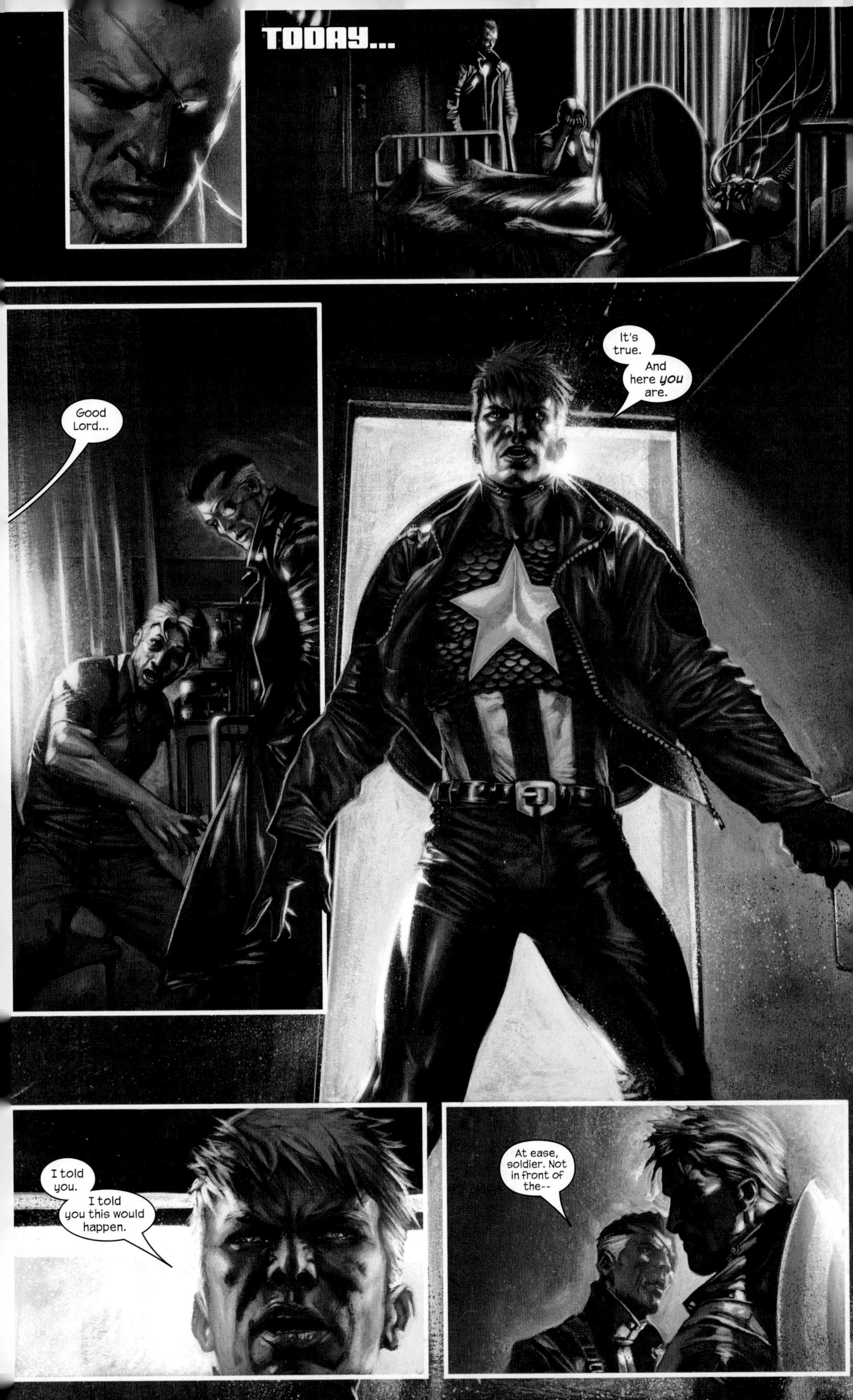
TODAY...
Good Lord...
It's true.
And here *you* are.
I told you.
I told you this would happen.
At ease, soldier. Not in front of the--

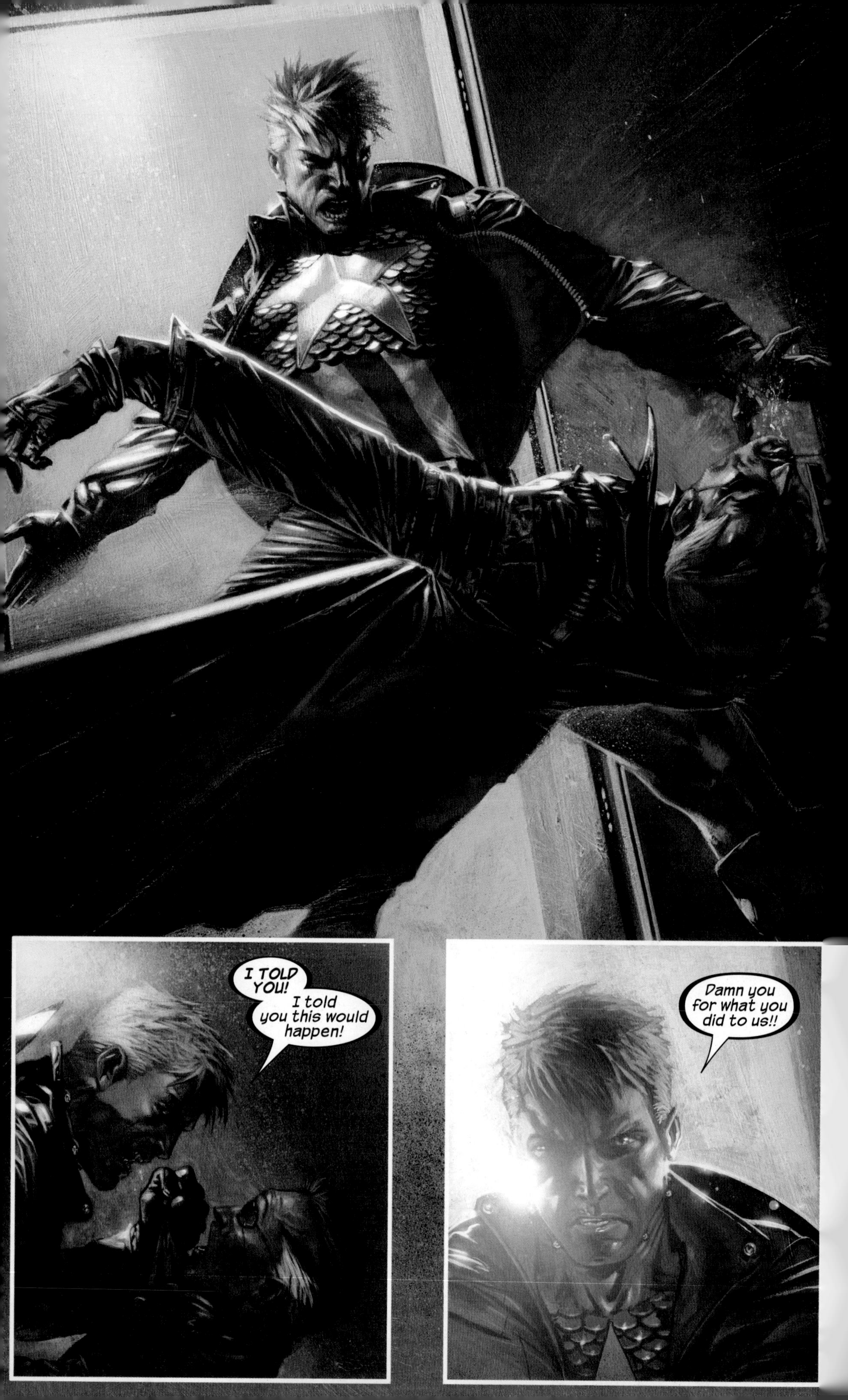
I TOLD YOU!
I told you this would happen!
Damn you for what you did to us!!

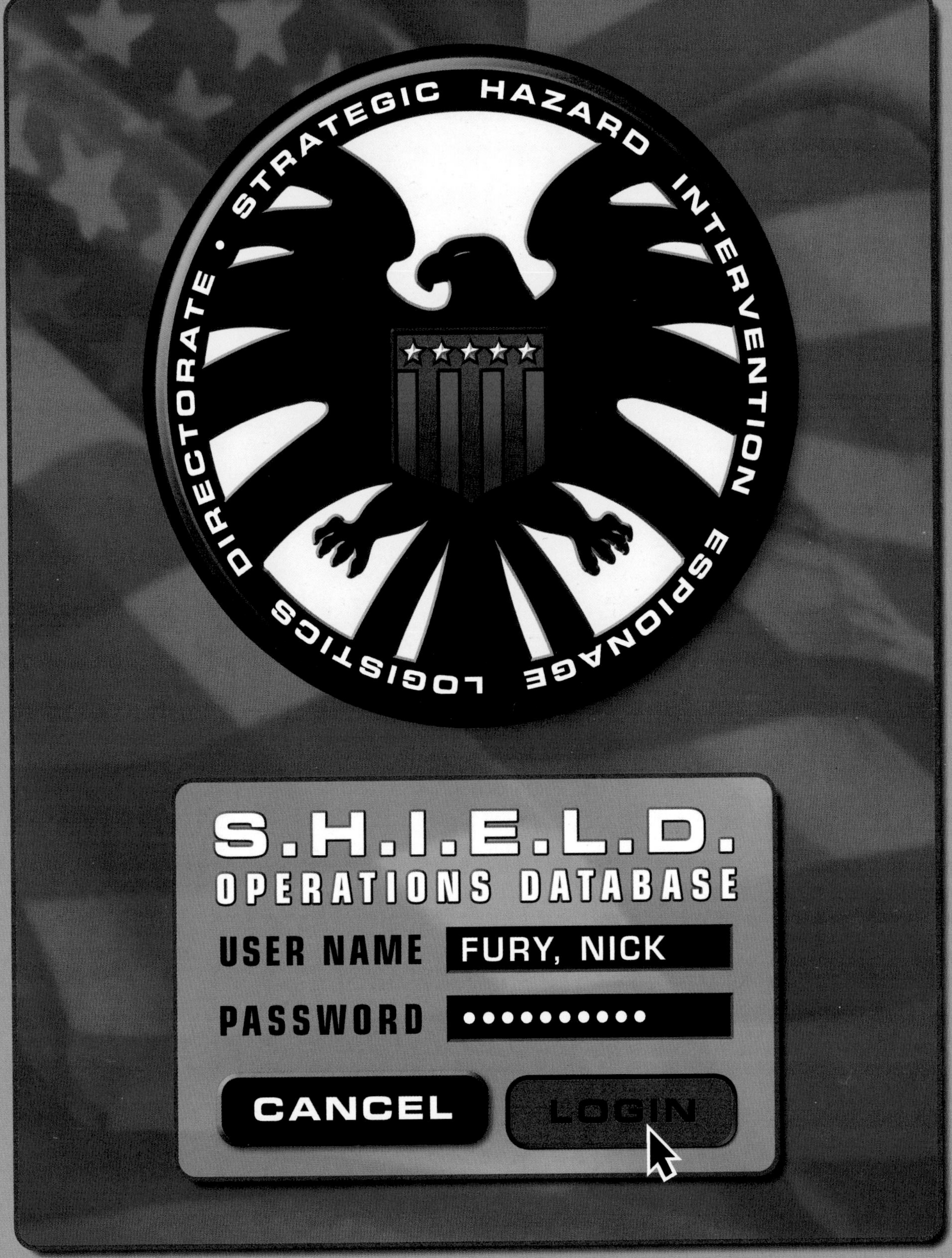
STRATEGIC HAZARD INTERVENTION ESPIONAGE LOGISTICS DIRECTORATE
S.H.I.E.L.D.
OPERATIONS DATABASE
USER NAME
FURY, NICK
PASSWORD
CANCEL
LOGIN

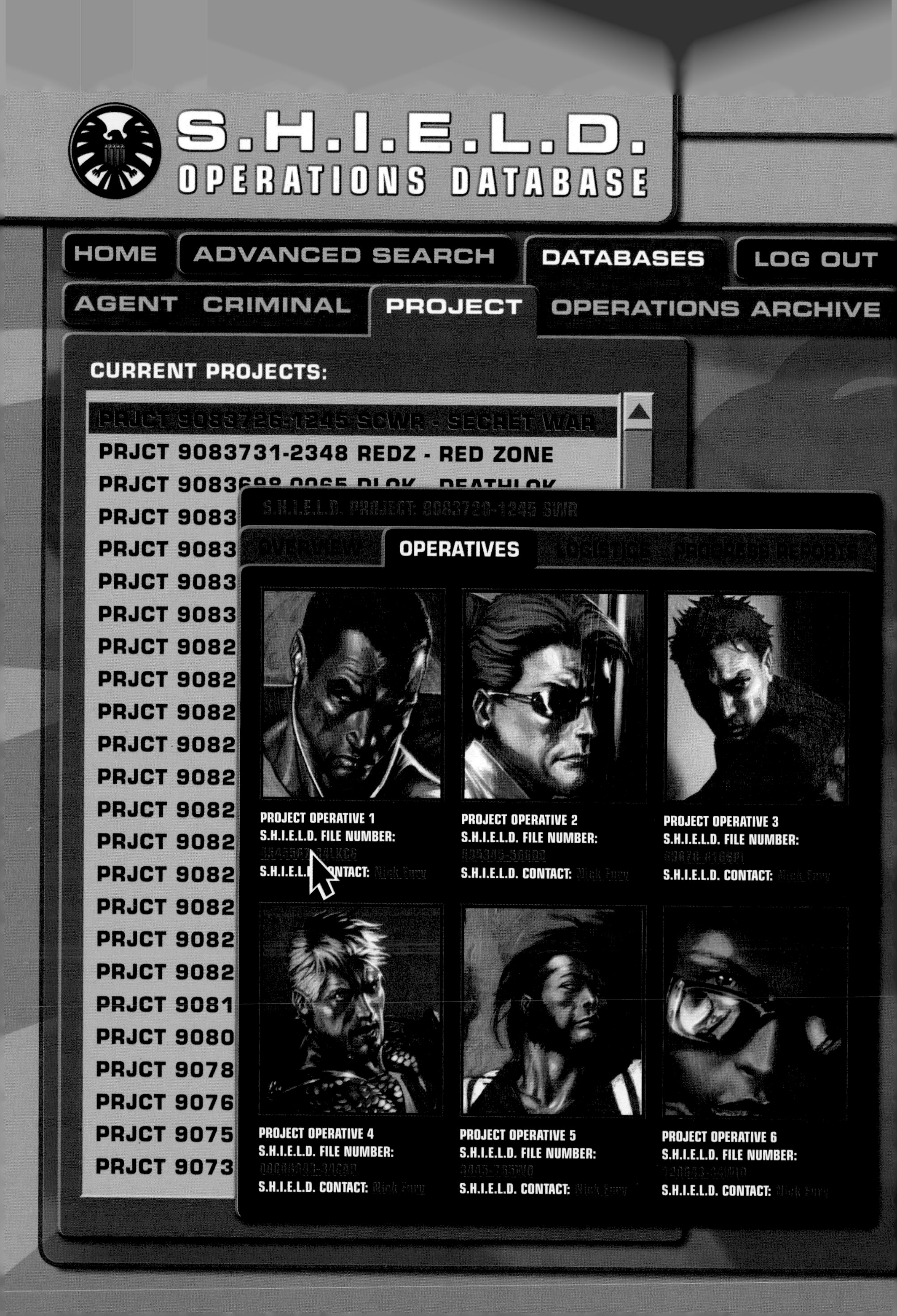

S.H.I.E.L.D.
OPERATIONS DATABASE

HOME ADVANCED SEARCH DATABASES LOG OUT

AGENT CRIMINAL PROJECT OPERATIONS ARCHIVE

CURRENT PROJECTS:

PRJCT 9083726-1245 SCWR - SECRET WAR
PRJCT 9083731-2348 REDZ - RED ZONE
PRJCT 9083698-0065 DLOK - DEATHLOK
PRJCT 9083
PRJCT 9083
PRJCT 9083
PRJCT 9083
PRJCT 9083
PRJCT 9082
PRJCT 9082
PRJCT 9082
PRJCT 9082
PRJCT 9082
PRJCT 9082
PRJCT 9082
PRJCT 9082
PRJCT 9082
PRJCT 9082
PRJCT 9082
PRJCT 9082
PRJCT 9081
PRJCT 9080
PRJCT 9078
PRJCT 9076
PRJCT 9075
PRJCT 9073

S.H.I.E.L.D. PROJECT: 9083726-1245 SWR

OVERVIEW **OPERATIVES** LOGISTICS PROGRESS REPORTS

PROJECT OPERATIVE 1
S.H.I.E.L.D. FILE NUMBER:
554560 241KCC
S.H.I.E.L.D. CONTACT: Nick Fury

PROJECT OPERATIVE 2
S.H.I.E.L.D. FILE NUMBER:
435345-56600
S.H.I.E.L.D. CONTACT: Nick Fury

PROJECT OPERATIVE 3
S.H.I.E.L.D. FILE NUMBER:
R9G7R-6164PI
S.H.I.E.L.D. CONTACT: Nick Fury

PROJECT OPERATIVE 4
S.H.I.E.L.D. FILE NUMBER:
00000032-3AGAP
S.H.I.E.L.D. CONTACT: Nick Fury

PROJECT OPERATIVE 5
S.H.I.E.L.D. FILE NUMBER:
3445-265WO
S.H.I.E.L.D. CONTACT: Nick Fury

PROJECT OPERATIVE 6
S.H.I.E.L.D. FILE NUMBER:
120033-34WIO
S.H.I.E.L.D. CONTACT: Nick Fury

SEARCH DATABASE OPERATIVES, SECRET WAR **SEARCH**

S.H.I.E.L.D. FILE NUMBER 4545567-34LKCG

PROJECT DATABASE >> PROJECT: 9083728-1245 SWR >> PROJECT OPERATIVE 1

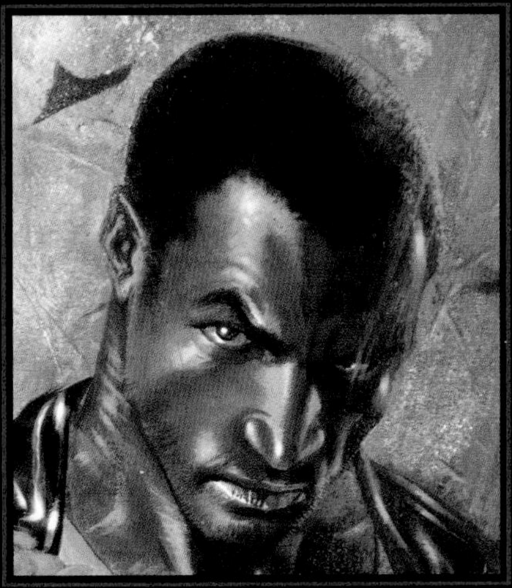

REAL NAME: *Carl Lucas*

ALIAS/ES: *Luke Cage, Hero for Hire, Power Man*

IDENTITY STATUS: *Public*

MARITAL STATUS: *Single*

RELATIVES: *Leonard Lucas (Father, Deceased), Esther Lucas (Mother, Deceased)*

BASE OF OPERATIONS: *Harlem, New York City*

PLACE OF BIRTH: *Harlem, New York City*

LEGAL STATUS: *American citizen acquitted of criminal charges*

OCCUPATION: *Hero for hire*

AFFILIATIONS: *Heroes for Hire Inc.*

HEIGHT: *6 ft. 6 in.* **WEIGHT:** *425 lbs.* **EYES:** *Brown* **HAIR:** *Black*

POWERS/WEAPONS: *Power level 8. Superhuman strength, dense muscle and bone tissue. Steel-hard skin.*

ENEMIES: *Diamondback (Deceased), Gideon Mace, Master Kahn, Constrictor, Bushmaster, Hardcore*

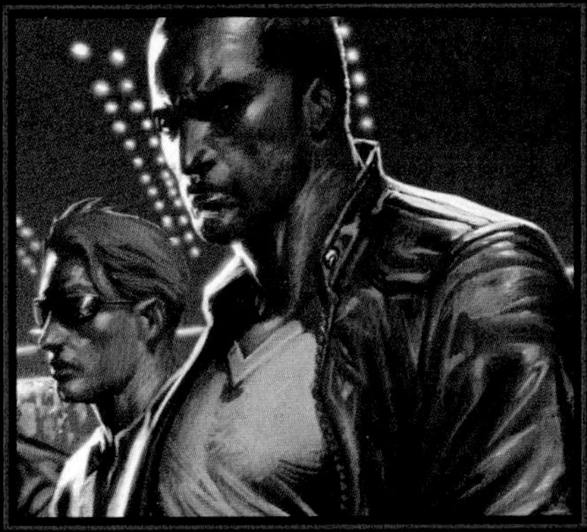

NICK FURY NOTE: *Cage will take money from anyone on the planet except me for services rendered, but he has an intense sense of patriotism and duty that can easily be manipulated. But only for the right kind of mission. He has a tendency to do interviews.*

S.H.I.E.L.D.
OPERATIONS DATABASE

HOME | **ADVANCED SEARCH** | **DATABASES** | **LOG OUT**

S.H.I.E.L.D. FILE NUMBER 535345-56GDD

PROJECT DATABASE >> PROJECT: 9083728-1245 SWR >> PROJECT OPERATIVE 2

REAL NAME: *Matthew Michael Murdock*

ALIAS/ES: *Daredevil, Mike Murdock, Jack Batlin*

IDENTITY STATUS: *Publicly Disputed*

MARITAL STATUS: *Unclear*

RELATIVES: *Jonathan "Jack" Murdock (Father, Deceased), Grace Murdock (Mother), Milla Donovan (Wife, Unmarried),*

BASE OF OPERATIONS: *Hell's Kitchen, New York City*

PLACE OF BIRTH: *Hell's Kitchen, New York City*

LEGAL STATUS: *Citizen of the United States. No criminal record.*

OCCUPATION: *Lawyer*

AFFILIATIONS: *Natasha Romanov aka Black Widow (See S.H.I.E.L.D. FILE NUMBER 56GDG56-870W)*

HEIGHT: *6'0" WEIGHT: 200 lbs EYES: Blue HAIR: Red*

POWERS/WEAPONS: *Power level 7. Superhuman senses. All senses register at a high level. Audio-radar sense. Olympic athlete and gymnast. Ninja martial arts training. Highly effective in combat with his customized billy club.*

ENEMIES: *Kingpin, Owl, Purple Man, Mister Fear, Stilt-Man, Gladiator, Bullseye, Typhoid Mary, Elektra.*

NICK FURY NOTE: *Murdock straddles the line between enforcing the law and upholding justice. Perfect for certain types of covert ops. Black Widow has him wrapped around her finger. Important to note for future.*

SEARCH DATABASE OPERATIVES, SECRET WAR **SEARCH**

S.H.I.E.L.D. FILE NUMBER 69678-616SPI

PROJECT DATABASE >> PROJECT: 9083728-1245 SWR >> PROJECT OPERATIVE 3

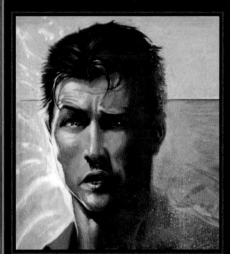

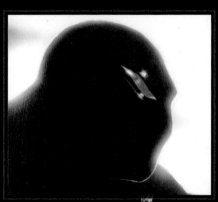

REAL NAME: *Peter Parker (Classified)*

ALIAS/ES: *Spider Man*

IDENTITY STATUS: *Secret.*

MARITAL STATUS: *Married*

RELATIVES: *Mary Jane Watson Parker (Wife), Ben Parker (Uncle, Deceased), May Parker (Aunt).*

BASE OF OPERATIONS: *New York City*

PLACE OF BIRTH: *Queens, New York City*

LEGAL STATUS: *American citizen with no criminal record*

OCCUPATION: *Freelance photographer, teacher*

AFFILIATIONS: *None*

HEIGHT: *5 ft. 10 in.* **WEIGHT:** *165 lbs.* **EYES:** *Brown* **HAIR:** *Brown*

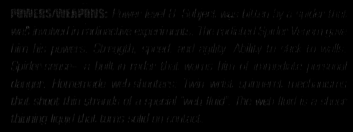

POWERS/WEAPONS: *Power level 8. Subject was bitten by a spider that was involved in radioactive experiments. The radiated Spider Venom gave him his powers. Strength, speed, and agility. Ability to stick to walls. Spider-sense— a built in radar that warns him of immediate personal danger. Homemade web-shooters: Twin wrist spinneret mechanisms that shoot thin strands of a special "web fluid". The web fluid is a sheer thinning liquid that turns solid on contact.*

ENEMIES: *Green Goblin, Doctor Octopus, Vulture, Lizard, Scorpion, Electro, Sandman, Mysterio, Kraven the Hunter, Venom, Carnage.*

NICK FURY NOTE: *Parker feeds off a staggering guilt that propels him to basically do anything you tell him he has to do. The public perception of him is a big negative. Keep a distance unless absolutely necessary.*

S.H.I.E.L.D.
OPERATIONS DATABASE

HOME | **ADVANCED SEARCH** | **DATABASES** | **LOG OUT**

S.H.I.E.L.D. FILE NUMBER 00008643-34CAP

PROJECT DATABASE >> PROJECT: 9083728-1245 SWR >> PROJECT OPERATIVE 4

REAL NAME: *Steve Rogers*

ALIAS/ES: *Captain America, The Captain, Nomad*

IDENTITY STATUS: *Public*

MARITAL STATUS: *Single*

RELATIVES: *Joseph Rogers & Sarah Rogers (Parents, both deceased)*

BASE OF OPERATIONS: *New York City*

PLACE OF BIRTH: *New York City*

LEGAL STATUS: *American citizen with no criminal record*

OCCUPATION: *Crimefighter, licensed freelance artist*

AFFILIATIONS: *Avengers, Former Invaders, partner to Bucky (Deceased), Nomad, the Falcon*

HEIGHT: *6 ft. 2 in.* **WEIGHT:** *240 lbs.* **EYES:** *Blue* **HAIR:** *Blond*

POWERS/WEAPONS: *Power Level 8. Steve is the product of a military experiment, super-soldier Operation: Rebirth, in which he was given the Super-Soldier Serum and bombarded with Vita-Rays (wavelengths of radiation). Peak human agility, strength, speed, endurance, master of the Martial Arts, Boxing, Judo. Virtually indestructible alloy shield.*

ENEMIES: *Red Skull, Batroc, Baron Zemo I & II, Modok, Hydra*

NICK FURY NOTE: *Cap is the most and least efficient agent. His public persona has become a large problem for stealth work, but for certain types of missions it's the perfect decoy. His patriotism is slanted and out of date. He rarely deals with his anger issues.*

SEARCH DATABASE OPERATIVES, SECRET WAR **SEARCH**

S.H.I.E.L.D. FILE NUMBER 3445-765WO

PROJECT DATABASE >> PROJECT: 9083728-1245 SWR >> PROJECT OPERATIVE 5

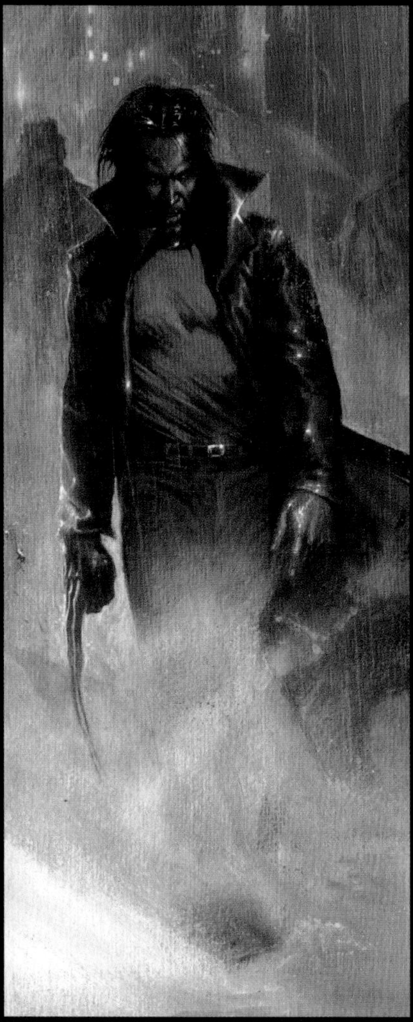

REAL NAME: *Classified*

ALIAS/ES: *Wolverine, Logan, Patch, Weapon X,*

IDENTITY STATUS: *Secret*

MARITAL STATUS: *Single*

RELATIVES: *Amiko (foster daughter)*

BASE OF OPERATIONS: *Westchester, NY*

PLACE OF BIRTH: *Classified*

LEGAL STATUS: *Canadian Citizen*

OCCUPATION: *Adventurer, member of the X-Men, former Samurai, former C.I.A. operative, Canada's Weapon X Program, Xavier Institute for Higher Learning, the Clan Yashida compound in Japan; Department H in Canada.*

AFFILIATIONS: *X-Men, (former) Clan Yashida, the Weapon X Program, Alpha Flight*

HEIGHT: *5 ft. 3 in.* **WEIGHT:** *With adamantium skeleton 300 lbs.*

EYES: *Blue* **HAIR:** *Black*

POWERS/WEAPONS: *Power level-9. Mutant. Regenerates damaged or destroyed areas of his body & internal organs. Immune to poisons & alcohol. Superhuman acute senses. Adamantium bonded to his entire skeleton. Three 1 foot long Adamantium claws on each hand which he can "sheathe." Adamantium skeleton result of a top secret Canadian project named Weapon X. Everything concerning Logan's origin is a mystery.*

ENEMIES: *Sabretooth, Magneto, Lady Deathstrike, Juggernaut, Hulk, Silver Samurai, Cyber (Deceased), Ogun, The Hand, Omega Red, The Reavers*

NICK FURY NOTE: *Logan is my secret weapon. He owes me his life five times over. His entire persona makes for the perfect ruthless stealth agent. In a perfect world, he would be a level ten S.H.I.E.L.D. Agent.*

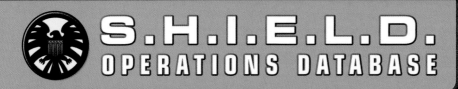

S.H.I.E.L.D.
OPERATIONS DATABASE

HOME | ADVANCED SEARCH | DATABASES | LOG OUT

S.H.I.E.L.D. FILE NUMBER 5605656- 67BW

PROJECT DATABASE >> PROJECT: 9083728-1245 SWR >> PROJECT OPERATIVE 6

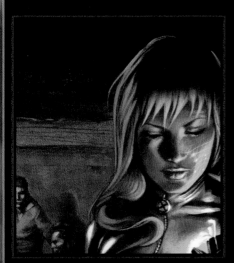

REAL NAME: *Classified*

ALIAS/ES: *Black Widow*

IDENTITY STATUS: *Classified*

MARITAL STATUS: *Single*

RELATIVES: *Classified*

BASE OF OPERATIONS: *Classified*

PLACE OF BIRTH: *Classified*

LEGAL STATUS: *Classified*

OCCUPATION: *Spy*

AFFILIATIONS: *Avengers*

HEIGHT: *5 ft. 6 in.* **WEIGHT:** *125 lbs* **EYES:** *Brown* **HAIR:** *Red*

POWERS/WEAPONS: *Classified*

ENEMIES: *Classified*

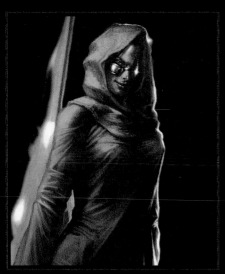

NICK FURY NOTE: *Classified*

SEARCH DATABASE JOHNSON, DAISY **SEARCH**

S.H.I.E.L.D. DOCUMENT 68785895-78795 HJFBK

CRIMINAL_DATABASE >> OPERATIONS_DOCUMENTS >> INTERROGATIONS
SECRET CODE: WHITE

Interrogation Transcript
Subject: Daisy_Johnson, minor, age 17

Interrogation conducted by S.H.I.E.L.D. Commander Nicholas Fury (level 10). Code clearance: White.
Interrogation observed by S.H.I.E.L.D. Agent Jasper Sitwell (level 5) and S.H.I.E.L.D. Agent Clay Quartermain (level 8)
Recording date: 4/5/2001
Place: S.H.I.E.L.D. Compound, Portland, Oregon

DAISY JOHNSON
Come on, how many of you cops I gotta talk to? It was just a record store.

NICK FURY
Stealing CDs? That how you plan on making a living?

DAISY JOHNSON
Oh my lord...

NICK FURY
Do you know who I am, Daisy?

DAISY JOHNSON
Daisy? My name is Cory.

NICK FURY
No, your name is Daisy. But my question is, do you know who I am?

DAISY JOHNSON
You do kinda look familiar.

NICK FURY
My name is Nick Fury.

DAISY JOHNSON
No *(beep)*.

NICK FURY
You're addressing a colonel, Daisy, watch your mouth.

DAISY JOHNSON
Stop calling me Daisy, you're freaking me out. Listen, I stole some CDs, I tried to—I can pay for them, it was two CDs. I didn't mean to, like, alert the National Guard.

NICK FURY
I'm not the National Guard. I'm the executive director of S.H.I.E.L.D. The Strategic Hazard Intervention Espionage Logistics Directorate.

DAISY JOHNSON
I really have no idea what is going on here.

NICK FURY
Then just sit still and listen. We're not talking to you because ya shoved some crappy music into your blouse...we're talkin' to you because of the tremor.

| HOME | ADVANCED SEARCH | DATABASES | LOG OUT |

CRIMINAL DATABASE >> S.H.I.E.L.D. DOCUMENT 696369-34934 THK (Cont.)

DAISY JOHNSON
The earthquake?

NICK FURY
That wasn't an earthquake. That was you.

DAISY JOHNSON
What?

NICK FURY
Rewind it in your head. You got caught stealing, you became agitated, you lost control of your body, you caused a tremor. A 3.2 on the Richter Scale.

DAISY JOHNSON
What?

NICK FURY
Daisy, Portland doesn't get earthquakes.

DAISY JOHNSON
Stop calling me Daisy!

NICK FURY
Your name, your real name is Daisy Johnson.

DAISY JOHNSON
My name is Cory Sutter. You're talking to the wrong girl.

NICK FURY
The Sutters adopted you when you were seven months old.

DAISY JOHNSON
They did not.

NICK FURY
(Opens the file and shows it to her.) They might not have told ya, but they did. Here. Your name before they changed it was Daisy Johnson. Your mother was a prostitute named Kim Johnson. Your father was a man named Calvin Zabo. Do you know the name?

DAISY JOHNSON
Calvin Zabo?

NICK FURY
He's known to the world as a mutation, calls himself Mister Hyde.

DAISY JOHNSON
Shut up.

NICK FURY
You've heard of Mister Hyde, criminal. Loud guy who fights super heroes?

DAISY JOHNSON
I—

NICK FURY
Not the one from the books, the one that fought Daredevil, and Thor, and Spider-Man, and—

DAISY JOHNSON
Shut up!

SEARCH DATABASE JOHNSON, DAISY SEARCH

S.H.I.E.L.D. DOCUMENT 68785895-78795 HJFBK (Cont.)

NICK FURY
Your dad was and is a bit of a wack job to begin with. He's a pretty good scientist but his whole theory of life was based on the idea that the book "Doctor Jekyll and Mister Hyde" was true. And he went about to try and prove it. He robbed and stole from every lab he ever got in the door to, all to finance his research. And he found a chemical process that—hold on, let me read it... blah blah blah—"chemical process is hormonal in nature, causing his cell structure to instantly manufacture mutated hormones that induce a physical transformation encompassing his entire figure. Blah blah blah... over 200 pounds of bone and muscle tissue are added to Zabo's body. Yeah yeah yeah... about 30 seconds, the entire metamorphosis is complete." Your father is the super criminal known as Mister Hyde. Your mother was a prostitute he had a longstanding 'business' relationship with. You are the result of a drunken binge in New Orleans. Your name is Daisy Johnson. Today you caused an earthquake.

DAISY JOHNSON
Please stop talking.

NICK FURY
Would you like to look at the file? Here.

DAISY JOHNSON
Why wouldn't they tell me this? My mom? Why would they *(beeeeeep)* me like that?

NICK FURY
Your adoptive parents don't know what I just told you. I don't know why they haven't told you you were adopted, that's their thing. See, your name is in our database. You were tagged as a possible caterpillar.

DAISY JOHNSON
Caterpillar?

NICK FURY
Do you want a tissue?

DAISY JOHNSON
The *(beep)* is a caterpillar?

NICK FURY
Your dad has been jacking hormones and crazy juice into his body for years. We have no idea what he has done to himself. What his specific anatomy is. We don't know—how do I put this?

DAISY JOHNSON
My dad's a freak, so he had a freak baby?

NICK FURY
You were a caterpillar, but now...

DAISY JOHNSON
I'm a butterfly.

NICK FURY
You have powers. You have seismic—

DAISY JOHNSON
I'm a mutant.

NICK FURY
We'll have to run tests to find that out. The mutant gene is specific. You might just have altered cell structure or brainwave activity.

DAISY JOHNSON
This *(beeeeep)* is my father? You know this for sure?

NICK FURY
It's my job to know these things.

S.H.I.E.L.D.
OPERATIONS DATABASE

HOME   ADVANCED SEARCH   DATABASES   LOG OUT

CRIMINAL DATABASE -> S.H.I.E.L.D. DOCUMENT 696369-34934 THK (Cont.)

DAISY JOHNSON
So, what? So now I'm going to prison. I didn't know this. I didn't know.

NICK FURY
I know.

DAISY JOHNSON
(Beep)

NICK FURY
Would you like some water?

DAISY JOHNSON
What's going on?
(At this time, the interrogation room starts to vibrate. Ms. Johnson stands and panics.)

NICK FURY
You should try to calm down.

DAISY JOHNSON
What's going on?

NICK FURY
You're causing an earthquake, but this room is fortified—specifically created to take the impact. No one else can feel it.

DAISY JOHNSON
I'm doing this?

NICK FURY
Try to get ahold of yourself.
(Ms. Johnson falls to her knees and touches the floor. She calms herself, the vibration stops.)

DAISY JOHNSON
I did that?

NICK FURY
You'll get better at it.

DAISY JOHNSON
Oh my...

NICK FURY
I know this is a big ball of crazy to swallow all at once, but I wanted to talk to you personally. Was wondering if you had any plans?

DAISY JOHNSON
Well, I was going to go to art school, but now I guess I have to join the freakin' X-Men or something. This sucks! My whole life is *(beeeeeep)*.

NICK FURY
You're seventeen years old, your life hasn't started yet.

DAISY JOHNSON
Future plans... You know, I get headaches.

NICK FURY
I know.

S.H.I.E.L.D. DOCUMENT 68785895-78795 HJFBK (Cont.)

DAISY JOHNSON
But, now—

NICK FURY
You feel pretty good.

DAISY JOHNSON
I do.

NICK FURY
Yeah, it's all part of it.

DAISY JOHNSON
You know this?

NICK FURY
Seen it before.

DAISY JOHNSON
What do you want from me?

NICK FURY
Was hoping I could offer you a place in the world. We have agents—a training facility—we can help you figure out what it is you can do, we can train you in all sorts of stuff.

DAISY JOHNSON
Not an X-Man?

NICK FURY
No, I'm actually offering you a paying job. Free training. Room, board, food. A career. Travel.

DAISY JOHNSON
What's the catch?

NICK FURY
The catch. Well, you basically do whatever I say for the rest of your life.

DAISY JOHNSON
Oh, is that all?

NICK FURY
But you'll be joining the single most powerful, most important organization on the planet Earth.

DAISY JOHNSON
Seriously?

NICK FURY
Yeah. You want to be a special agent of S.H.I.E.L.D.? I'll let you keep the CDs.

(End transcript)

Recording device switched off at 3:12:04.

Transcript reviewed and edited by Colonel Nick Fury for security clearance.

090-278

CRIMSON
DYNAMO_

MR_FANTASTIC_

NICK FURY_

BLACK WIDOW_

THING_

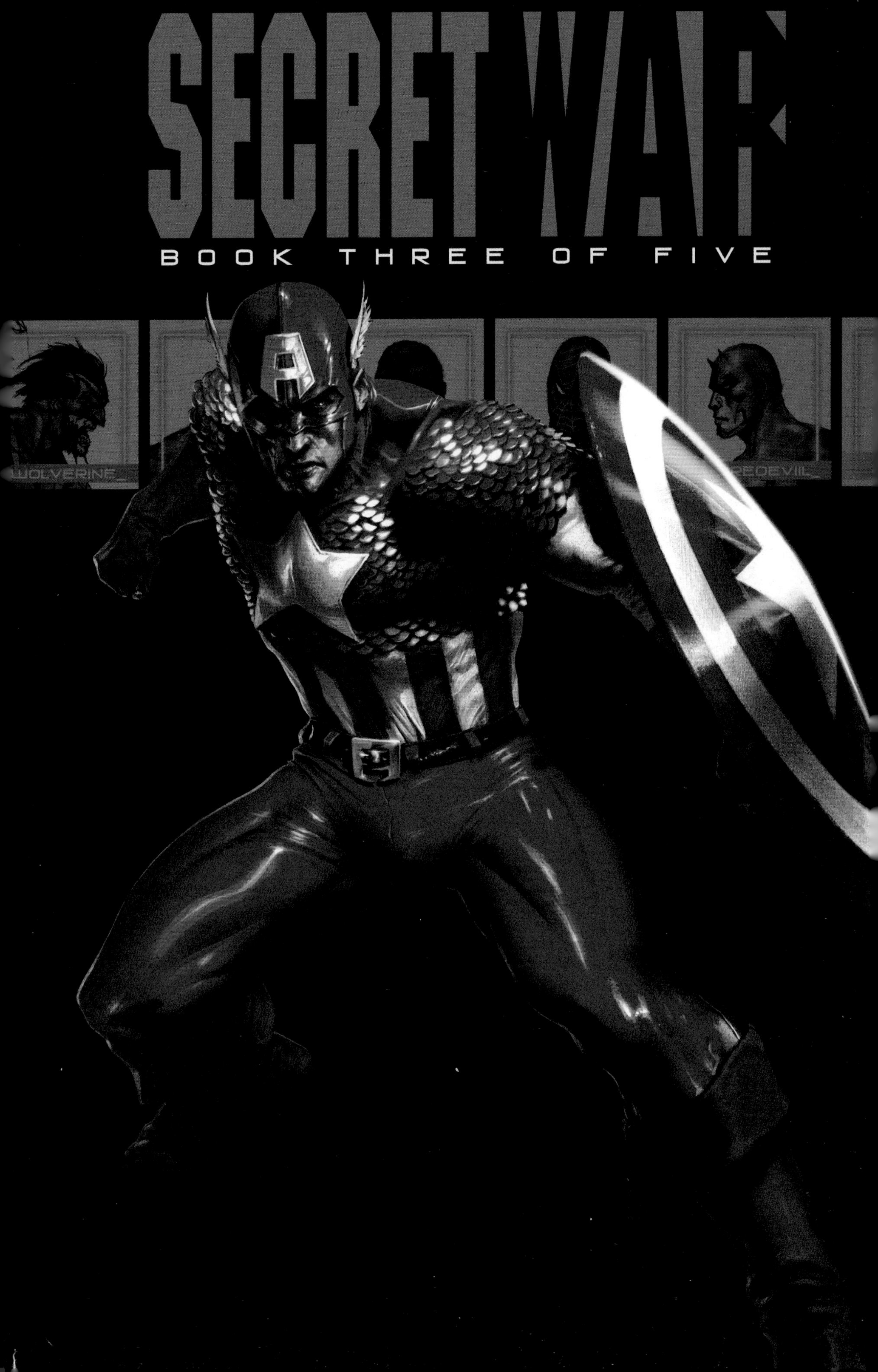
SECRET WAR
BOOK THREE OF FIVE
WOLVERINE_

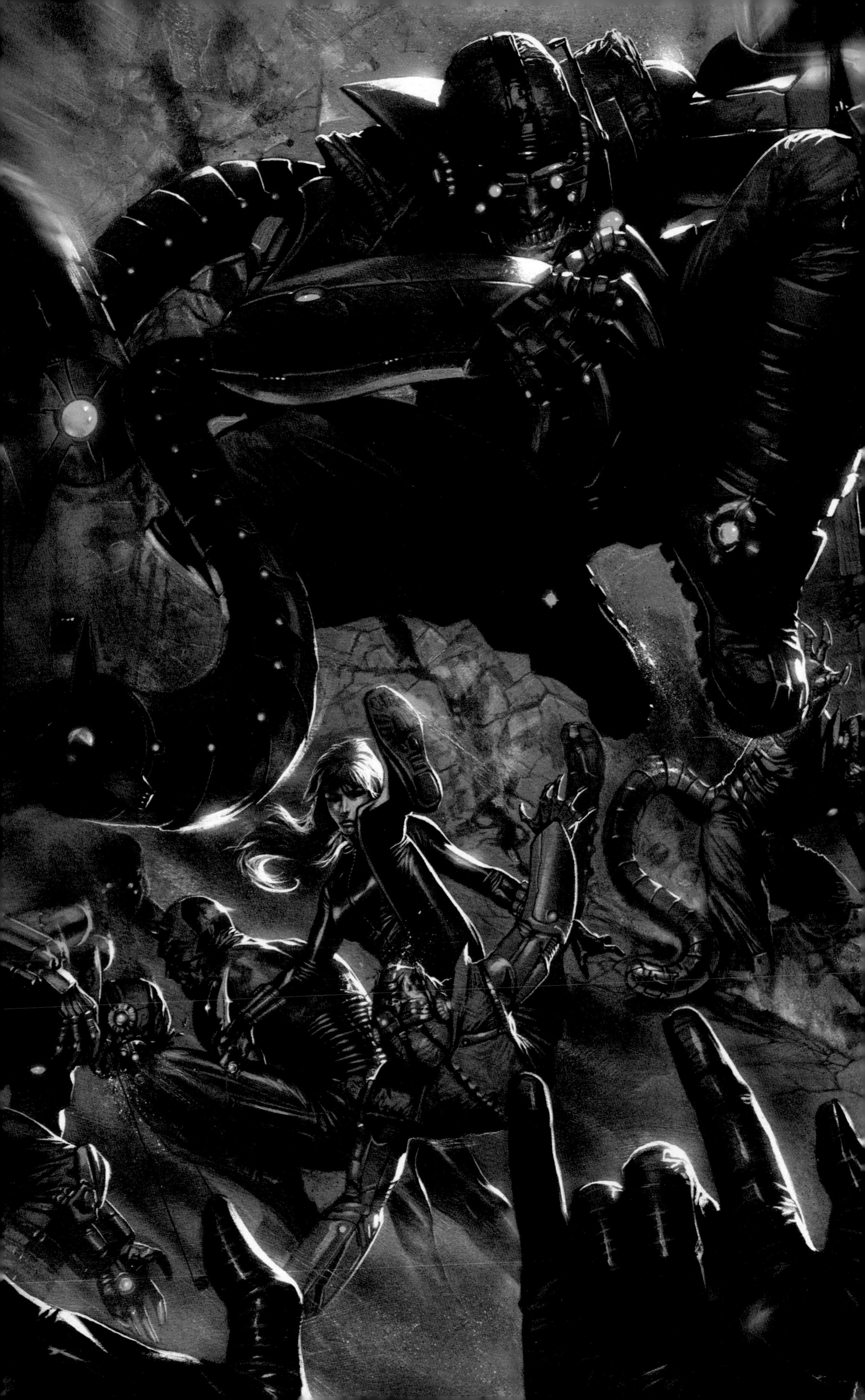

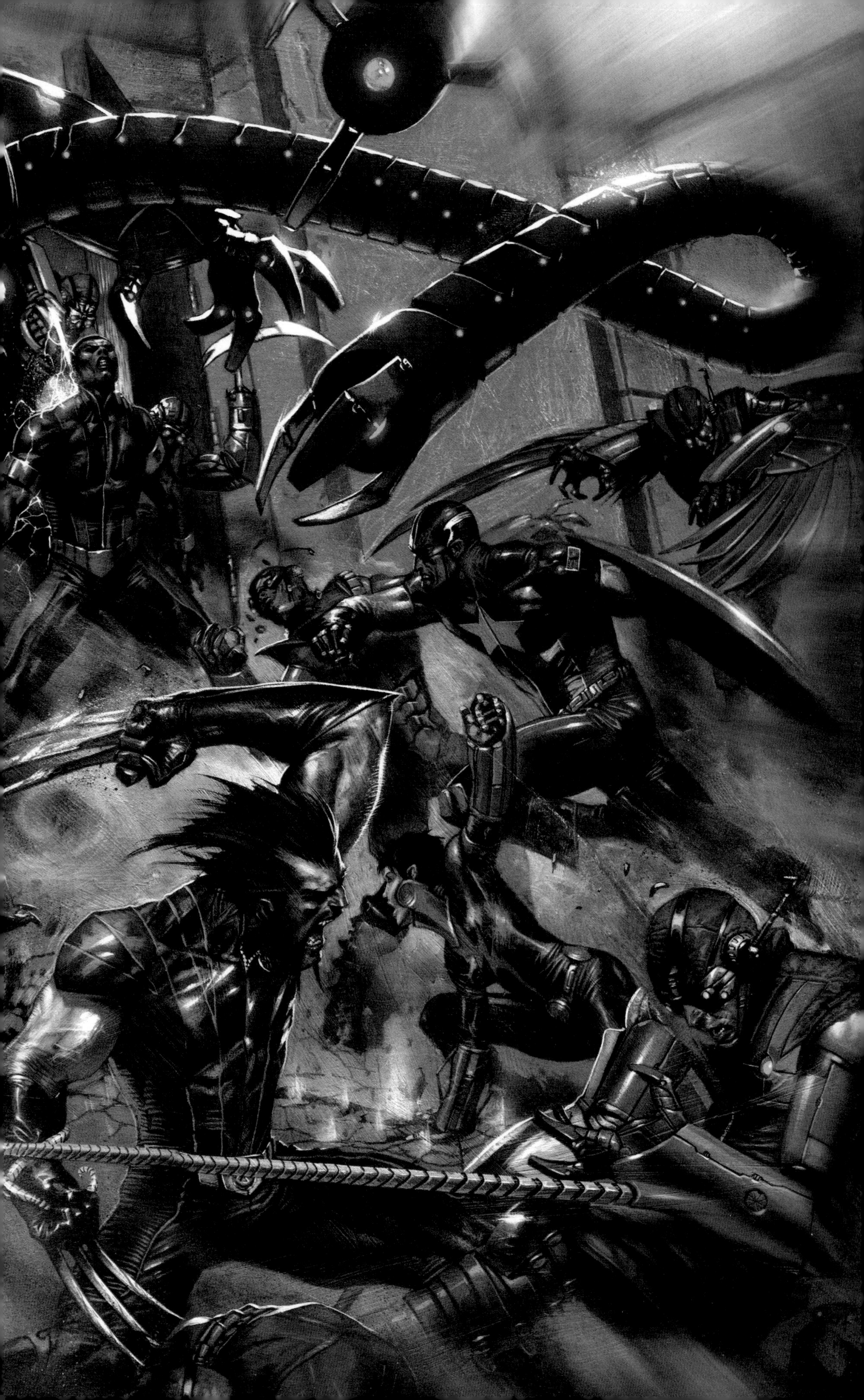

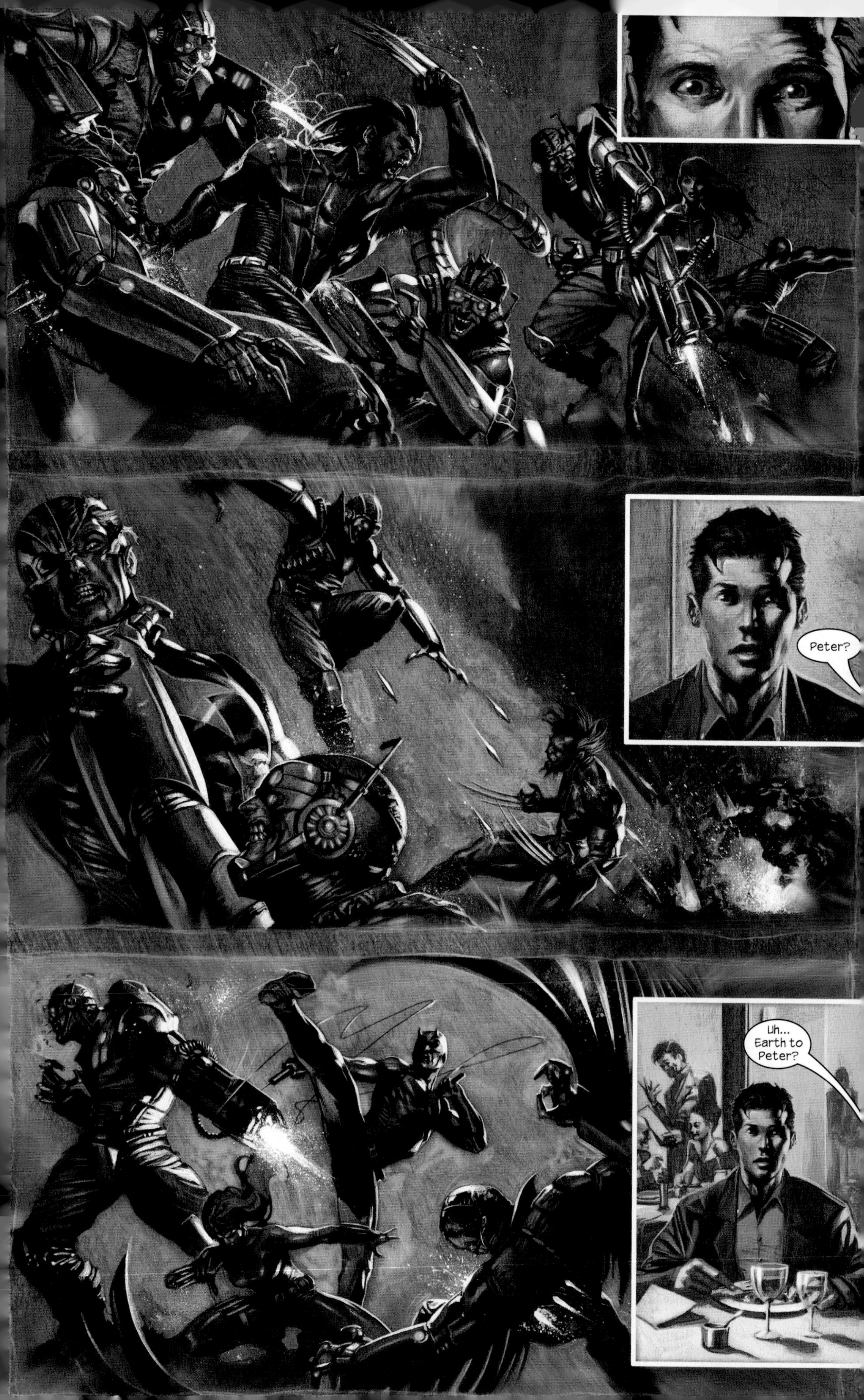
Peter?
Uh... Earth to Peter?

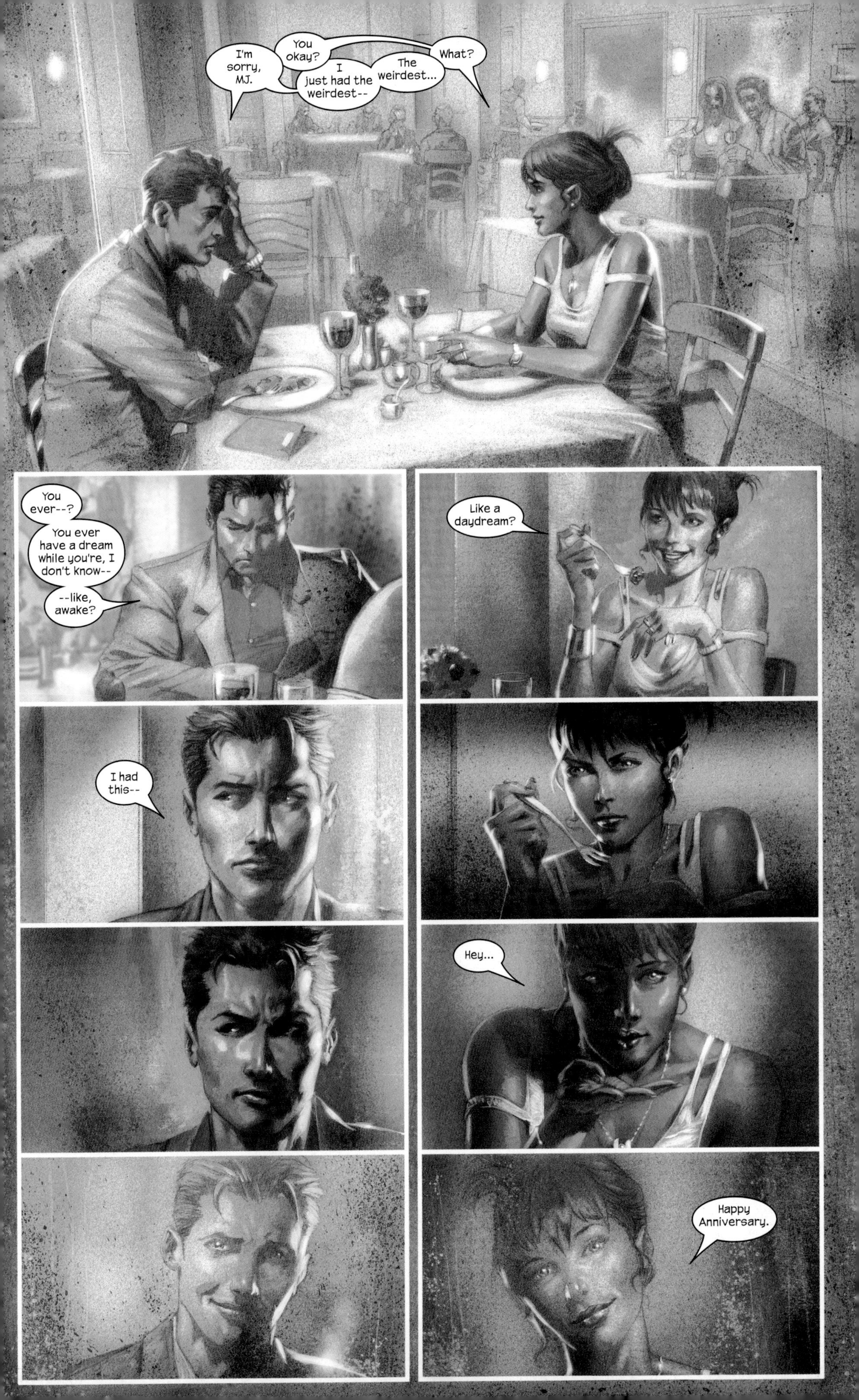

I'm sorry, MJ.
You okay?
I just had the weirdest--
The weirdest...
What?
You ever--?
You ever have a dream while you're, I don't know--
--like, awake?
Like a daydream?
I had this--
Hey...
Happy Anniversary.

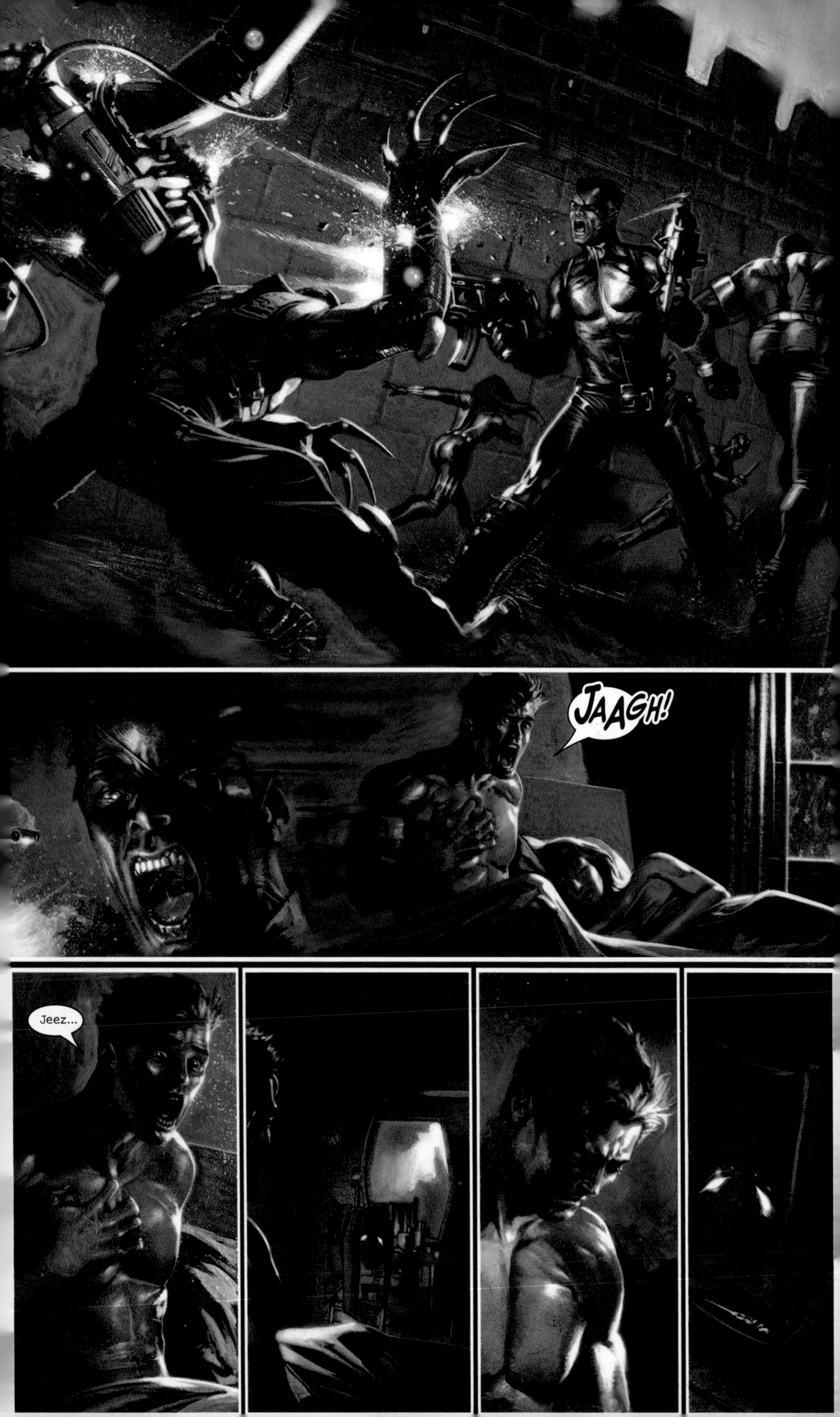
JAAGH!
Jeez...

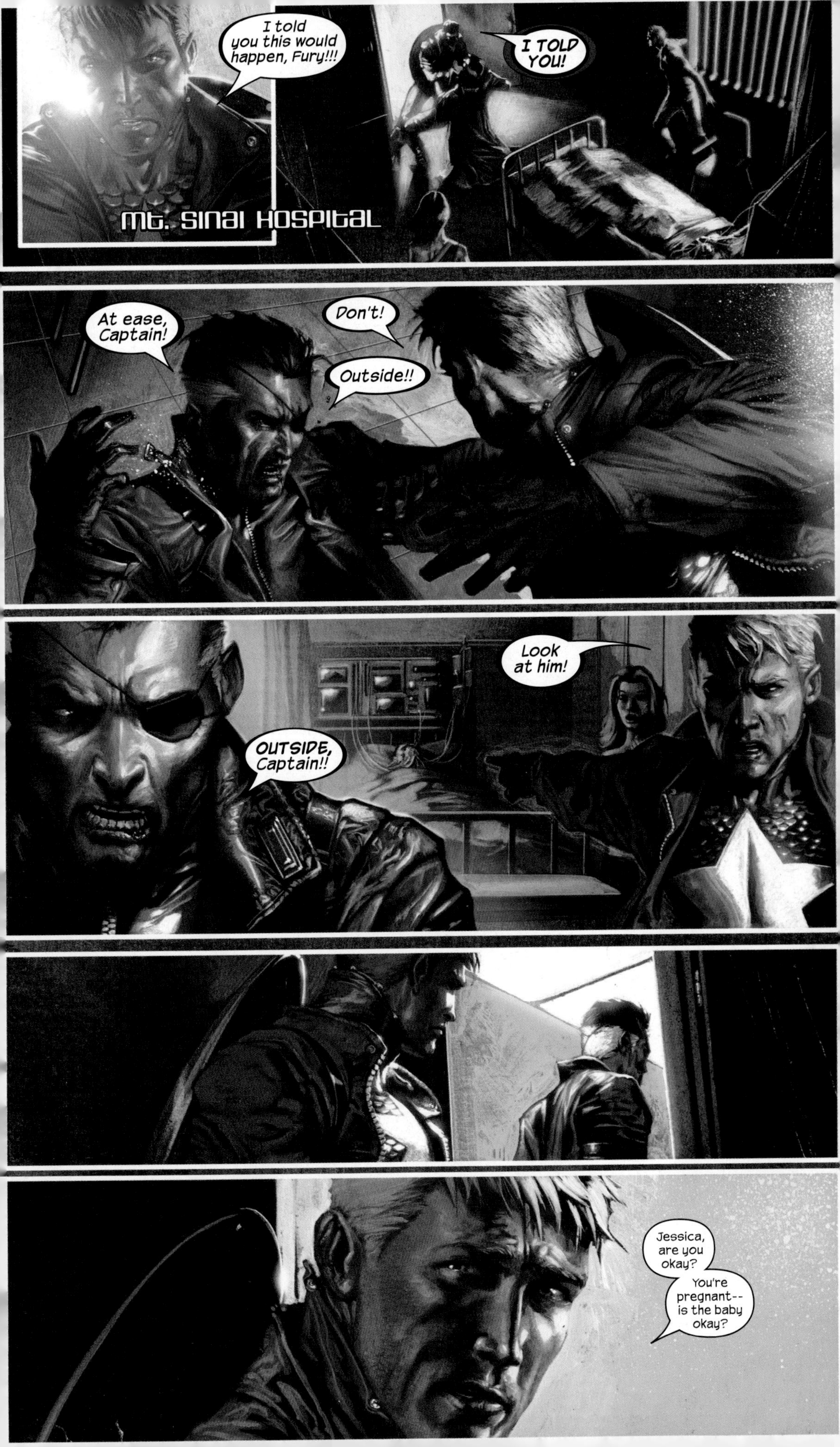
I told you this would happen, Fury!!!
MT. SINAI HOSPITAL
I TOLD YOU!
At ease, Captain!
Don't!
Outside!!
Look at him!
OUTSIDE, Captain!!
Jessica, are you okay?
You're pregnant-- is the baby okay?

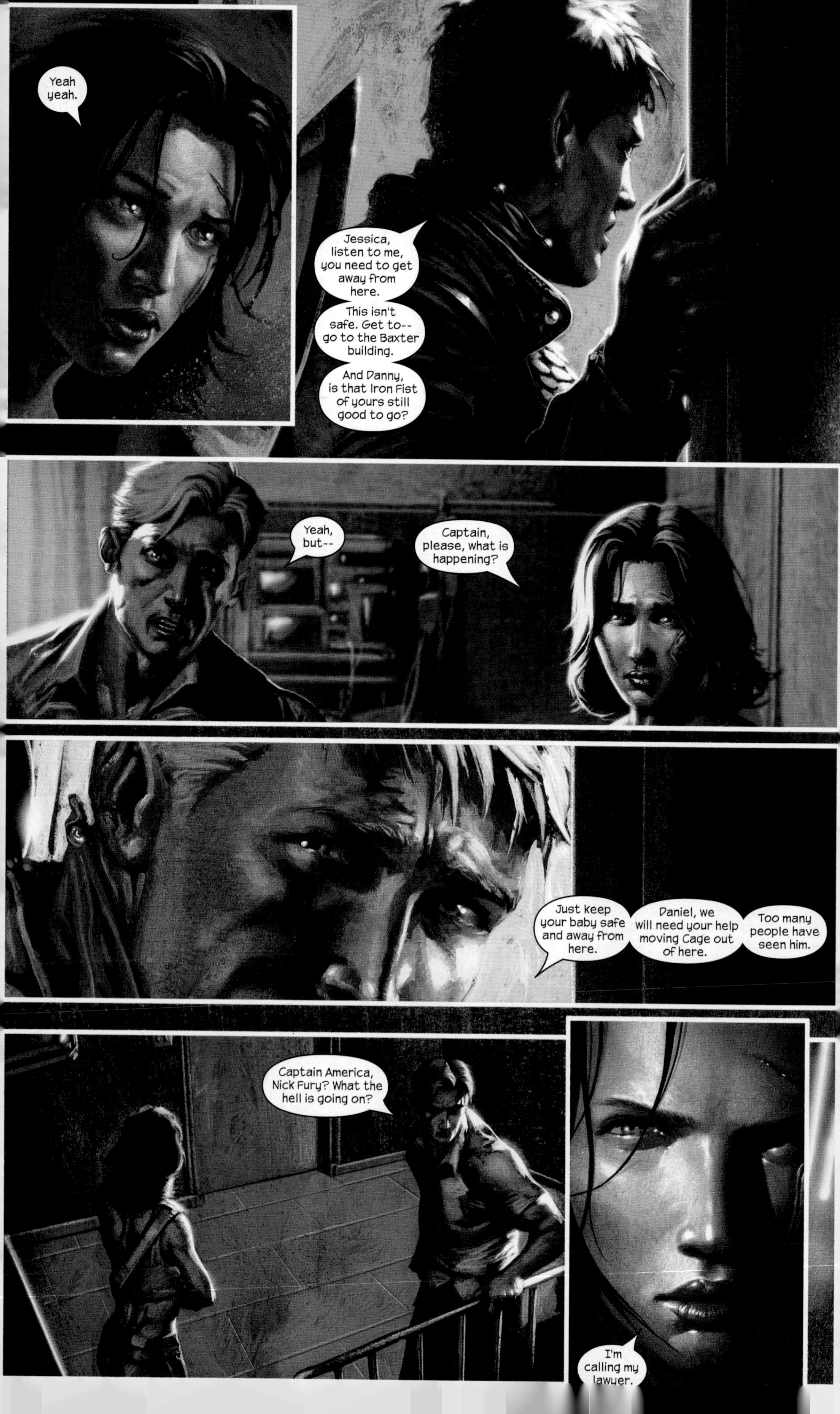
Yeah yeah.
Jessica, listen to me, you need to get away from here.
This isn't safe. Get to-- go to the Baxter building.
And Danny, is that Iron Fist of yours still good to go?
Yeah, but--
Captain, please, what is happening?
Just keep your baby safe and away from here.
Daniel, we will need your help moving Cage out of here.
Too many people have seen him.
Captain America, Nick Fury? What the hell is going on?
I'm calling my lawyer.

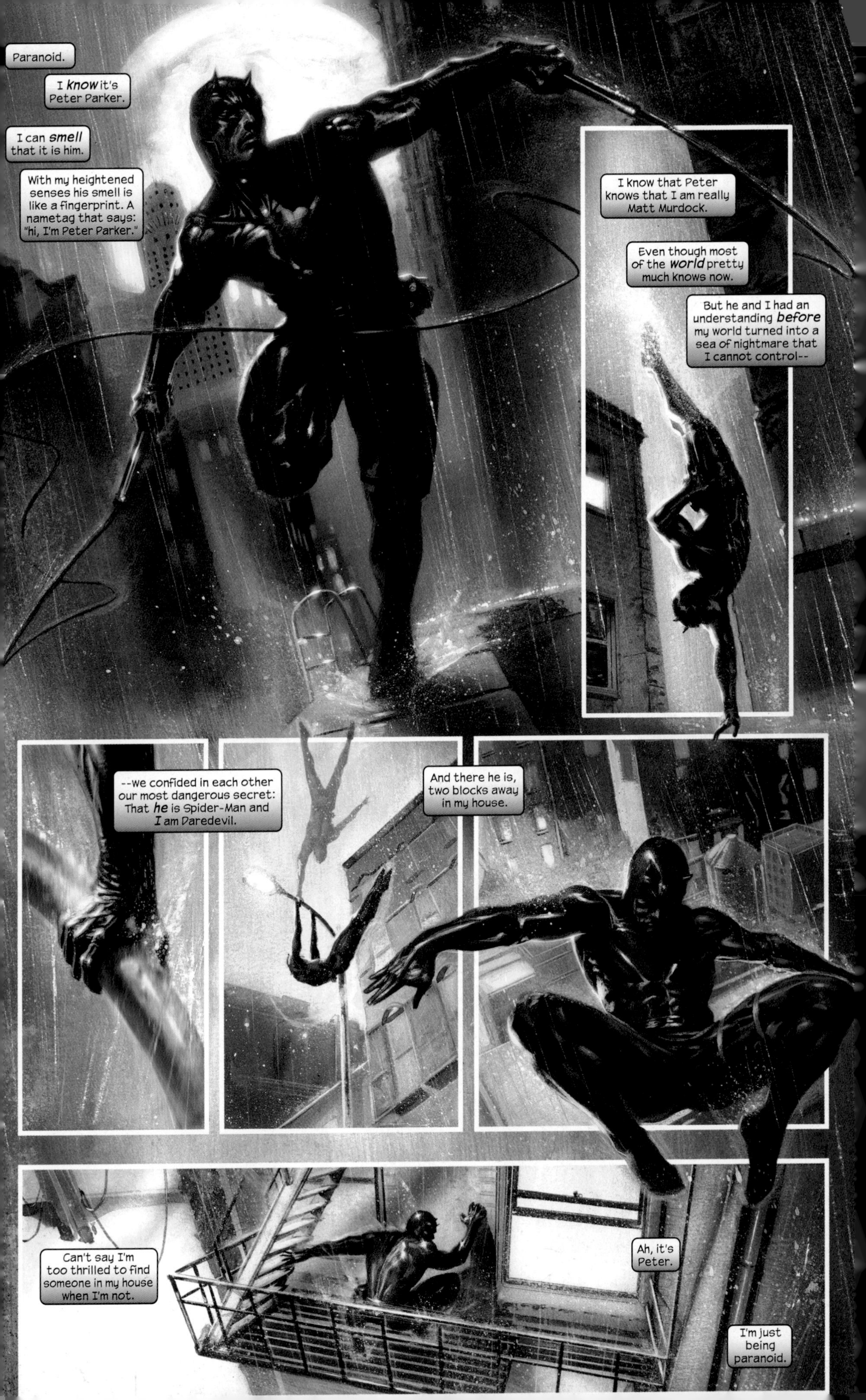
Paranoid.
I know it's Peter Parker.
I can smell that it is him.
With my heightened senses his smell is like a fingerprint. A nametag that says: "hi, I'm Peter Parker."
I know that Peter knows that I am really Matt Murdock.
Even though most of the world pretty much knows now.
But he and I had an understanding before my world turned into a sea of nightmare that I cannot control--
--we confided in each other our most dangerous secret: That he is Spider-Man and I am Daredevil.
And there he is, two blocks away in my house.
Can't say I'm too thrilled to find someone in my house when I'm not.
Ah, it's Peter.
I'm just being paranoid.

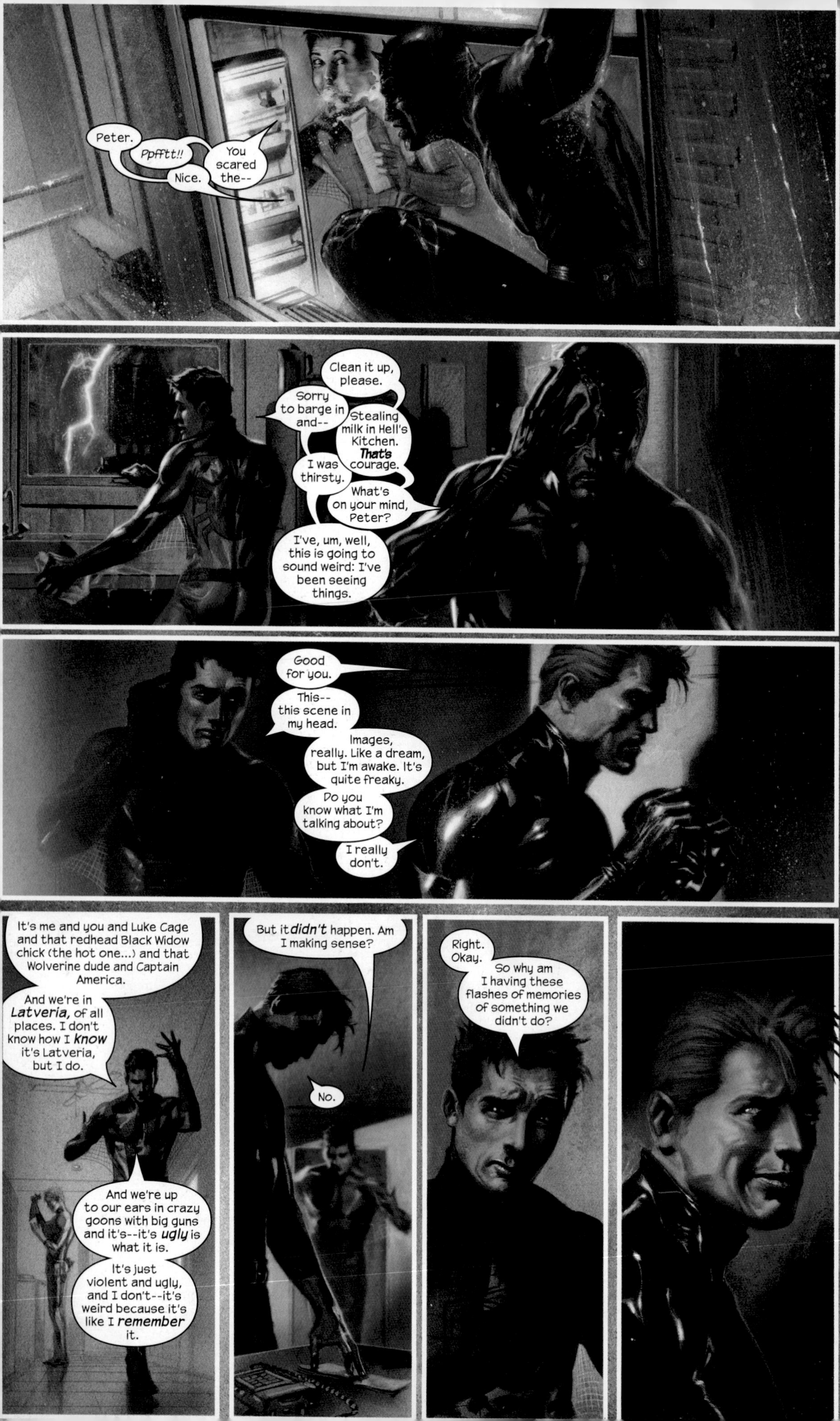
Peter.
Ppffft!!
You scared the--
Nice.
Clean it up, please.
Sorry to barge in and--
Stealing milk in Hell's Kitchen. *That's* courage.
I was thirsty.
What's on your mind, Peter?
I've, um, well, this is going to sound weird: I've been seeing things.
Good for you.
This-- this scene in my head.
Images, really. Like a dream, but I'm awake. It's quite freaky.
Do you know what I'm talking about?
I really don't.
It's me and you and Luke Cage and that redhead Black Widow chick (the hot one...) and that Wolverine dude and Captain America.
And we're in *Latveria*, of all places. I don't know how I *know* it's Latveria, but I do.
And we're up to our ears in crazy goons with big guns and it's--it's *ugly* is what it is.
It's just violent and ugly, and I don't--it's weird because it's like I *remember* it.
But it *didn't* happen. Am I making sense?
No.
Right. Okay.
So why am I having these flashes of memories of something we didn't do?

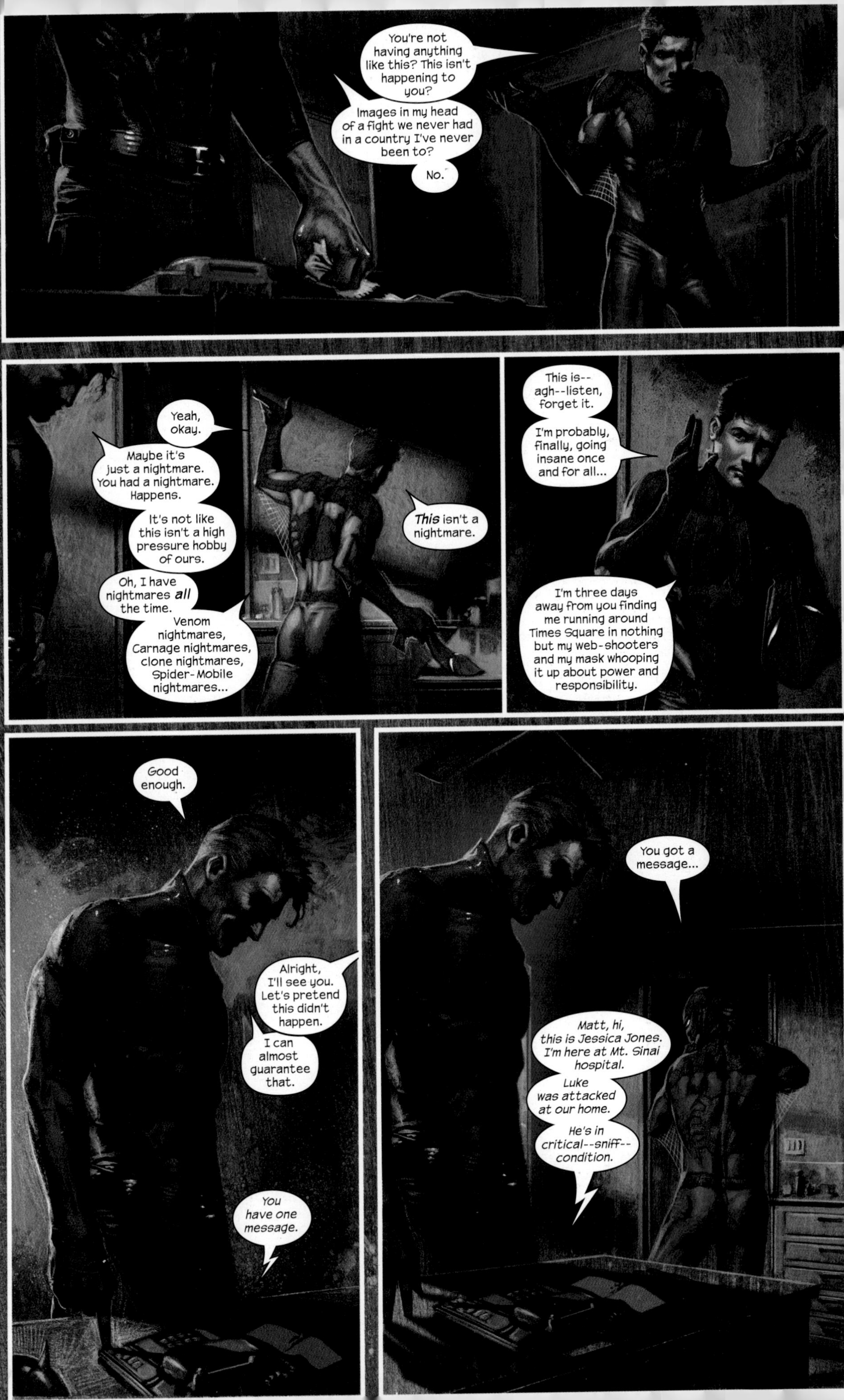

You're not having anything like this? This isn't happening to you?
Images in my head of a fight we never had in a country I've never been to?
No.
Yeah, okay.
Maybe it's just a nightmare. You had a nightmare. Happens.
It's not like this isn't a high pressure hobby of ours.
Oh, I have nightmares *all* the time.
Venom nightmares, Carnage nightmares, clone nightmares, Spider-Mobile nightmares...
This isn't a nightmare.
This is-- agh--listen, forget it.
I'm probably, finally, going insane once and for all...
I'm three days away from you finding me running around Times Square in nothing but my web-shooters and my mask whooping it up about power and responsibility.
Good enough.
Alright, I'll see you. Let's pretend this didn't happen.
I can almost guarantee that.
You have one message.
You got a message...
Matt, hi, this is Jessica Jones. I'm here at Mt. Sinai hospital.
Luke was attacked at our home.
He's in critical--sniff-- condition.

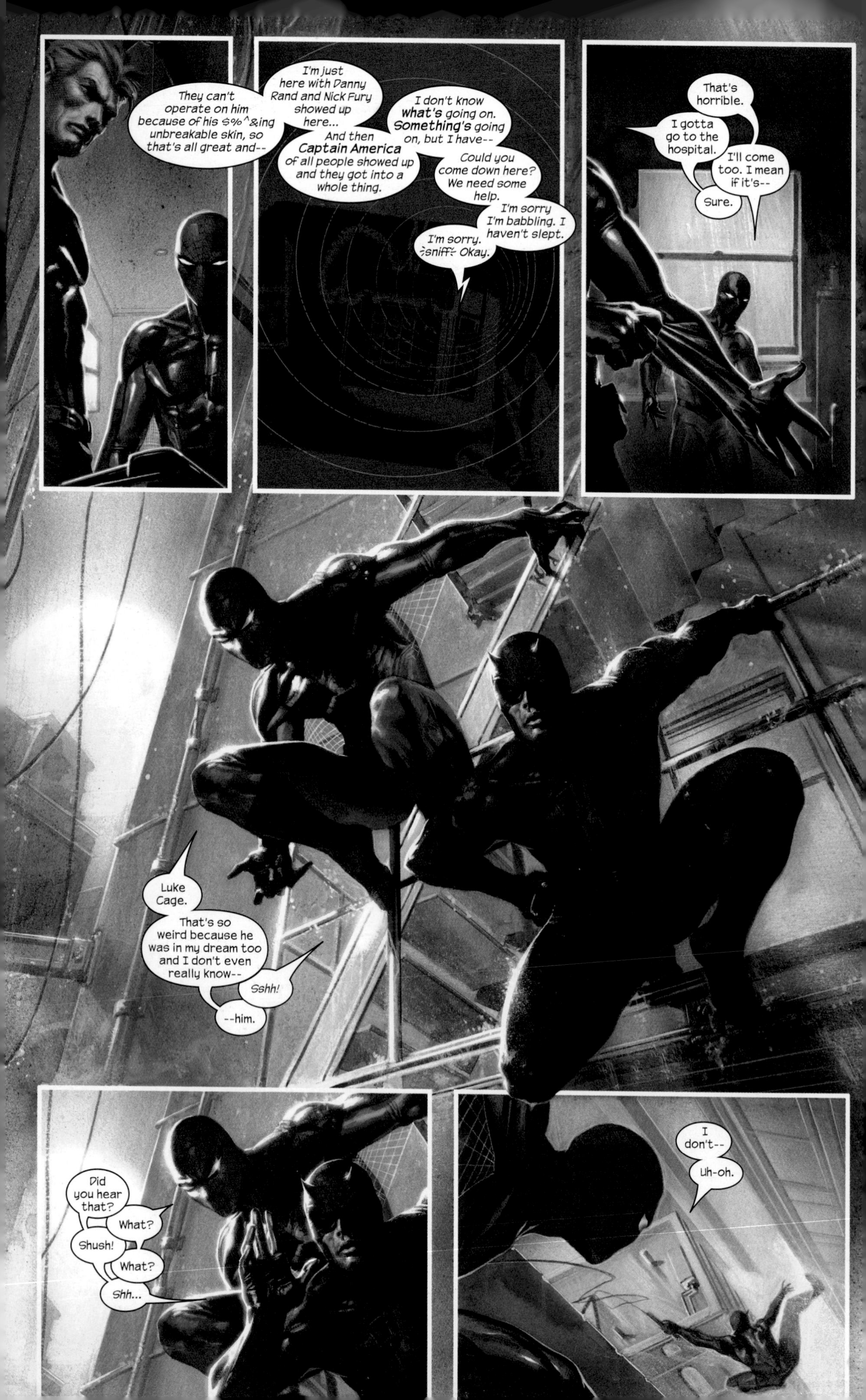
They can't operate on him because of his $%^&ing unbreakable skin, so that's all great and--
I'm just here with Danny Rand and Nick Fury showed up here...
And then Captain America of all people showed up and they got into a whole thing.
I don't know what's going on. Something's going on, but I have--
Could you come down here? We need some help.
I'm sorry I'm babbling. I haven't slept.
I'm sorry. *sniff* Okay.
That's horrible.
I gotta go to the hospital.
I'll come too. I mean if it's--
Sure.
Luke Cage.
That's so weird because he was in my dream too and I don't even really know--
Sshh!
--him.
Did you hear that?
What?
Shush!
What?
Shh...
I don't--
Uh-oh.

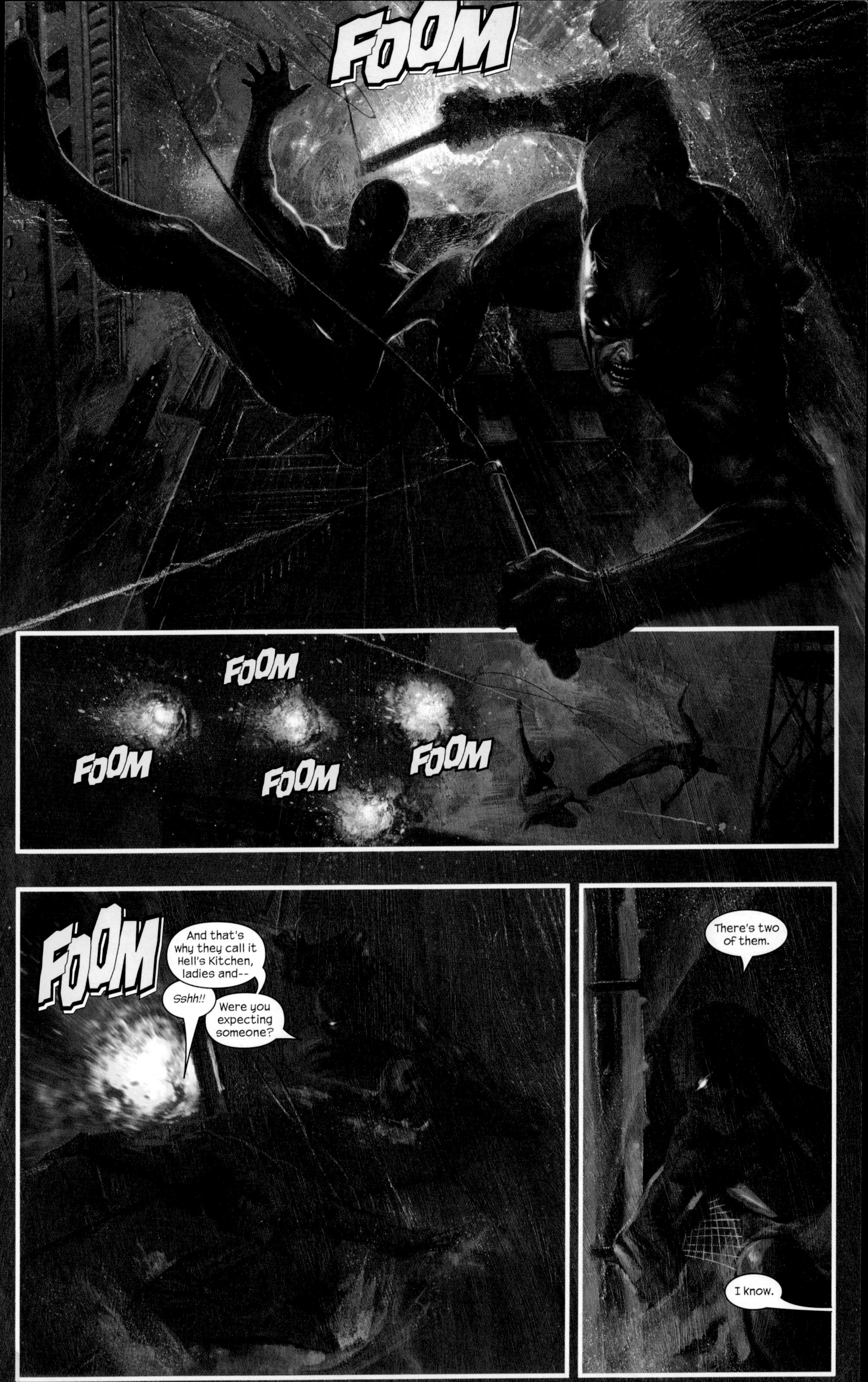
FOOM
FOOM
FOOM
FOOM
FOOM
FOOM
And that's why they call it Hell's Kitchen, ladies and--
Sshh!!
Were you expecting someone?
There's two of them.
I know.

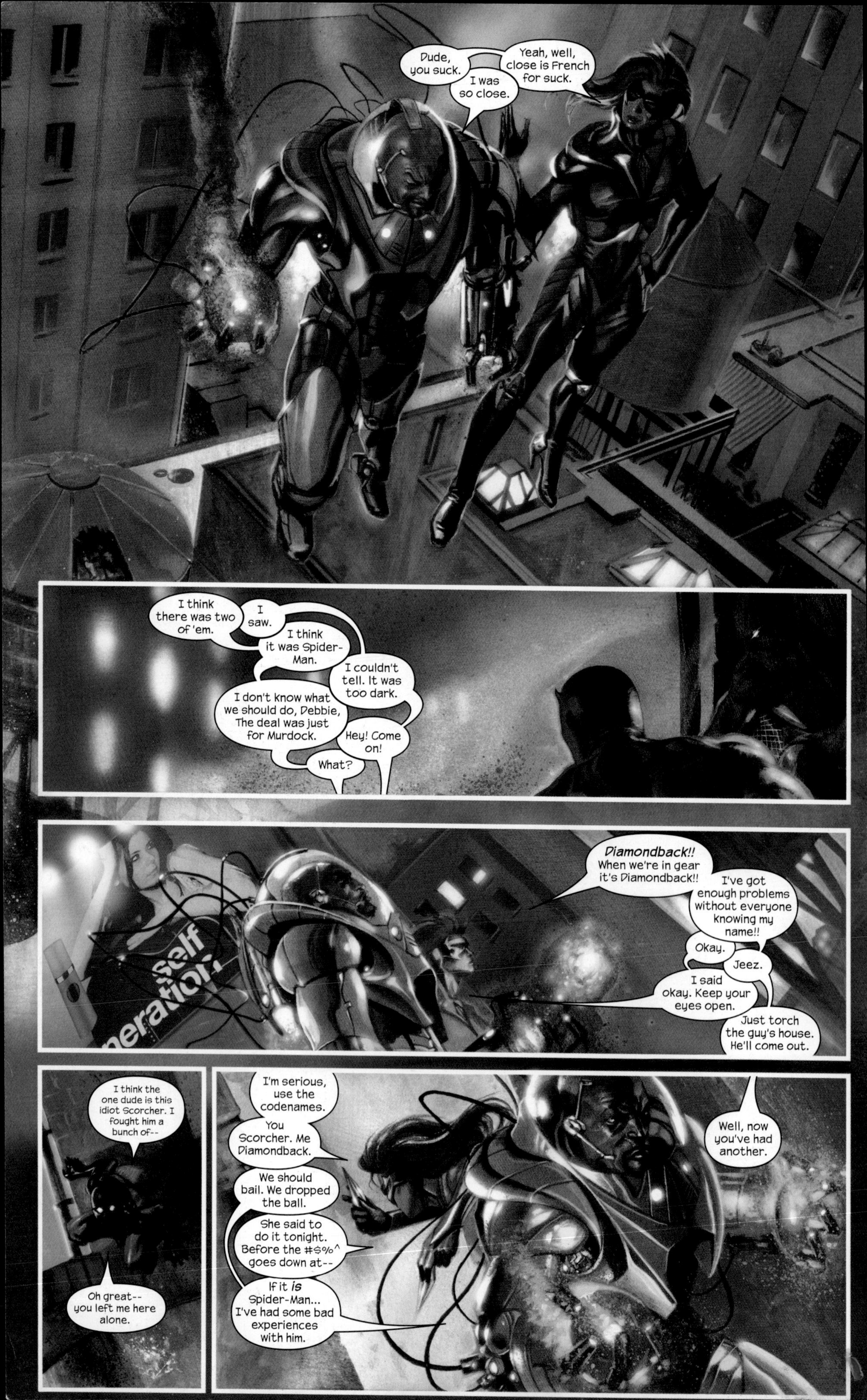
Dude, you suck.
I was so close.
Yeah, well, close is French for suck.
I think there was two of 'em.
I saw.
I think it was Spider-Man.
I couldn't tell. It was too dark.
I don't know what we should do, Debbie, The deal was just for Murdock.
Hey! Come on!
What?
self
neration
Diamondback!! When we're in gear it's Diamondback!!
I've got enough problems without everyone knowing my name!!
Okay.
Jeez.
I said okay. Keep your eyes open.
Just torch the guy's house. He'll come out.
I think the one dude is this idiot Scorcher. I fought him a bunch of--
Oh great-- you left me here alone.
I'm serious, use the codenames.
You Scorcher. Me Diamondback.
We should bail. We dropped the ball.
She said to do it tonight. Before the #$%^ goes down at--
If it *is* Spider-Man... I've had some bad experiences with him.
Well, now you've had another.

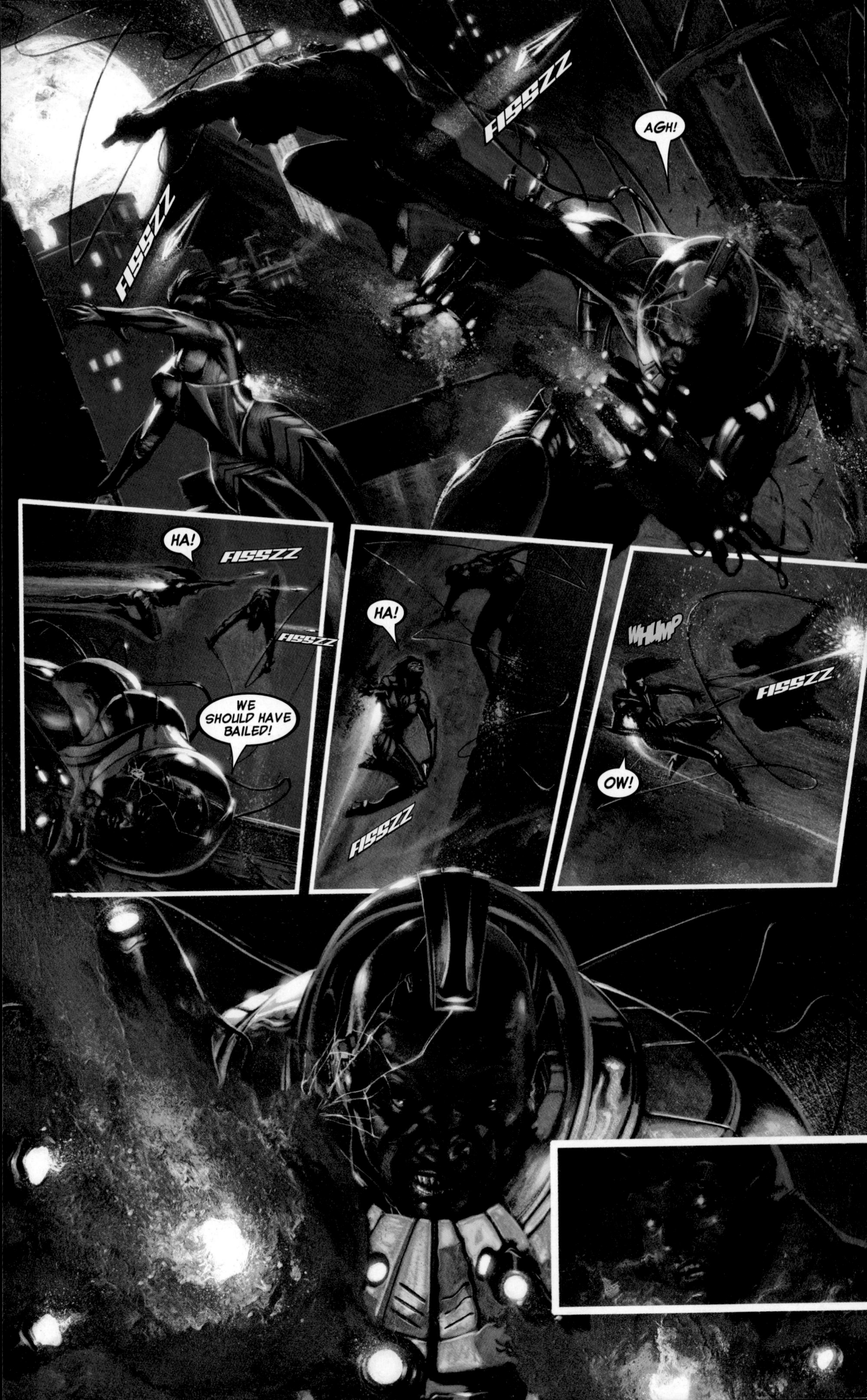
FISSZZ
FISSZZ
AGH!
HA!
FISSZZ
FISSZZ
WE SHOULD HAVE BAILED!
HA!
FISSZZ
WHUMP
FISSZZ
OW!

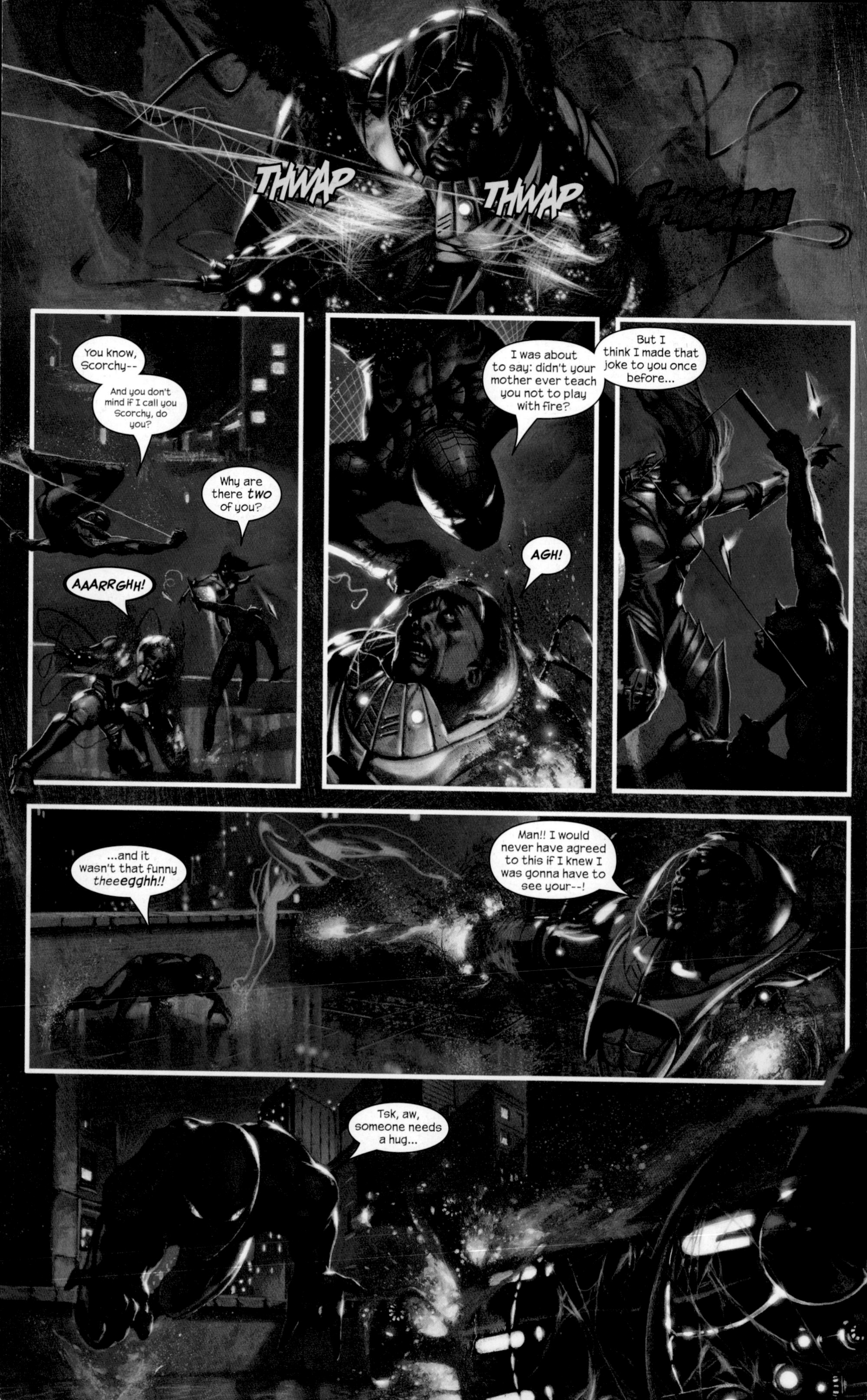
THWAP
THWAP
You know, Scorchy--
And you don't mind if I call you Scorchy, do you?
Why are there two of you?
AAARRGHH!
I was about to say: didn't your mother ever teach you not to play with fire?
AGH!
But I think I made that joke to you once before...
...and it wasn't that funny theeegghh!!
Man!! I would never have agreed to this if I knew I was gonna have to see your--!
Tsk, aw, someone needs a hug...

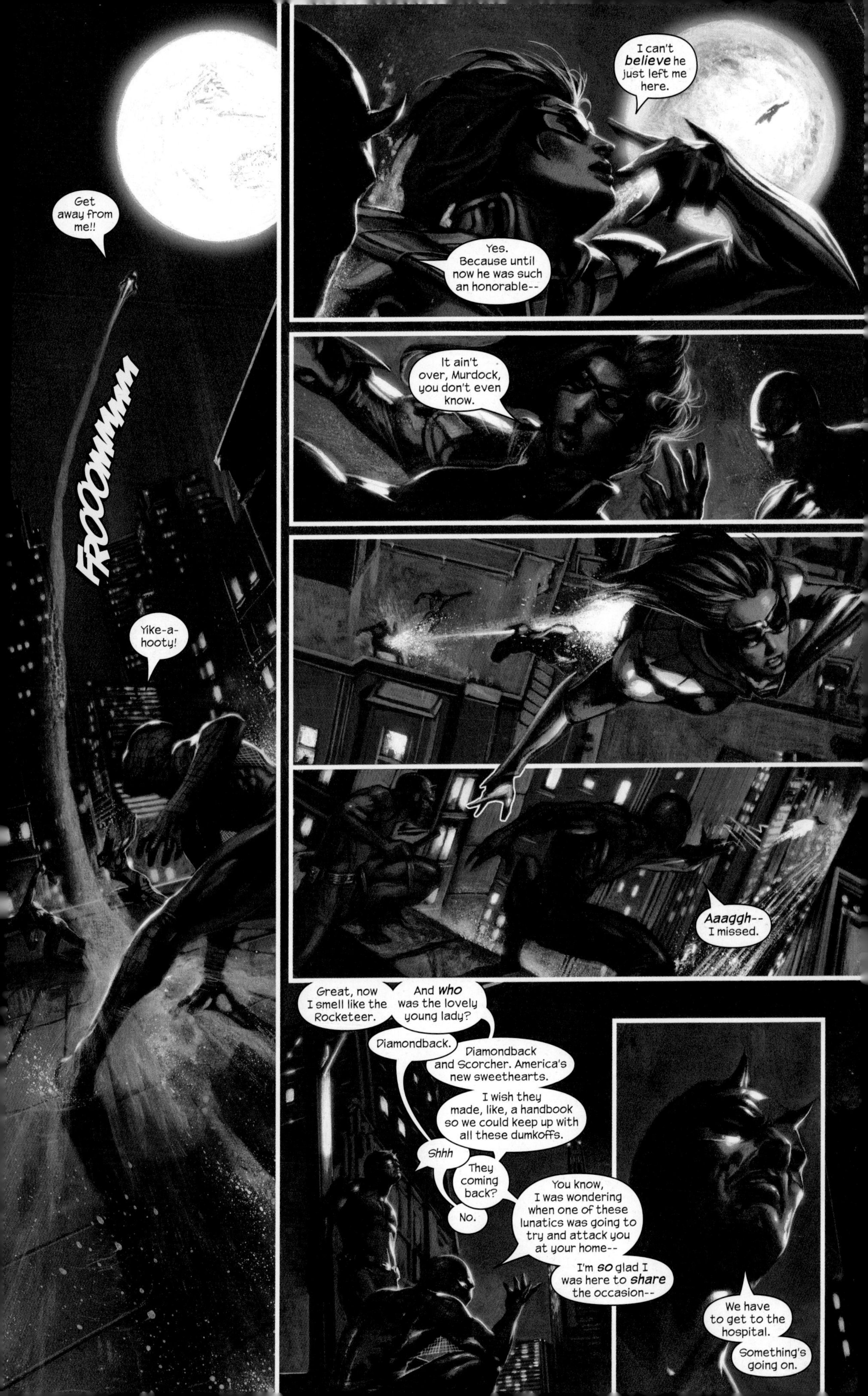

Get away from me!!
FROOOMMMM
Yike-a-hooty!
I can't *believe* he just left me here.
Yes. Because until now he was such an honorable--
It ain't over, Murdock, you don't even know.
Aaaggh-- I missed.
Great, now I smell like the Rocketeer.
And *who* was the lovely young lady?
Diamondback.
Diamondback and Scorcher. America's new sweethearts.
I wish they made, like, a handbook so we could keep up with all these dumkoffs.
Shhh
They coming back?
No.
You know, I was wondering when one of these lunatics was going to try and attack you at your home--
I'm *so* glad I was here to *share* the occasion--
We have to get to the hospital.
Something's going on.

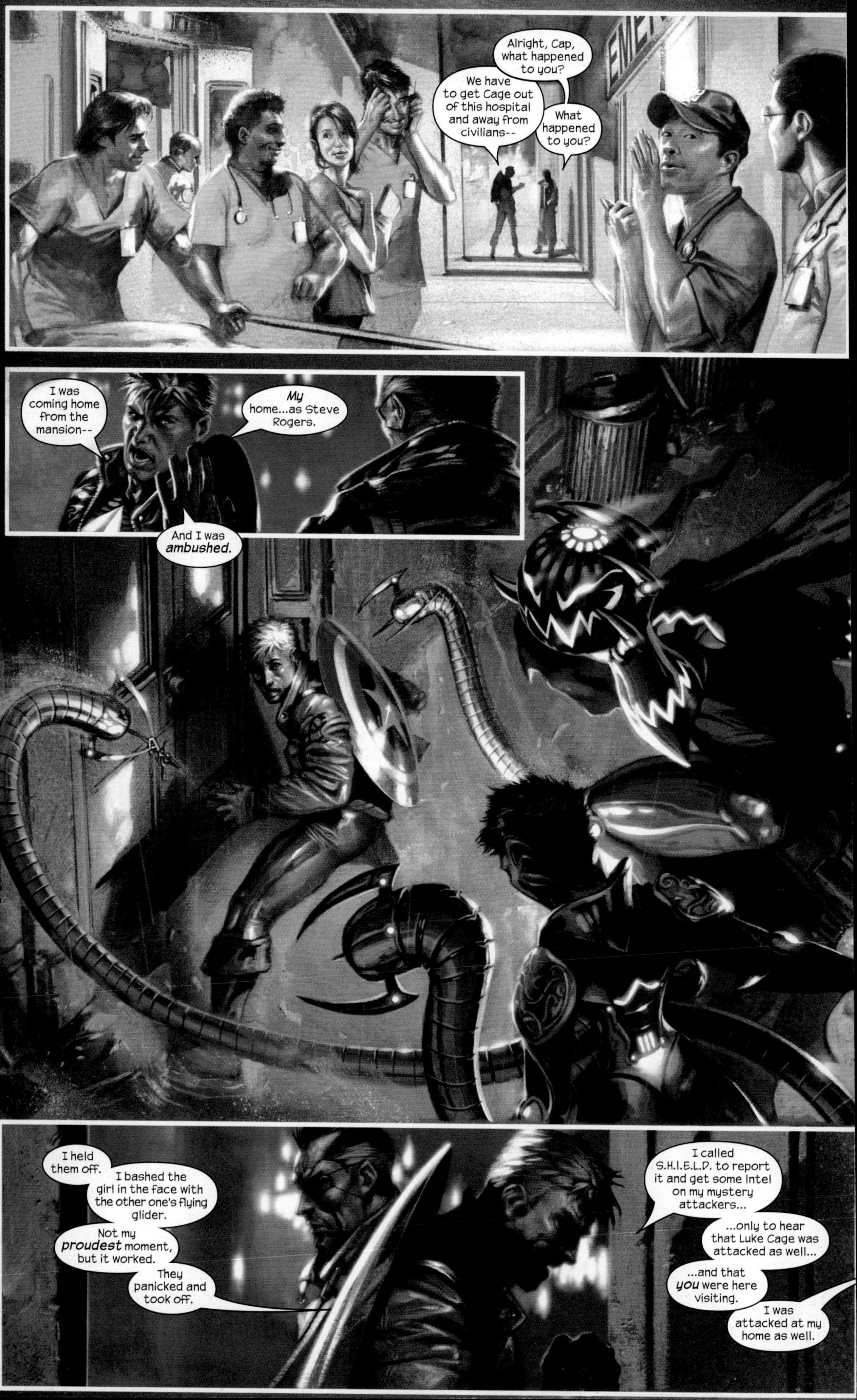
Alright, Cap, what happened to you?
We have to get Cage out of this hospital and away from civilians--
What happened to you?
I was coming home from the mansion--
My home...as Steve Rogers.
And I was *ambushed.*
I held them off.
I bashed the girl in the face with the other one's flying glider.
Not my *proudest* moment, but it worked.
They panicked and took off.
I called S.H.I.E.L.D. to report it and get some Intel on my mystery attackers...
...only to hear that Luke Cage was attacked as well...
...and that *you* were here visiting.
I was attacked at my home as well.

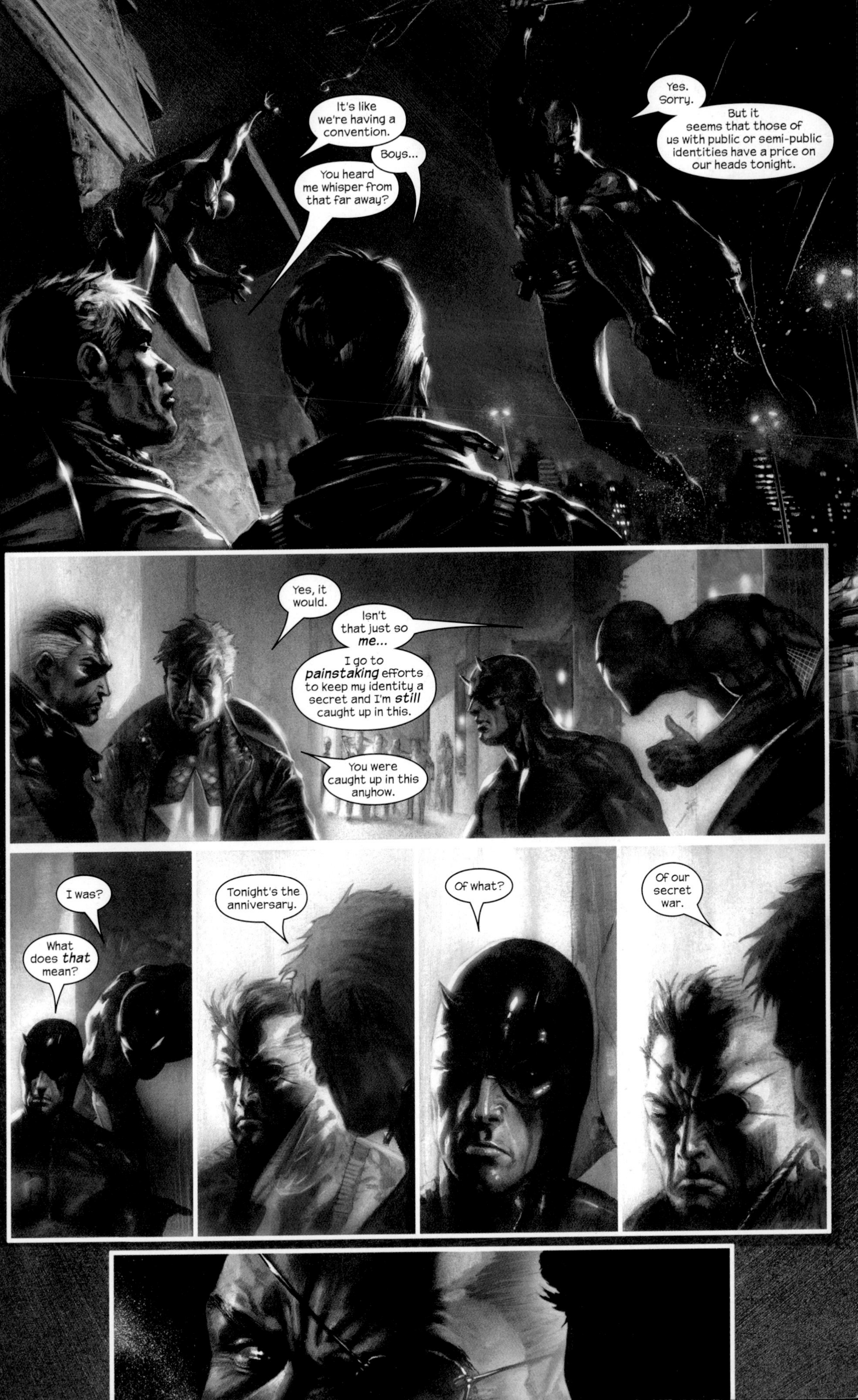
It's like we're having a convention.
Boys...
You heard me whisper from that far away?
Yes. Sorry.
But it seems that those of us with public or semi-public identities have a price on our heads tonight.
Yes, it would.
Isn't that just so *me*...
I go to *painstaking* efforts to keep my identity a secret and I'm *still* caught up in this.
You were caught up in this anyhow.
I was?
What does *that* mean?
Tonight's the anniversary.
Of what?
Of our secret war.

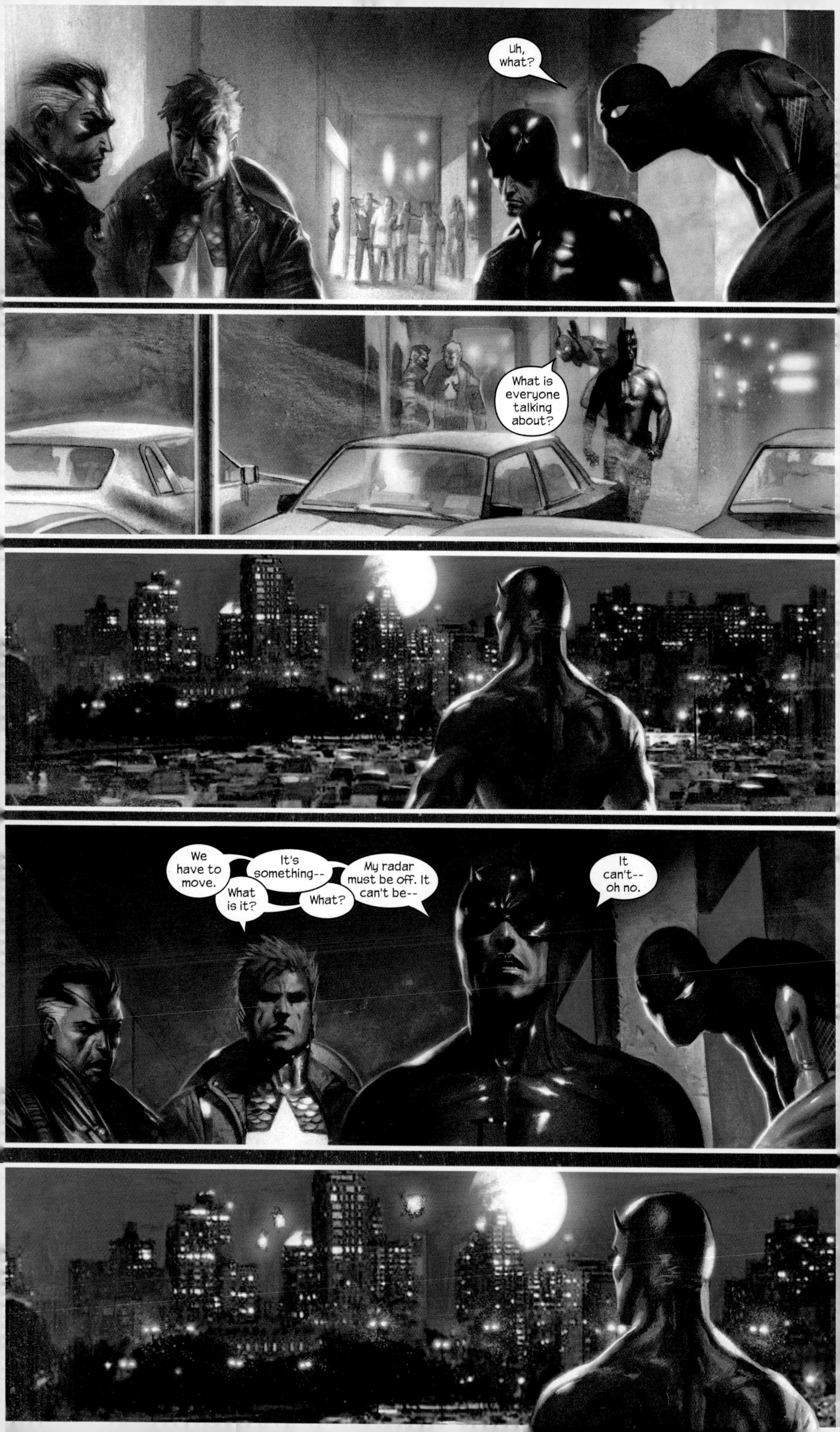

Uh, what?
What is everyone talking about?
We have to move.
It's something--
What is it?
What?
My radar must be off. It can't be--
It can't-- oh no.

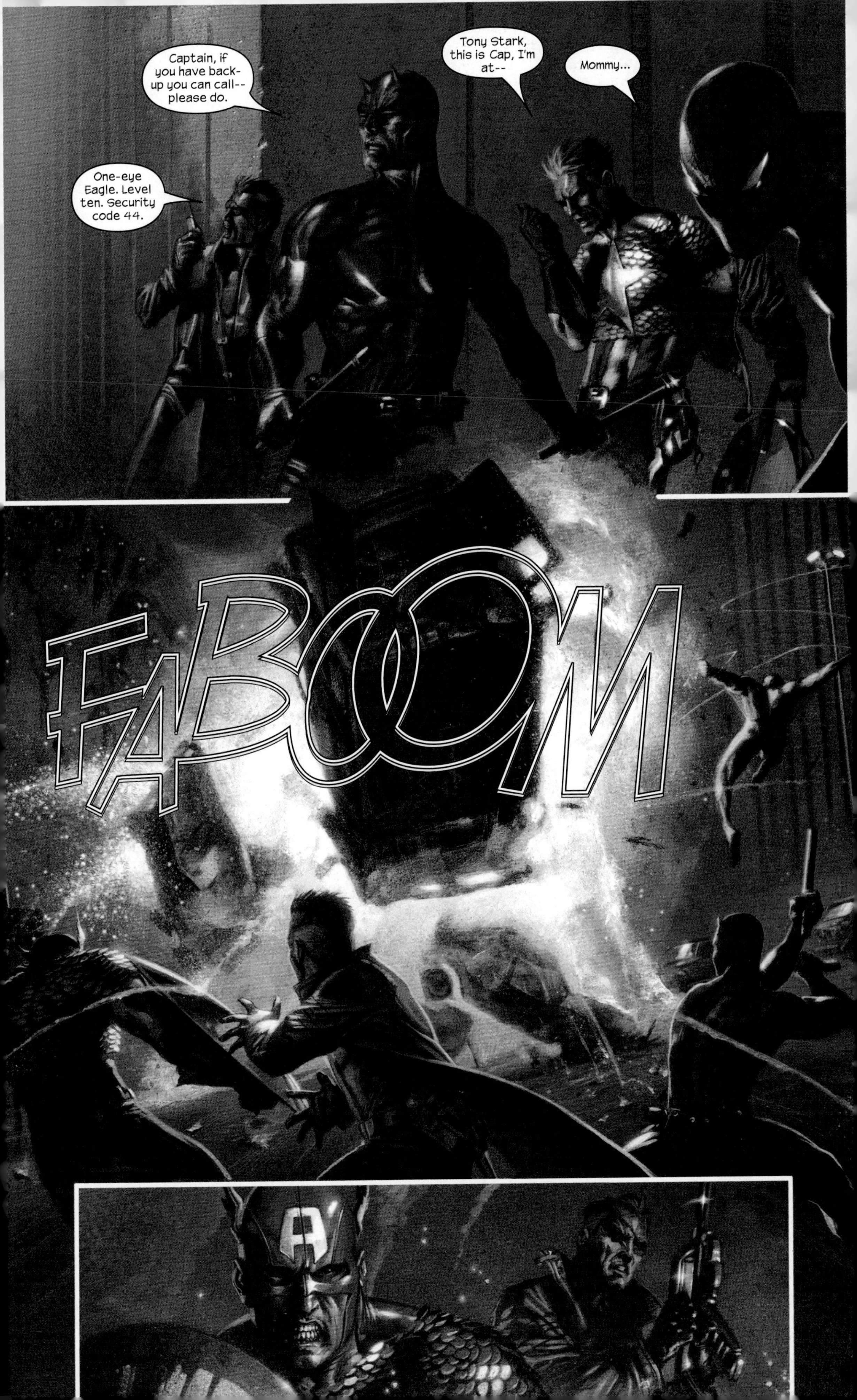
Captain, if you have back-up you can call-- please do.
One-eye Eagle. Level ten. Security code 44.
Tony Stark, this is Cap, I'm at--
Mommy...
FABOOM

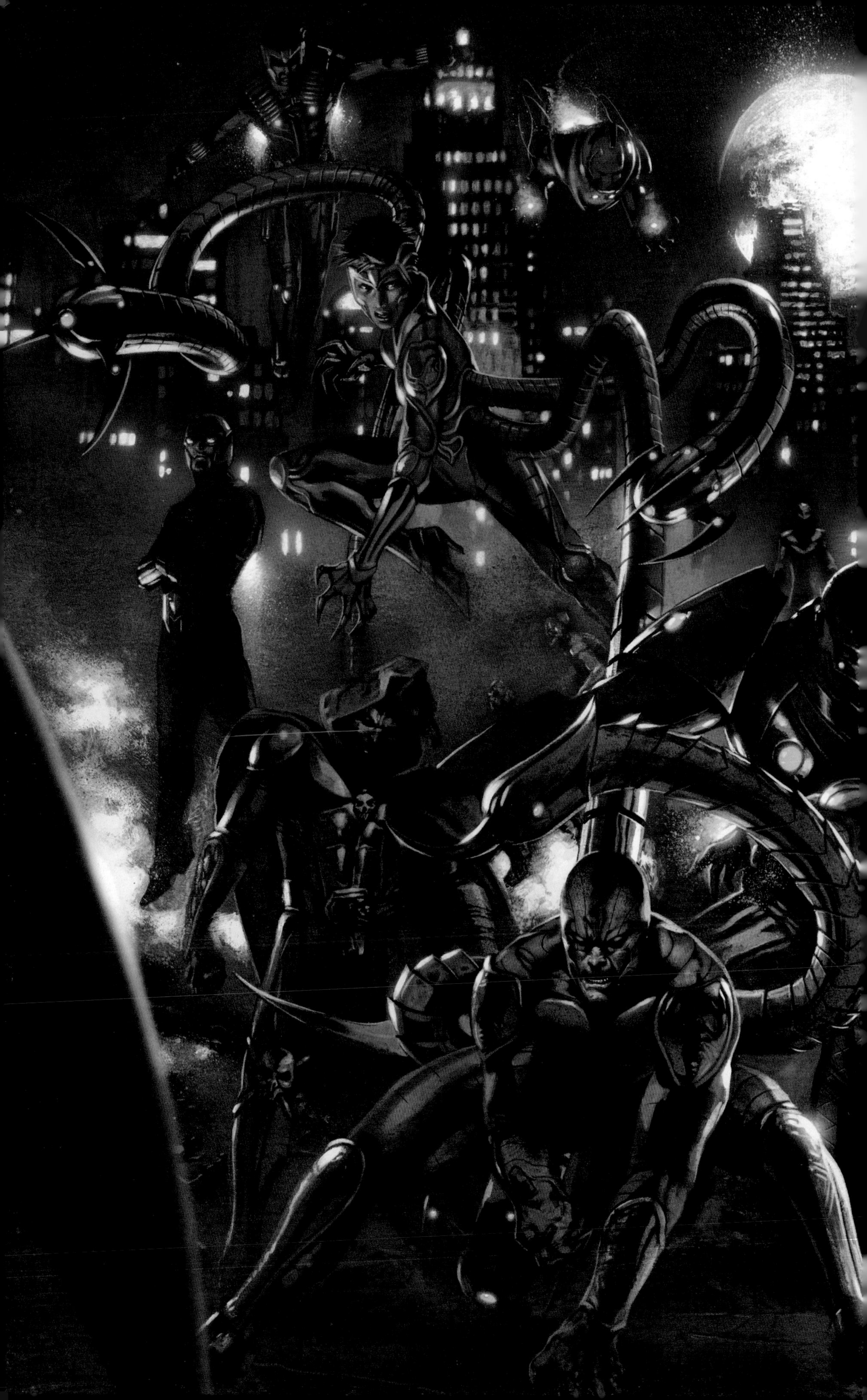

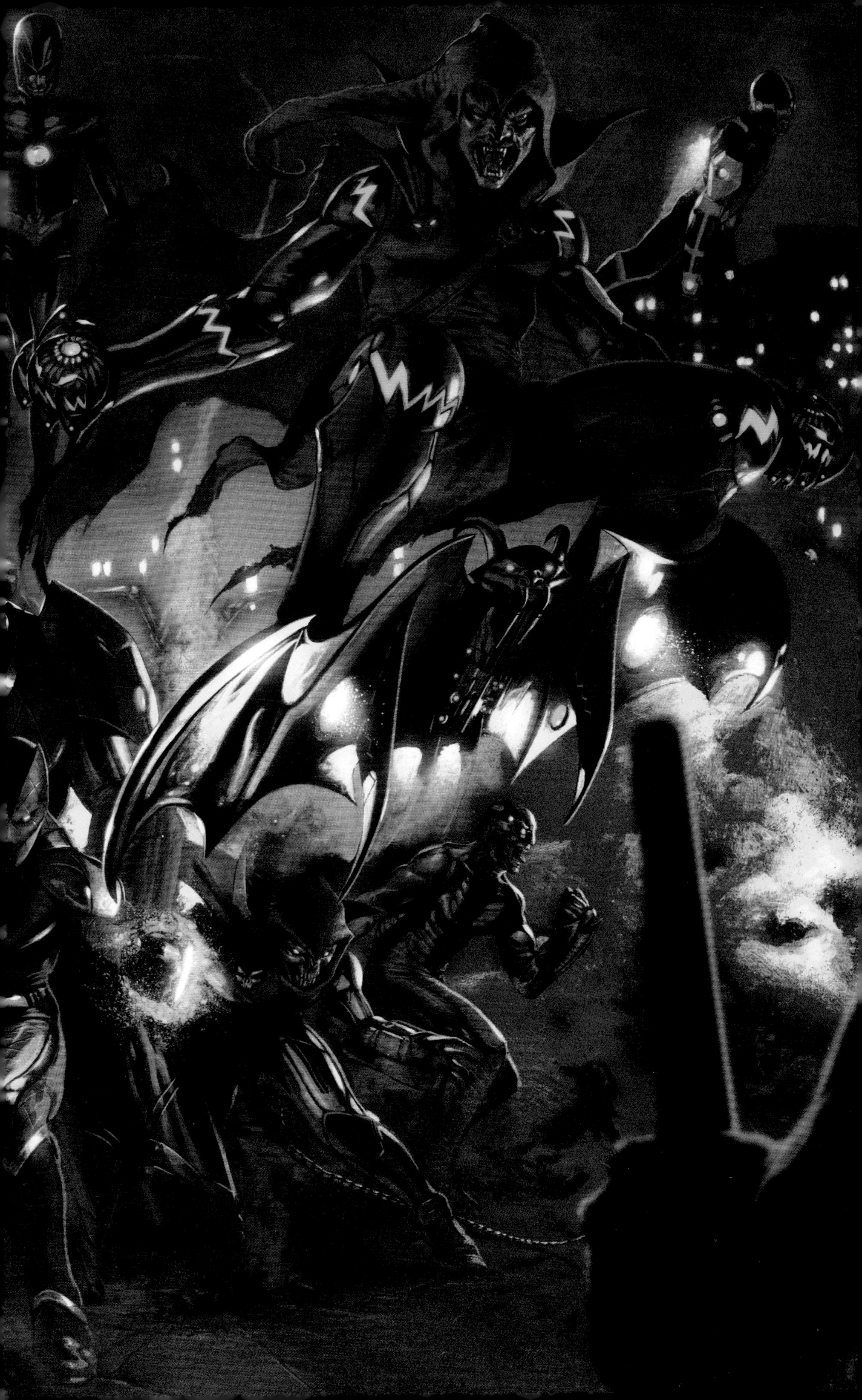

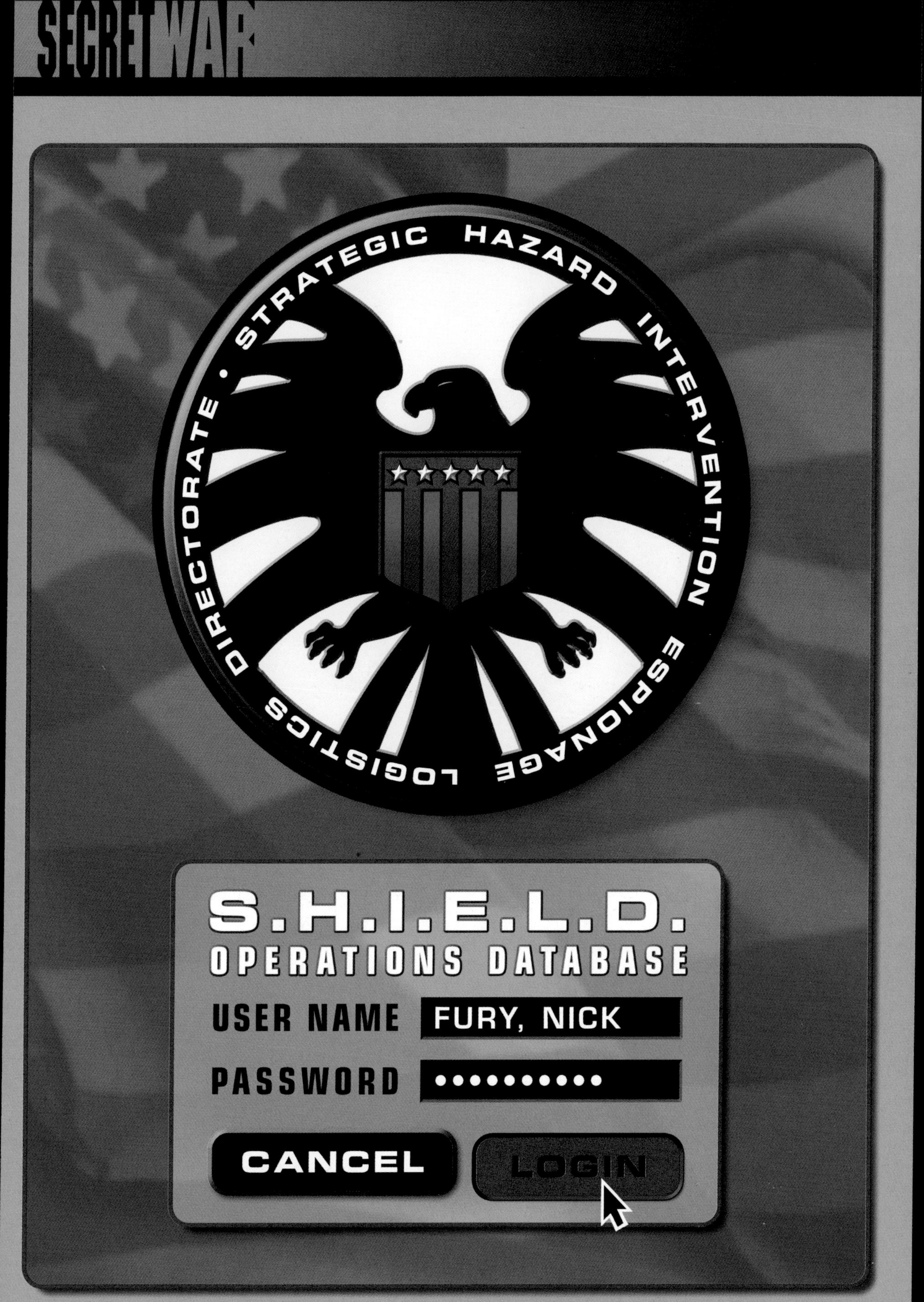
STRATEGIC HAZARD INTERVENTION ESPIONAGE LOGISTICS DIRECTORATE
S.H.I.E.L.D.
OPERATIONS DATABASE
USER NAME
FURY, NICK
PASSWORD
••••••••••
CANCEL
LOGIN

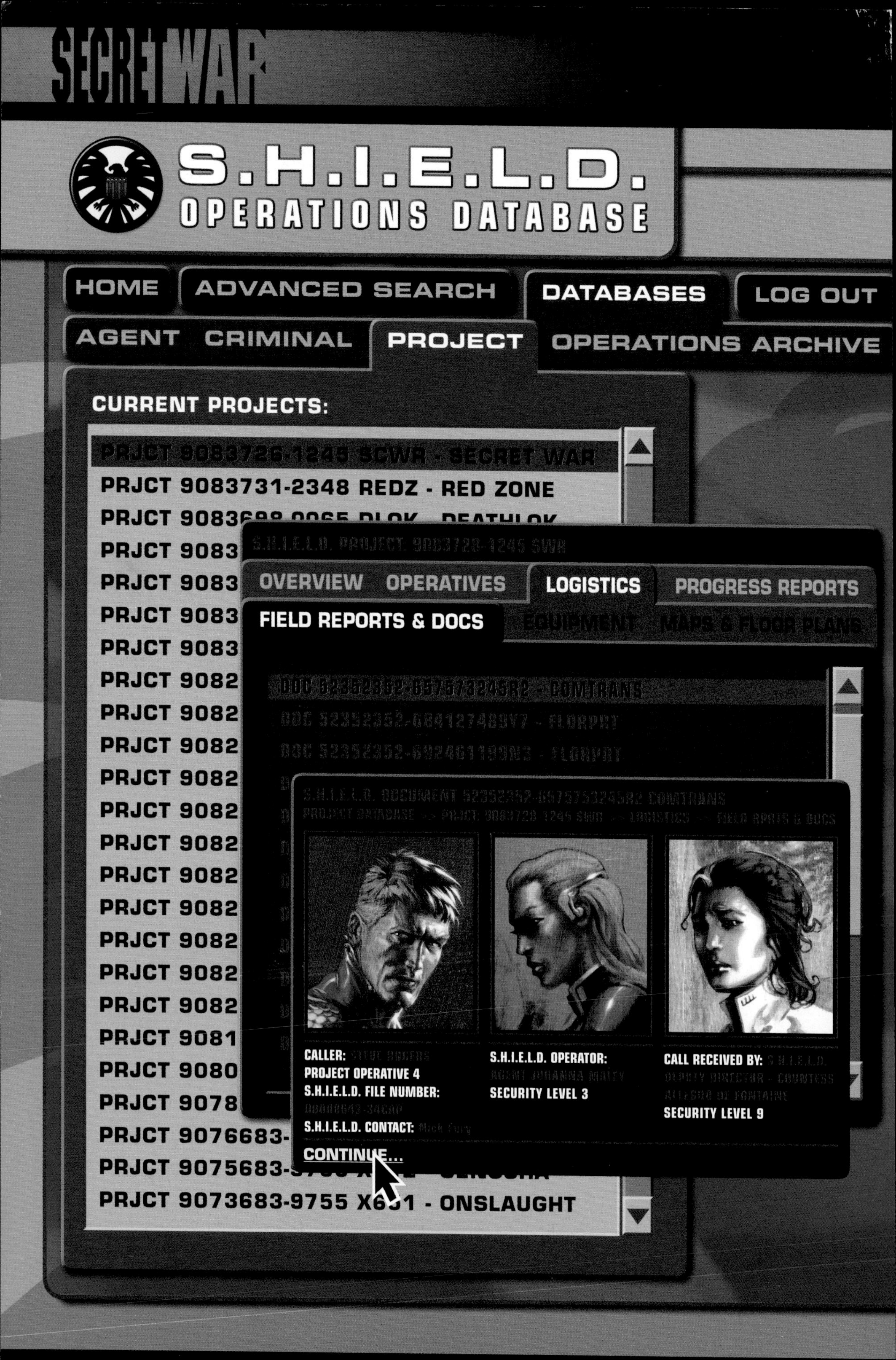

S.H.I.E.L.D.
OPERATIONS DATABASE

HOME	ADVANCED SEARCH	DATABASES	LOG OUT

AGENT   CRIMINAL   **PROJECT**   OPERATIONS ARCHIVE

CURRENT PROJECTS:

PRJCT 9083726-1245 SCWR - SECRET WAR
PRJCT 9083731-2348 REDZ - RED ZONE
PRJCT 9083688-0065 DLOK - DEATHLOK
PRJCT 9083
PRJCT 9083
PRJCT 9083
PRJCT 9083
PRJCT 9082
PRJCT 9082
PRJCT 9082
PRJCT 9082
PRJCT 9082
PRJCT 9082
PRJCT 9082
PRJCT 9082
PRJCT 9082
PRJCT 9082
PRJCT 9081
PRJCT 9080
PRJCT 9078
PRJCT 9076683-
PRJCT 9075683-9766 X-MEN - GENOSHA
PRJCT 9073683-9755 X631 - ONSLAUGHT

S.H.I.E.L.D. PROJECT. 9083726-1245 SWR

OVERVIEW   OPERATIVES   **LOGISTICS**   PROGRESS REPORTS

FIELD REPORTS & DOCS   EQUIPMENT   MAPS & FLOOR PLANS

DOC 52352352-657573245R2 - COMTRANS
DOC 52352352-684127489V7 - FLORPRT
DOC 52352352-692461199N3 - FLORPRT

S.H.I.E.L.D. DOCUMENT 52352352-657573245R2 COMTRANS
PROJECT DATABASE -> PRJCT 9083726 1245 SWR -> LOGISTICS -> FIELD RPRTS & DOCS

CALLER: STEVE ROGERS
PROJECT OPERATIVE 4
S.H.I.E.L.D. FILE NUMBER:
086608643-3468P
S.H.I.E.L.D. CONTACT: Nick Fury

S.H.I.E.L.D. OPERATOR:
AGENT JOHANNA MAITZ
SECURITY LEVEL 3

CALL RECEIVED BY: S.H.I.E.L.D.
DEPUTY DIRECTOR - COUNTESS
ALLEGRO DE FONTAINE
SECURITY LEVEL 9

CONTINUE...

SEARCH DATABASE ROGERS, STEVE SEARCH

S.H.I.E.L.D. DOCUMENT 52352352-6575753245R2 COMTRANS

PROJECT DATABASE >> PROJECT: 9083728-1245 SWR >> LOGISTICS >> FIELD REPORTS & DOCS >> COMMUNICATION TRANSCRIPTS

SECRET CODE: WHITE

Recording date: 6/12/05 11: 43 P.M.
Operator: S.H.I.E.L.D. Agent Johanna Maley - Level 3
Call Origin: Pay Phone 34521
Phone location: Bronx, New York
Broadcast locked. Coded and scrambled using nic-7 code block.

S.H.I.E.L.D. OPERATOR
Jackpot Records.

VOICE
Rogers, Steven. Code name: Soldier. Password: Modok 555.

S.H.I.E.L.D. OPERATOR
One moment.

VOICE
I don't have a moment.

S.H.I.E.L.D. OPERATOR
Waiting for computer confirmation of voiceprint.

VOICE
Nightmare.

S.H.I.E.L.D. OPERATOR
Confirmed. How can I help you, Captain?

CAPTAIN AMERICA
I need to talk to Fury, and I need a S.H.I.E.L.D. Containment crew down here now!

S.H.I.E.L.D. OPERATOR
What's the situation and location?

CAPTAIN AMERICA
The location is my home! I was just attacked in front of my home. You understand what I am saying? Get me Fury on the line A.S.A.P.

S.H.I.E.L.D. OPERATOR
Um, I'm having trouble locating Colonel Fury.

CAPTAIN AMERICA
What?

S.H.I.E.L.D. OPERATOR
He's off the grid.

CAPTAIN AMERICA
Off the grid?

S.H.I.E.L.D. OPERATOR
I'm looking now. Would you like to talk to Deputy Director Allegro De Fontaine?

CAPTAIN AMERICA
I -- Damn it. Yeah.

S.H.I.E.L.D. OPERATOR
Patching through. One moment.

S.H.I.E.L.D.
OPERATIONS DATABASE

HOME ADVANCED SEARCH DATABASES LOG OUT

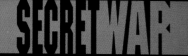

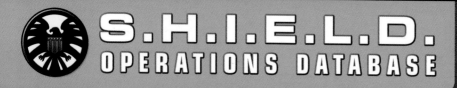

S.H.I.E.L.D. DOCUMENT 52352352-6575753245R2 COMTRANS (Cont.)

CAPTAIN AMERICA
Off the grid?

Countess Valentina Allegro De Fontaine patched into the call via tktek server nine.
Countess Valentina Allegro De Fontaine location S.H.I.E.L.D. Helicarrier.
Broadcast locked. Coded and scrambled using nic 7 code block.

COUNTESS VALENTINA ALLEGRO DE FONTAINE
This is De Fontaine.

CAPTAIN AMERICA
It's Steve Rogers.

COUNTESS VALENTINA ALLEGRO DE FONTAINE
What's going on, Captain?

CAPTAIN AMERICA
I need Fury.

COUNTESS VALENTINA ALLEGRO DE FONTAINE
Um, can I help you?

CAPTAIN AMERICA
Why is he off the grid?

COUNTESS VALENTINA ALLEGRO DE FONTAINE
I don't know, Cap. What happened?

CAPTAIN AMERICA
I went home. My home...my civilian home. And I was ambushed.

COUNTESS VALENTINA ALLEGRO DE FONTAINE
Ambushed?

CAPTAIN AMERICA
Attacked.

COUNTESS VALENTINA ALLEGRO DE FONTAINE
Can you identify the attackers?

CAPTAIN AMERICA
They--no, they were masked. But one of them--both of them were themed tech attacks.

COUNTESS VALENTINA ALLEGRO DE FONTAINE
And this just happened now?

CAPTAIN AMERICA
Yes!

COUNTESS VALENTINA ALLEGRO DE FONTAINE
You're where now?

CAPTAIN AMERICA
Across the street from my apartment. Two blocks away. But I can still see my apartment. One looked and moved very similarly to those goblin types that are always attacking Spider-Man.

COUNTESS VALENTINA ALLEGRO DE FONTAINE
Goblin? Like the Green Goblin?

CAPTAIN AMERICA
Yes. He was in full armor and he had a powered low-flying glider.

COUNTESS VALENTINA ALLEGRO DE FONTAINE
Did you get a good look at his face?

SEARCH DATABASE

ROGERS, STEVE

SEARCH

S.H.I.E.L.D. DOCUMENT 52352352-6575753245R2 COMTRANS (Cont.)

CAPTAIN AMERICA
No. It was a full mask.

COUNTESS VALENTINA ALLEGRO DE FONTAINE
Did anyone identify themselves?

CAPTAIN AMERICA
No.

COUNTESS VALENTINA ALLEGRO DE FONTAINE
Do you believe it was Norman Osborn?

CAPTAIN AMERICA
I couldn't tell you, the confrontation was--it was very quick. There was very little actual speaking. They attacked and I attacked back. The face--it was covered by a goblin mask but I don't think it was the actual Green Goblin. The armor was more high tech. It looked new. Higher tech than I believe I've seen Osborn with--

COUNTESS VALENTINA ALLEGRO DE FONTAINE
And the other one?

CAPTAIN AMERICA
It was a woman. But she had metal arms like that Octavius person.

COUNTESS VALENTINA ALLEGRO DE FONTAINE
Like Doctor Octopus?

CAPTAIN AMERICA
Yes.

COUNTESS VALENTINA ALLEGRO DE FONTAINE
The one Spider-Man is always dealing with?

CAPTAIN AMERICA
Yes. But a woman. She also had a flying apparatus strapped to her back. Like a rocket pack. Like the rocket-men serials.

COUNTESS VALENTINA ALLEGRO DE FONTAINE
A female Doctor Octopus with a jet pack?

CAPTAIN AMERICA
Yes.

COUNTESS VALENTINA ALLEGRO DE FONTAINE
Short hair. Kind of butch?

CAPTAIN AMERICA
I suppose.

COUNTESS VALENTINA ALLEGRO DE FONTAINE
Dr. Carolyn Trainer.

CAPTAIN AMERICA
Is that her name?

COUNTESS VALENTINA ALLEGRO DE FONTAINE
Pretty sure. Got the file right here. We got her on file. She had body armor too.

CAPTAIN AMERICA
Thin armor, yes. Who is she?

COUNTESS VALENTINA ALLEGRO DE FONTAINE
The female Doctor Octopus.

CAPTAIN AMERICA
What's her story? Who is she working for?

COUNTESS VALENTINA ALLEGRO DE FONTAINE
I don't know. What happened to them?

S.H.I.E.L.D. OPERATIONS DATABASE

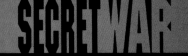

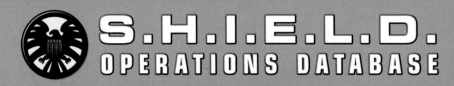

S.H.I.E.L.D. DOCUMENT 52352352-657575324582 COMTRANS (Cont.)

CAPTAIN AMERICA
I held them off. I bashed the octopus woman in the face with the other one's flying glider. Not my proudest moment, but it worked. They panicked and took off. It was my impression that they thought I was just going to fold like a cheap card table and were pretty surprised when I didn't. She yelled out something about "this not being the deal." Or something--

COUNTESS VALENTINA ALLEGRO DE FONTAINE
I'm cross-searching goblin files.

CAPTAIN AMERICA
Any idea why Spider-Man's enemies are attacking me at my home? Or know how they know where I live?

COUNTESS VALENTINA ALLEGRO DE FONTAINE
I'm cross-referencing files right now.

CAPTAIN AMERICA
It might not have been a goblin or Osborn, but it looked like it.

COUNTESS VALENTINA ALLEGRO DE FONTAINE
Hold on. First Luke Cage and now this.

CAPTAIN AMERICA
What?

COUNTESS VALENTINA ALLEGRO DE FONTAINE
Um...

CAPTAIN AMERICA
Was Luke Cage attacked?

COUNTESS VALENTINA ALLEGRO DE FONTAINE
We don't know for sure.

CAPTAIN AMERICA
Valentina, what's going on?

COUNTESS VALENTINA ALLEGRO DE FONTAINE
Cage was attacked in his home. By--by a mystery assailant.

CAPTAIN AMERICA
Is he alright?

COUNTESS VALENTINA ALLEGRO DE FONTAINE
No.

CAPTAIN AMERICA
Is he dead?

COUNTESS VALENTINA ALLEGRO DE FONTAINE
No. Hospital.

CAPTAIN AMERICA
Is Jessica Jones all right?

COUNTESS VALENTINA ALLEGRO DE FONTAINE
Who is that?

CAPTAIN AMERICA
His girlfriend or fiancé.

COUNTESS VALENTINA ALLEGRO DE FONTAINE
I don't know.

CAPTAIN AMERICA
She's pregnant.

S.H.I.E.L.D. DOCUMENT 52352352-6575753245R2 COMTRANS (Cont.)

COUNTESS VALENTINA ALLEGRO DE FONTAINE
I don't even know who she is.

CAPTAIN AMERICA
Valentina, where's Fury?

COUNTESS VALENTINA ALLEGRO DE FONTAINE
He went off the grid.

CAPTAIN AMERICA
But you know where he is. You always know where he is.

COUNTESS VALENTINA ALLEGRO DE FONTAINE
Cap...

CAPTAIN AMERICA
Is he in hiding?

COUNTESS VALENTINA ALLEGRO DE FONTAINE
No.

CAPTAIN AMERICA
Did he go to visit Cage?

COUNTESS VALENTINA ALLEGRO DE FONTAINE
Cap, don't. I hate lying to you. You know that.

CAPTAIN AMERICA
He went off the grid to go to see...oh my God.

COUNTESS VALENTINA ALLEGRO DE FONTAINE
What?

CAPTAIN AMERICA
What that man did.

COUNTESS VALENTINA ALLEGRO DE FONTAINE
Cap, just calm down. We'll send a S.H.I.E.L.D. Containment crew. We'll send--

CAPTAIN AMERICA
What hospital?

COUNTESS VALENTINA ALLEGRO DE FONTAINE
Cap.

CAPTAIN AMERICA
Valentina. What hospital?

COUNTESS VALENTINA ALLEGRO DE FONTAINE
I'll call you back on another line, stay at that phone.

[End transcript]

Transcript reviewed and edited by Nick Fury for security clearance.
566-788

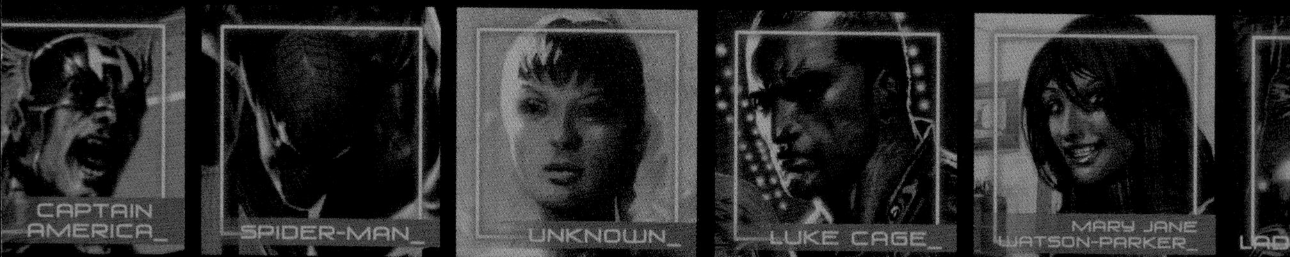
CAPTAIN AMERICA_
SPIDER-MAN_
UNKNOWN_
LUKE CAGE_
MARY JANE WATSON-PARKER_

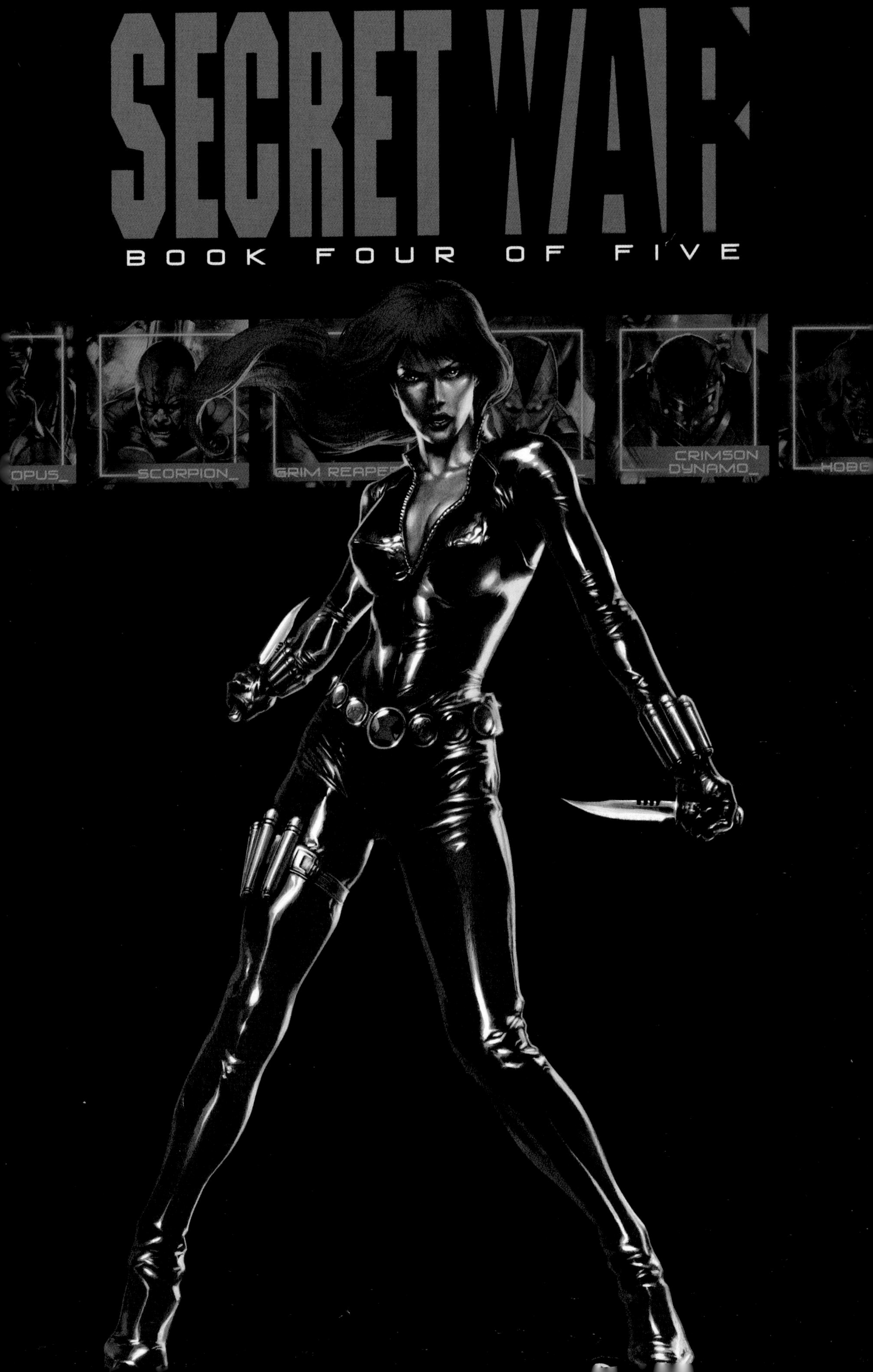
SECRET WAR
BOOK FOUR OF FIVE
OPUS_
SCORPION_
GRIM REAPE
CRIMSON DYNAMO_
HOBG

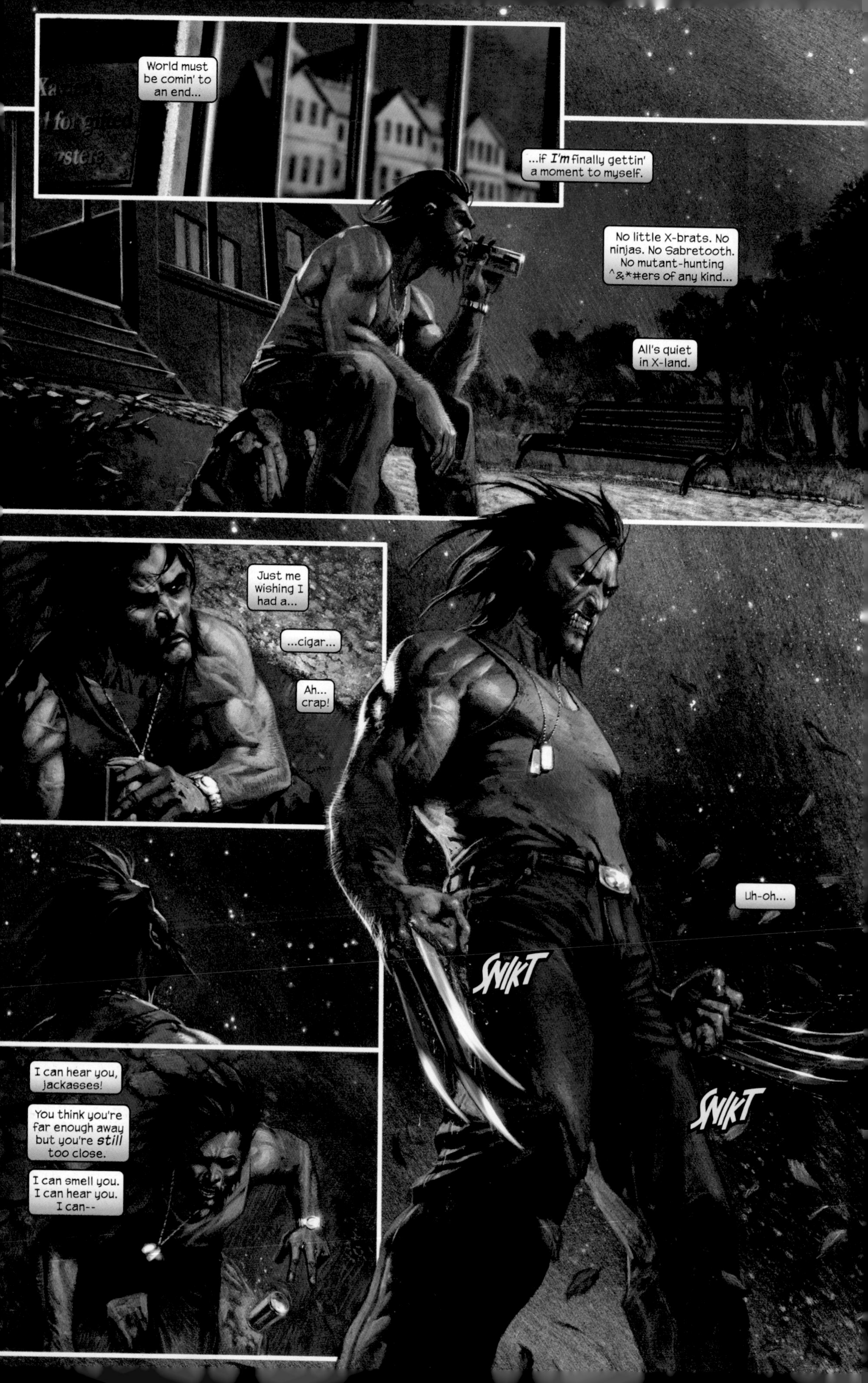
World must be comin' to an end...
...if I'm finally gettin' a moment to myself.
No little X-brats. No ninjas. No Sabretooth. No mutant-hunting ^&*#ers of any kind...
All's quiet in X-land.
Just me wishing I had a...
...cigar...
Ah... crap!
Uh-oh...
SNIKT
SNIKT
I can hear you, jackasses!
You think you're far enough away but you're still too close.
I can smell you. I can hear you. I can--

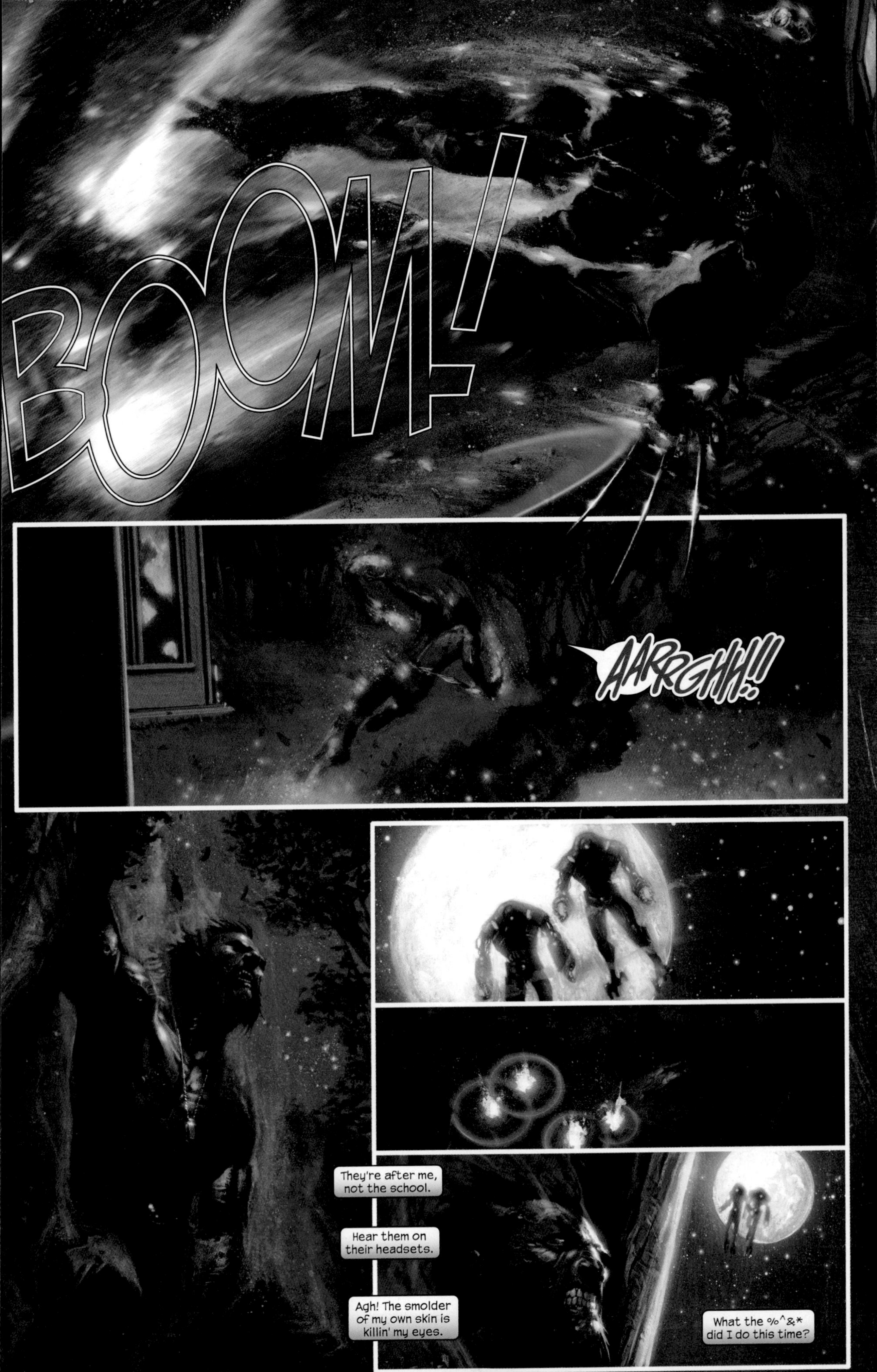
BOOM!
AARRGHH!!
They're after me, not the school.
Hear them on their headsets.
Agh! The smolder of my own skin is killin' my eyes.
What the %^&* did I do this time?

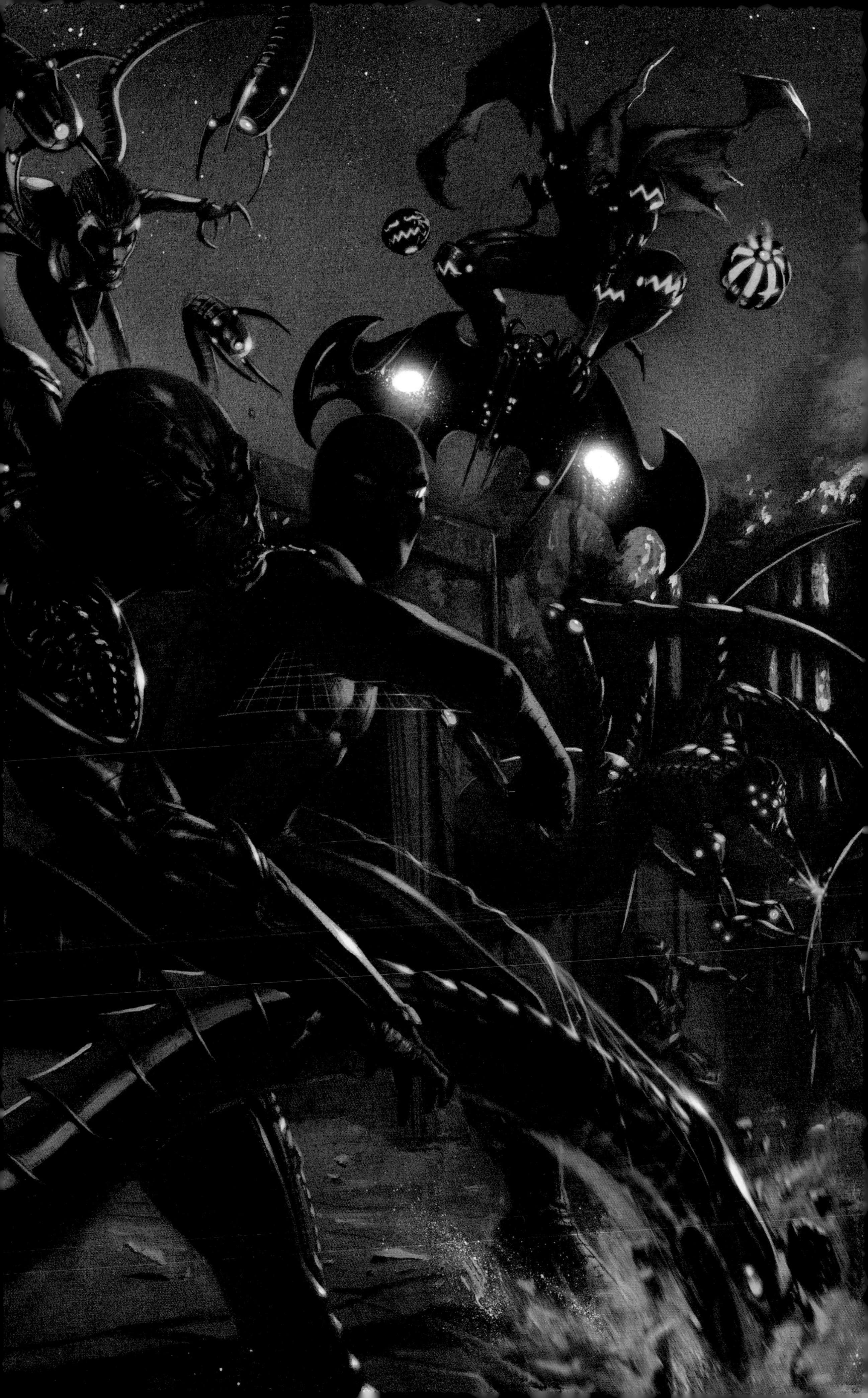

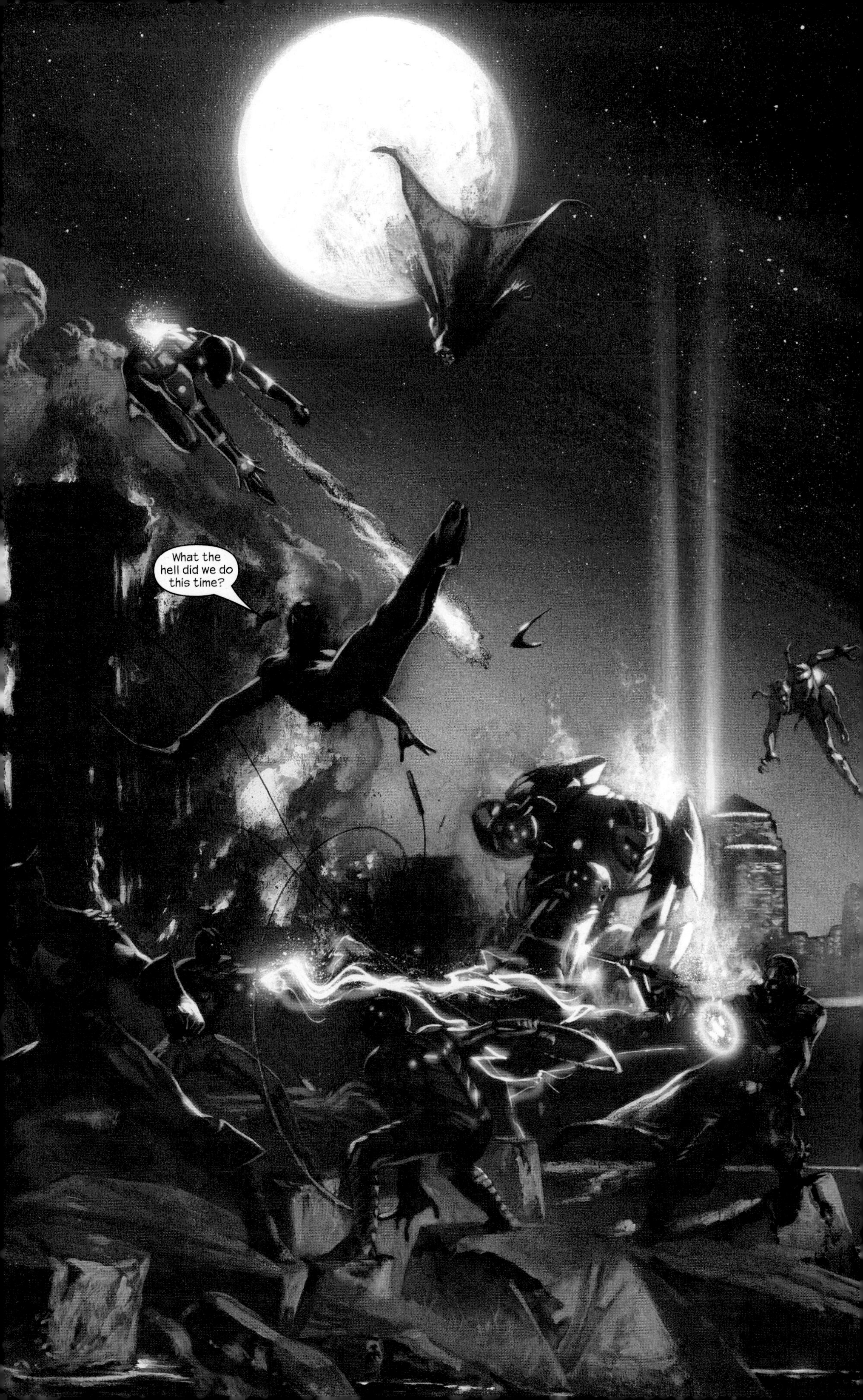
What the hell did we do this time?

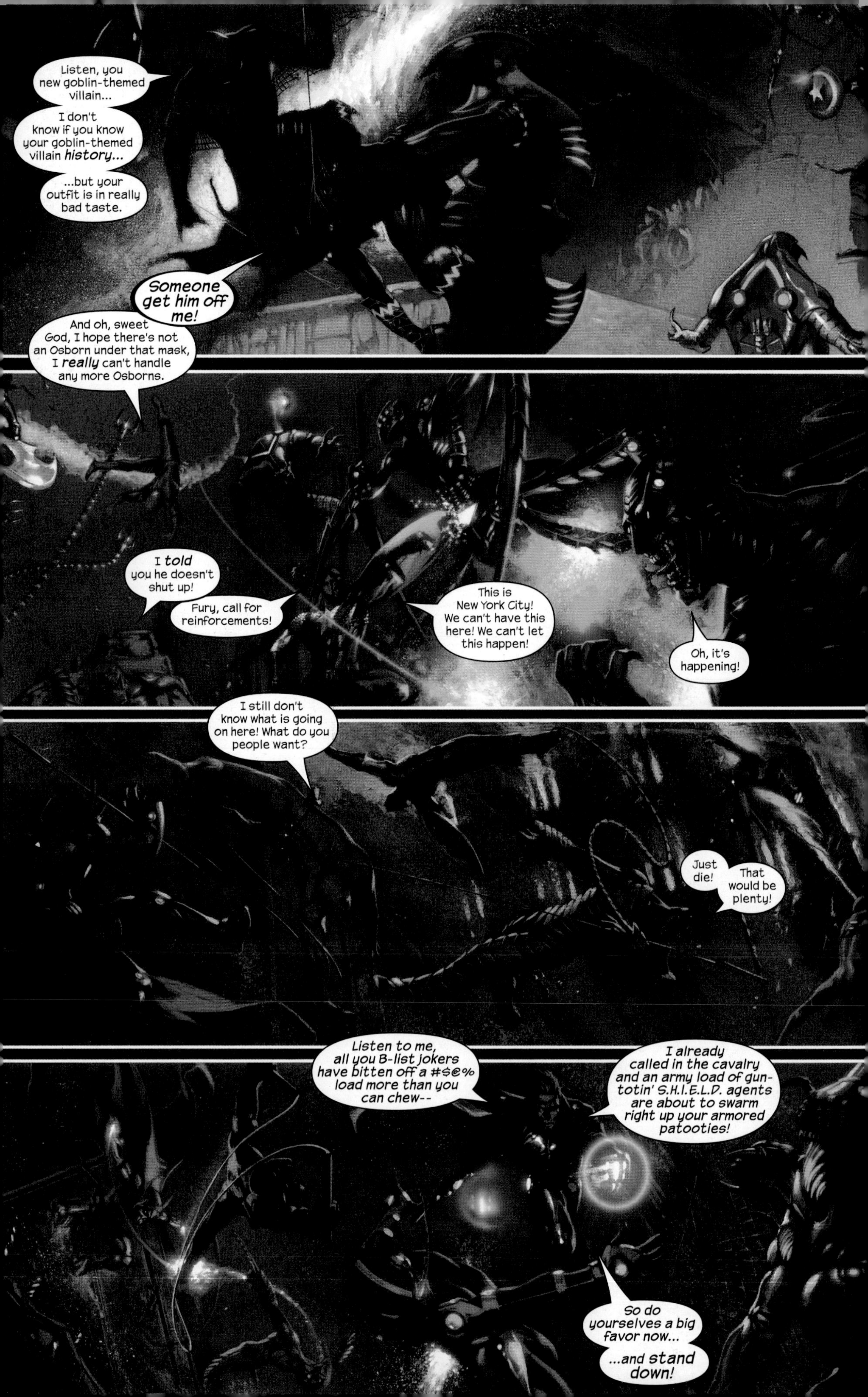

Listen, you new goblin-themed villain...
I don't know if you know your goblin-themed villain *history...*
...but your outfit is in really bad taste.
Someone get him off me!
And oh, sweet God, I hope there's not an Osborn under that mask, I *really* can't handle any more Osborns.
I *told* you he doesn't shut up!
Fury, call for reinforcements!
This is New York City! We can't have this here! We can't let this happen!
Oh, it's happening!
I still don't know what is going on here! What do you people want?
Just die!
That would be plenty!
Listen to me, all you B-list jokers have bitten off a #$@% load more than you can chew--
I already called in the cavalry and an army load of gun-totin' S.H.I.E.L.D. agents are about to swarm right up your armored patooties!
So do yourselves a big favor now...
...and *stand down!*

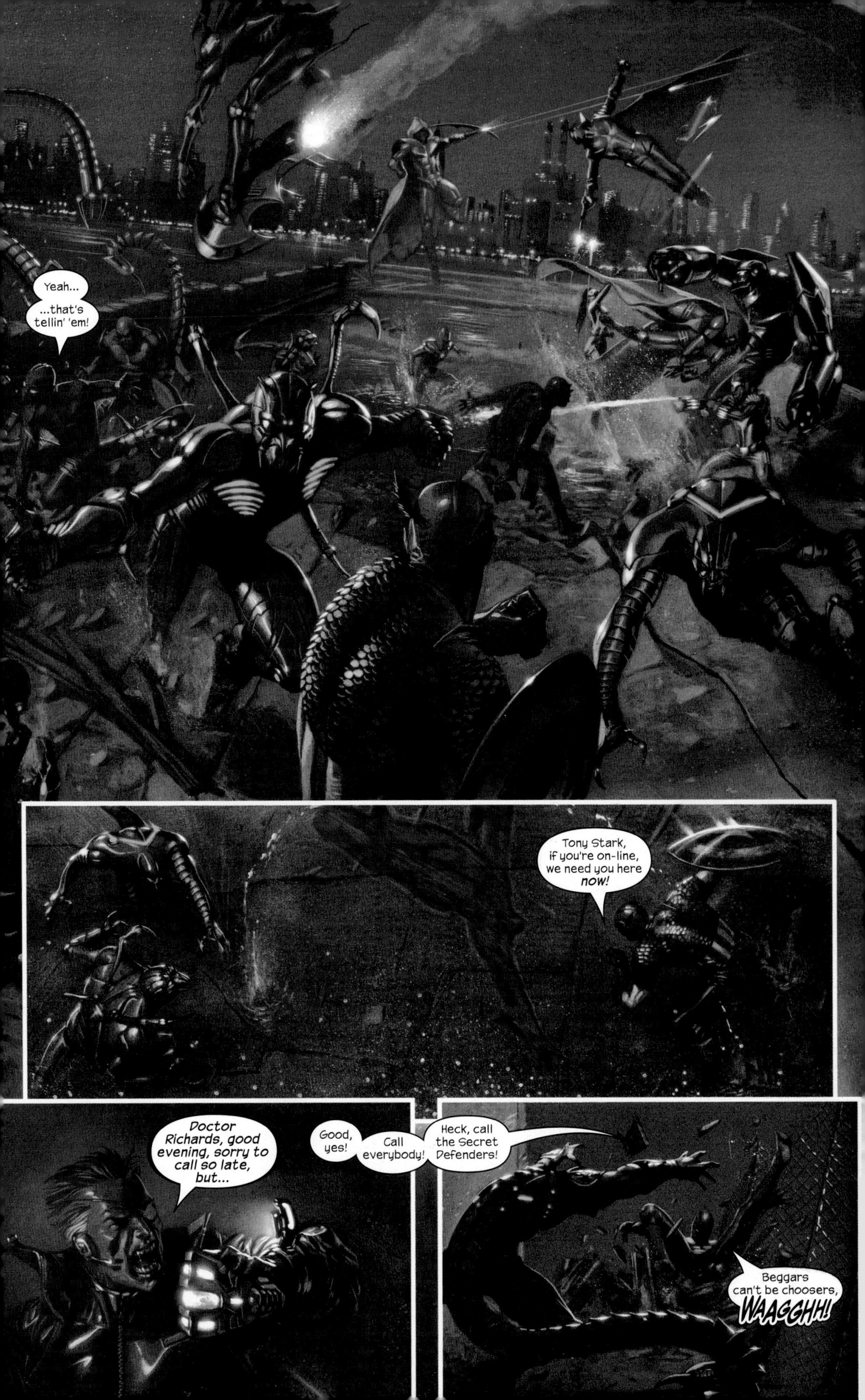
Yeah...
...that's tellin' 'em!
Tony Stark, if you're on-line, we need you here now!
Doctor Richards, good evening, sorry to call so late, but...
Good, yes!
Call everybody!
Heck, call the Secret Defenders!
Beggars can't be choosers, WAAGGHH!!

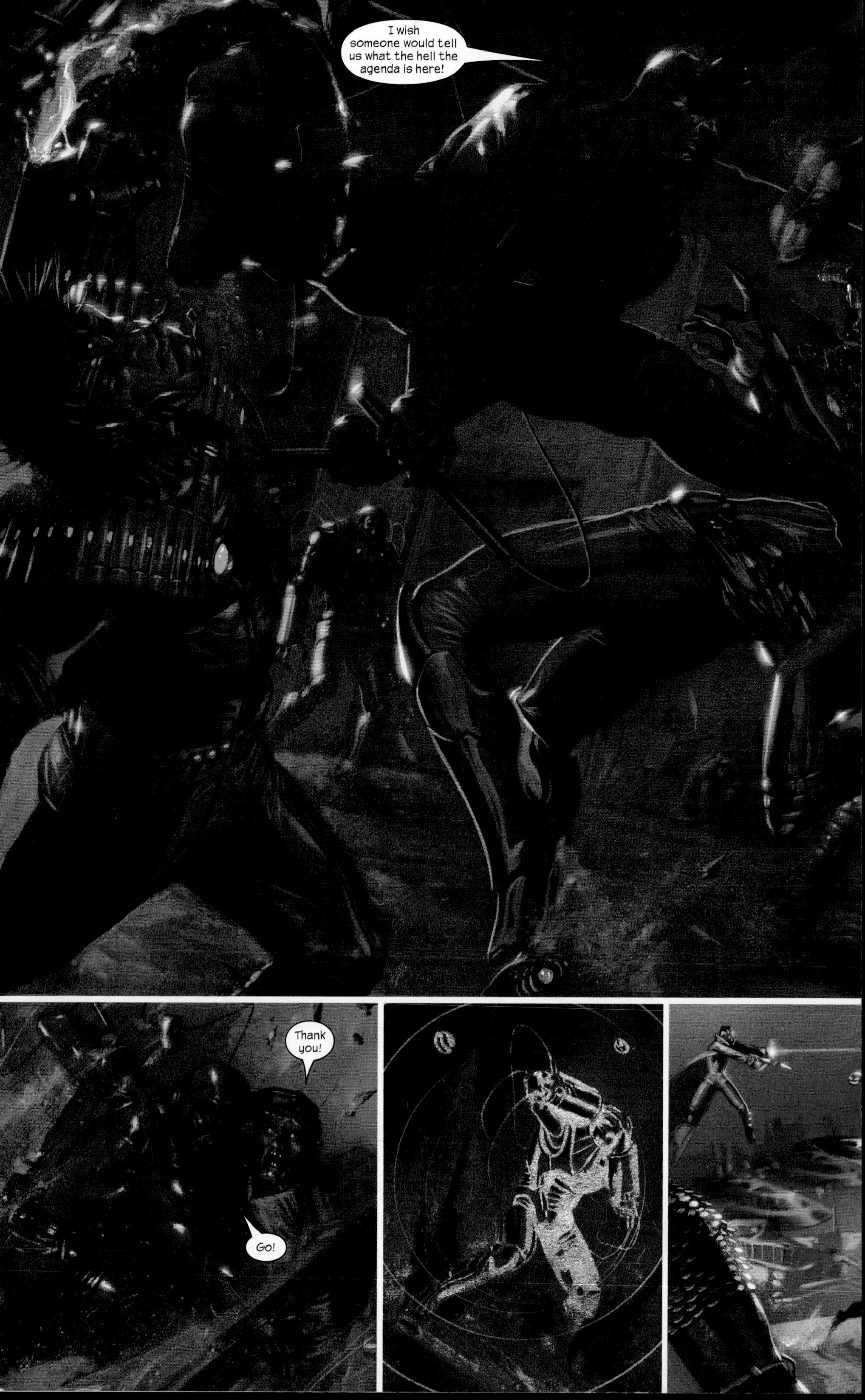
I wish someone would tell us what the hell the agenda is here!
Thank you!
Go!

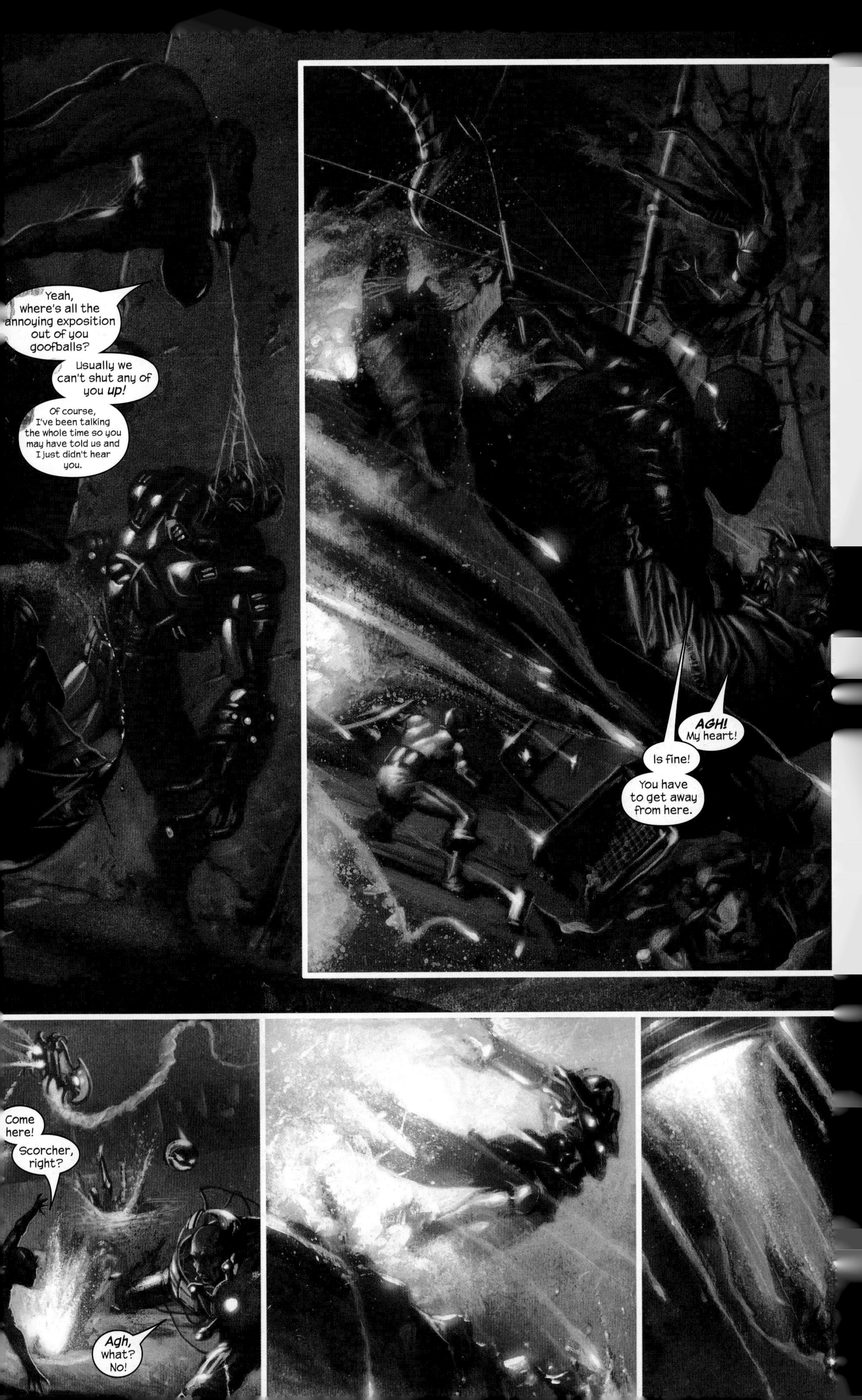
Yeah, where's all the annoying exposition out of you goofballs?
Usually we can't shut any of you *up!*
Of course, I've been talking the whole time so you may have told us and I just didn't hear you.
AGH! My heart!
Is fine!
You have to get away from here.
Come here!
Scorcher, right?
Agh, what? No!

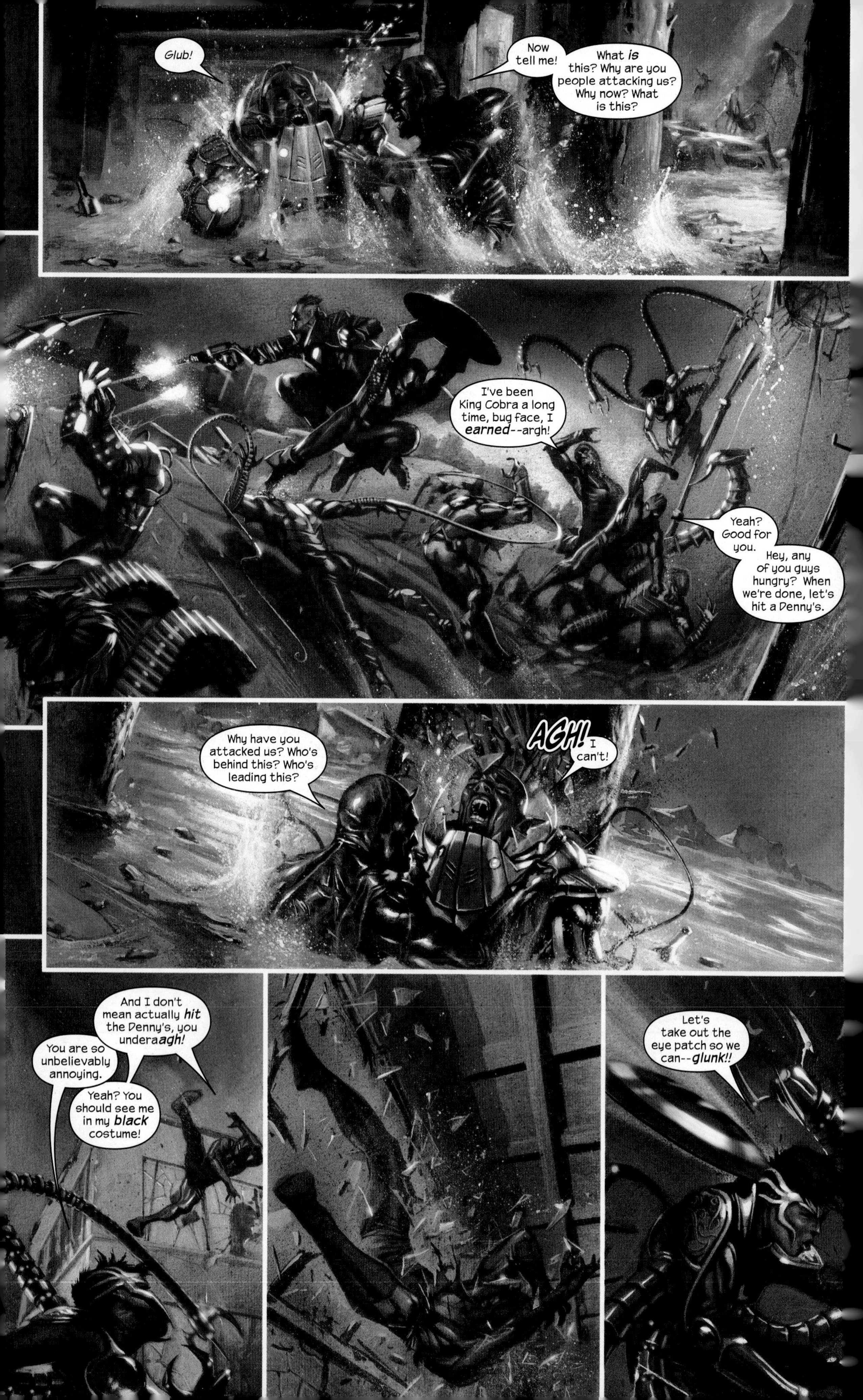
Glub!
Now tell me!
What is this? Why are you people attacking us? Why now? What is this?
I've been King Cobra a long time, bug face, I earned--argh!
Yeah? Good for you.
Hey, any of you guys hungry? When we're done, let's hit a Denny's.
Why have you attacked us? Who's behind this? Who's leading this?
AGH!
I can't!
And I don't mean actually hit the Denny's, you underaagh!
You are so unbelievably annoying.
Yeah? You should see me in my black costume!
Let's take out the eye patch so we can--glunk!!

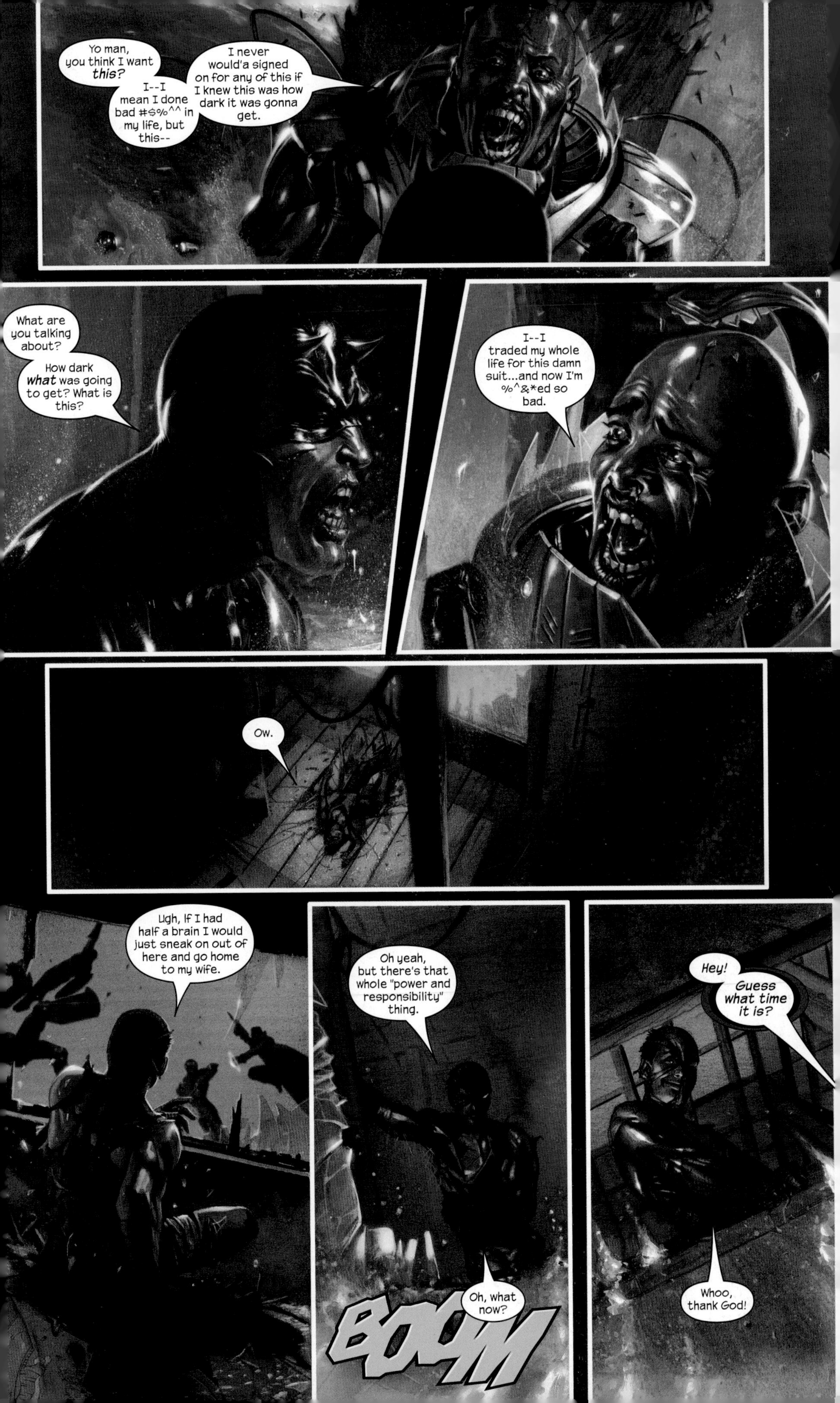
Yo man, you think I want *this?*
I--I mean I done bad #$%^^ in my life, but this--
I never would'a signed on for any of this if I knew this was how dark it was gonna get.
What are you talking about?
How dark *what* was going to get? What is this?
I--I traded my whole life for this damn suit...and now I'm %^&*ed so bad.
Ow.
Ugh, If I had half a brain I would just sneak on out of here and go home to my wife.
Oh yeah, but there's that whole "power and responsibility" thing.
BOOM
Oh, what now?
Hey!
Guess what time it is?
Whoo, thank God!

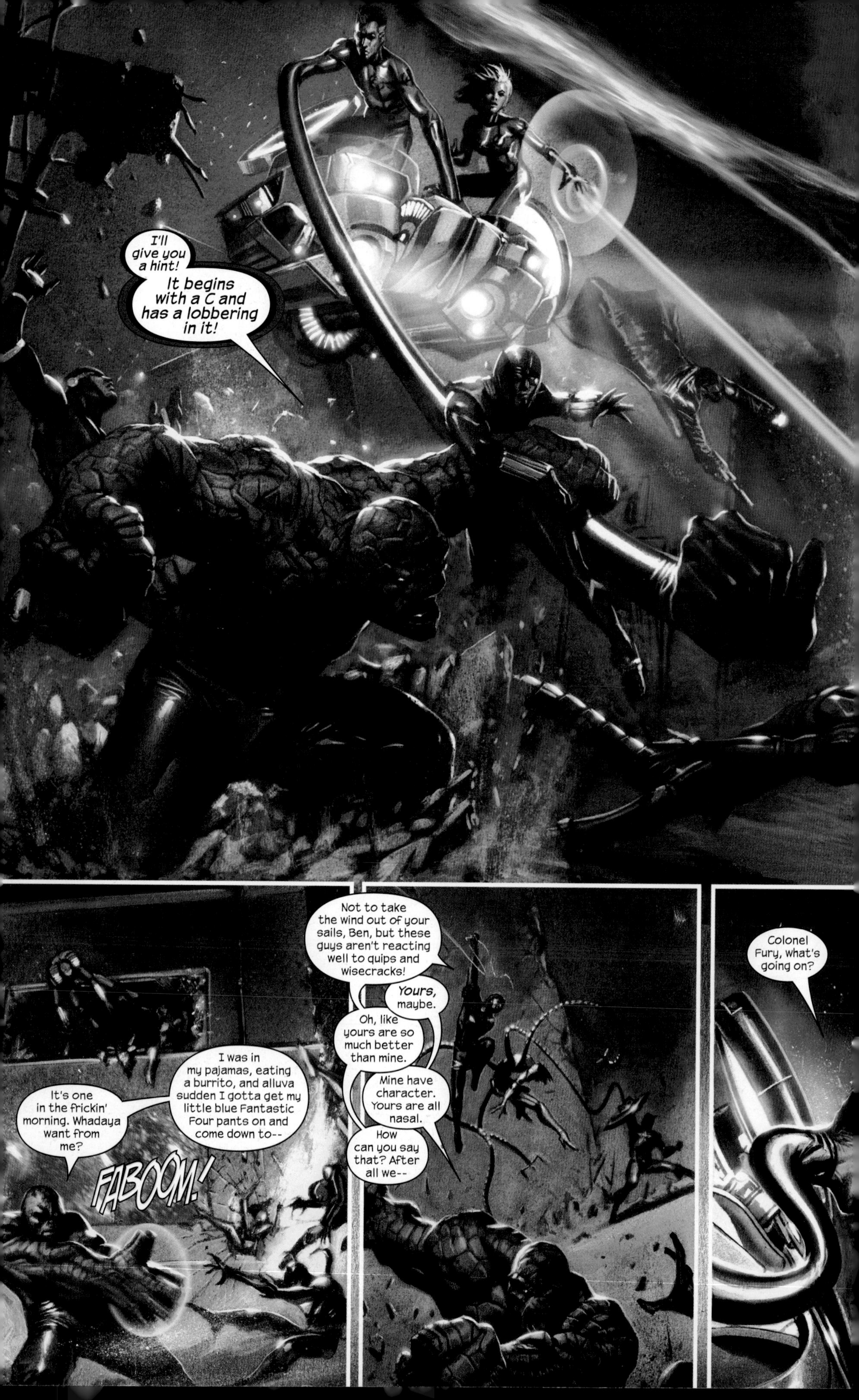

I'll give you a hint! It begins with a C and has a lobbering in it!
It's one in the frickin' morning. Whadaya want from me?
I was in my pajamas, eating a burrito, and alluva sudden I gotta get my little blue Fantastic Four pants on and come down to--
FABOOM!
Not to take the wind out of your sails, Ben, but these guys aren't reacting well to quips and wisecracks!
Yours, maybe.
Oh, like yours are so much better than mine.
Mine have character. Yours are all nasal.
How can you say that? After all we--
Colonel Fury, what's going on?

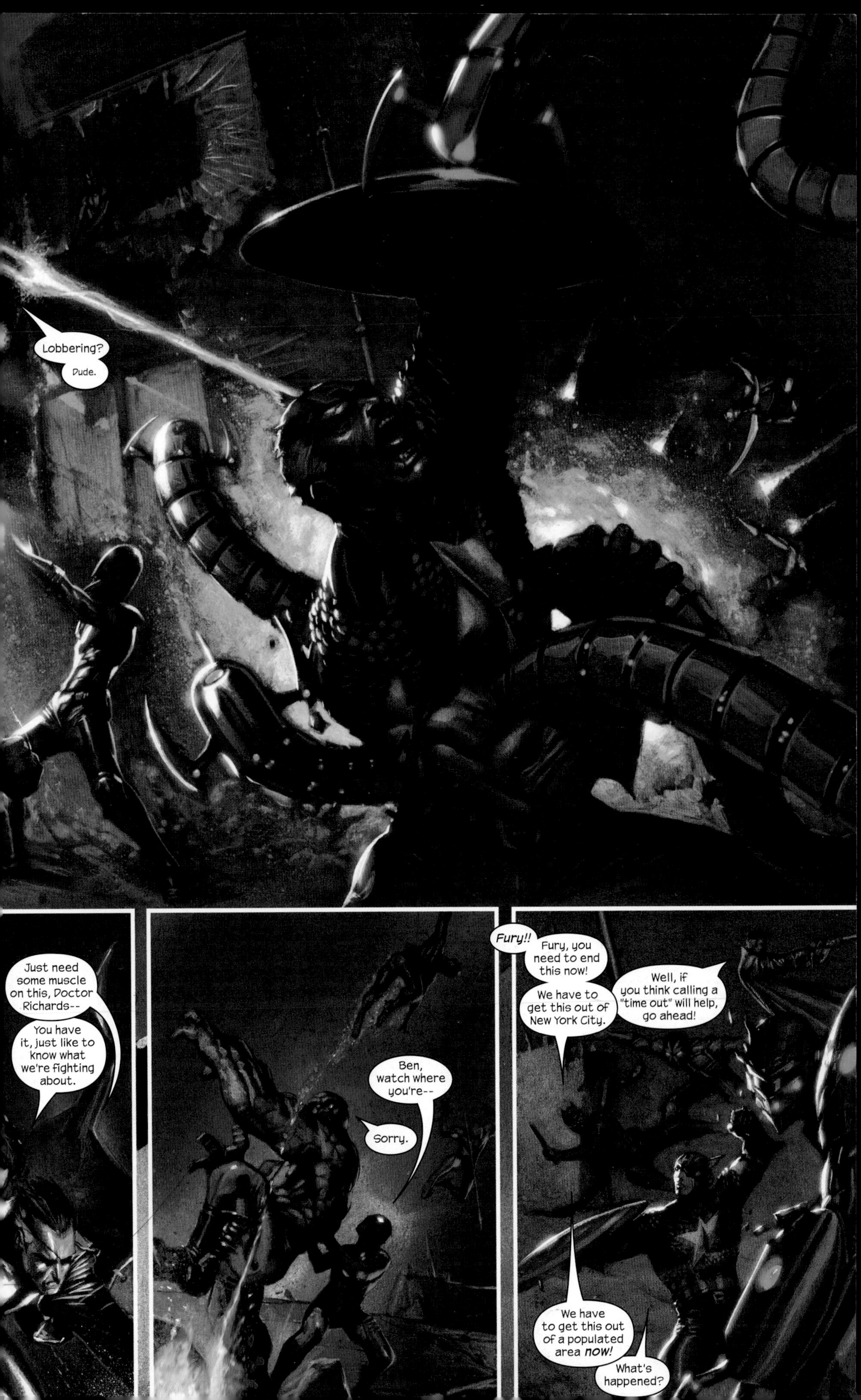
Lobbering?
Dude.
Just need some muscle on this, Doctor Richards--
You have it, just like to know what we're fighting about.
Ben, watch where you're--
Sorry.
Fury!!
Fury, you need to end this now!
We have to get this out of New York City.
Well, if you think calling a "time out" will help, go ahead!
We have to get this out of a populated area *now!*
What's happened?

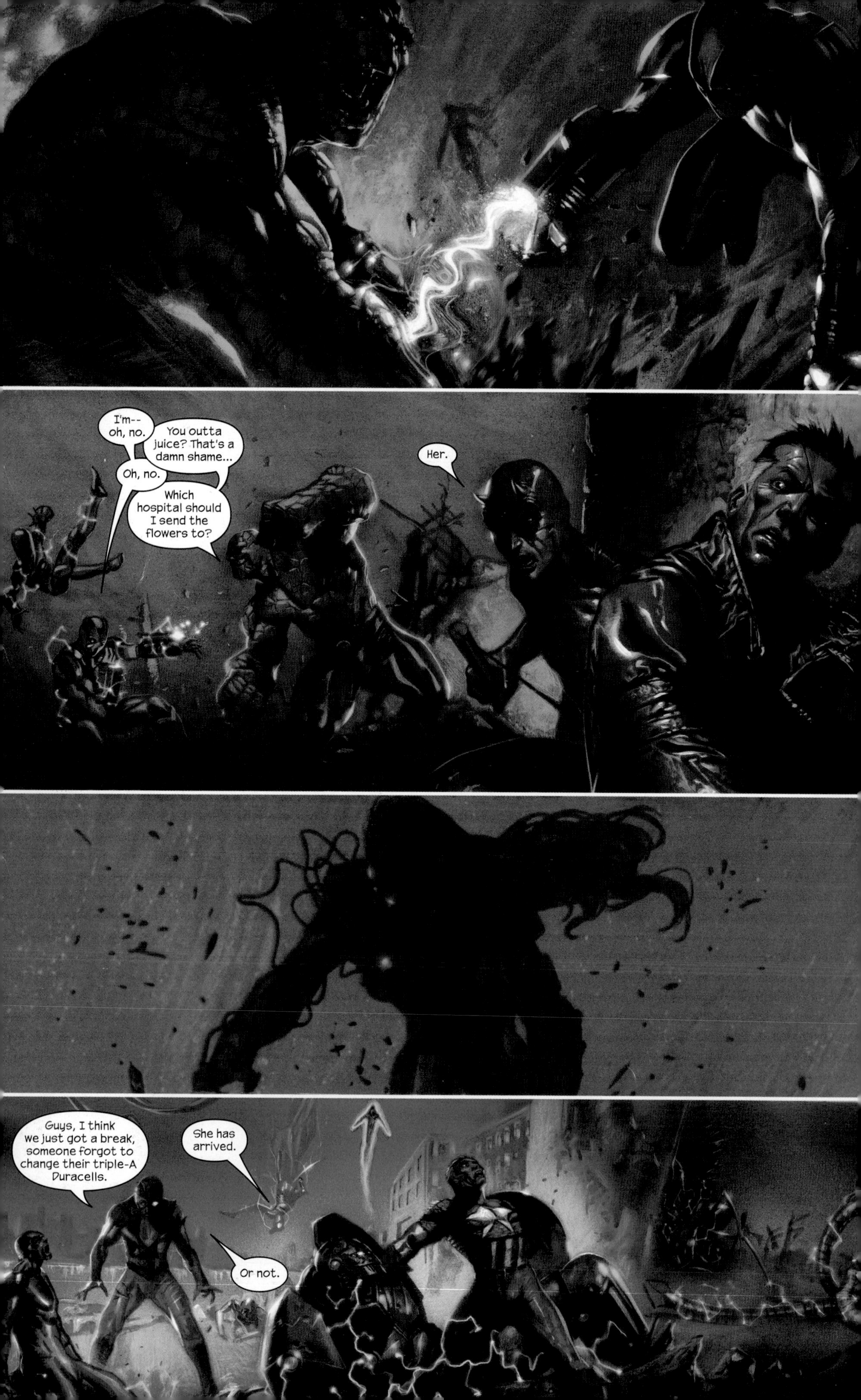

I'm-- oh, no.
You outta juice? That's a damn shame...
Oh, no.
Which hospital should I send the flowers to?
Her.
Guys, I think we just got a break, someone forgot to change their triple-A Duracells.
She has arrived.
Or not.

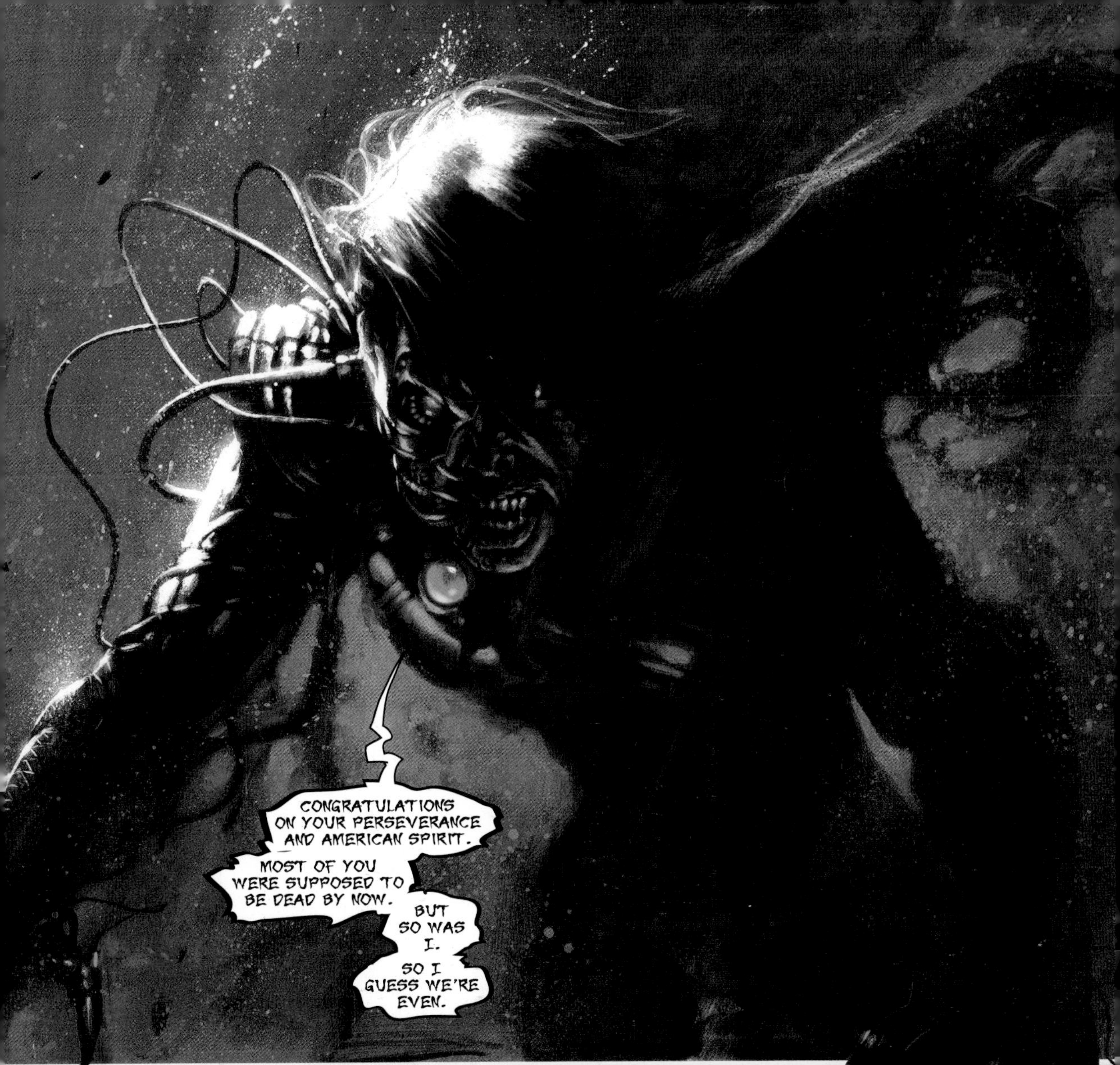
CONGRATULATIONS ON YOUR PERSEVERANCE AND AMERICAN SPIRIT.
MOST OF YOU WERE SUPPOSED TO BE DEAD BY NOW.
BUT SO WAS I.
SO I GUESS WE'RE EVEN.

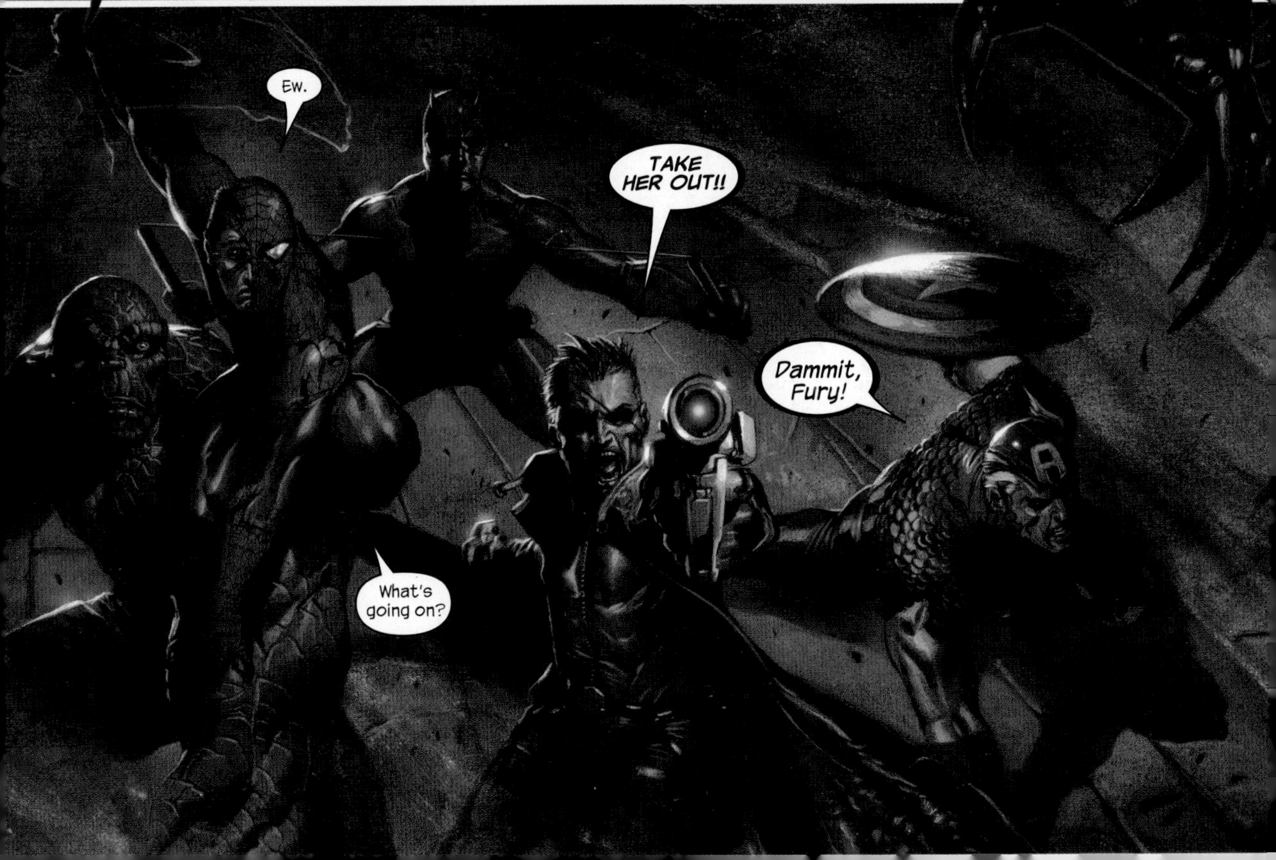
Ew.
TAKE HER OUT!!
Dammit, Fury!
What's going on?

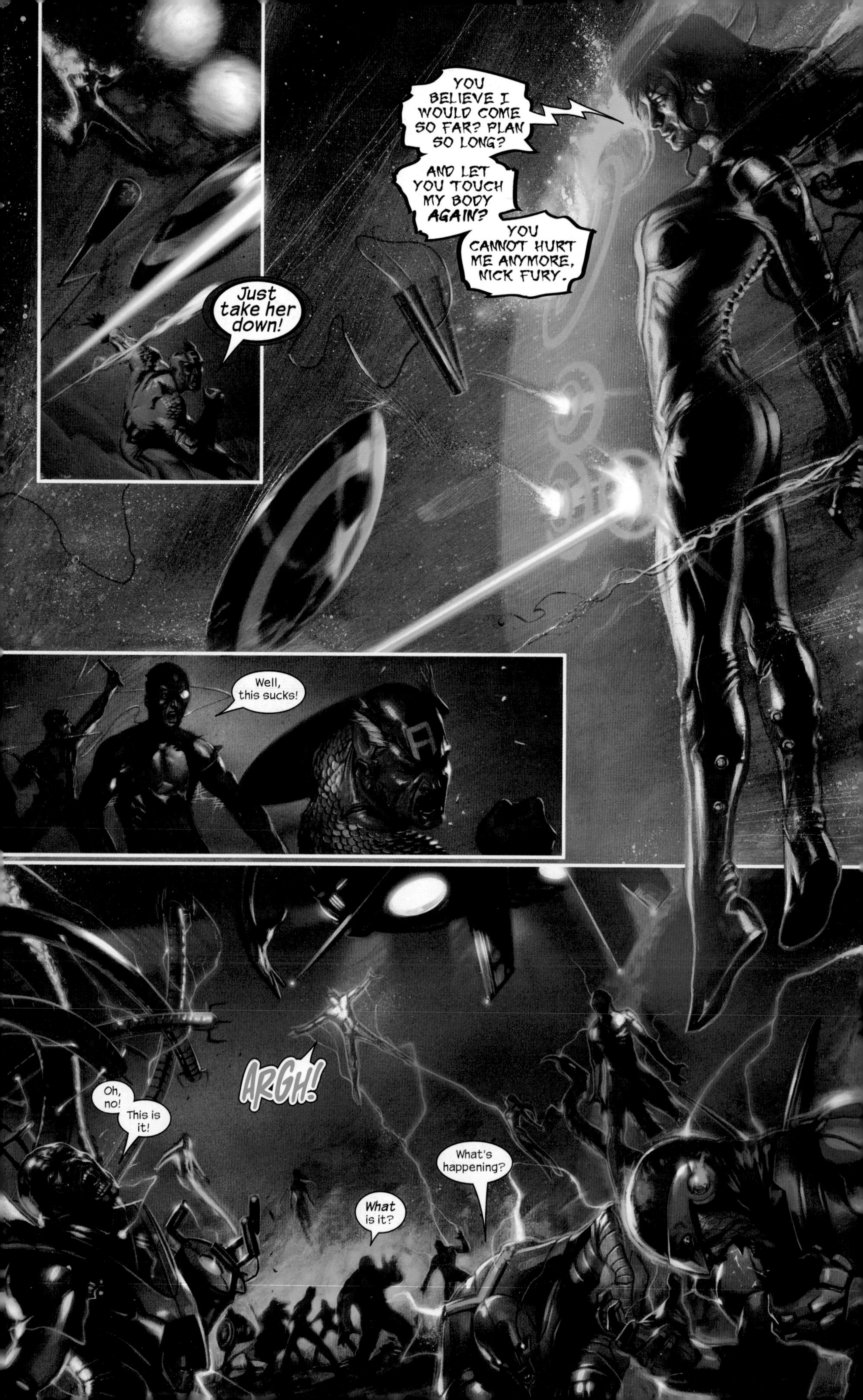
YOU BELIEVE I WOULD COME SO FAR? PLAN SO LONG?
AND LET YOU TOUCH MY BODY AGAIN?
YOU CANNOT HURT ME ANYMORE, NICK FURY.
Just take her down!
Well, this sucks!
ARGH!
Oh, no!
This is it!
What's happening?
What is it?

TAKE THESE WORDS TO HELL WITH YOU, FURY!
THIS IS THE DAY YOU PAY FOR ALL YOUR SINS!
YOUR COSTUMED SOLDIERS HAVE BEEN GATHERED AND BEATEN.
THOSE WHO SURVIVED WERE PURPOSELY GATHERED HERE--ROUNDED UP--
--FOR ONE PURPOSE.
TO WATCH THIS.
TO LET THE LAST THING THEY SEE ON THIS EARTH BE THE CULMINATION OF ALL YOUR LIES AND BETRAYALS!

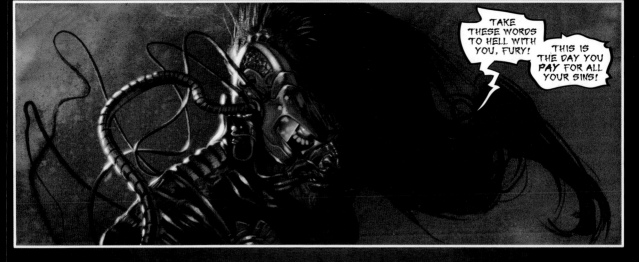

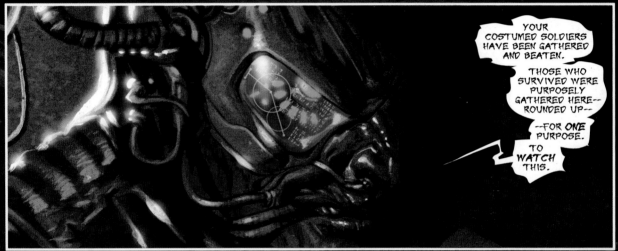

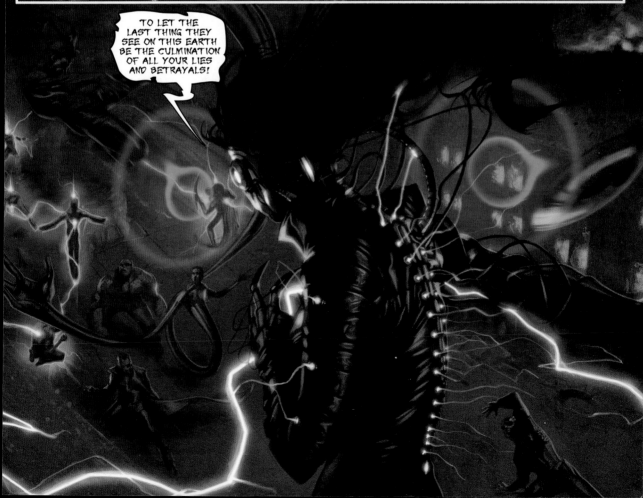

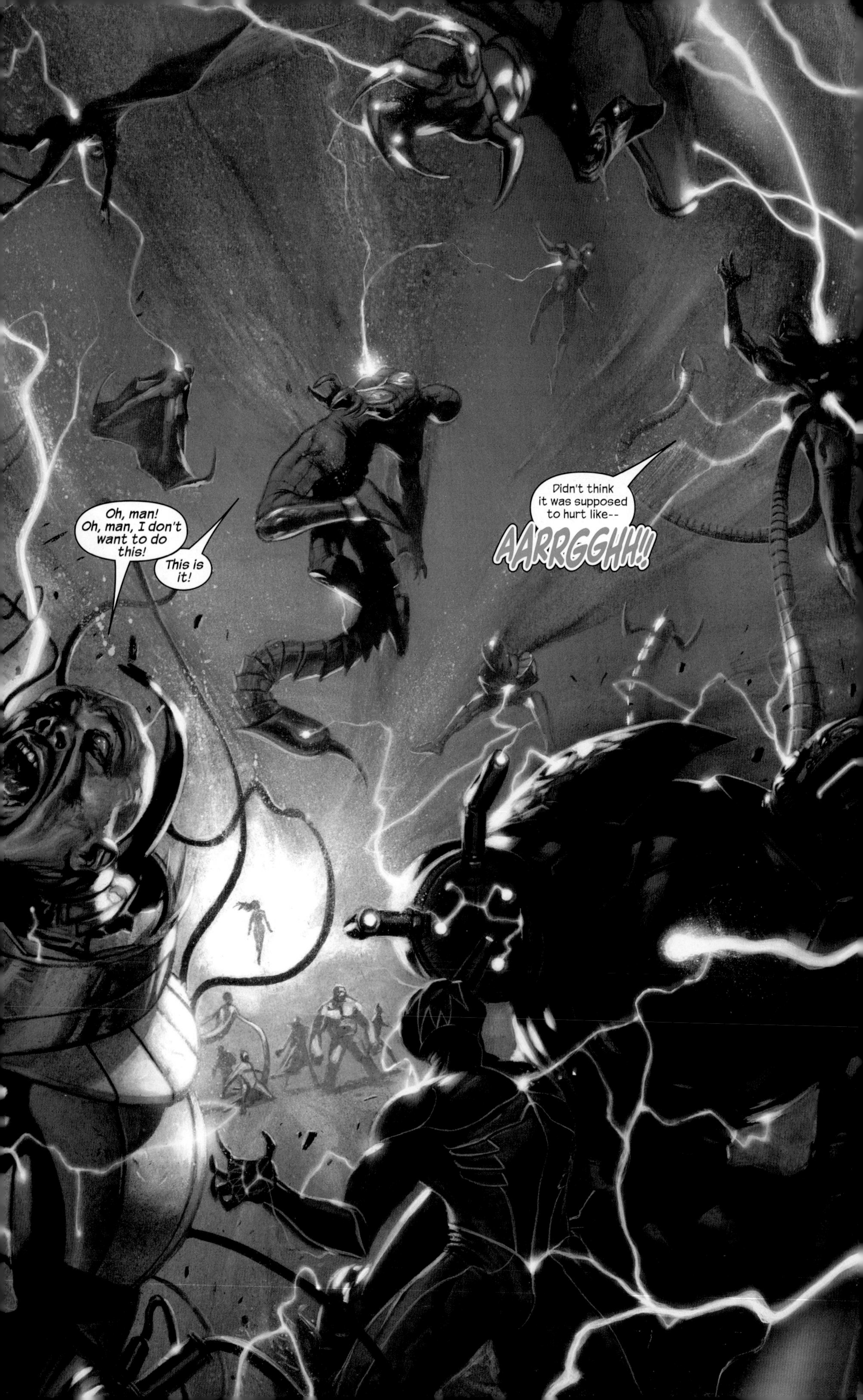
Oh, man!
Oh, man, I don't want to do this!
This is it!
Didn't think it was supposed to hurt like--
AARRGGHH!!

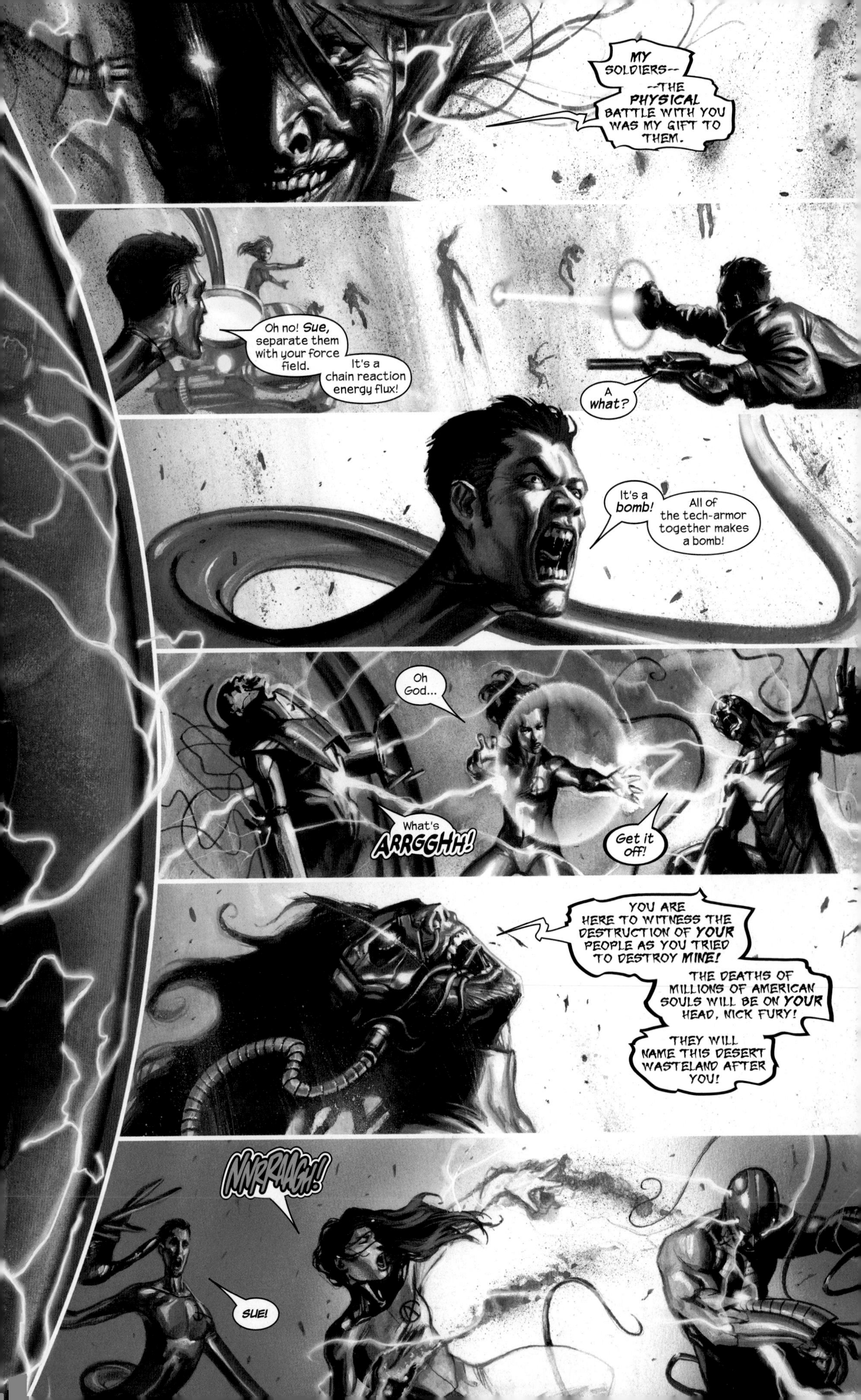

MY SOLDIERS--
--THE PHYSICAL BATTLE WITH YOU WAS MY GIFT TO THEM.
Oh no! Sue, separate them with your force field.
It's a chain reaction energy flux!
A what?
It's a bomb!
All of the tech-armor together makes a bomb!
Oh God...
What's
ARRGGHH!
Get it off!
YOU ARE HERE TO WITNESS THE DESTRUCTION OF YOUR PEOPLE AS YOU TRIED TO DESTROY MINE!
THE DEATHS OF MILLIONS OF AMERICAN SOULS WILL BE ON YOUR HEAD, NICK FURY!
THEY WILL NAME THIS DESERT WASTELAND AFTER YOU!
NNRRAAGH!
SUE!

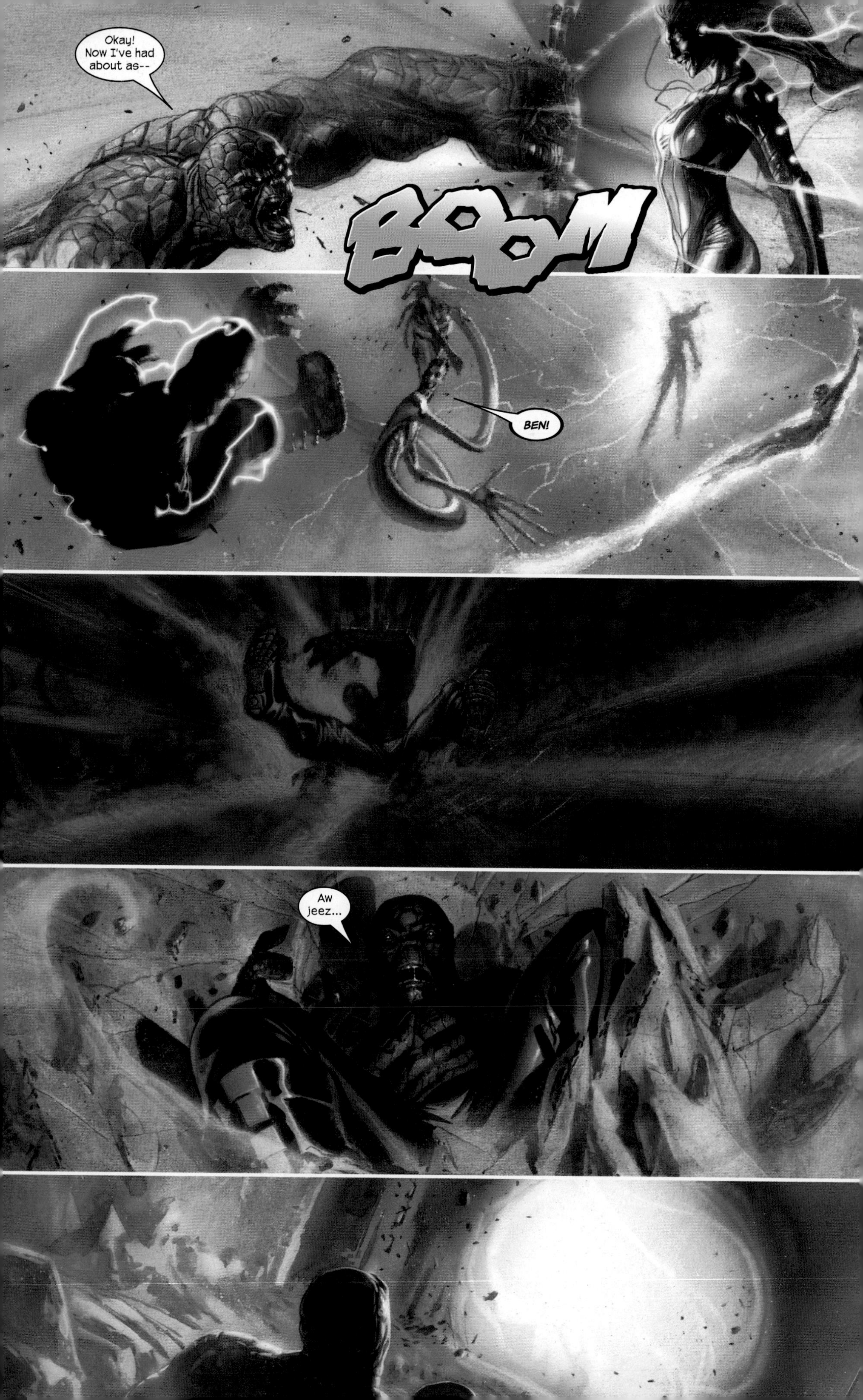
Okay! Now I've had about as--
BOOM
BEN!
Aw jeez...

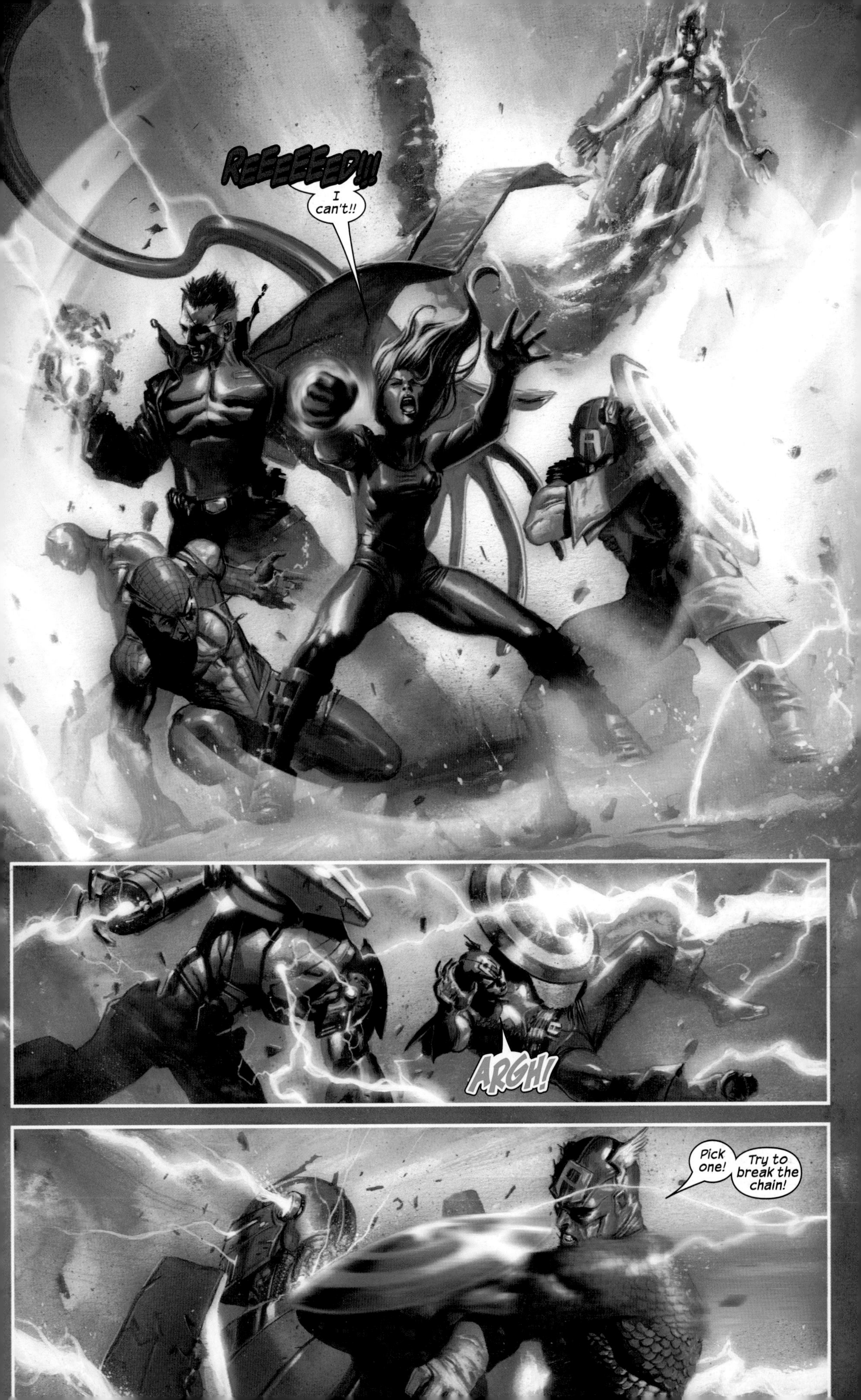
REEEEEEED!!!
I can't!!
ARGH!
Pick one!
Try to break the chain!

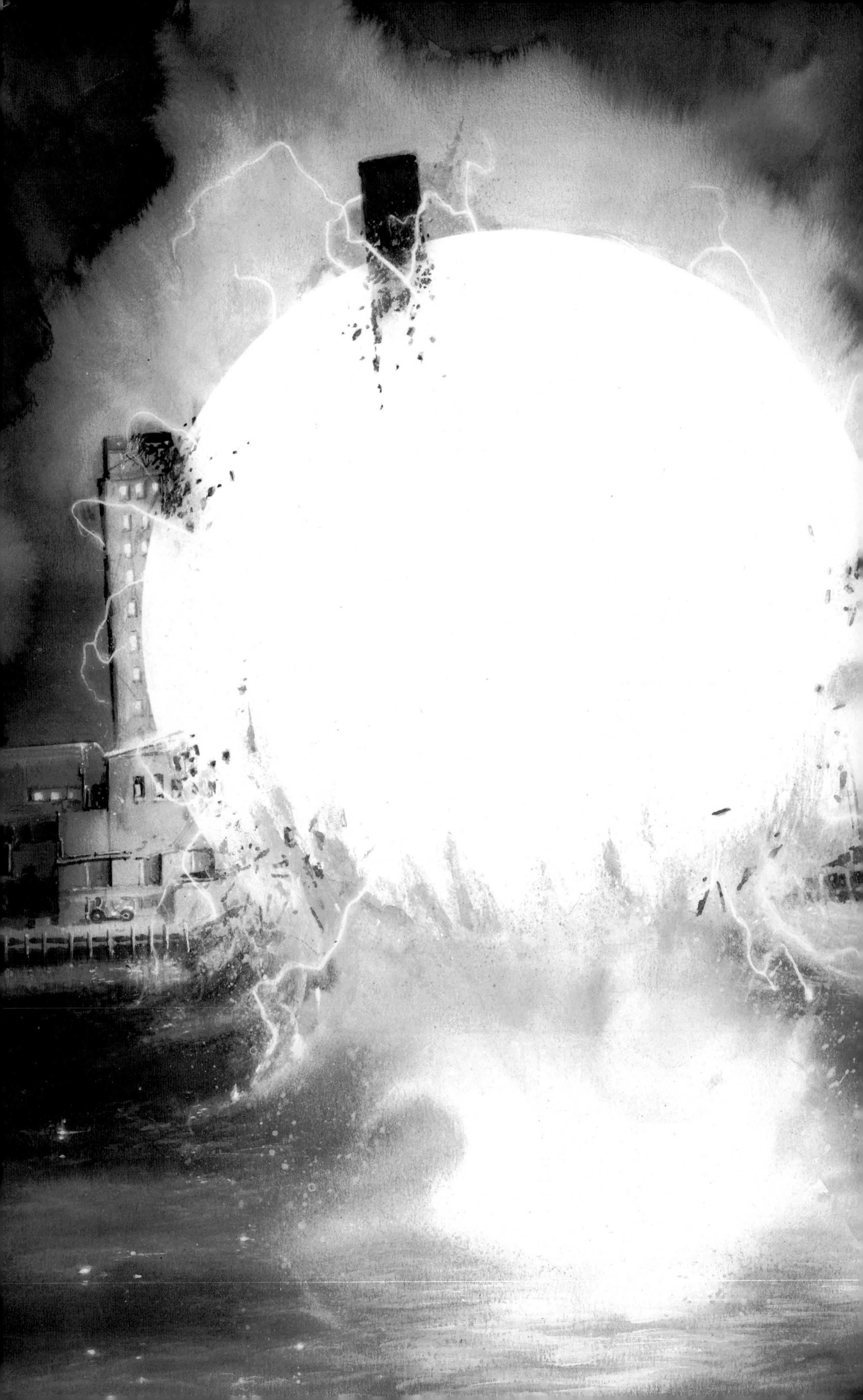

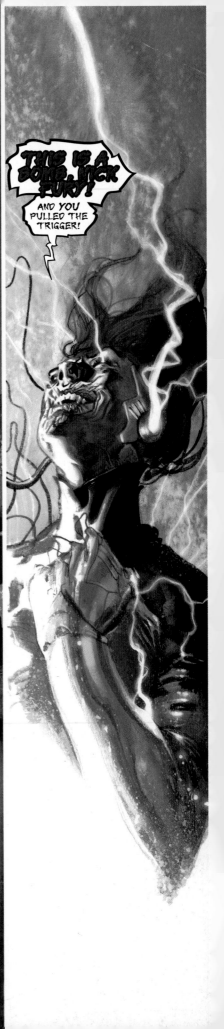

THIS IS A BOMB, JACK FURY!

AND YOU PULLED THE TRIGGER!

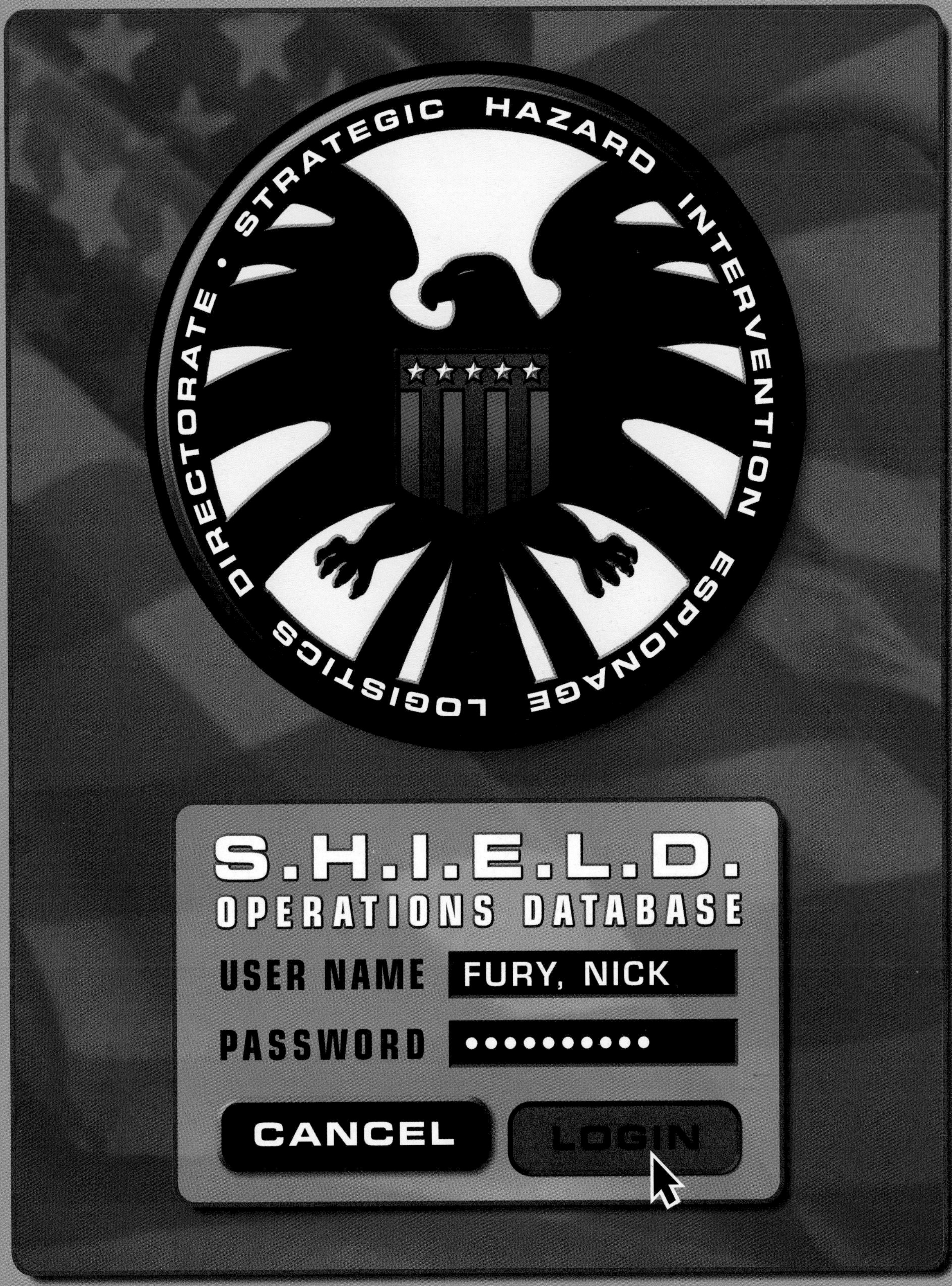
STRATEGIC HAZARD INTERVENTION ESPIONAGE LOGISTICS DIRECTORATE
S.H.I.E.L.D.
OPERATIONS DATABASE
USER NAME
FURY, NICK
PASSWORD
••••••••••
CANCEL
LOGIN

S.H.I.E.L.D.
OPERATIONS DATABASE

HOME | ADVANCED SEARCH | DATABASES | LOG OU

AGENT | CRIMINAL | PROJECT | OPERATIONS ARCHIV

CRIMINAL PROFILE

GARGAN, MACDONALD "MAC" aka SCORPION ▼

S.H.I.E.L.D. FILE NUMBER HMN-0000014773-001
CRIMINAL DATABASE >> CRIMINAL PROFILES >> BOOMERANG

REAL NAME: *Fred Myers*

ALIASES: *Boomerang, Fred Slade*

IDENTITY STATUS: *Secret*

MARITAL STATUS: *Single*

RELATIVES: *Unknown*

BASE OF OPERATIONS: *Mobile*

PLACE OF BIRTH: *Alice Springs, Northern Territory, Australia*

LEGAL STATUS: *Naturalized American citizen with a criminal record*

OCCUPATION: *Ex-criminal athlete, now full-time mercenary*

AFFILIATIONS: *Former employee of the Secret Empire, former ally of Viper, Boost, the Silver Samurai, Jester, and others of the Rangers*

HEIGHT: *5 ft. 11 in.* WEIGHT: *175 lbs.* EYES: *Blue* HAIR: *Brown*

POWERS/WEAPONS: *A great pitcher with amazing hand-eye coordination, Boomerang is a master of throwing bladed and non-bladed weapons. Various custom-designed boomerangs include shatterangs, gasarangs, razorangs, screamerangs...*

ENEMIES: *The Hulk, Iron Fist, Spider-Man, Hawkeye, Iron Man*

NICK FURY NOTE: *Armed and extremely deadly. Myers is a trained professional...*

MARKO, FLINT aka SANDMAN

MYERS, FRED aka BOOMERANG

NATCHIOS, ELEKTRA

OCTAVIUS, OTTO aka DOCTOR OCTOPUS

OSBORN, HARRY aka GREEN GOBLIN II

OSBORN, NORMAN aka GREEN GOBLIN

S.H.I.E.L.D. FILE NUMBER HMN-0000012517-001
CRIMINAL DATABASE >> CRIMINAL PROFILES >> CONSTRICTOR

REAL NAME: *Frank Schlichting*

ALIAS/ES: *Constrictor*

IDENTITY STATUS: *Secret*

MARITAL STATUS: *Divorced*

RELATIVES: *Unknown*

BASE OF OPERATIONS: *Mobile*

PLACE OF BIRTH: *Racine, Wisconsin*

LEGAL STATUS: *Citizen of the United States with a criminal record*

OCCUPATION: *Professional criminal and assassin*

AFFILIATIONS: *Former partner of Sabretooth, former employee of The Corporation, Justin Hammer, Stewart Montenegro, Viper II*

HEIGHT: *5 ft. 11 in.* **WEIGHT:** *190 lbs.* **EYES:** *Blue-gray* **HAIR:** *Black*

POWERS/WEAPONS: *Electrically insulated, partially bullet-proofed battlesuit with twin lengths of cybernetically controlled, electronically powered cables, which eject and retract from special appliances running from shoulder to wrist. Made of an Adamantium alloy, they extend to a maximum length of 30 feet. Suit is capable of generating a powerful electrical charge through the cables, with a maximum charge of 35,000 volts of high-frequency electricity for up to 3 minutes.*

ENEMIES: *The Hulk, Luke Cage, Captain America, Anaconda, Scourge*

NICK FURY NOTE: *Frank is a mercenary through and through. If you can pay the price, he'll do anything you want to anyone you want. He's a professional — that means he's smart, efficient and has a good business sense. Lucia has to have bank in order to get Frank to stick his neck out. That, or he one heck of a liar.*

S.H.I.E.L.D. FILE NUMBER HMN-0000019951-009
CRIMINAL DATABASE >> CRIMINAL PROFILES >> CRIMSON DYNAMO

REAL NAME: *UNKNOWN*

ALIAS/ES: *UNKNOWN*

IDENTITY STATUS: *SECRET*

MARITAL STATUS: *UNKNOWN*

RELATIVES: *UNKNOWN*

BASE OF OPERATIONS: *UNKNOWN*

PLACE OF BIRTH: *UNKNOWN*

LEGAL STATUS: *UNKNOWN*

OCCUPATION: *UNKNOWN, possible mercenary*

AFFILIATIONS: *Lucia Von Bardas (former president of Latveria); Phineas Mason a.k.a. The Tinkerer*

HEIGHT: *UNKNOWN*

POWERS/WEAPONS: *Specially designed suit of armor made of carborundum matrix alloy. Powered by various battery arrays throughout the suit. Jet boots enable flight of up to 110 miles per hour. With the suit, can lift approximately 1,200 lbs. Offensive hand blasters that carry a 1,000,000 volt frequency.*

ENEMIES: *UNKNOWN*

NICK FURY NOTES: *I hate that I don't know who's in the CD armor. I don't like unknown quantities and they seem to be increasing daily. I'll probably wind up leaking this to Stark and letting him take care of it.*

S.H.I.E.L.D. OPERATIONS DATABASE

S.H.I.E.L.D. FILE NUMBER HMN-0000027497-002

CRIMINAL DATABASE >> CRIMINAL PROFILES >> DIAMONDBACK

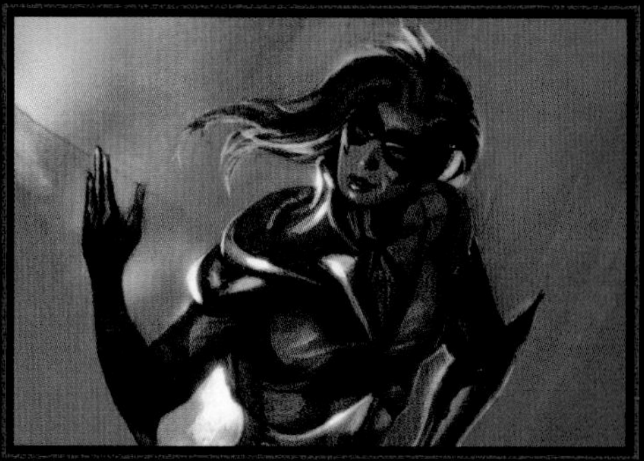

REAL NAME: *Debbie (surname unknown)*

ALIAS/ES: *Diamondback*

IDENTITY STATUS: *Secret*

MARITAL STATUS: *UNKNOWN*

RELATIVES: *UNKNOWN*

BASE OF OPERATIONS: *UNKNOWN*

PLACE OF BIRTH: *UNKNOWN*

LEGAL STATUS: *UNKNOWN*

OCCUPATION: *UNKNOWN, possible mercenary*

AFFILIATIONS: *Lucia Von Bardas (former president of Latveria), Phineas Mason a.k.a. The Tinkerer, Scorcher*

HEIGHT: *5 ft. 8 in.* **WEIGHT:** *135 lbs.* **EYES:** *blue* **HAIR:** *brown*

POWERS/WEAPONS: *Olympic-level athlete excelling in gymnastics. Accomplished hand-to-hand combatant. Expert knife thrower. Numerous 4-inch elongated diamond-shaped throwing spikes. Carries needle-sharp "diamonds," that are occasionally filled with various substances.*

ENEMIES: *UNKNOWN*

NICK FURY NOTE: *This new Diamondback is going to have a problem when the real deal finds out someone has taken her shtick. Rachel is going to flat out kick this girl's butt. Debbie here seems new to the game, but her actions and attitude suggest she's a first-timer and is extremely paranoid that she'll get caught—that's exactly why it'll be so easy. She'll overplan and doesn't seem to adapt well.*

S.H.I.E.L.D. FILE NUMBER HMN-0000014173-001

CRIMINAL DATABASE >> CRIMINAL PROFILES >> GOLDBUG

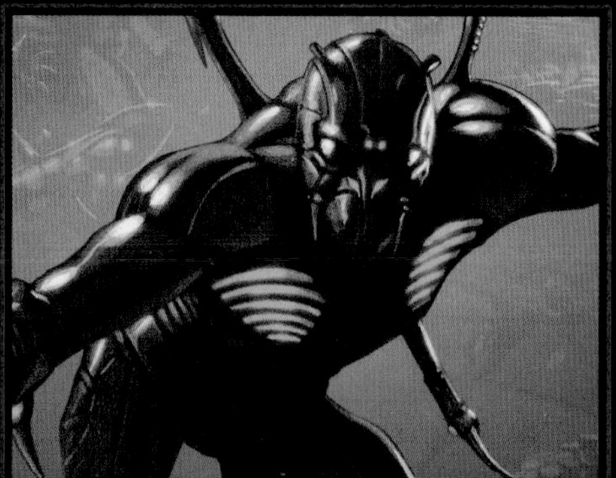

REAL NAME: *Unrevealed*

ALIAS/ES: *Jack Smith, Goldbug*

IDENTITY STATUS: *Known to the United States authorities*

MARITAL STATUS: *Presumed single*

RELATIVES: *None*

BASE OF OPERATIONS: *New York area*

PLACE OF BIRTH: *Unknown*

LEGAL STATUS: *Criminal record in the United States*

OCCUPATION: *Executive at Shank's Armored Couriers, New York City*

AFFILIATIONS: *Unknown*

HEIGHT: *5 ft. 9 in.* **WEIGHT:** *170 lbs.* **EYES:** *Blue* **HAIR:** *Blond, possibly now bald*

POWERS/WEAPONS: *Costume made of steel mesh coated with gold foil, contains electrically powered exoskeleton that amplifies Goldbug's strength, wafer-thin parachute sewn inside costume. "Gold gun" that shoots gold dust that hardens on contact. Lasers mounted on hovercraft and submarine, aqua regia solution used to dissolve metals.*

ENEMIES: *Luke Cage, Spider-Man, Namor the Sub-Mariner, Thunderbolt, the Maggia, Tyrannus*

NICK FURY NOTES: *Goldbug isn't hard to pin down. He does his thing as an extension of his business. Another techie with a high price. Note to self: track down Lucia's funds and take out her bank rollers; she can't be waging her war alone.*

S.H.I.E.L.D. FILE NUMBER HMN-0000002688-001

CRIMINAL DATABASE >> CRIMINAL PROFILES >> GRIM REAPER

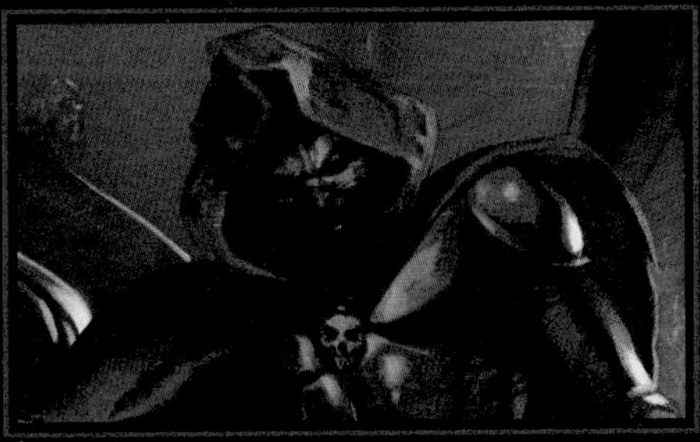

REAL NAME: *Eric Williams*

ALIAS/ES: *Grim Reaper*

IDENTITY STATUS: *Publicly Known*

MARITAL STATUS: *Single*

RELATIVES: *Sanford (father; deceased), Martha (mother; deceased), Simon (alias Wonder Man, brother), Vision (brother; deceased), Wanda (alias the Scarlet Witch, sister-in-law)*

BASE OF OPERATIONS: *Mobile*

PLACE OF BIRTH: *Paterson, New Jersey*

LEGAL STATUS: *Citizen of the United States with a criminal record*

OCCUPATION: *Professional criminal*

AFFILIATIONS: *Leader of the first Lethal Legion, former partner of the Space Phantom and leader (with him) of New York City fragment of HYDRA; ally of Ultron, Nekra, Black Talon II, Goliath, and Man-Ape; former member of the Maggia; former minion of Count Nefaria*

HEIGHT: *6 ft. 4 in.* **WEIGHT:** *225 lbs.* **EYES:** *Blue* **HAIR:** *Blond, later grey*

POWERS/WEAPONS: *Multi-purpose stainless steel scythe whose handle's basket fits over his right hand. The scythe, a four-foot, single edged blade mounted on a two-foot handle, has a power blaster mounted in the handle which releases a concussive ray of low-density plasma. The handle is equipped with a miniaturized cerebral-frequency generator that can induce a deep coma in any living being it comes in contact with and also revive them. The scythe also contains an array of batteries that power a motor that moves the blade like a miniature helicopter rotor.*

ENEMIES: *Wonder Man, Scarlet Witch, Avengers, Madame Masque*

NICK FURY NOTES: *Eric has me worried. We can't seem to keep him down, heck, he's even been dead before. He's passionate and smart. Frankly, I'm surprised to see he's involved in all this. Lucia probably promised Eric his brother's head in return for him joining up. I wish his brother (the AVENGER Wonder Man) was here, we could use his raw power, but I don't dare risk getting more heroes than necessary involved.*

S.H.I.E.L.D. FILE NUMBER HMN-0000019950-004

CRIMINAL DATABASE >> CRIMINAL PROFILES >> HOBGOBLIN

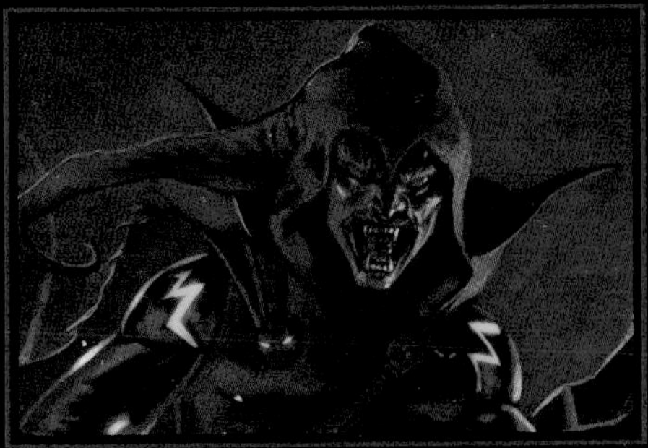

REAL NAME: *UNKNOWN*

ALIAS/ES: *UNKNOWN*

IDENTITY STATUS: *SECRET*

MARITAL STATUS: *UNKNOWN*

RELATIVES: *UNKNOWN*

BASE OF OPERATIONS: *UNKNOWN*

PLACE OF BIRTH: *UNKNOWN*

LEGAL STATUS: *UNKNOWN*

OCCUPATION: *UNKNOWN, possible mercenary*

AFFILIATIONS: *Lucia Von Bardas (former president of Latveria); Phineas Mason a.k.a. The Tinkerer*

HEIGHT: *UNKNOWN*

POWERS/WEAPONS: *Superhuman strength. Various concussion and incendiary grenades, smoke and gas emitting bombs, and a number of case-hardened razor-edged throwing blades. Weaponry is carried in a shoulder bag. His gloves are interwoven with micro circuit-powered conducting filaments capable of channeling pulsed discharges of 10,000 volts of high-frequency electrical power from rechargeable power packs in both his glove cuffs and costume tunic, which have the capacity to discharge for up to five minutes of sustained fire before depleting their power supply. He rides a one-man, miniature turbo-fan powered, vertical thrust "goblin-glider," capable of great maneuverability and speeds of up to 90 miles per hour.*

ENEMIES: *UNKNOWN*

NICK FURY NOTES: *A new Goblin, just what the world needs. I don't know who's behind the mask this time, but he'd better watch out. I won't have to raise a finger after what Parker's been through recently with the "real" Goblin. Parker won't let another Goblin hurt anyone ever again. I pity this guy, he just picked up the wrong duds.*

S.H.I.E.L.D.
OPERATIONS DATABASE

S.H.I.E.L.D. FILE NUMBER HMN-0000015884-001
CRIMINAL DATABASE >> CRIMINAL PROFILES >> KING COBRA

REAL NAME: *Klaus Voorhees*

ALIAS/ES: *King Cobra, Cobra*

IDENTITY STATUS: *Publicly known*

MARITAL STATUS: *Single*

RELATIVES: *Unknown*

BASE OF OPERATIONS: *Serpent Society Citadel*

PLACE OF BIRTH: *Rotterdam, Holland*

LEGAL STATUS: *Former citizen of Holland, now citizen of the United States with a criminal record*

OCCUPATION: *Former scientific research assistant, now professional criminal*

AFFILIATIONS: *Former partner of Mister Hyde, member of the original and second Serpent Squad, leader of the Serpent Society*

HEIGHT: *5 ft. 11 in.* **WEIGHT:** *180 lbs.* **EYES:** *Blue* **HAIR:** *Black*

POWERS/WEAPONS: *All the bones in his body are malleable and his muscles loose to an exceedingly resilient, making his body very flexible and pliant. He is extremely quick and has a great degree of independent control over his muscles. He has a very slippery costume and suction devices for his fingers and feet. His wrist shooters are capable of shooting missiles containing venom, smoke and nerve gas.*

ENEMIES: *Thor, Daredevil, Captain America, Spider-Man*

NICK FURY NOTES: *Klaus frightens me. He's no dummy, so his involvement here is particularly surprising. What's his angle? Is the Serpent Society rebuilding? Is it just money? Revenge? Another loose cannon in the mess. It's spiraling out of control.*

S.H.I.E.L.D. FILE NUMBER HMN-0000018265-002
CRIMINAL DATABASE >> CRIMINAL PROFILES >> LADY OCTOPUS

REAL NAME: *Dr. Carolyn Trainer*

ALIAS/ES: *Lady Octopus, Doctor Octopus*

IDENTITY STATUS: *Known*

MARITAL STATUS: *Unknown*

RELATIVES: *Seward Trainer (father)*

BASE OF OPERATIONS: *Unknown*

PLACE OF BIRTH: *Unknown*

LEGAL STATUS: *Citizen of the United States with a criminal record*

OCCUPATION: *Professional criminal*

AFFILIATIONS: *Ally of Doctor Octopus, Master Programmer, Stunner, Baron III, Delilah, The Hand, Employee of the Pro-Tooler, Overrode Area*

HEIGHT: *5 ft. 2 in.* **WEIGHT:** *100 lbs.* **EYES:** *Brown* **HAIR:** *Unknown*

POWERS/WEAPONS: *Can download information from the global net directly into her brain via computer chips implanted there. Four mentally controlled, electrically powered, telescoping, titanium steel tentacles attached to a stainless steel harness, which she wears on her body. Each tentacle has three single-jointed pinchers, and is able to move at 90 feet per second. Her harness gives her superhuman strength, and she wears body armor for extra protection. Ability to create an impenetrable personal force field for defensive purposes. Shoots explosive force from her tentacles.*

ENEMIES: *Spider-Man*

NICK FURY NOTES: *I've always mistrusted this with no regard, but Dr. Trainer is smart. Her eyes are often bigger than her stomach, so I can see how she can be twisted and used by a powerful personality. Too Spider-centric for my taste, too.*

S.H.I.E.L.D. FILE NUMBER HMN-0000014398-001

CRIMINAL DATABASE >> CRIMINAL PROFILES >> MENTALLO

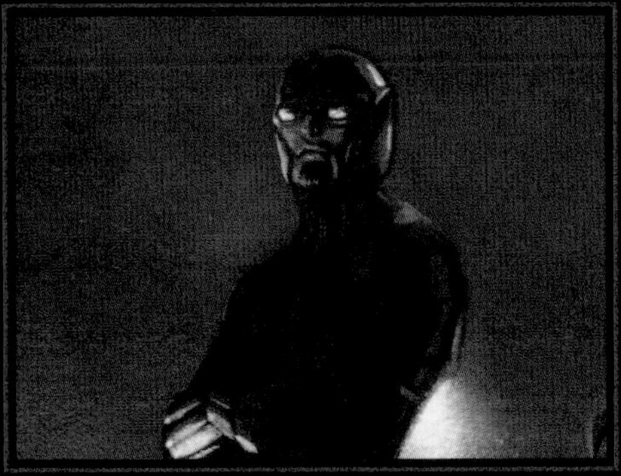

REAL NAME: *Marvin Flumm*

ALIAS/ES: *Mentallo*

IDENTITY STATUS: *Known to the authorities*

MARITAL STATUS: *Single*

RELATIVES: *Unknown*

BASE OF OPERATIONS: *Mobile*

PLACE OF BIRTH: *Watford City, North Dakota*

LEGAL STATUS: *Citizen of the United States with a criminal record*

OCCUPATION: *Professional Criminal*

AFFILIATIONS: *Former S.H.I.E.L.D. agent, former HYDRA division leader, frequent ally of the Fixer (now known as Techno)*

HEIGHT: *5 ft. 10 in.* **WEIGHT:** *175 lbs.* **EYES:** *Brown* **HAIR:** *Brown*

POWERS/WEAPONS: *Limited telepathic powers, which can be amplified through scientific means. Can "read" the thoughts of any human mind within an approximate radius of 5 miles. Capable of scanning an area to locate a particular brain pattern. Can project his thoughts. Capable of contacting as many as three minds at a time. Can project visual images.*

ENEMIES: *Nick Fury, S.H.I.E.L.D., Professor X, Super-Adaptoid, Thing, Fantastic Four, Deathlok I, Micronauts, US Agent, Iron Man, Avengers, Hulk*

NICK FURY NOTES: *Flumm's background makes him an ideal choice for Lucia's mission. He hates the spy community, and nothing represents spies like me. I'll remember to give him a personal visit as soon as I get out of this mess.*

S.H.I.E.L.D. FILE NUMBER HMN-0000016894-004

CRIMINAL DATABASE >> CRIMINAL PROFILES >> MISTER FEAR

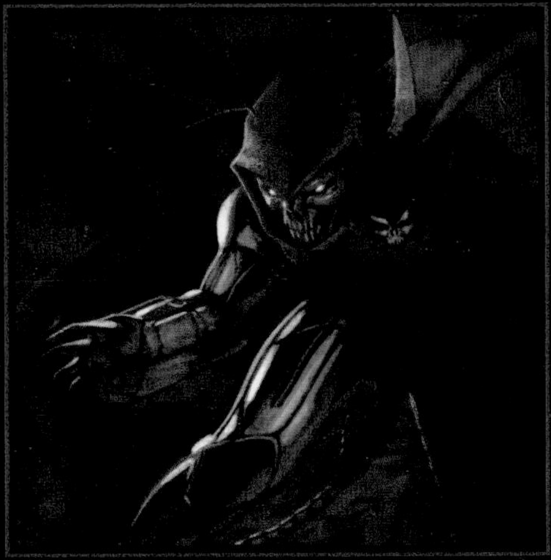

REAL NAME: *Alan Fagan*

ALIAS/ES: *Mister Fear*

IDENTITY STATUS: *Known to the police*

MARITAL STATUS: *Single*

RELATIVES: *Larry Cranston (uncle, deceased)*

BASE OF OPERATIONS: *New York City*

PLACE OF BIRTH: *Madison, Wisconsin*

LEGAL STATUS: *American citizen with criminal record*

OCCUPATION: *Businessman*

AFFILIATIONS: *None*

HEIGHT: *5 ft. 11 in.* **WEIGHT:** *165 lbs.* **EYES:** *Hazel* **HAIR:** *Silver*

POWERS/WEAPONS: *Uses a compound based on light scent pheromones, tailored for human beings, which causes severe anxiety, fear and panic in victims, rendering them incapable of fighting or resisting his will. He employs the gas in the form of gas pellets shot from a gun. The gas works for about 15 minutes on a normal adult male, and 5 on an exceptionally fit adult male.*

ENEMIES: *Daredevil, Spider-Man, Hawkeye, Betty Brant Leeds*

NICK FURY NOTES: *Oddly, a guy named Mr. Fear is the least of my worries during this Secret War. He's nasty and deadly, but ultimately any one of my team can take him down.*

S.H.I.E.L.D.
OPERATIONS DATABASE

S.H.I.E.L.D. FILE NUMBER HMN-0000008422-001
CRIMINAL DATABASE >> CRIMINAL PROFILES >> SCORPION

REAL NAME: *MacDonald "Mac" Gargan*
ALIAS/ES: *Scorpion*
IDENTITY STATUS: *Secret*
MARITAL STATUS: *Unknown*
RELATIVES: *Unknown*
BASE OF OPERATIONS: *Unknown*
PLACE OF BIRTH: *Unknown*
LEGAL STATUS: *Citizen of the United States with a criminal record*
OCCUPATION: *Professional criminal*
AFFILIATIONS: *Former member of The Masters of Evil, Ally of Mr. Hyde, Justin Hammer, Chameleon, Terrible Tinkerer*

HEIGHT: *5 ft. 11 in.* **WEIGHT:** *175 lbs.* **EYES:** *Green* **HAIR:** *Unknown*

POWERS/WEAPONS: *Superhuman strength, speed, agility and stamina. Battlesuit constructed of two layers of steel mesh with one layer of insulated rubber within. 7 foot long tail, cybernetically controlled, can whip with speeds up to 90 feet per second and can spring distances up to 30 feet. The tip has a spike that can ram, and or fire force blasts.*

ENEMIES: *Spider-Man, Captain America, Avengers, Iron Man*

NICK FURY NOTES: *However, pure and simple, that's what I use to get Mac wrapped up in the mess. He's made mistake after mistake since he was, 18, allying with Hydra could be his last.*

S.H.I.E.L.D. FILE NUMBER HMN-0000010978-001
CRIMINAL DATABASE >> CRIMINAL PROFILES >> SCORCHER

REAL NAME: *Hubik, first name unknown*
ALIAS/ES: *Scorcher*
IDENTITY STATUS: *Secret*
MARITAL STATUS: *Unknown*
RELATIVES: *Unknown*
BASE OF OPERATIONS: *Unknown*
PLACE OF BIRTH: *Unknown*
LEGAL STATUS: *Citizen of the United States with a criminal record*
OCCUPATION: *Professional criminal*
AFFILIATIONS: *Employee of Norman Osborn, leader of an unnamed Strikersquad, Member of The Masters of Evil*

HEIGHT: *5 ft. 11 in.* **WEIGHT:** *210 lbs.* **EYES:** *Brown* **HAIR:** *Unknown*

POWERS/WEAPONS: *Can direct enormous fire-powered force blasts. Intense heat generation from powered armored suit. Flame/Tables connected to the suit's personal helmet, jet pod.*

ENEMIES: *Spider-Man, Thunderbolts*

NICK FURY NOTES: *Hubik is scared, dumb, and angry. He's not the real threat here, but he's being played hard. I'm hoping he's the one guy I can pull out at the end help reverse. I could be wrong there with his revenge.*

S.H.I.E.L.D. FILE NUMBER HMN-0000009971-001

CRIMINAL DATABASE >> CRIMINAL PROFILES >> SHOCKER

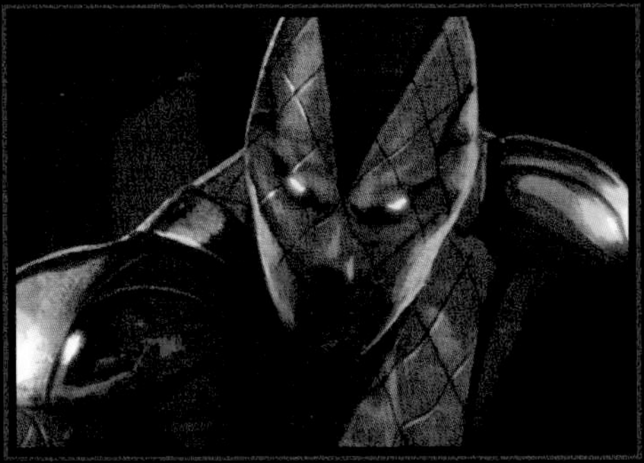

REAL NAME: *Herman Schultz*

ALIAS/ES: *Shocker*

IDENTITY STATUS: *Publicly Known*

MARITAL STATUS: *Unknown*

RELATIVES: *Unknown*

BASE OF OPERATIONS: *Unknown*

PLACE OF BIRTH: *Unknown*

LEGAL STATUS: *Citizen of the United States with a criminal record*

OCCUPATION: *Professional criminal*

AFFILIATIONS: *Former member of the Masters of Evil III, Sinister Seven, former ally of The Chameleon, Hammerhead, and The Trapster*

HEIGHT: *5 ft. 8 in.* **WEIGHT:** *175 lbs.* **EYES:** *Green* **HAIR:** *Unknown*

POWERS/WEAPONS: *Dual Vibro-Shock units that create high pressure air blasts that are very powerful and very destructive. Vibrational shield that deflects blows. Uniform of foam-lined fabric to absorb the impact caused by his Vibro-Shock units.*

ENEMIES: *Spider-Man, the Avengers, Electro*

NICK FURY NOTES: *Schultz has a rocky history, he's been a bit player and one of the big dogs. But his bark is worse than his bite. There's something inside him that genuinely doesn't want to hurt people. He's always held back. I'd hate to think what he could do if he ever let loose.*

S.H.I.E.L.D. FILE NUMBER AI-0000019952-020

CRIMINAL DATABASE >> CRIMINAL PROFILES >> SPIDER-SLAYER

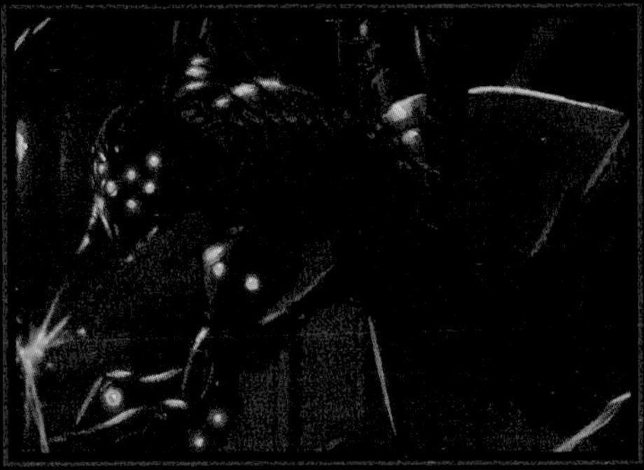

REAL NAME: *N/A*

ALIAS/ES: *N/A*

IDENTITY STATUS: *N/A*

MARITAL STATUS: *N/A*

RELATIVES: *N/A*

BASE OF OPERATIONS: *UNKNOWN*

PLACE OF BIRTH: *UNKNOWN*

LEGAL STATUS: *N/A*

OCCUPATION: *UNKNOWN*

AFFILIATIONS: *UNKNOWN*

HEIGHT: *UNKNOWN*

POWERS/WEAPONS: *Made of extremely durable metals. Weapons on past versions have included: nullifier for Spider-Man's spider-sense, ethylchloride spray, grappling and cutting devices, laser beams, whiplike arms. This newest version most likely contains other new and unknown weapons also.*

ENEMIES: *UNKNOWN*

NICK FURY NOTES: *Another unknown. The last, 19th version, of the Spider-Slayer was trouble enough. I have no idea what drives this version, but ultimately, it doesn't matter—we'll take him down.*

S.H.I.E.L.D.
OPERATIONS DATABASE

S.H.I.E.L.D. FILE NUMBER HMN-0000012689-001

CRIMINAL DATABASE — CRIMINAL PROFILES — TRAPSTER

REAL NAME

ALIASES

IDENTITY STATUS

MARITAL STATUS

RELATIVES

BASE OF OPERATIONS

PLACE OF BIRTH

LEGAL STATUS

OCCUPATION

AFFILIATIONS

HEIGHT   WEIGHT   EYES   HAIR

POWERS/WEAPONS

FRIENDS

MISC FILE NOTES

S.H.I.E.L.D. FILE NUMBER HMN-0000001422-001

CRIMINAL DATABASE — CRIMINAL PROFILES — WIZARD

REAL NAME

ALIASES

IDENTITY STATUS

MARITAL STATUS

RELATIVES

BASE OF OPERATIONS

PLACE OF BIRTH

LEGAL STATUS

OCCUPATION

AFFILIATIONS

HEIGHT   WEIGHT   EYES   HAIR

POWERS/WEAPONS

FRIENDS

MISC FILE NOTES

SECRET WAR

BOOK FIVE OF FIVE

ASTIC_   NICK FURY_   THING_   LUCIA VON BARDAS_   CY

S.H.I.E.L.D.
OPERATIONS DATABASE

HOME | ADVANCED SEARCH | DATABASES | LOG OUT

S.H.I.E.L.D. FILE NUMBER 4545567-01NFRY

PROJECT DATABASE >> PROJECT: 9083728-1245 SWR >> PROJECT OPERATIVE 1

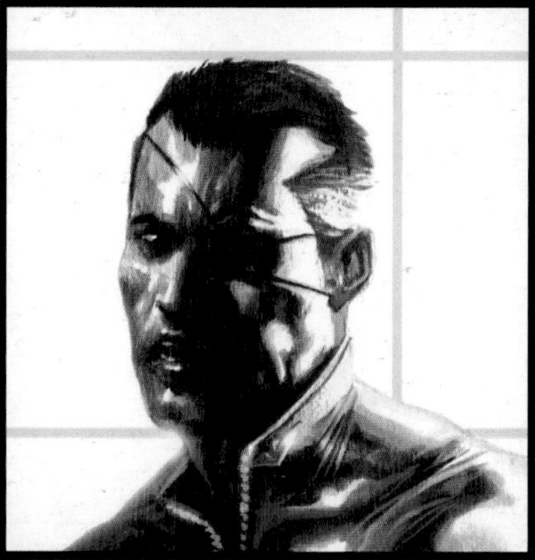

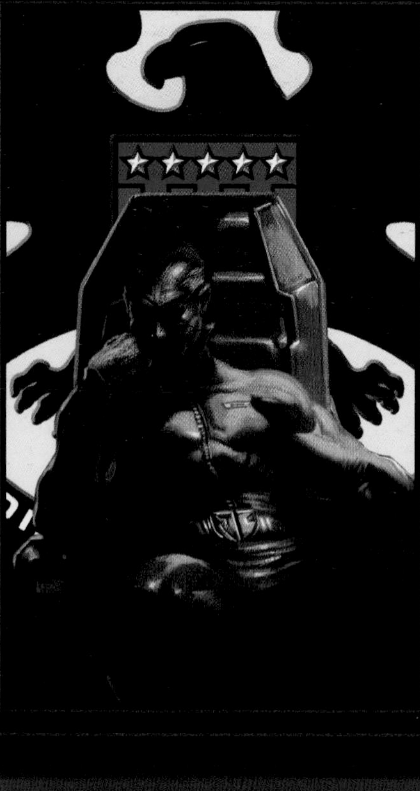

REAL NAME: *Nicholas Joseph Fury*

OCCUPATION: *Agent of S.H.I.E.L.D. (Stategic Hazard Intervention Espionage Logistics Directorate)*

IDENTITY: *Publicly known*

LEGAL STATUS: *Citizen of the United States with no criminal record.*

OTHER ALIASES: *None*

PLACE OF BIRTH: *New York City, New York*

KNOWN RELATIVES: *Jack Fury (Father, Deceased), Jacob Fury (Brother, Deceased), Dawn Fury (Sister), Jacob Fury II (Son, Deceased).*

GROUP AFFILIATION: *S.H.I.E.L.D.; Formerly the U.S. Army and the Central Intelligence Agency*

S.H.I.E.L.D. AGENT CLEARANCE LEVEL: *10*

BASE OF OPERATIONS: *S.H.I.E.L.D. Headquarters; apartment in Manhattan*

HEIGHT: *6'1"* **WEIGHT:** *225 lbs.*

EYES: *Brown* **HAIR:** *Brown, with graying temples*

ABILITIES: *Trained paratrooper, Ranger, demolitions expert and vehicle specialist. He holds an unlimited tonnage, all-seas license as a commander of ocean-going vessels. Fury has completed Green and Black Beret Special Forces training, is an agent of the O.S.S. (Office of Special Services) and a liaison of the M5 (British Secret Intelligence). He is a seasoned unarmed and armed-combat expert. A heavyweight boxer in the Army, holds a black belt in Tae Kwon Do and a brown belt in Jiu Jitsu.*

NOTE: *Ingests the Infinity Formula annually, slowing the process of aging in his body.*

SEARCH DATABASE SECRET WAR **SEARCH**

S.H.I.E.L.D. FILE NUMBER 4545567-22DJNSN

PROJECT DATABASE >> PROJECT: 9083728-1245 SWR >> PROJECT OPERATIVE 2

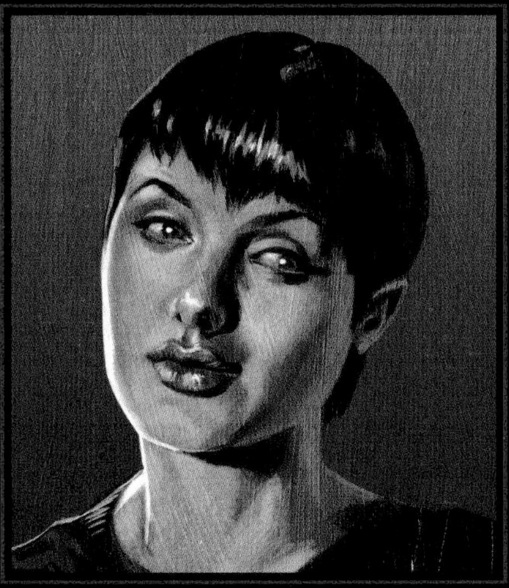

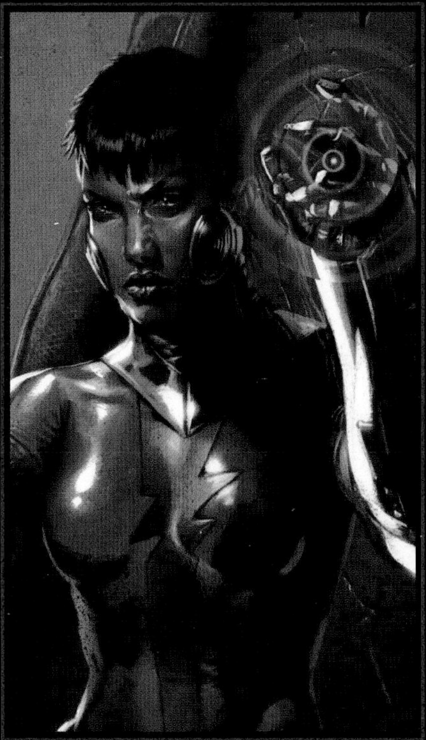

REAL NAME: *Daisy Louise Johnson*

OCCUPATION: *Special Field Officer of S.H.I.E.L.D.*

IDENTITY: *Secret*

LEGAL STATUS: *Citizen of the United States with no criminal record*

OTHER ALIASES: *None*

PLACE OF BIRTH: *Portland, Oregon*

KNOWN RELATIVES: *Calvin Zabo, father, a.k.a. Mr. Hyde*

GROUP AFFILIATION: *S.H.I.E.L.D.*

S.H.I.E.L.D. AGENT CLEARANCE LEVEL: *10*

BASE OF OPERATIONS: *S.H.I.E.L.D. Headquarters, New York City, New York*

HISTORY: *Daisy Johnson is the illegitimate daughter of Calvin Zabo.*

See S.H.I.E.L.D. File MTNT0000000034524297-001
See S.H.I.E.L.D. Caterpillar file 45345-234252

HEIGHT: *5'4"* **WEIGHT:** *115 lbs.* **EYES:** *Blue* **HAIR:** *Black*

STRENGTH LEVEL: *Possesses the normal human strength of a woman her age, height, and build who engages in intensive regular exercise.*

KNOWN SUPERHUMAN POWERS: *Daisy generates powerful waves of vibrations which can produce effects resembling those of earthquakes. She is immune to any harmful effects of the vibrations.*

ABILITIES: *A superb hand-to-hand combatant, skilled all-around athlete, and excellent marksman. She was a leading espionage agent, adept at undercover assignments.*

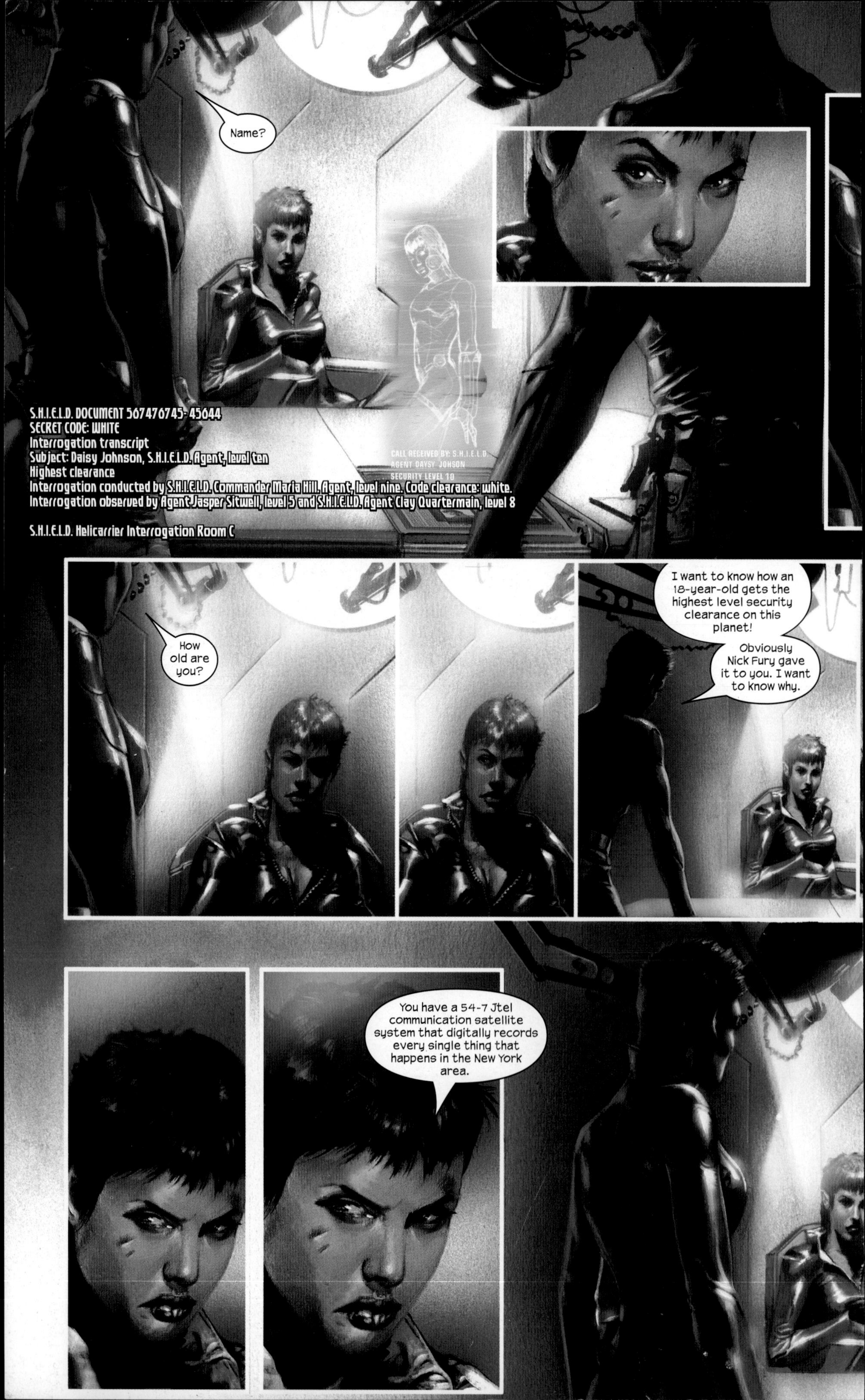
Name?
S.H.I.E.L.D. DOCUMENT 567476745- 45644
SECRET CODE: WHITE
Interrogation transcript
Subject: Daisy Johnson, S.H.I.E.L.D. Agent, level ten
Highest clearance
Interrogation conducted by S.H.I.E.L.D. Commander Maria Hill. Agent, level nine. Code clearance: white.
Interrogation observed by Agent Jasper Sitwell, level 5 and S.H.I.E.L.D. Agent Clay Quartermain, level 8
S.H.I.E.L.D. Helicarrier Interrogation Room C
CALL RECEIVED BY: S.H.I.E.L.D. AGENT DAYSY JOHSON SECURITY LEVEL 10
How old are you?
I want to know how an 18-year-old gets the highest level security clearance on this planet!
Obviously Nick Fury gave it to you. I want to know why.
You have a 54-7 Jtel communication satellite system that digitally records every single thing that happens in the New York area.

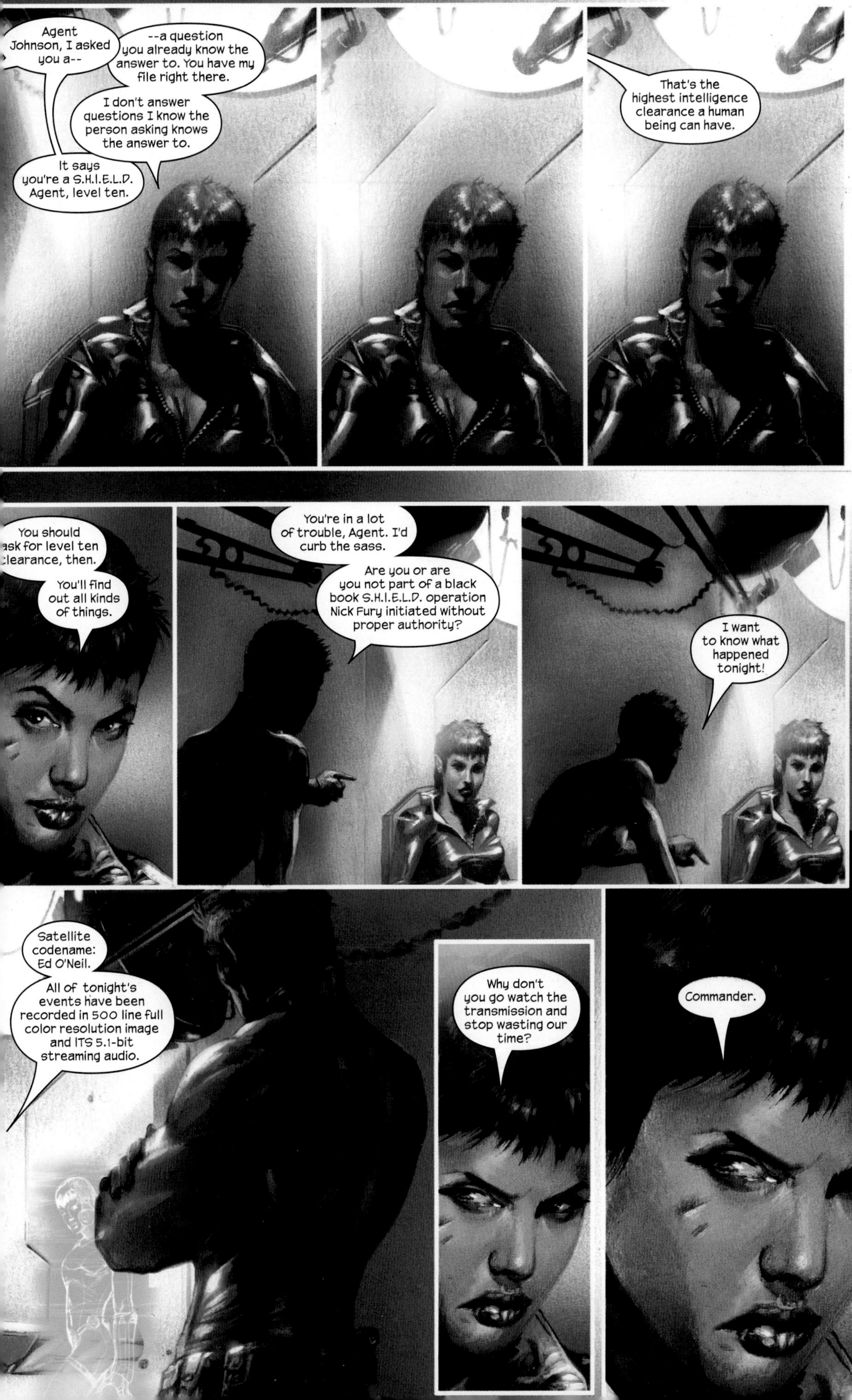
Agent Johnson, I asked you a--
--a question you already know the answer to. You have my file right there.
I don't answer questions I know the person asking knows the answer to.
It says you're a S.H.I.E.L.D. Agent, level ten.
That's the highest intelligence clearance a human being can have.
You should ask for level ten clearance, then.
You'll find out all kinds of things.
You're in a lot of trouble, Agent. I'd curb the sass.
Are you or are you not part of a black book S.H.I.E.L.D. operation Nick Fury initiated without proper authority?
I want to know what happened tonight!
Satellite codename: Ed O'Neil.
All of tonight's events have been recorded in 500 line full color resolution image and ITS 5.1-bit streaming audio.
Why don't you go watch the transmission and stop wasting our time?
Commander.

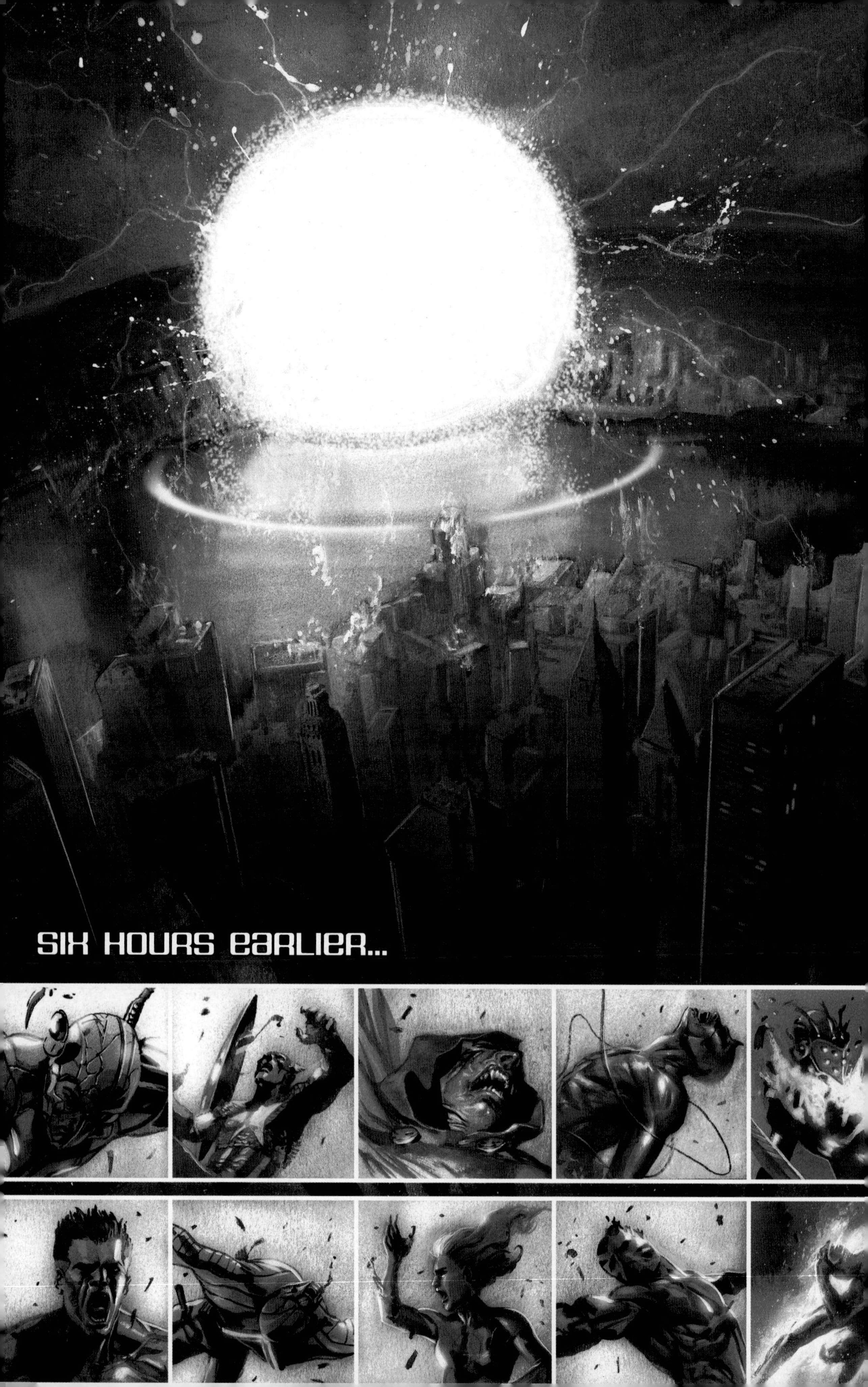
SIX HOURS EARLIER...

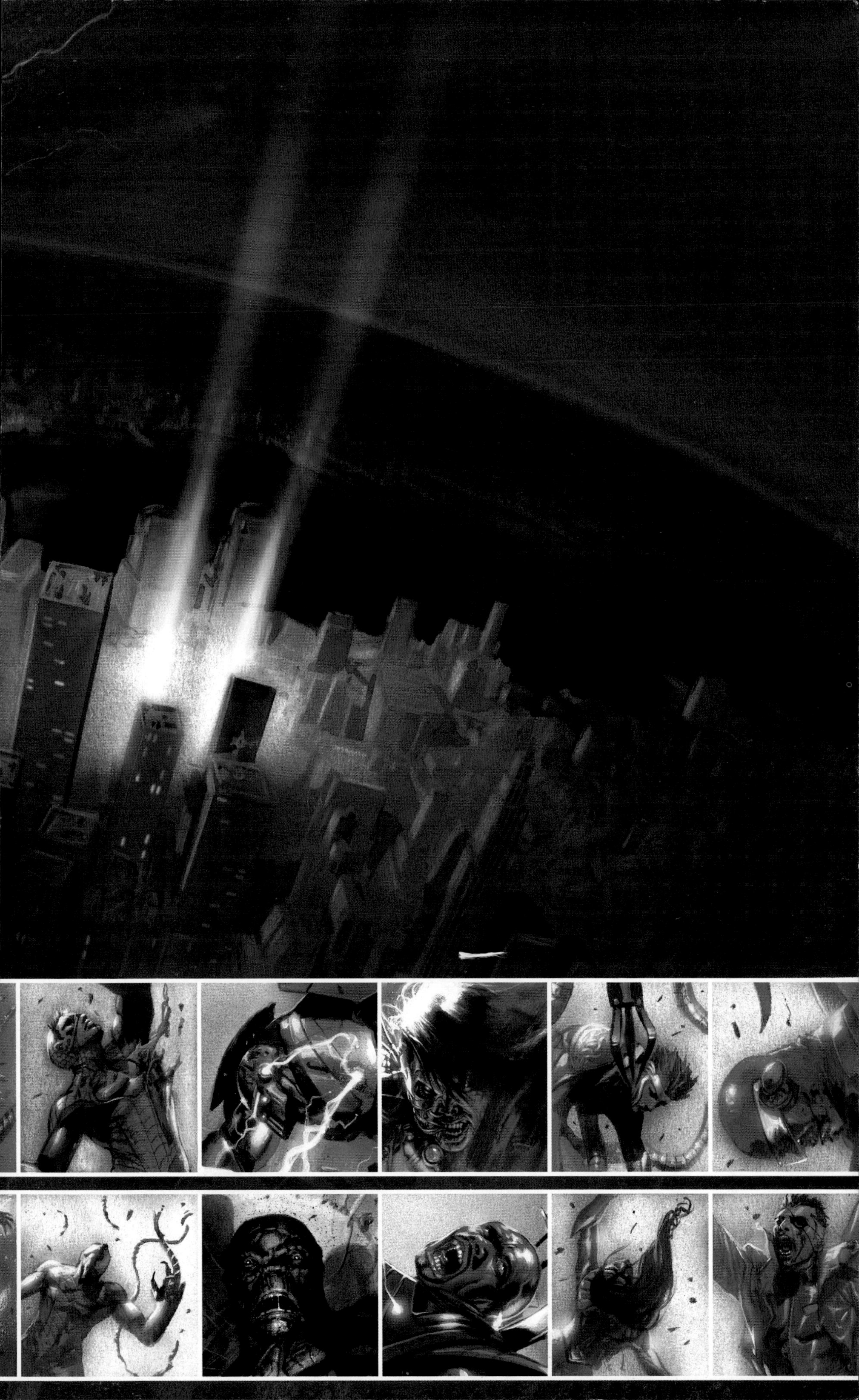

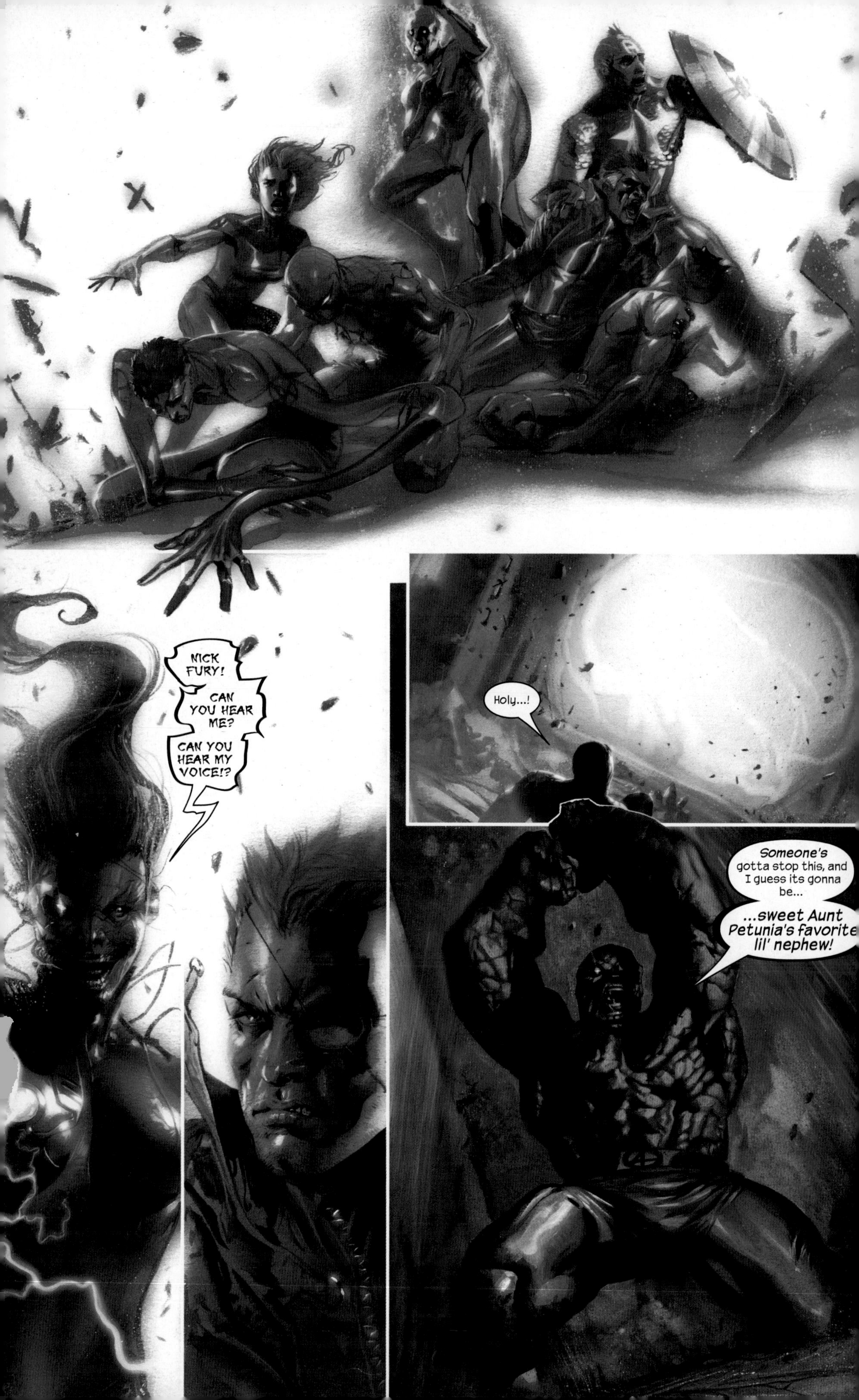
NICK FURY!
CAN YOU HEAR ME?
CAN YOU HEAR MY VOICE!?
Holy...!
Someone's gotta stop this, and I guess its gonna be...
...sweet Aunt Petunia's favorite lil' nephew!

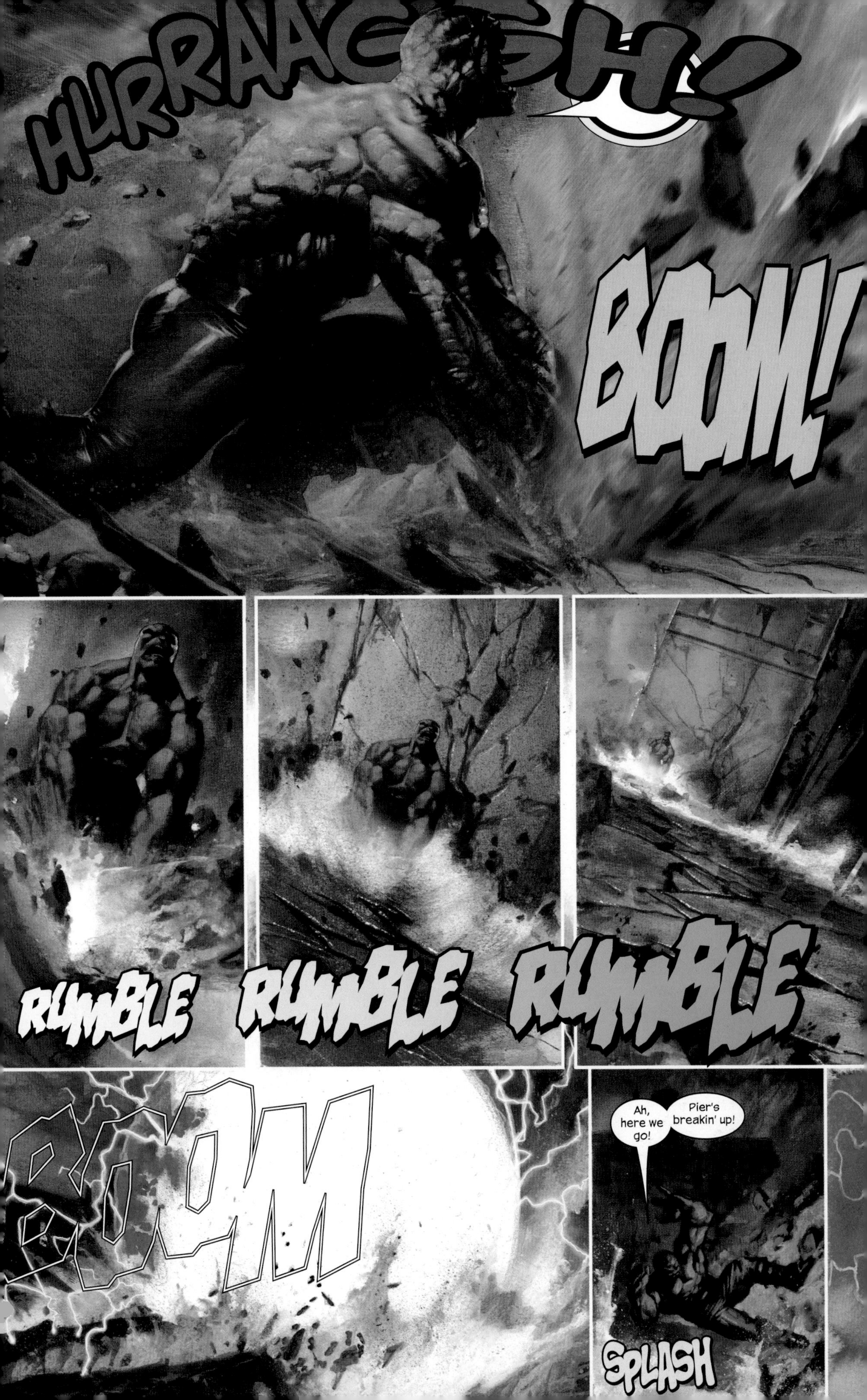
HURRAAGGGH!
BOOM!
RUMBLE
RUMBLE
RUMBLE
BOOOM
Ah, here we go!
Pier's breakin' up!
SPLASH

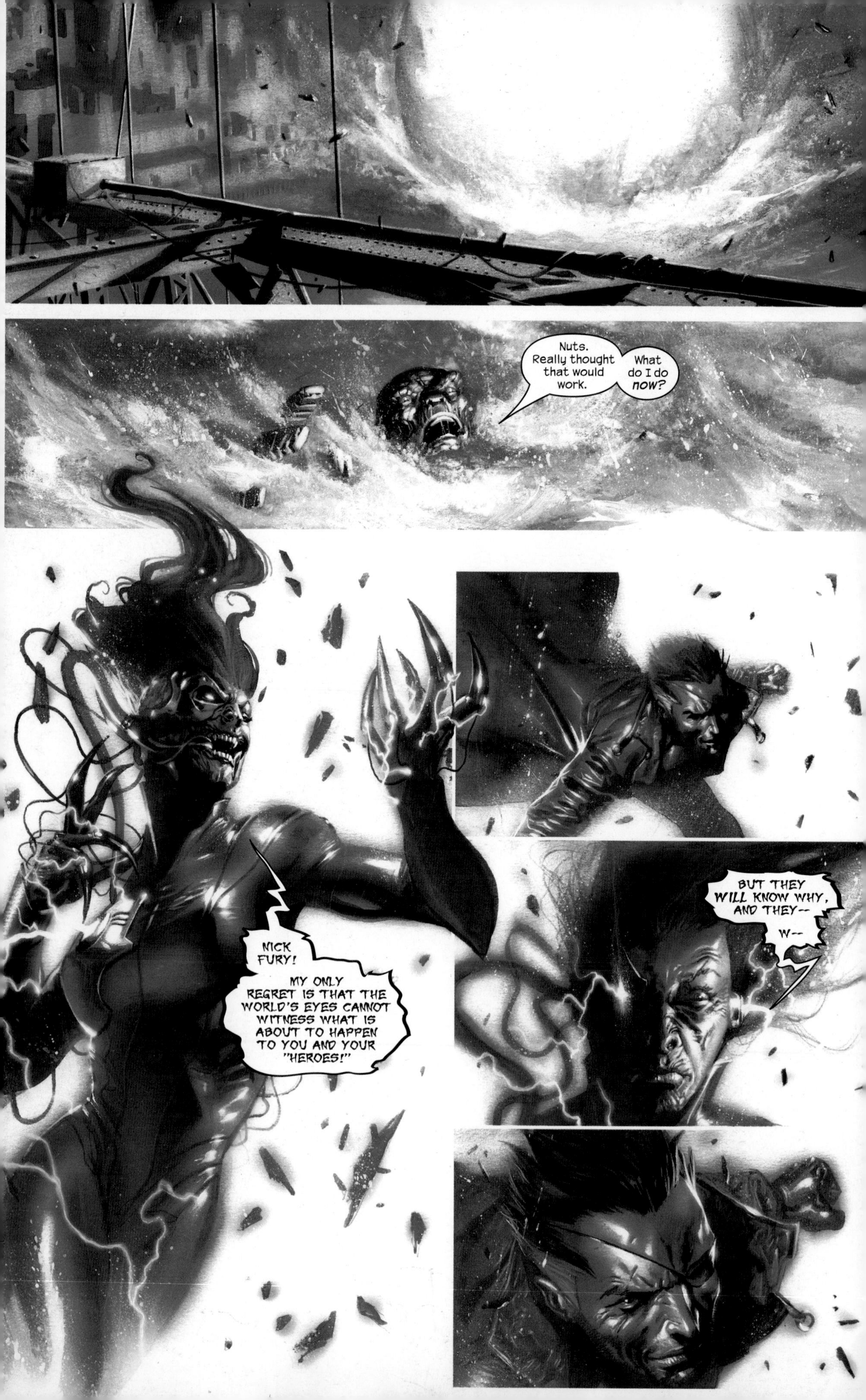
Nuts. Really thought that would work.
What do I do now?
NICK FURY!
MY ONLY REGRET IS THAT THE WORLD'S EYES CANNOT WITNESS WHAT IS ABOUT TO HAPPEN TO YOU AND YOUR "HEROES!"
BUT THEY WILL KNOW WHY, AND THEY--
W--

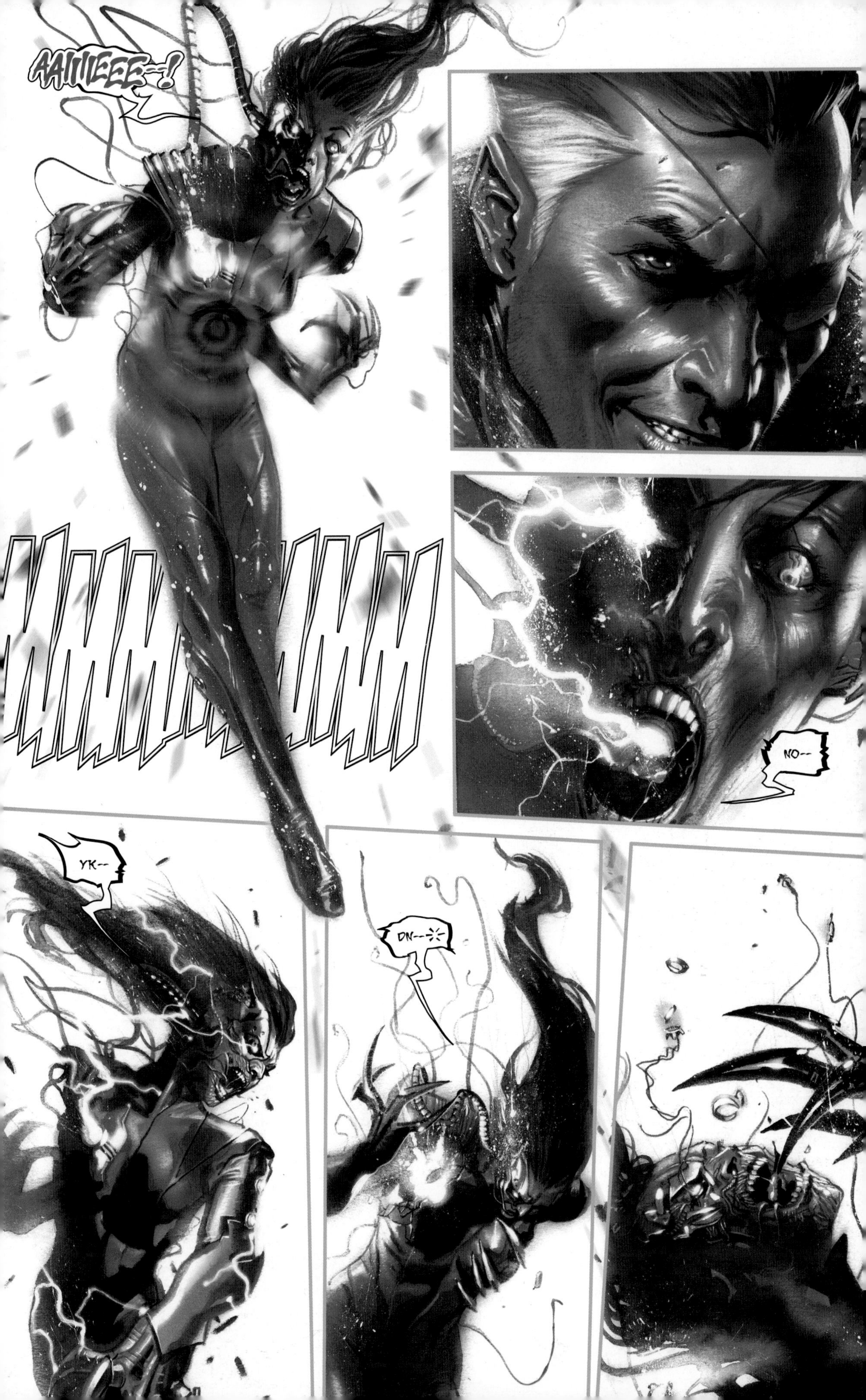
AAIIIIEEE--!
HMMMMMMMMMMM
NO--
YK--
DN--

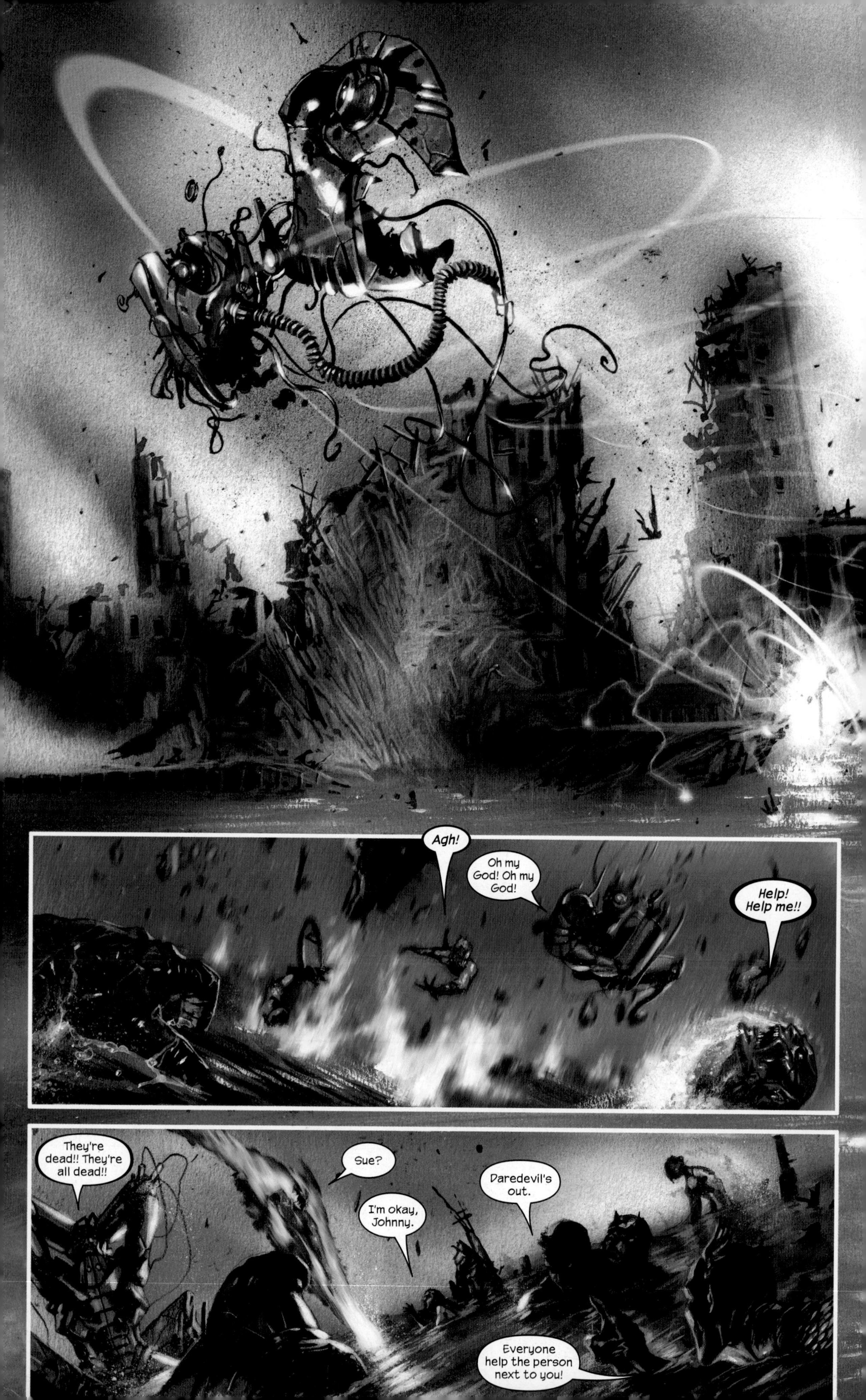
Agh!
Oh my God! Oh my God!
Help! Help me!!
They're dead!! They're all dead!!
Sue?
I'm okay, Johnny.
Daredevil's out.
Everyone help the person next to you!

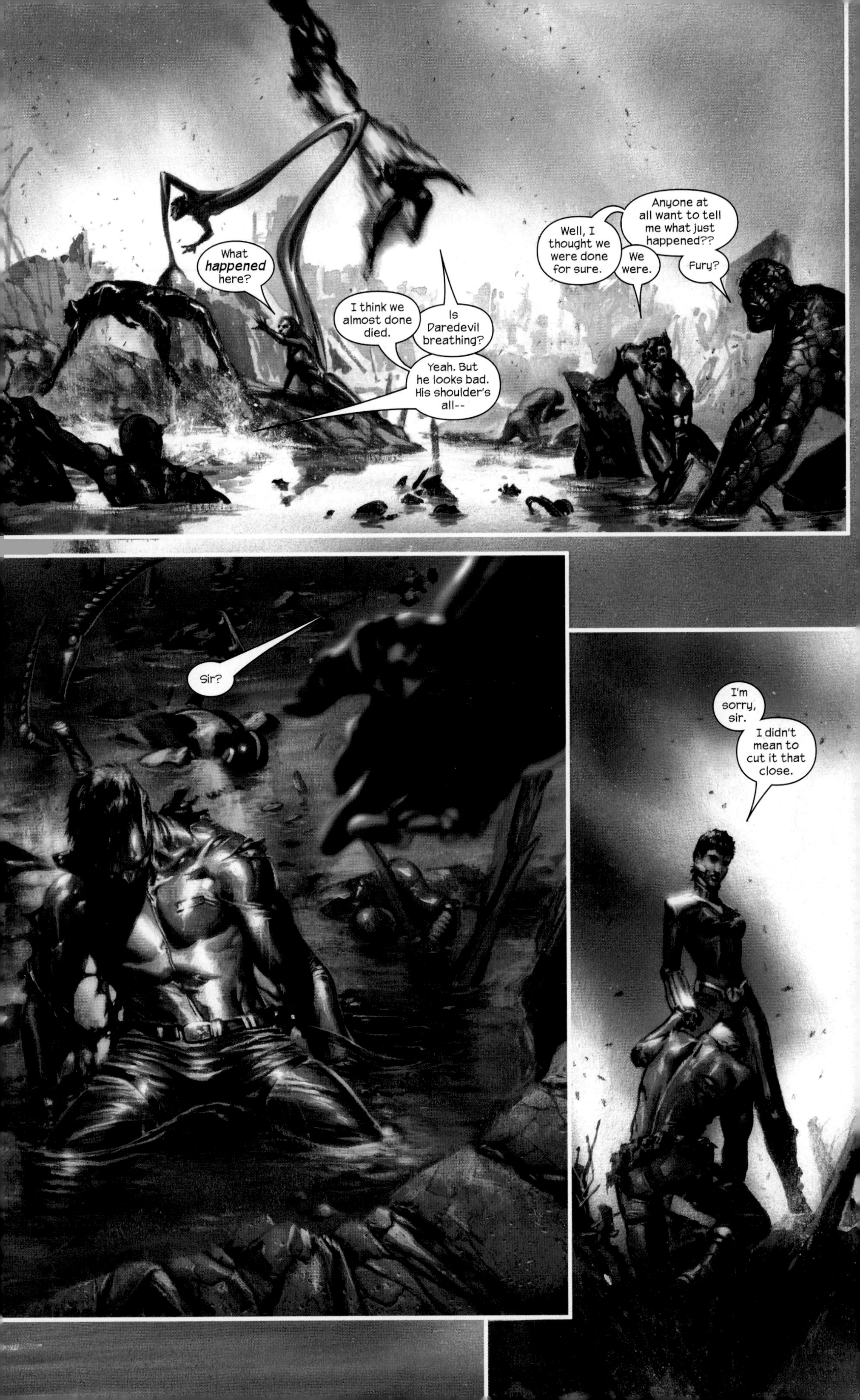
What *happened* here?
I think we almost done died.
Is Daredevil breathing?
Yeah. But he looks bad. His shoulder's all--
Well, I thought we were done for sure.
Anyone at all want to tell me what just happened??
We were.
Fury?
Sir?
I'm sorry, sir.
I didn't mean to cut it that close.

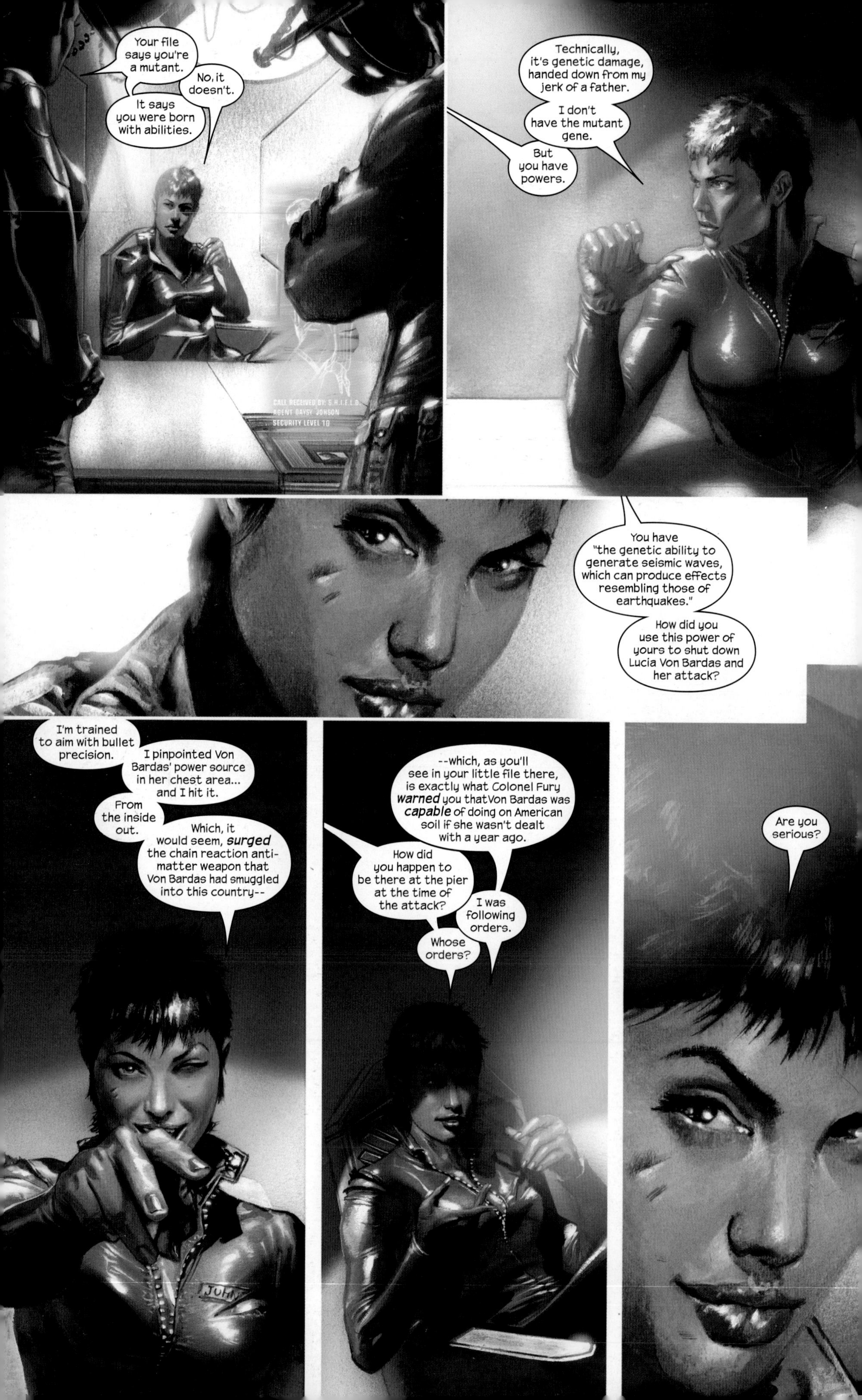
Your file says you're a mutant.
No, it doesn't.
It says you were born with abilities.
CALL RECEIVED BY: S.H.I.E.L.D.
SECURITY LEVEL 10
Technically, it's genetic damage, handed down from my jerk of a father.
I don't have the mutant gene.
But you have powers.
You have "the genetic ability to generate seismic waves, which can produce effects resembling those of earthquakes."
How did you use this power of yours to shut down Lucia Von Bardas and her attack?
I'm trained to aim with bullet precision.
I pinpointed Von Bardas' power source in her chest area... and I hit it.
From the inside out.
Which, it would seem, **surged** the chain reaction anti-matter weapon that Von Bardas had smuggled into this country--
--which, as you'll see in your little file there, is exactly what Colonel Fury ***warned*** you that Von Bardas was ***capable*** of doing on American soil if she wasn't dealt with a year ago.
How did you happen to be there at the pier at the time of the attack?
I was following orders.
Whose orders?
Are you serious?

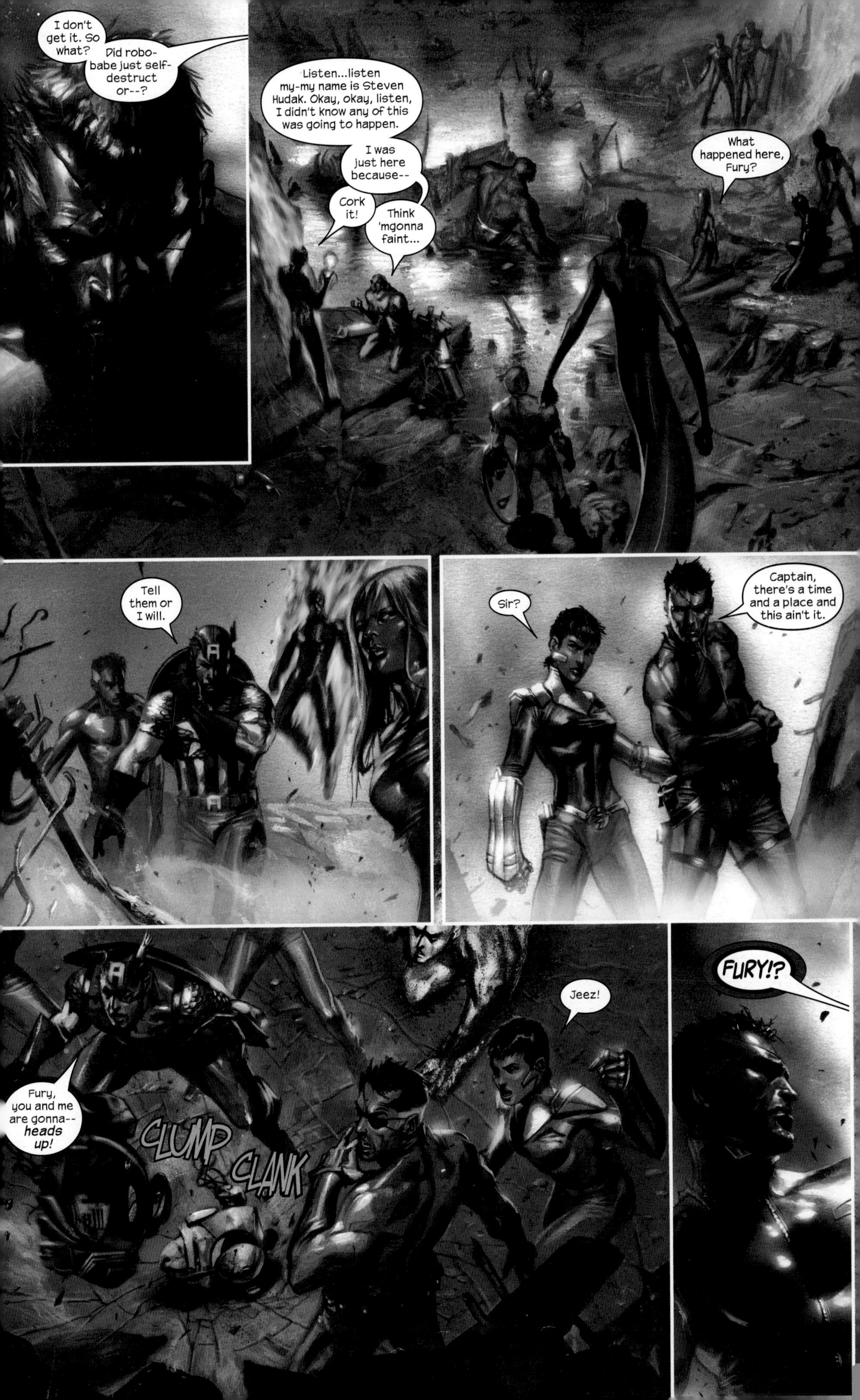

I don't get it. So what?
Did robo-babe just self-destruct or--?
Listen...listen my-my name is Steven Hudak. Okay, okay, listen, I didn't know any of this was going to happen.
I was just here because--
Cork it!
Think 'mgonna faint...
What happened here, Fury?
Tell them or I will.
Sir?
Captain, there's a time and a place and this ain't it.
Fury, you and me are gonna-- *heads up!*
CLUMP
CLANK
Jeez!
FURY!?

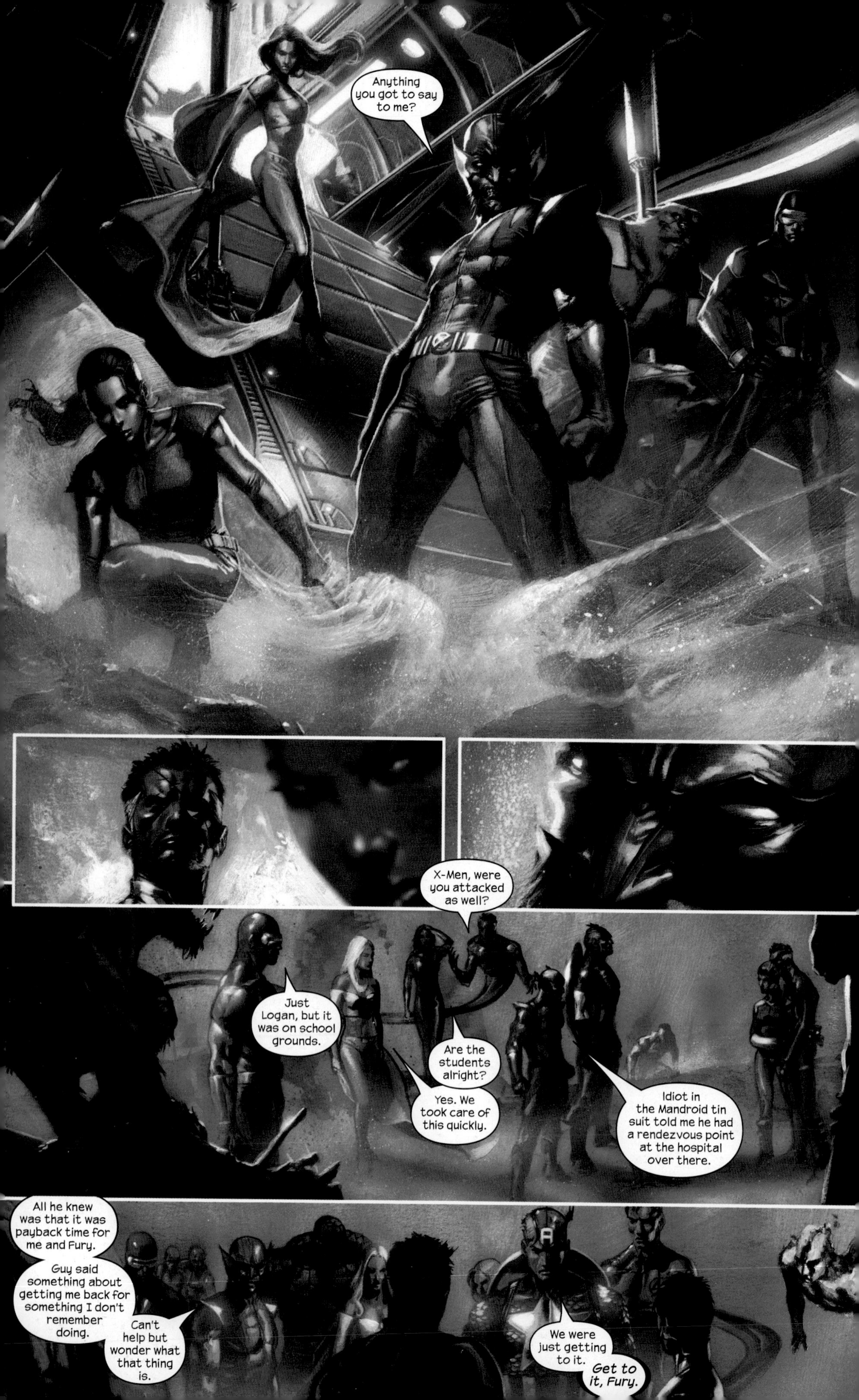
Anything you got to say to me?
X-Men, were you attacked as well?
Just Logan, but it was on school grounds.
Are the students alright?
Yes. We took care of this quickly.
Idiot in the Mandroid tin suit told me he had a rendezvous point at the hospital over there.
All he knew was that it was payback time for me and Fury.
Guy said something about getting me back for something I don't remember doing.
Can't help but wonder what that thing is.
We were just getting to it.
Get to it, Fury.

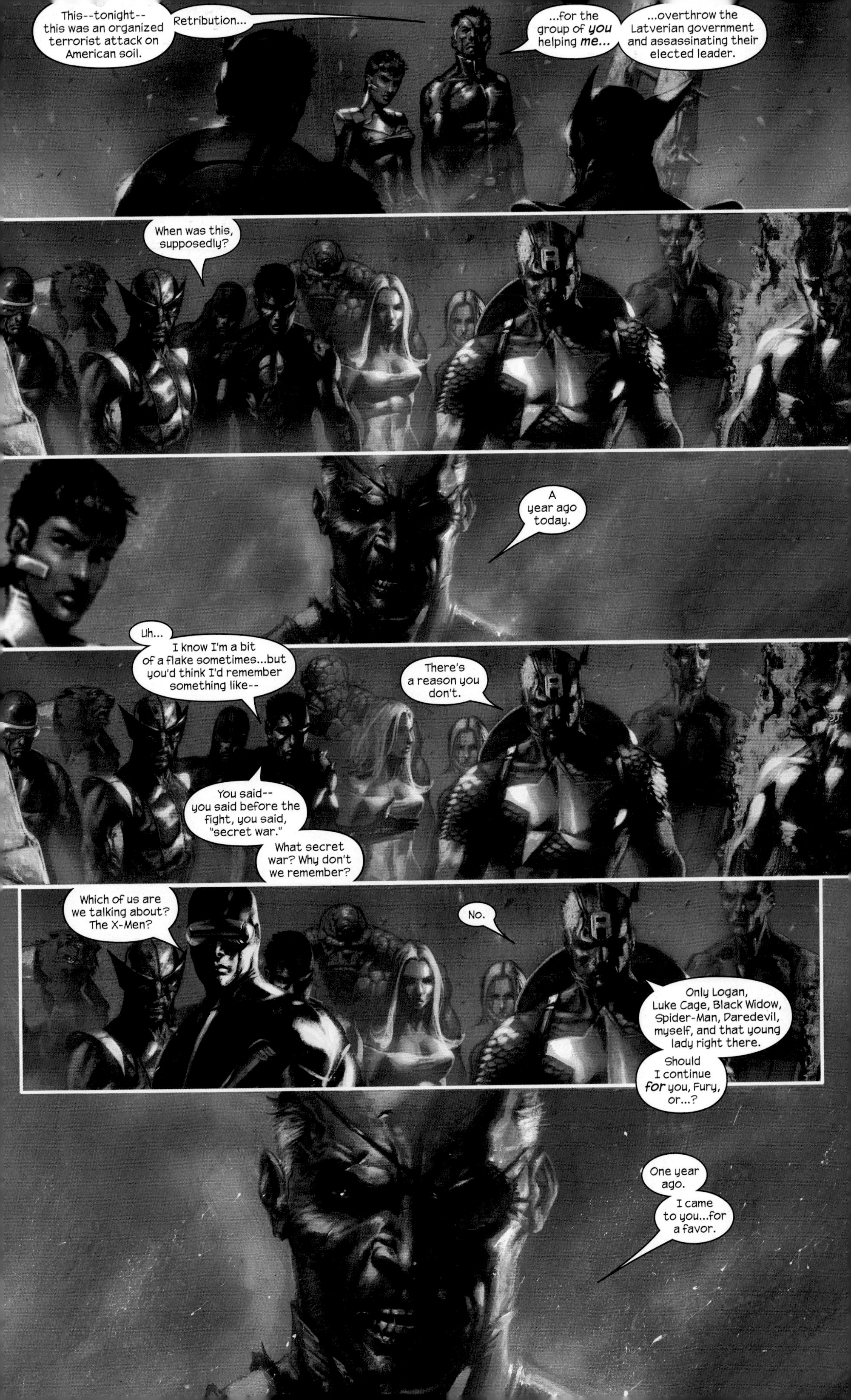
This--tonight--
this was an organized
terrorist attack on
American soil.
Retribution...
...for the
group of *you*
helping *me*...
...overthrow the
Latverian government
and assassinating their
elected leader.
When was this,
supposedly?
A
year ago
today.
Uh...
I know I'm a bit
of a flake sometimes...but
you'd think I'd remember
something like--
There's
a reason you
don't.
You said--
you said before the
fight, you said,
"secret war."
What secret
war? Why don't
we remember?
Which of us are
we talking about?
The X-Men?
No.
Only Logan,
Luke Cage, Black Widow,
Spider-Man, Daredevil,
myself, and that young
lady right there.
Should
I continue
for you, Fury,
or...?
One year
ago.
I came
to you...for
a favor.

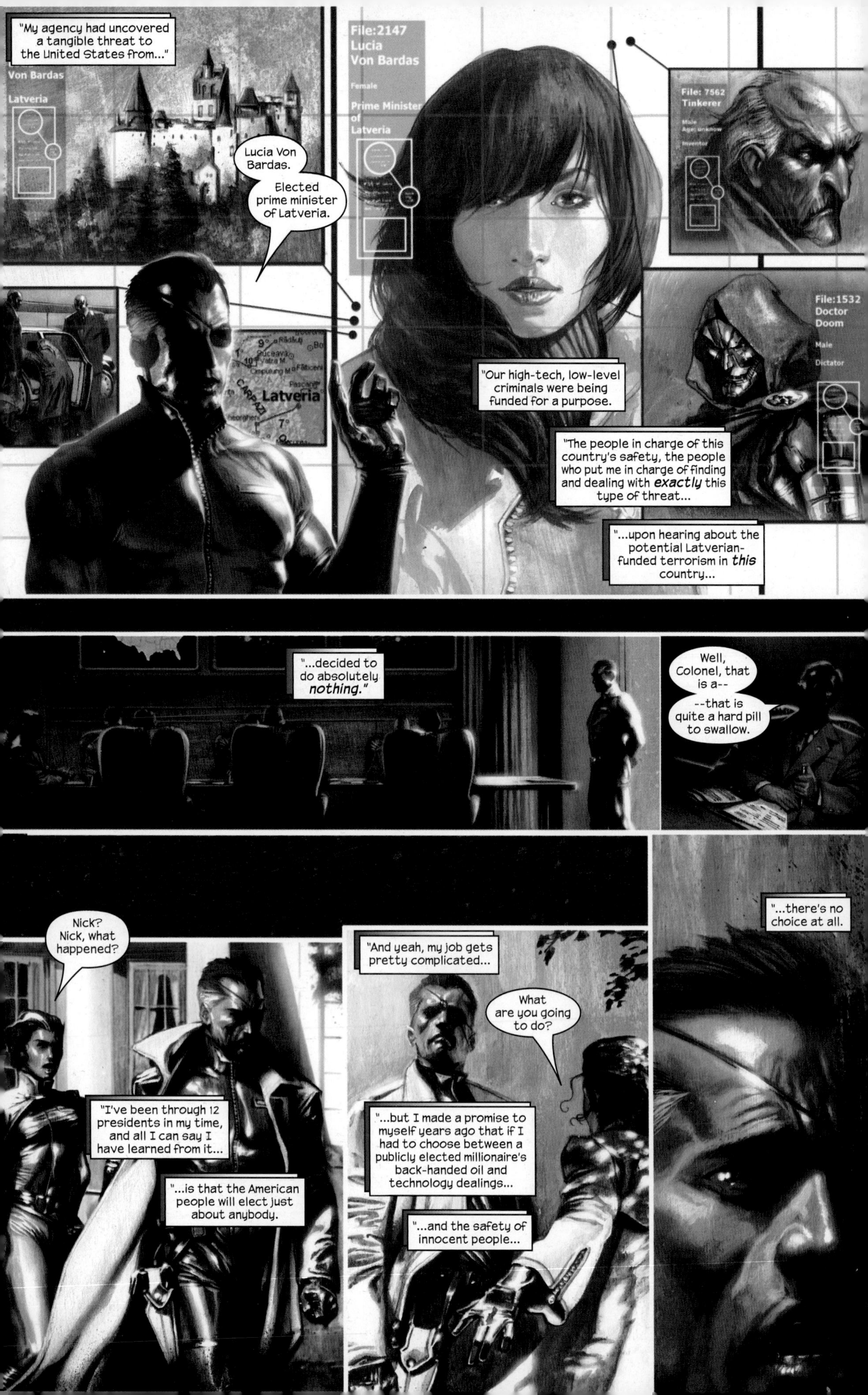
"My agency had uncovered a tangible threat to the United States from..."
Von Bardas
Latveria
File:2147
Lucia
Von Bardas
Female
Prime Minister of Latveria
File: 7562
Tinkerer
Lucia Von Bardas.
Elected prime minister of Latveria.
Latveria
File:1532
Doctor
Doom
Male
Dictator
"Our high-tech, low-level criminals were being funded for a purpose.
"The people in charge of this country's safety, the people who put me in charge of finding and dealing with *exactly* this type of threat...
"...upon hearing about the potential Latverian-funded terrorism in *this* country...
"...decided to do absolutely *nothing*."
Well, Colonel, that is a--
--that is quite a hard pill to swallow.
Nick? Nick, what happened?
"I've been through 12 presidents in my time, and all I can say I have learned from it...
"...is that the American people will elect just about anybody.
"And yeah, my job gets pretty complicated...
What are you going to do?
"...but I made a promise to myself years ago that if I had to choose between a publicly elected millionaire's back-handed oil and technology dealings...
"...and the safety of innocent people...
"...there's no choice at all.

"Problem was, I made too much of a stink about what I found.

"And my reputation of being someone who doesn't take this kind of crap from people preceded me by decades.

"They knew I was going to move on this.

"I didn't *care* that they knew-- I just wanted to get it *done* before they tried to stop me.

"Then the thought occurred to me--did my president *want* me to go off on my own and take care of it *for* him because his hands were tied--or too dirty?

"Is that what the blow-off was about?

"Or had they invested so much money into rebuilding Latveria that the idea that maybe it *had* backfired on them was too much?

"Or did they actually think they could *negotiate* with people like that?

"Then I thought, I don't *care*.

"All that mattered was that this had to be stopped.

"But I couldn't use S.H.I.E.L.D. materials--not only would it tip my hat--it was an act of war.

"Actually, without permission from the U.N. and the World Court--it was worse than that.

"An act of global treason-- *terrorism!*

"But the thing is--what I wanted to do here wouldn't mean half as much if I *had* used my men.

"Von Bardas wanted to punish us by funding our criminals--use our criminal system against us...

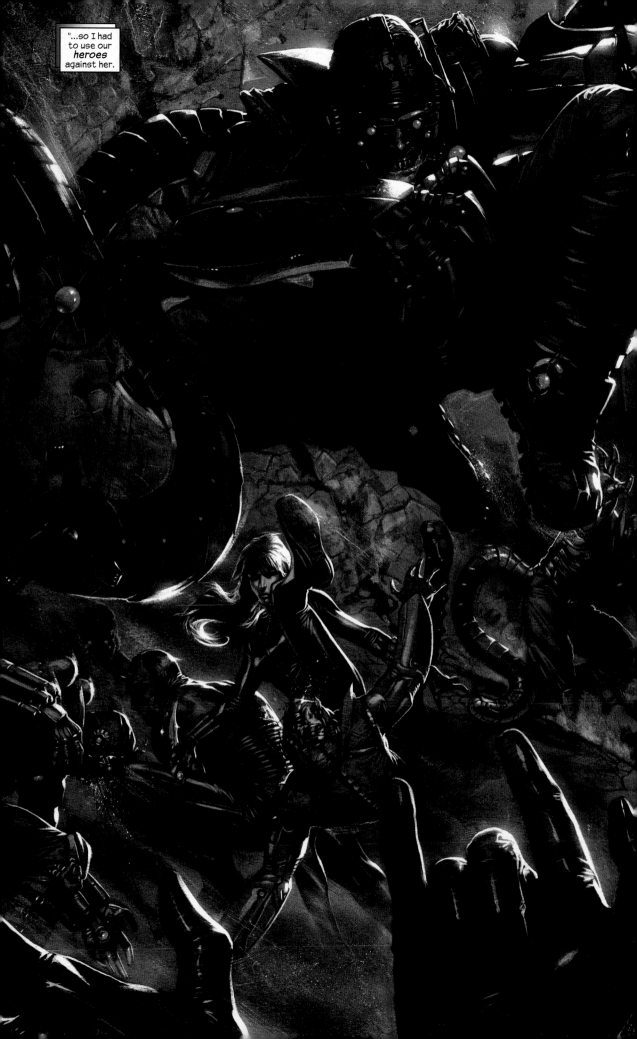

"...so I had to use our *heroes* against her.

"...so I had to use our *heroes* against her.

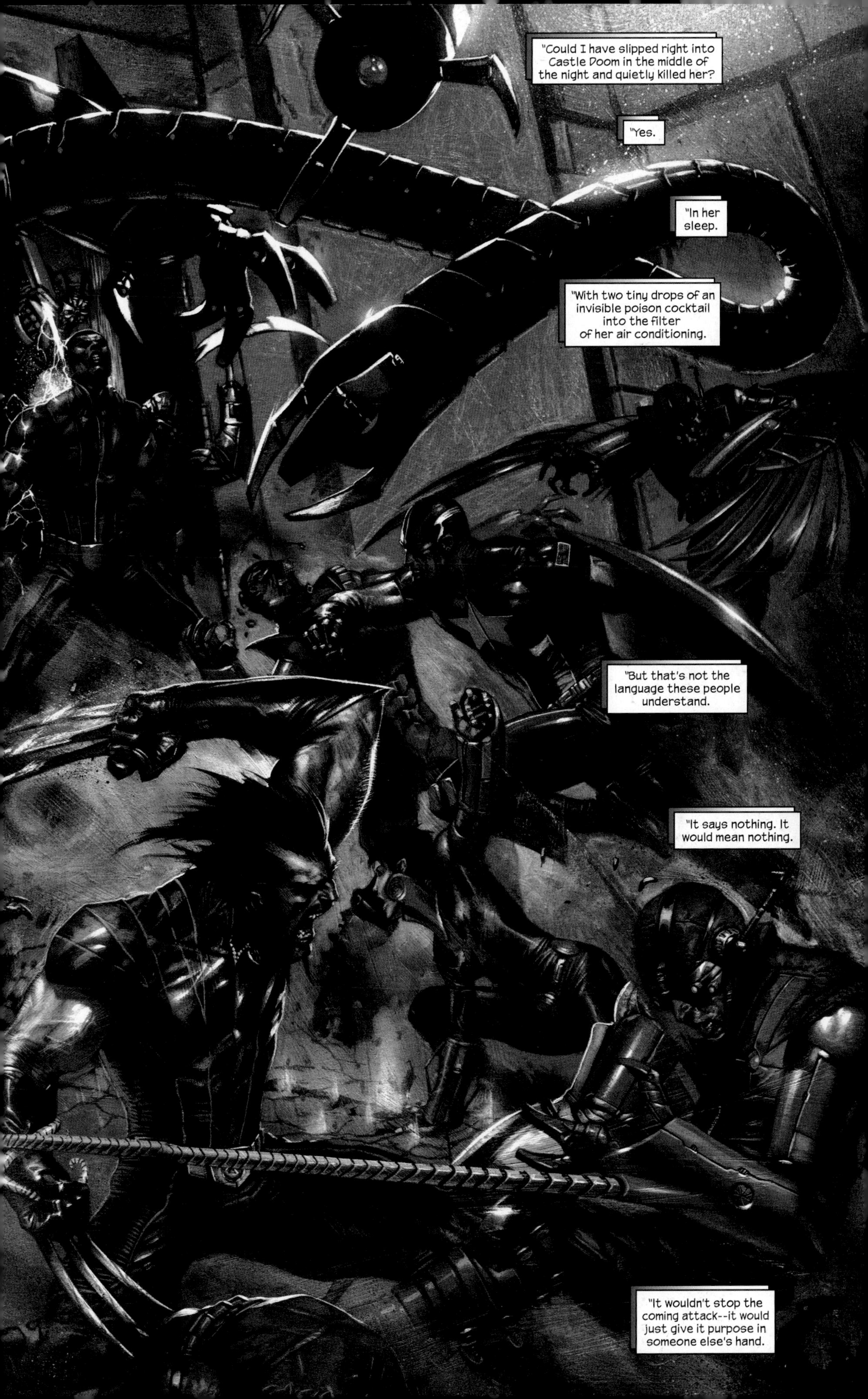
"Could I have slipped right into Castle Doom in the middle of the night and quietly killed her?
"Yes.
"In her sleep.
"With two tiny drops of an invisible poison cocktail into the filter of her air conditioning.
"But that's not the language these people understand.
"It says nothing. It would mean nothing.
"It wouldn't stop the coming attack--it would just give it purpose in someone else's hand.

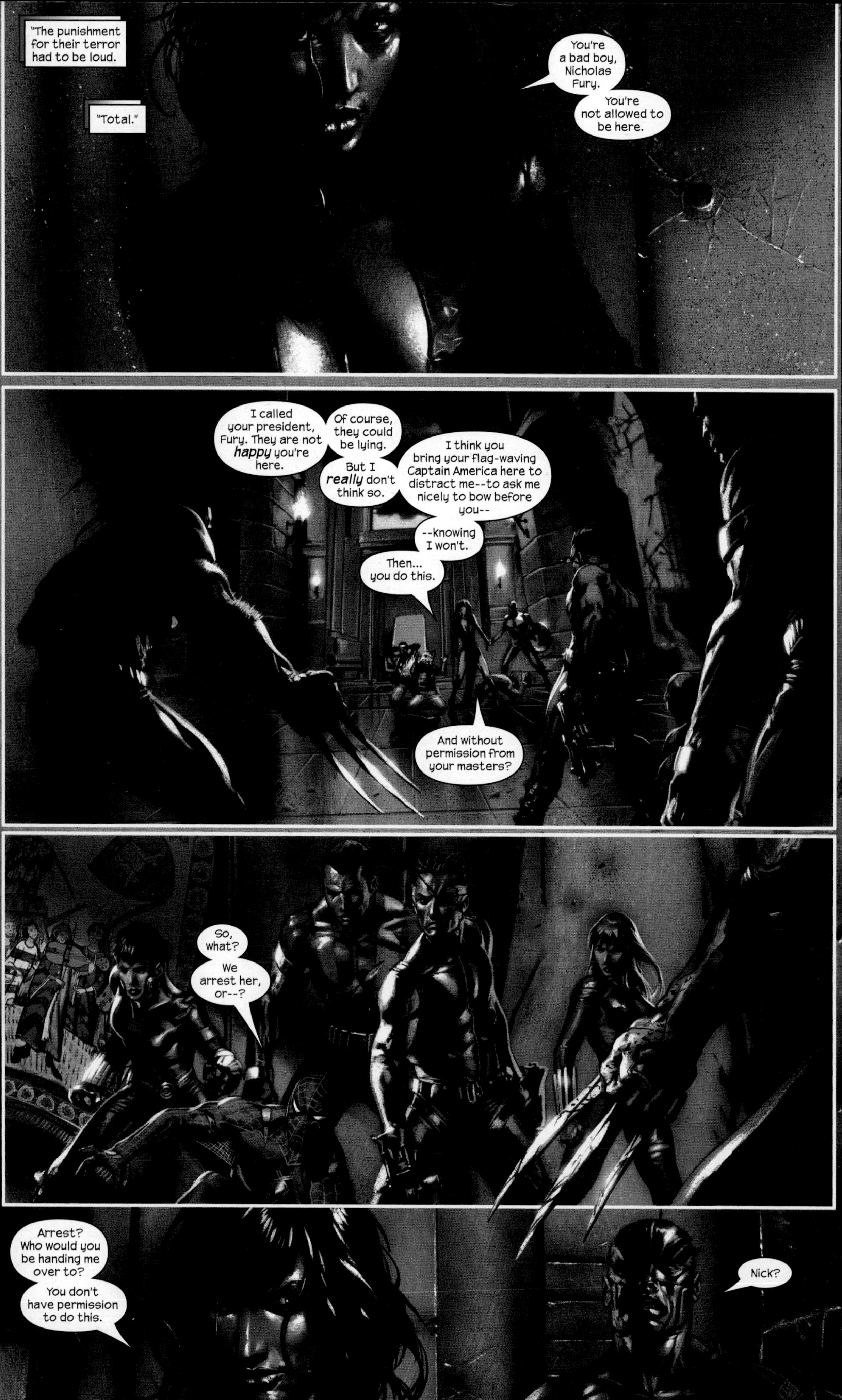

"The punishment for their terror had to be loud.
"Total."
You're a bad boy, Nicholas Fury.
You're not allowed to be here.
I called your president, Fury. They are not *happy* you're here.
Of course, they could be lying.
But I *really* don't think so.
I think you bring your flag-waving Captain America here to distract me--to ask me nicely to bow before you--
--knowing I won't.
Then... you do this.
And without permission from your masters?
So, what?
We arrest her, or--?
Arrest? Who would you be handing me over to?
You don't have permission to do this.
Nick?

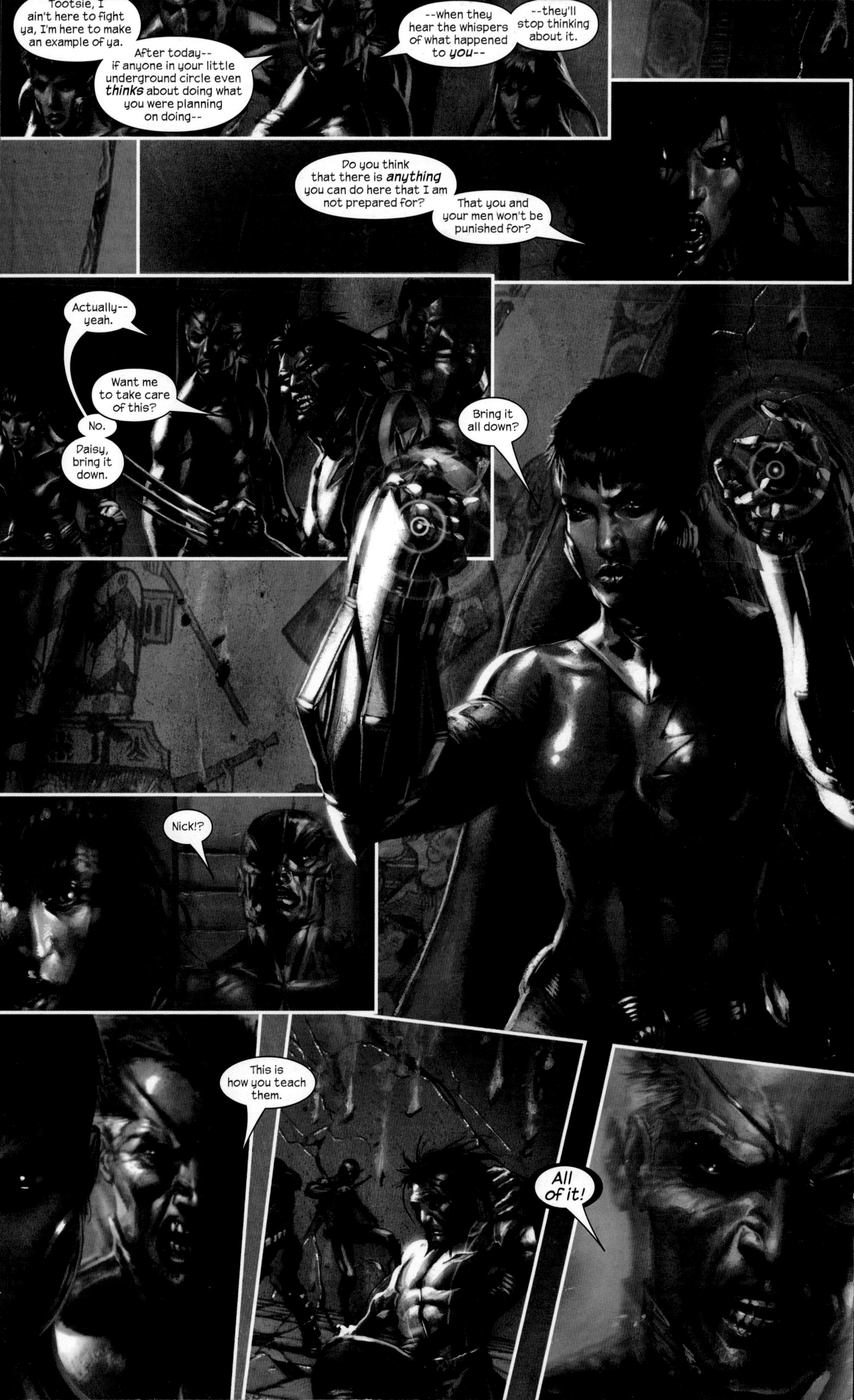
Tootsie, I ain't here to fight ya, I'm here to make an example of ya.
After today-- if anyone in your little underground circle even *thinks* about doing what you were planning on doing--
--when they hear the whispers of what happened to *you*--
--they'll stop thinking about it.
Do you think that there is *anything* you can do here that I am not prepared for?
That you and your men won't be punished for?
Actually-- yeah.
Want me to take care of this?
No.
Daisy, bring it down.
Bring it all down?
Nick!?
This is how you teach them.
All of it!

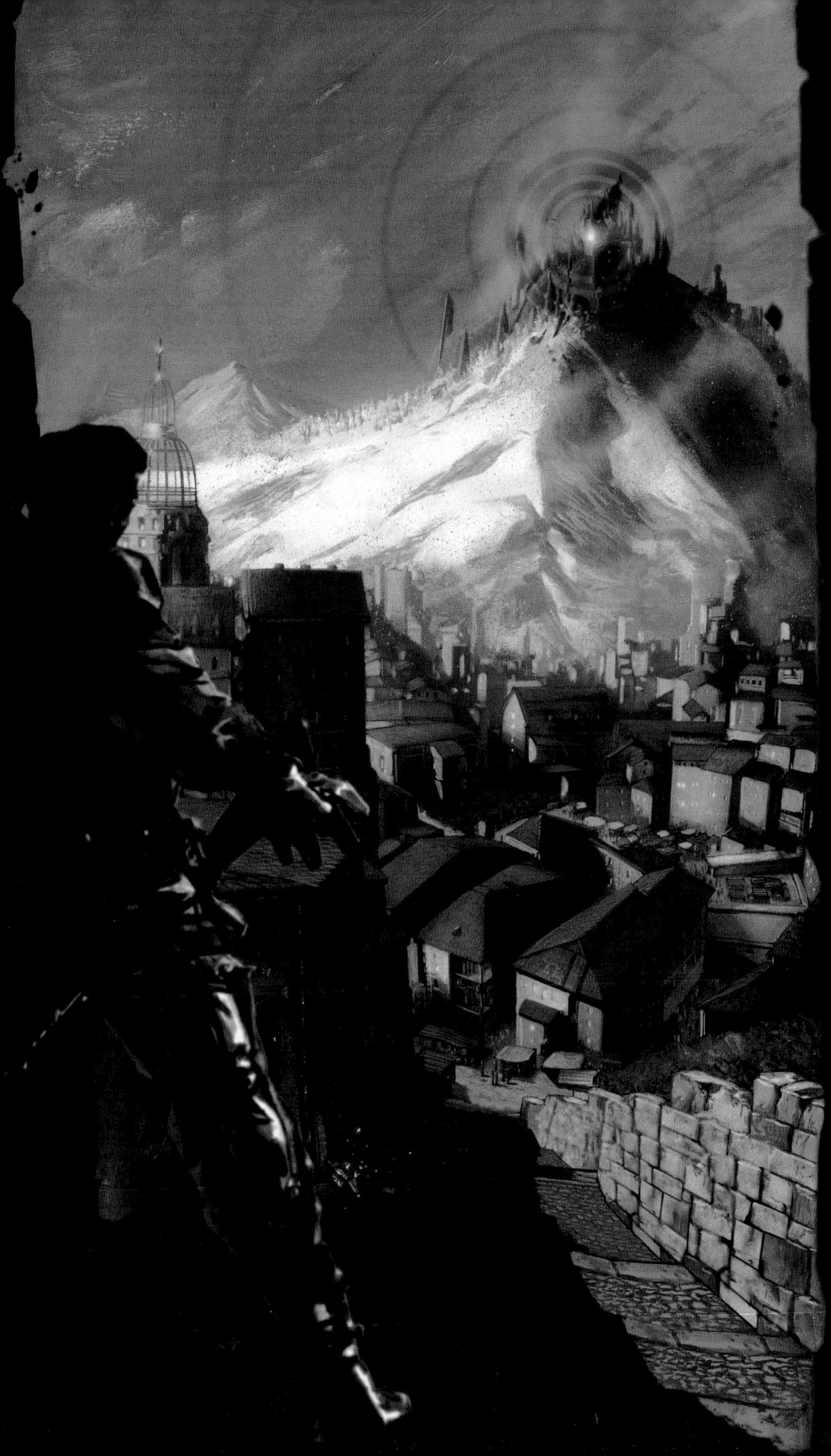

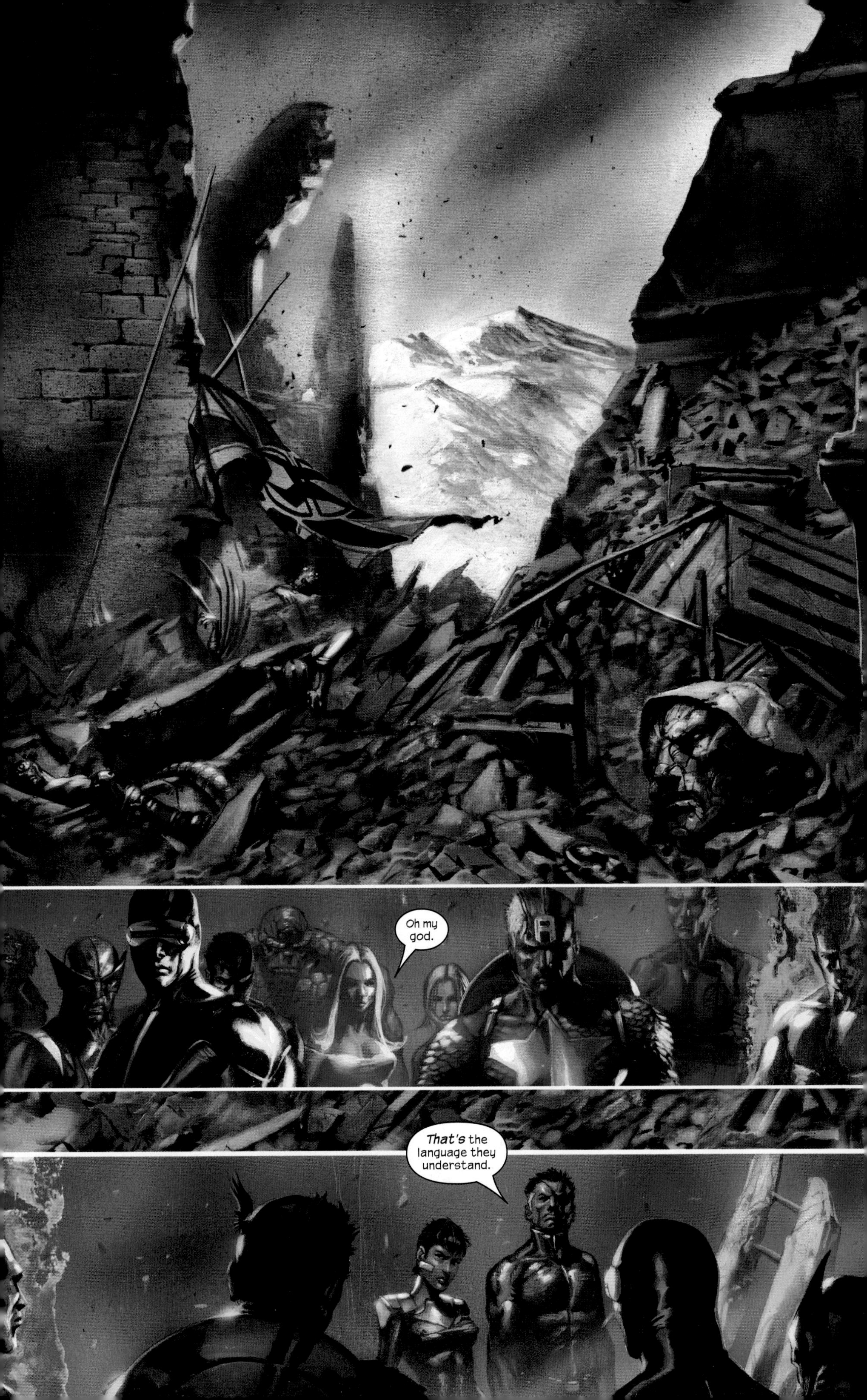
Oh my god.
That's the language they understand.

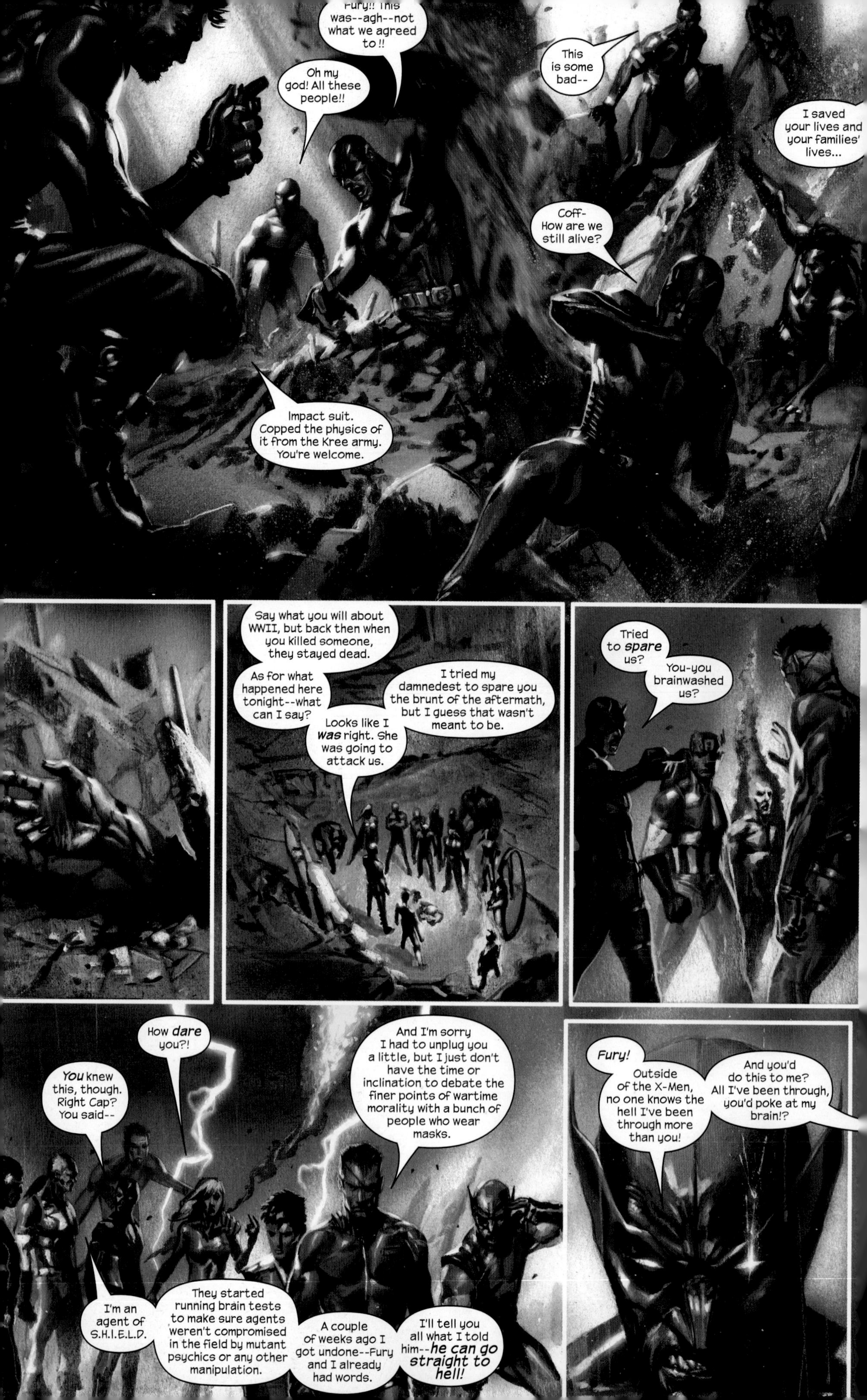
Fury!! This was--agh--not what we agreed to!!
Oh my god! All these people!!
This is some bad--
I saved your lives and your families' lives...
Coff- How are we still alive?
Impact suit. Copped the physics of it from the Kree army. You're welcome.
Say what you will about WWII, but back then when you killed someone, they stayed dead.
As for what happened here tonight--what can I say?
I tried my damnedest to spare you the brunt of the aftermath, but I guess that wasn't meant to be.
Looks like I *was* right. She was going to attack us.
Tried to *spare* us?
You-you brainwashed us?
How *dare* you?!
You knew this, though. Right Cap? You said--
And I'm sorry I had to unplug you a little, but I just don't have the time or inclination to debate the finer points of wartime morality with a bunch of people who wear masks.
I'm an agent of S.H.I.E.L.D.
They started running brain tests to make sure agents weren't compromised in the field by mutant psychics or any other manipulation.
A couple of weeks ago I got undone--Fury and I already had words.
I'll tell you all what I told him--***he can go straight to hell!***
Fury!
Outside of the X-Men, no one knows the hell I've been through more than you!
And you'd do this to me? All I've been through, you'd poke at my brain!?

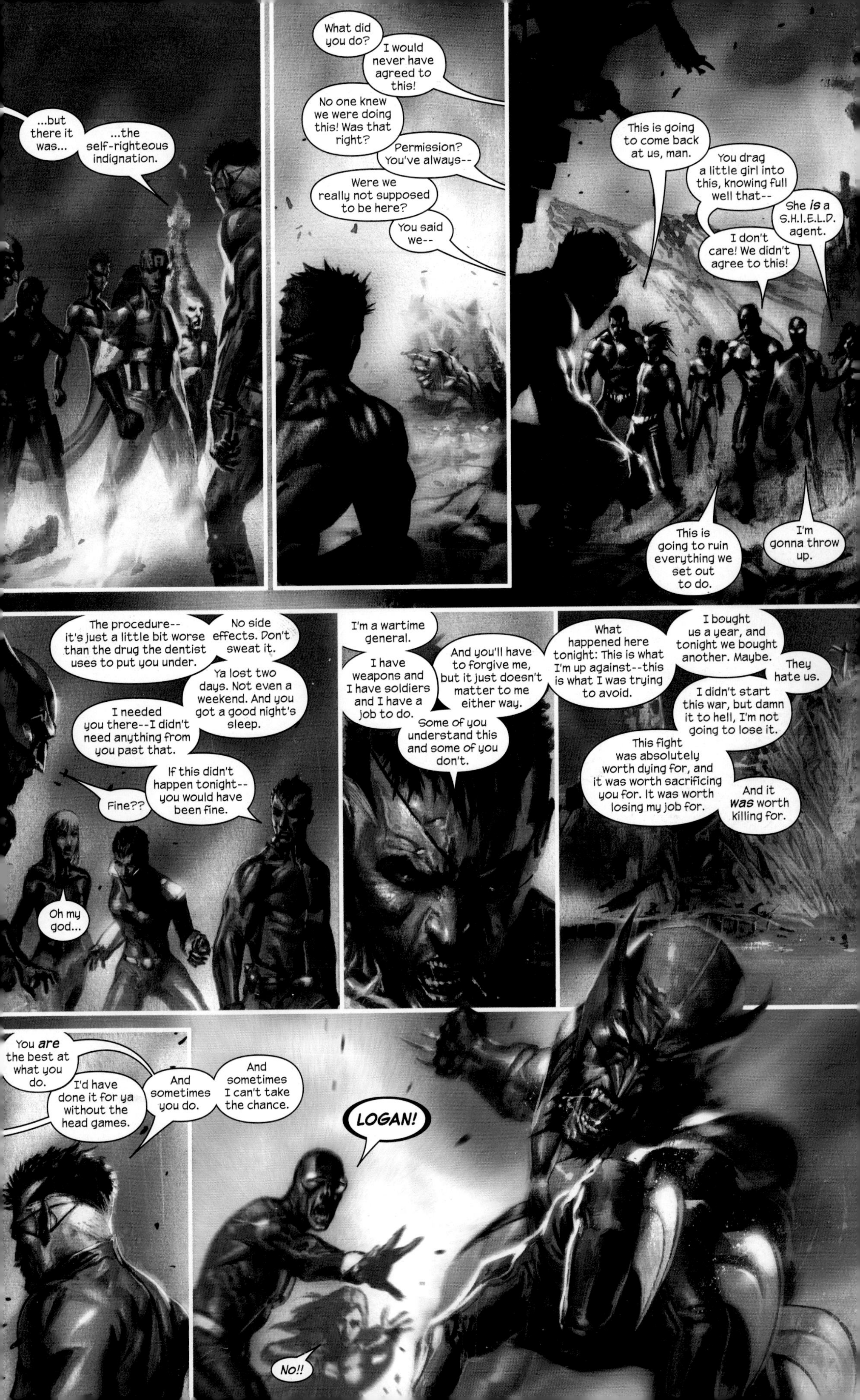
...but there it was...
...the self-righteous indignation.
What did you do?
I would never have agreed to this!
No one knew we were doing this! Was that right?
Permission? You've always--
Were we really not supposed to be here?
You said we--
This is going to come back at us, man.
You drag a little girl into this, knowing full well that--
She *is* a S.H.I.E.L.D. agent.
I don't care! We didn't agree to this!
This is going to ruin everything we set out to do.
I'm gonna throw up.
The procedure-- it's just a little bit worse than the drug the dentist uses to put you under.
No side effects. Don't sweat it.
Ya lost two days. Not even a weekend. And you got a good night's sleep.
I needed you there--I didn't need anything from you past that.
If this didn't happen tonight-- you would have been fine.
Fine??
Oh my god...
I'm a wartime general.
I have weapons and I have soldiers and I have a job to do.
And you'll have to forgive me, but it just doesn't matter to me either way.
Some of you understand this and some of you don't.
What happened here tonight: This is what I'm up against--this is what I was trying to avoid.
I bought us a year, and tonight we bought another. Maybe.
They hate us.
I didn't start this war, but damn it to hell, I'm not going to lose it.
This fight was absolutely worth dying for, and it was worth sacrificing you for. It was worth losing my job for.
And it *was* worth killing for.
You *are* the best at what you do.
I'd have done it for ya without the head games.
And sometimes you do.
And sometimes I can't take the chance.
LOGAN!
No!!

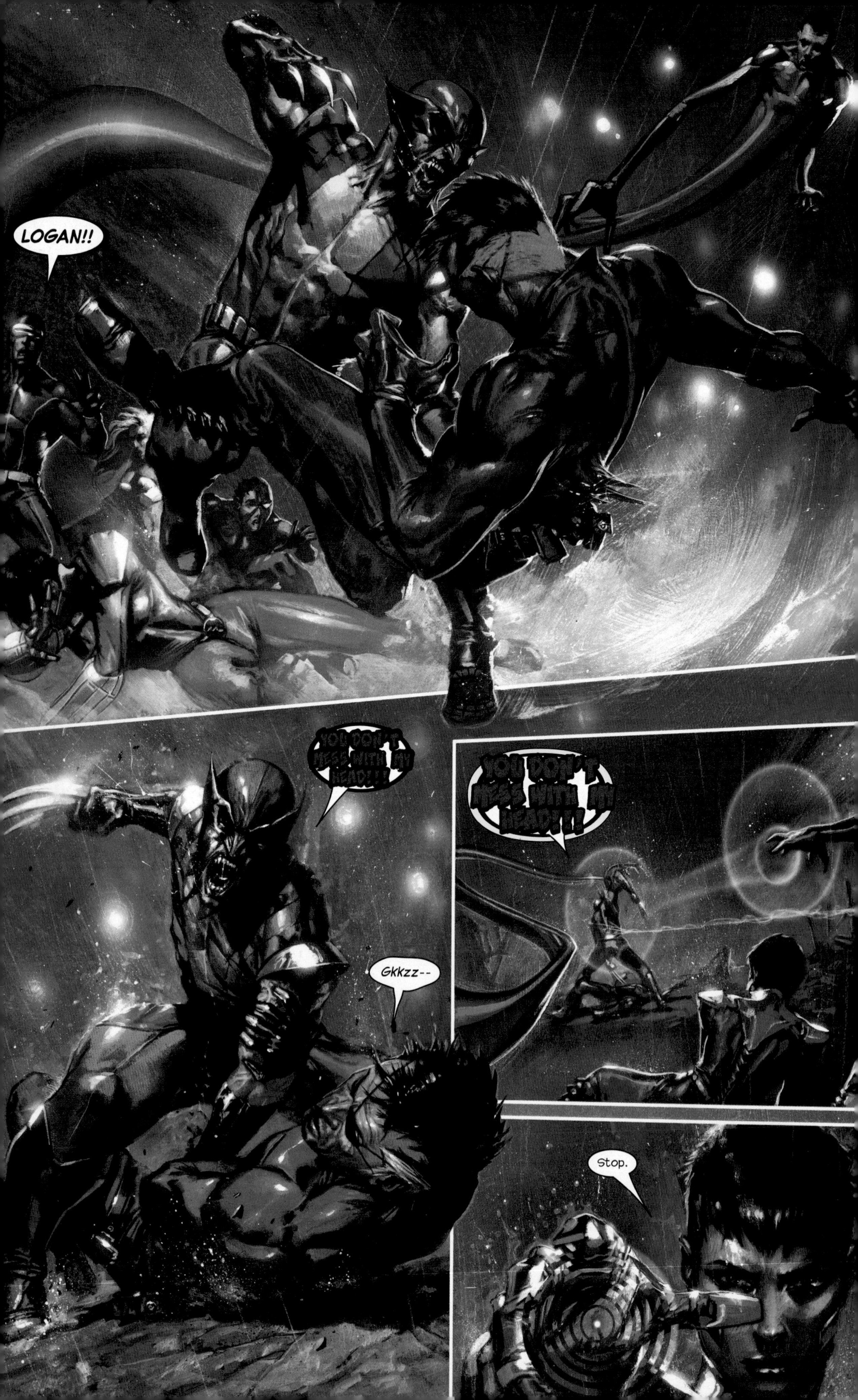
LOGAN!!
YOU DON'T MESS WITH MY HEAD!!!
Gkkzz--
YOU DON'T MESS WITH MY HEAD!!!
Stop.

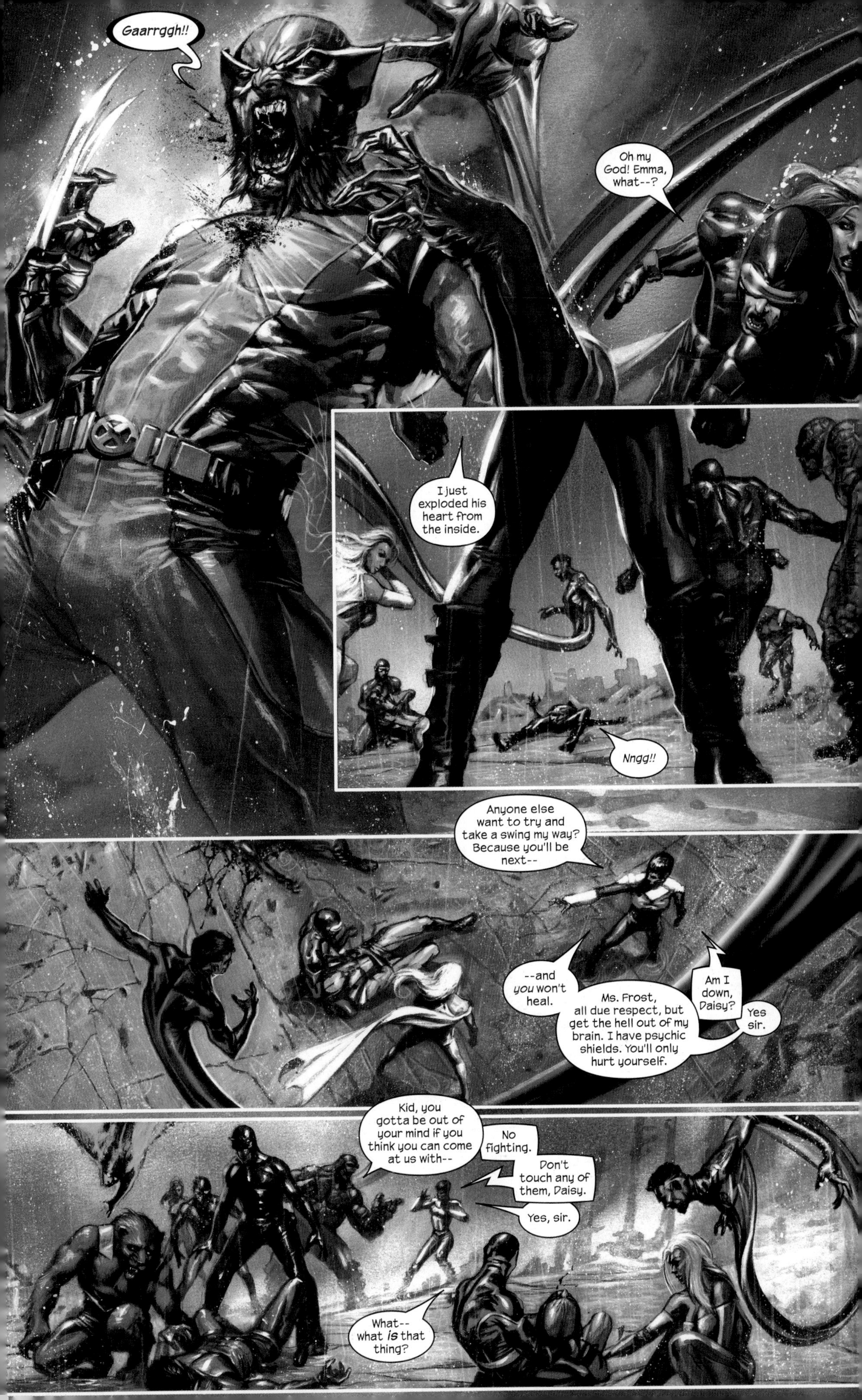
Gaarrggh!!
Oh my God! Emma, what--?
I just exploded his heart from the inside.
Nngg!!
Anyone else want to try and take a swing my way? Because you'll be next--
--and *you* won't heal.
Ms. Frost, all due respect, but get the hell out of my brain. I have psychic shields. You'll only hurt yourself.
Am I down, Daisy?
Yes sir.
Kid, you gotta be out of your mind if you think you can come at us with--
No fighting.
Don't touch any of them, Daisy.
Yes, sir.
What-- what *is* that thing?

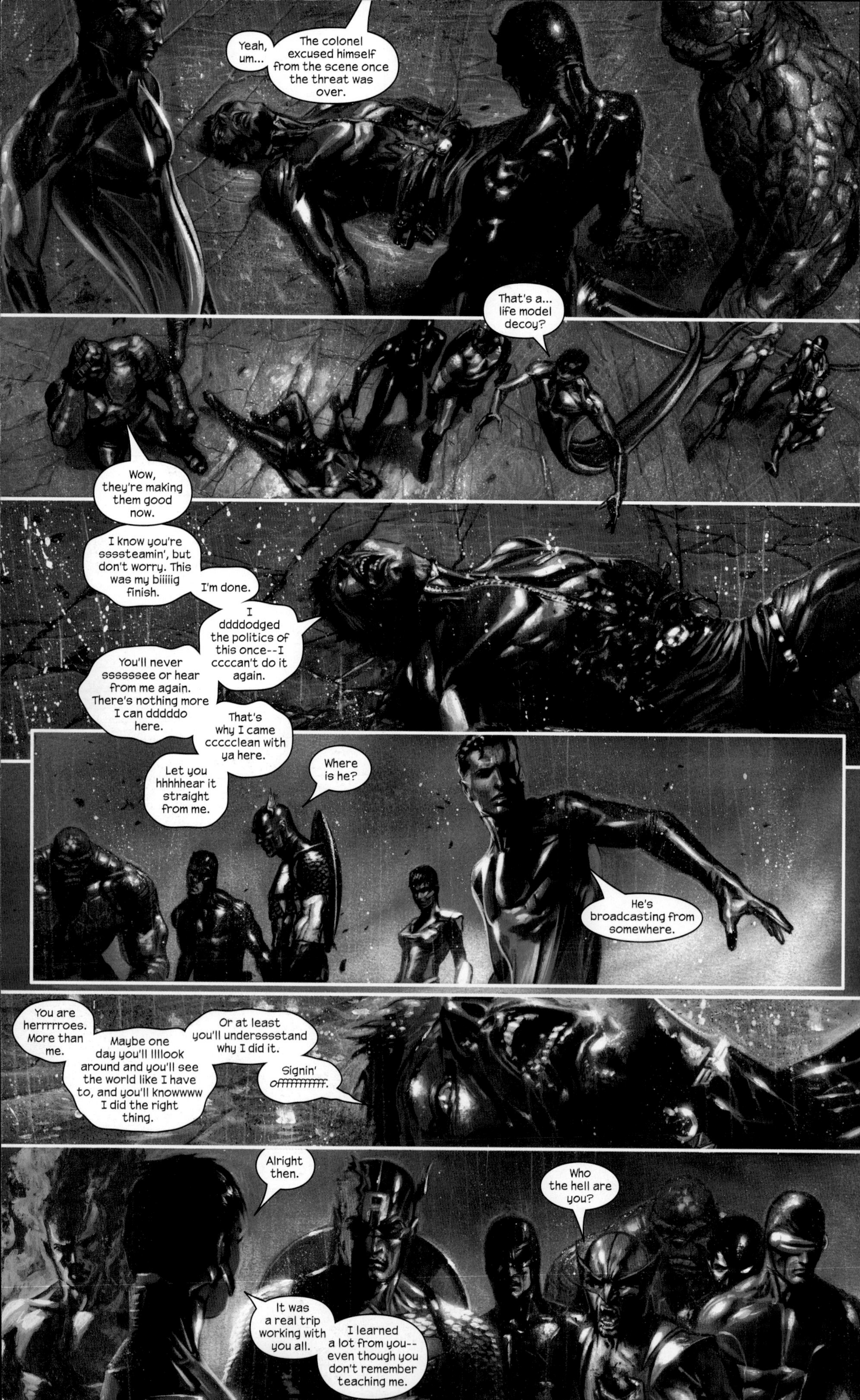
Yeah, um...
The colonel excused himself from the scene once the threat was over.
That's a... life model decoy?
Wow, they're making them good now.
I know you're sssssteamin', but don't worry. This was my biiiiig finish.
I'm done.
I ddddodged the politics of this once--I cccccan't do it again.
You'll never sssssssee or hear from me again. There's nothing more I can ddddddo here.
That's why I came cccccclean with ya here.
Let you hhhhhear it straight from me.
Where is he?
He's broadcasting from somewhere.
You are herrrrroes. More than me.
Maybe one day you'll lllllook around and you'll see the world like I have to, and you'll knowwww I did the right thing.
Or at least you'll undersssstand why I did it.
Signin' offffffffffff.
Alright then.
Who the hell are you?
It was a real trip working with you all.
I learned a lot from you--even though you don't remember teaching me.

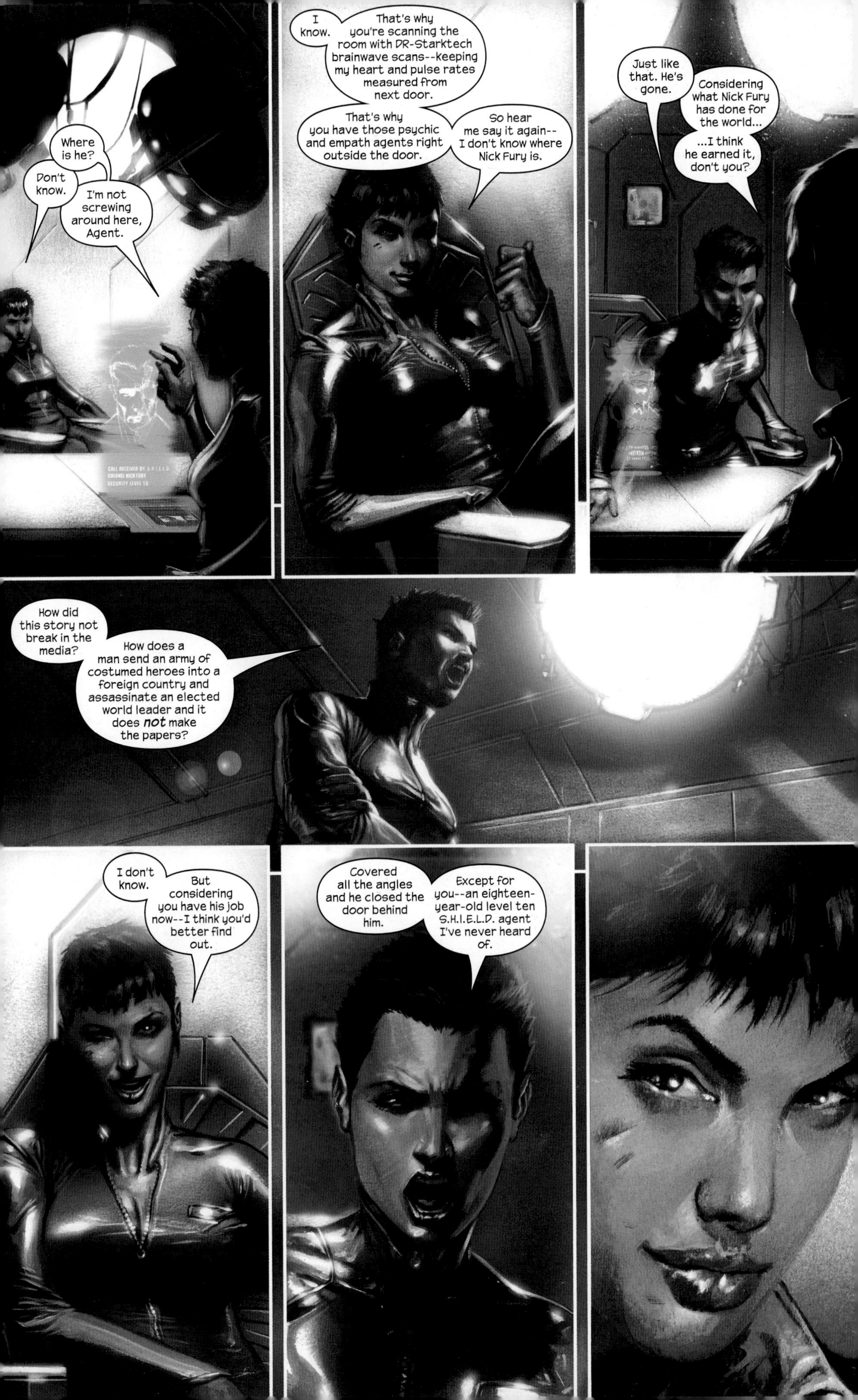
Where is he?
Don't know.
I'm not screwing around here, Agent.
CALL RECEIVED BY: S.H.I.E.L.D.
COLONEL NICK FURY
SECURITY LEVEL 10
I know.
That's why you're scanning the room with DR-Starktech brainwave scans--keeping my heart and pulse rates measured from next door.
That's why you have those psychic and empath agents right outside the door.
So hear me say it again--I don't know where Nick Fury is.
Just like that. He's gone.
Considering what Nick Fury has done for the world...
...I think he earned it, don't you?
How did this story not break in the media?
How does a man send an army of costumed heroes into a foreign country and assassinate an elected world leader and it does *not* make the papers?
I don't know.
But considering you have his job now--I think you'd better find out.
Covered all the angles and he closed the door behind him.
Except for you--an eighteen-year-old level ten S.H.I.E.L.D. agent I've never heard of.

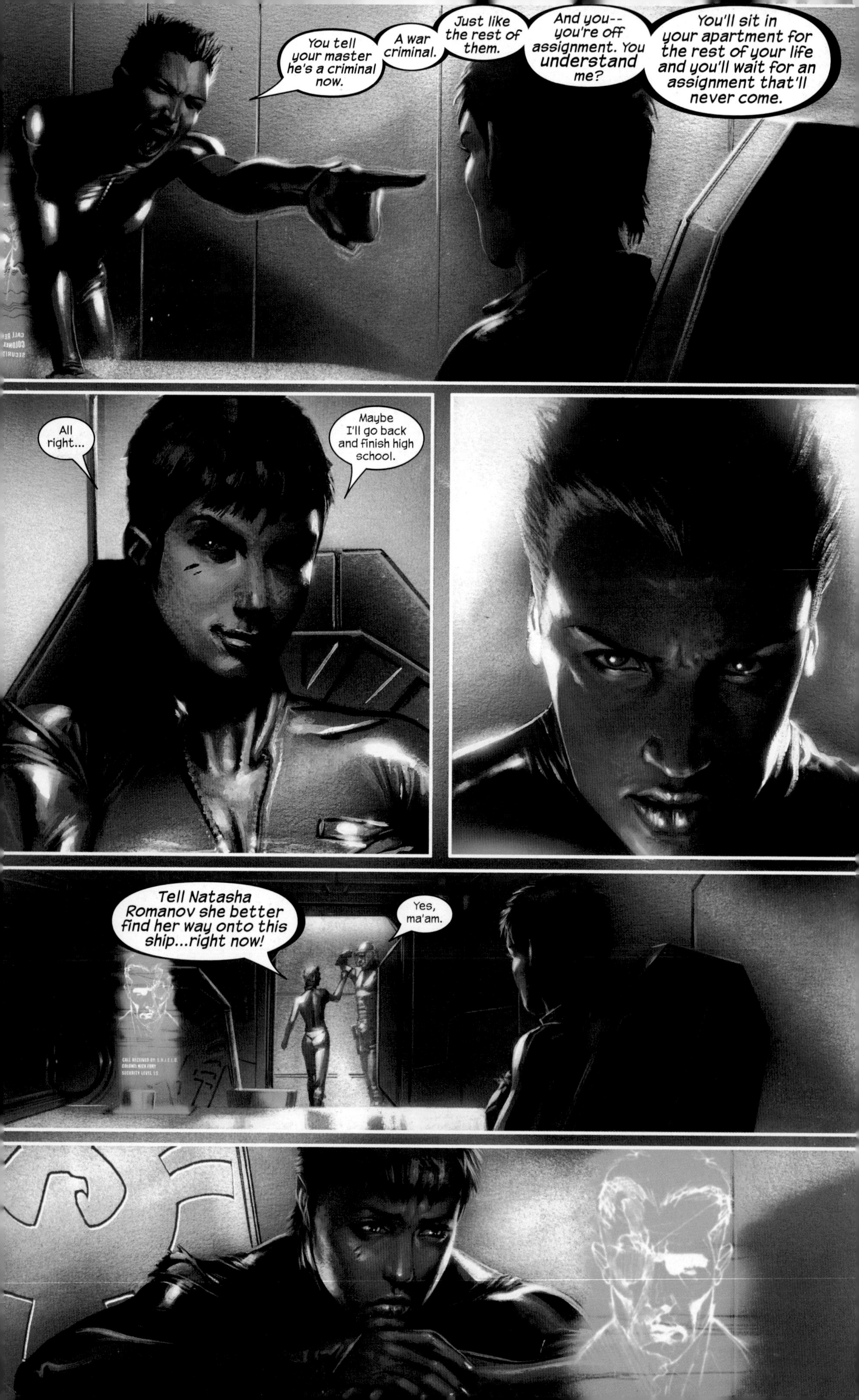
You tell your master he's a criminal now.
A war criminal.
Just like the rest of them.
And you-- you're off assignment. You understand me?
You'll sit in your apartment for the rest of your life and you'll wait for an assignment that'll never come.
All right...
Maybe I'll go back and finish high school.
Tell Natasha Romanov she better find her way onto this ship...right now!
Yes, ma'am.

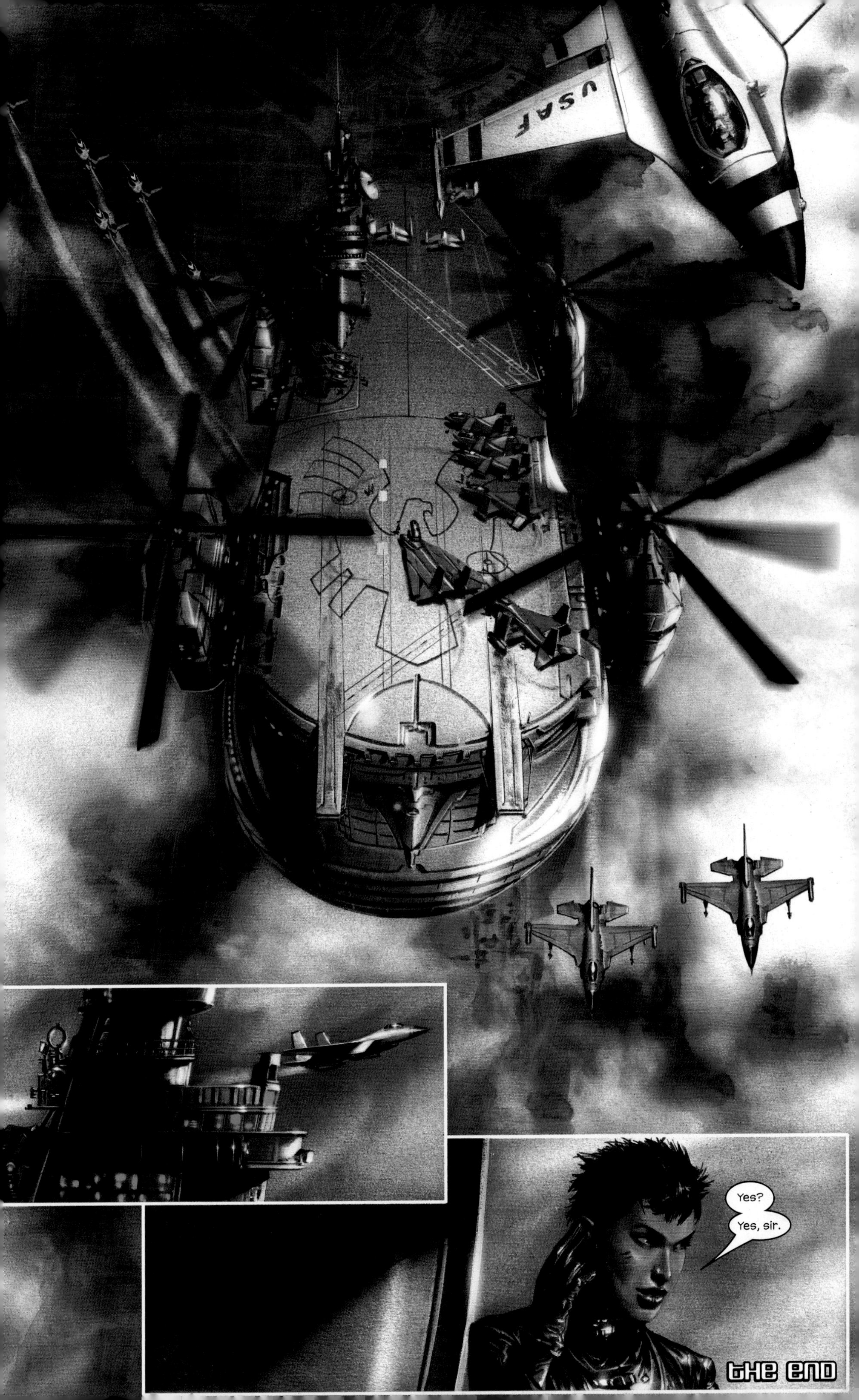
USAF
Yes?
Yes, sir.
THE END

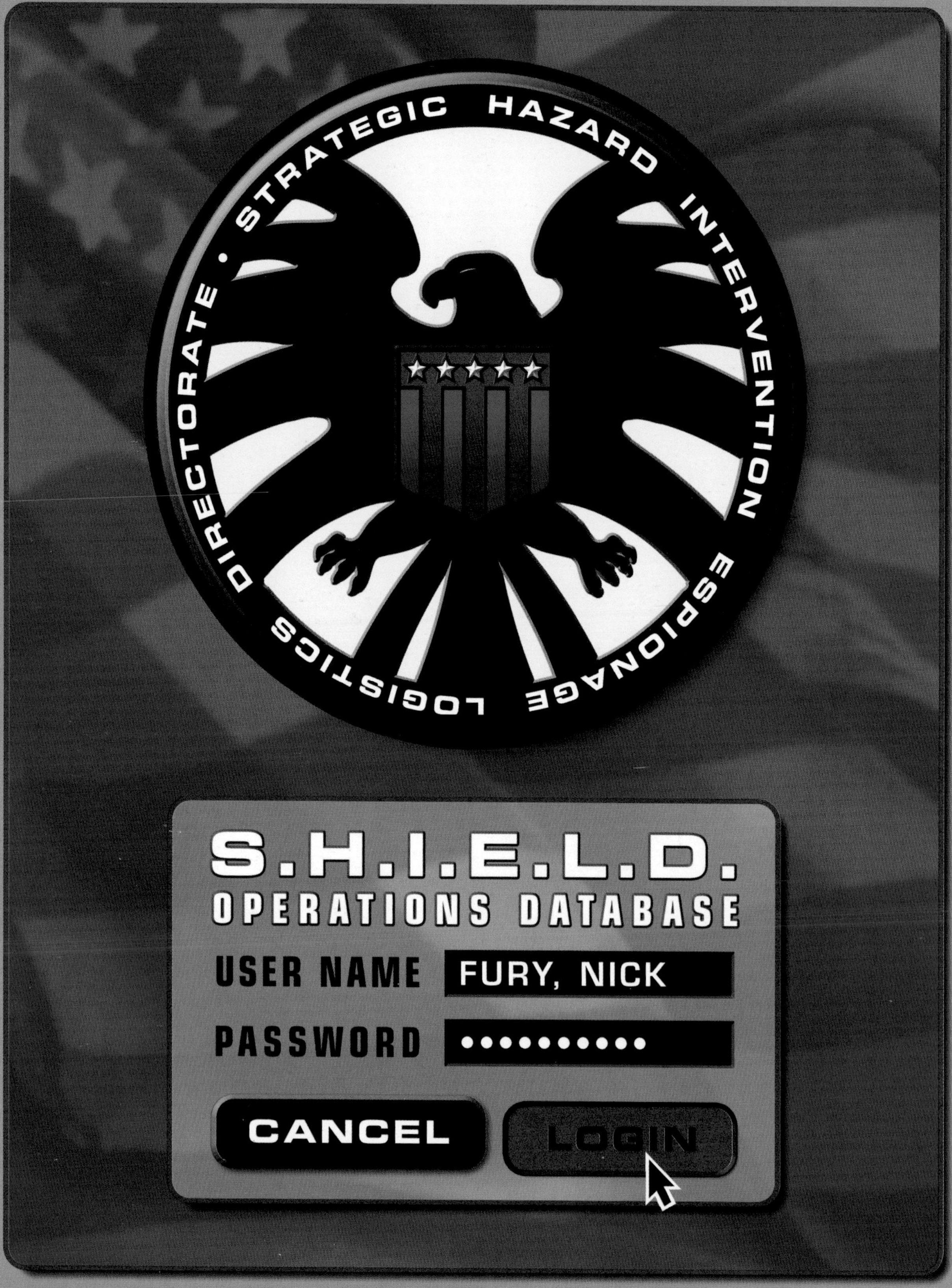
STRATEGIC HAZARD INTERVENTION ESPIONAGE LOGISTICS DIRECTORATE
S.H.I.E.L.D.
OPERATIONS DATABASE
USER NAME
FURY, NICK
PASSWORD
•••••••••••
CANCEL
LOGIN

SEARCH DATABASE SECRET WAR SEARCH

S.H.I.E.L.D. DOCUMENT 68785895-34825 APSMDT

CRIMINAL DATABASE >> OPERATIONS DOCUMENTS >> INTERROGATIONS

SECRET CODE: WHITE

Interrogation Transcript

Subject: Hudak

A.K.A. Scorcher (see S.H.I.E.L.D. FILE HMN-0000018978-001).

Interrogation conducted by: S.H.I.E.L.D. Agent Jasper Sitwell -- level 5

Recording date: 6/22/06 12: 43 PM EST

Place: S.H.I.E.L.D. Medical center: Atlanta, Georgia — Address classified

S.H.I.E.L.D. AGENT JASPER SITWELL
You rang?
HUDAK
Who are you?
S.H.I.E.L.D. AGENT JASPER SITWELL
S.H.I.E.L.D Agent Jasper Sitwell. You said you had further information regarding the incident in New York?
HUDAK
How long have I been in a hospital?
S.H.I.E.L.D. AGENT JASPER SITWELL
Couple of weeks.
HUDAK
I thought I died.
S.H.I.E.L.D. AGENT JASPER SITWELL
Better luck next time.
HUDAK
How-how many of the others made it?
S.H.I.E.L.D. AGENT JASPER SITWELL
Oh, you mean, the other scum bags who helped you try to evaporate New York City? Well, all your buddies lived.
HUDAK
They're not my—
S.H.I.E.L.D. AGENT JASPER SITWELL
Sure, it's hard to believe there's a god when you hear news like this, but look at it this way, at least when you all get out of your comas and such, none of you will ever see the light of day again. So there's that.
HUDAK
They're not my buddies. We're not a group. I don't even know most of--
S.H.I.E.L.D. AGENT JASPER SITWELL
What was your connection to Lucia Von Bardas?
HUDAK
None. I had none. I never met her before that night. I did all my business with the Tinkerer in Philly. I'm telling you—that's why I asked you guys to come here—I want it on the record. I want it known. I didn't know this was going to happen. I'm a bank robber, not a terrorist. Check my record. This isn't how I roll. Okay, you see? This-this was beyond anything I would have ever purposely involved myself with. And I sure as hell wasn't going on no kamikaze mission. I ain't going to blow myself up for anything.
S.H.I.E.L.D. AGENT JASPER SITWELL
Who funded this?
HUDAK
She did, didn't she? You think there's someone behind her?
S.H.I.E.L.D. AGENT JASPER SITWELL
You tell me.

S.H.I.E.L.D. OPERATIONS DATABASE

HOME ADVANCED SEARCH **DATABASES** LOG OUT

S.H.I.E.L.D. DOCUMENT 68785095-34825 APSMDT (Cont.)

HUDAK
I don't know. I only did business with the—
S.H.I.E.L.D. AGENT JASPER SITWELL
I know. I know all of this. I know who you are. I know what happened to you. What do you want from me?
HUDAK
I want a change of life, man, I want to switch my game.
S.H.I.E.L.D. AGENT JASPER SITWELL
Change of life.
HUDAK
I'm out of the robbing and all that. I'm putting the Scorcher away. I want to work with you guys to stop aggression like what almost happened from happening. I'll go underground. I'll go to Latveria. I'll hit the--
S.H.I.E.L.D. AGENT JASPER SITWELL
Uh-huh.
HUDAK
Are you listening to me? I want in. I want to help. I got mad skills. I got years on me. You think there's more to all of this? I want to help. I want to repay my debt to you guys.
S.H.I.E.L.D. AGENT JASPER SITWELL
You'd go underground? You'd go to Latveria?
HUDAK
Yeah, I said, yeah.
S.H.I.E.L.D. AGENT JASPER SITWELL
You know, a couple of your peers, they asked for the same thing. A similar thing in exchange for freedom.
HUDAK
I ain't askin' to cop a deal. I'm telling you I'll just do it to do it. Who? Which others? I'm telling the truth. I'll do it.
S.H.I.E.L.D. AGENT JASPER SITWELL
Oh, I know you're telling the truth. We have all kinds of ways of knowing.
(Agent Jasper Sitwell exits the hospital room.)
HUDAK
So what then?
S.H.I.E.L.D. AGENT JASPER SITWELL
We're thinking about it.
(End transcript)

See file folder OPERATION: CROSSFIRE

cc: S.H.I.E.L.D. DIRECTOR MARIA HILL

S.H.I.E.L.D. DOCUMENT 9996369-31231 USPRSDNT

AGENT DATABASE >> AGENT SCREENINGS >> WHITE HOUSE TRANSCRIPT
SECRET CODE: WHITE
S.H.I.E.L.D. Presidential Briefing
Subject: Acting S.H.I.E.L.D. Director Maria Hill. First meeting with President
Recording date: 4/15/2007
Place: White House Situation Room - West Wing

S.H.I.E.L.D. COMMANDER MARIA HILL
Mister President.
PRESIDENT
Ms. Hill. It is a pleasure to meet you. Finally.
S.H.I.E.L.D. COMMANDER MARIA HILL
Thank you, sir. Will the secretary be joining us?
PRESIDENT
No. No, I wanted to talk to you man-to-man, as it were.
S.H.I.E.L.D. COMMANDER MARIA HILL
Yes, sir.
PRESIDENT
Feeling a bit out of your skin lately?
S.H.I.E.L.D. COMMANDER MARIA HILL
Yes, sir. You could say that, sir.
PRESIDENT
My first three months in office were like a fever dream.
S.H.I.E.L.D. COMMANDER MARIA HILL
Yes, sir.
PRESIDENT
I'm here to help you help the world. Whatever you need, whatever's on your mind.
S.H.I.E.L.D. COMMANDER MARIA HILL
OK, um...why me sir? Why was I chosen to run S.H.I.E.L.D? There's—as far as I can see—and this isn't humility—there's a dozen people in line to succeed Fury. I have no idea how my name even came into—
PRESIDENT
Those people were Fury loyalists. And I've had enough of that in my lifetime.
S.H.I.E.L.D. COMMANDER MARIA HILL
Yes, sir.
PRESIDENT
You did a great job in Madripoor. It's a crap detail and you did a great job. We've had our eye on you for a couple of years now.
S.H.I.E.L.D. COMMANDER MARIA HILL
Thank you, sir.
PRESIDENT
I know that a year ago you were courted.
S.H.I.E.L.D. COMMANDER MARIA HILL
Yes, sir.
PRESIDENT
We thought that Fury was going to have to go then, but he held on. Bastard always found a way to hold on.
S.H.I.E.L.D. COMMANDER MARIA HILL
Yes, sir. Why was that, sir? Why after the situation in Latveria was Fury allowed to continue on?
PRESIDENT
Well, this is it—see, he created a situation that—if we were to let him go or court-martial him, or whatever the thing they call it when we

S.H.I.E.L.D.
OPERATIONS DATABASE

HOME ADVANCED SEARCH DATABASES LOG OUT

S.H.I.E.L.D. DOCUMENT 9996369-31231 USPRSDNT [Cont.]

oust one of you guys, that the whole thing would have gone public. So we either had to back him and cover it, or we had to publicly admit we lost all control of things. It's a tough choice, it makes for sleepless nights. But y'see what I mean? Fury's little tantrum. We couldn't answer the public the hows and whys. We just couldn't. It's too technical. It was better to sit him back behind his desk and turn the spin machine on. Thankfully most of the world doesn't rightly care what's happening down the street, let alone half a world away in some tiny backwards thingamadoo. Think he kind of knew that too-Fury. Which really twists my twister.

S.H.I.E.L.D. COMMANDER MARIA HILL

See, I thought then that it was just a misunderstanding that—

PRESIDENT

Let's skip all that now. Let's talk about you. This appointment is a serious one. Doesn't get much more serious. One that the U.N. and world leaders take very seriously. You're serving the world peace now, Director. The world's safety is actually in your hands.

S.H.I.E.L.D. COMMANDER MARIA HILL

I'll do everything in my power to—

PRESIDENT

But you're also an American.

S.H.I.E.L.D. COMMANDER MARIA HILL

Yes, sir.

PRESIDENT

Where are you from, Director?

S.H.I.E.L.D. COMMANDER MARIA HILL

Chicago.

PRESIDENT

Chicago!! American through and through.

S.H.I.E.L.D. COMMANDER MARIA HILL

Yes, sir.

PRESIDENT

I was hoping, Director, though you'll clearly need to keep the world's safety as your primary concern, that being an American citizen, you and I could have a robust relationship.

S.H.I.E.L.D. COMMANDER MARIA HILL

Yes, sir. I would like that, sir.

PRESIDENT

Honesty and forthrightness.

S.H.I.E.L.D. COMMANDER MARIA HILL

Yes, sir.

PRESIDENT

Good, good, I knew I backed the right horse here. Good for you. So, anything you need to discuss here? Anything I can do to help make the transition—

S.H.I.E.L.D. COMMANDER MARIA HILL

Well, sir. Yes, actually.

PRESIDENT

Shoot.

S.H.I.E.L.D. COMMANDER MARIA HILL

Fury's secret war.

PRESIDENT

Nnff. Anything else?

S.H.I.E.L.D. COMMANDER MARIA HILL

Sir, why did he do it?

PRESIDENT

I don't know.

SEARCH DATABASE SECRET WAR SEARCH

S.H.I.E.L.D. DOCUMENT 9996369-31231 USPRSONT (Cont.)

S.H.I.E.L.D. COMMANDER MARIA HILL

May I ask why you were reluctant to move on the intel he presented to you? I'm not pointing fingers. I'm just trying to understand my job.

PRESIDENT

We were going to use the information to put Lucia in her place. We were going to blackmail her with it. You see, that region, for as long as the world has turned, has been oppressed by people like that Victor Von Doom. We finally got his arrogant ass out of there, and it's insane to expect total peace and cooperation. They hate us there. It's in their blood. Give them money to rebuild and they only resent you more. Von Bardas was someone we felt we could ultimately control—or at least overpower. Fury jumped the gun. Was he right or wrong? Can't say. But he's a military man and he broke rank. He broke the law to serve who? Eh. I half-wish Doom was back in there. Him I could deal with. At least you knew where he stood. Now we gotta—or I should say you gotta—find out who knew von Bardas was still alive and clean up the loose ends, the money trail. These idiots in the costumes...

S.H.I.E.L.D. COMMANDER MARIA HILL

Yes, sir. Fury thought that—

PRESIDENT

I know what Fury thought. You know what I think? I think Fury's old and tired. And-and all that juice he's been taking to keep himself alive so long, I think it's made him goofy.

S.H.I.E.L.D. COMMANDER MARIA HILL

Yes, sir. But Fury is—

PRESIDENT

Missing. Yes. I know.

S.H.I.E.L.D. COMMANDER MARIA HILL

How important is it to you that we find him?

PRESIDENT

I'm not going to answer that question, Director. That's your call. But I think—we all think—Fury's gonna stay lost as long as he wants to stay lost. He kinda, from what I understand, wrote the book on it.

S.H.I.E.L.D. COMMANDER MARIA HILL

Yes, sir.

PRESIDENT

I tell ya—I more than hope we find him in a bathtub with a face full of bullets and pills. Hope he puts himself out of our misery. As far as this Latverian situation, don't forget, it's one of twelve I have to deal with every day. You understand? There's a bigger picture. There's larger considerations. You figure that out fast, will you do that for me?

S.H.I.E.L.D. COMMANDER MARIA HILL

Um, I think so.

PRESIDENT

Good, I'm glad we had this talk. One more thing...

S.H.I.E.L.D. COMMANDER MARIA HILL

Yes, sir?

PRESIDENT

The costumes.

S.H.I.E.L.D. COMMANDER MARIA HILL

The super heroes?

PRESIDENT

I don't like them. Never have, never will. I was half willing to let all this secret war crap out in the open just to bury a few of them. My point is that the less I hear your name and the word "costume" in the same sentence...the happier I'll be. And I speak for the rest of my peers. You get me?

S.H.I.E.L.D. COMMANDER MARIA HILL

Yes, sir.

PRESIDENT

Good girl.

(End transcript)- code fghsth-4534gev

.H.I.E.L.D.
ERATIONS DATABASE

S.H.I.E.L.D.
OPERATIONS DATABASE

CLOSING & SEALING FILE...

CANCEL

MARVEL
PSR
SPECIAL EDITION

SECRET WAR

FROM THE FILES OF NICK FURY

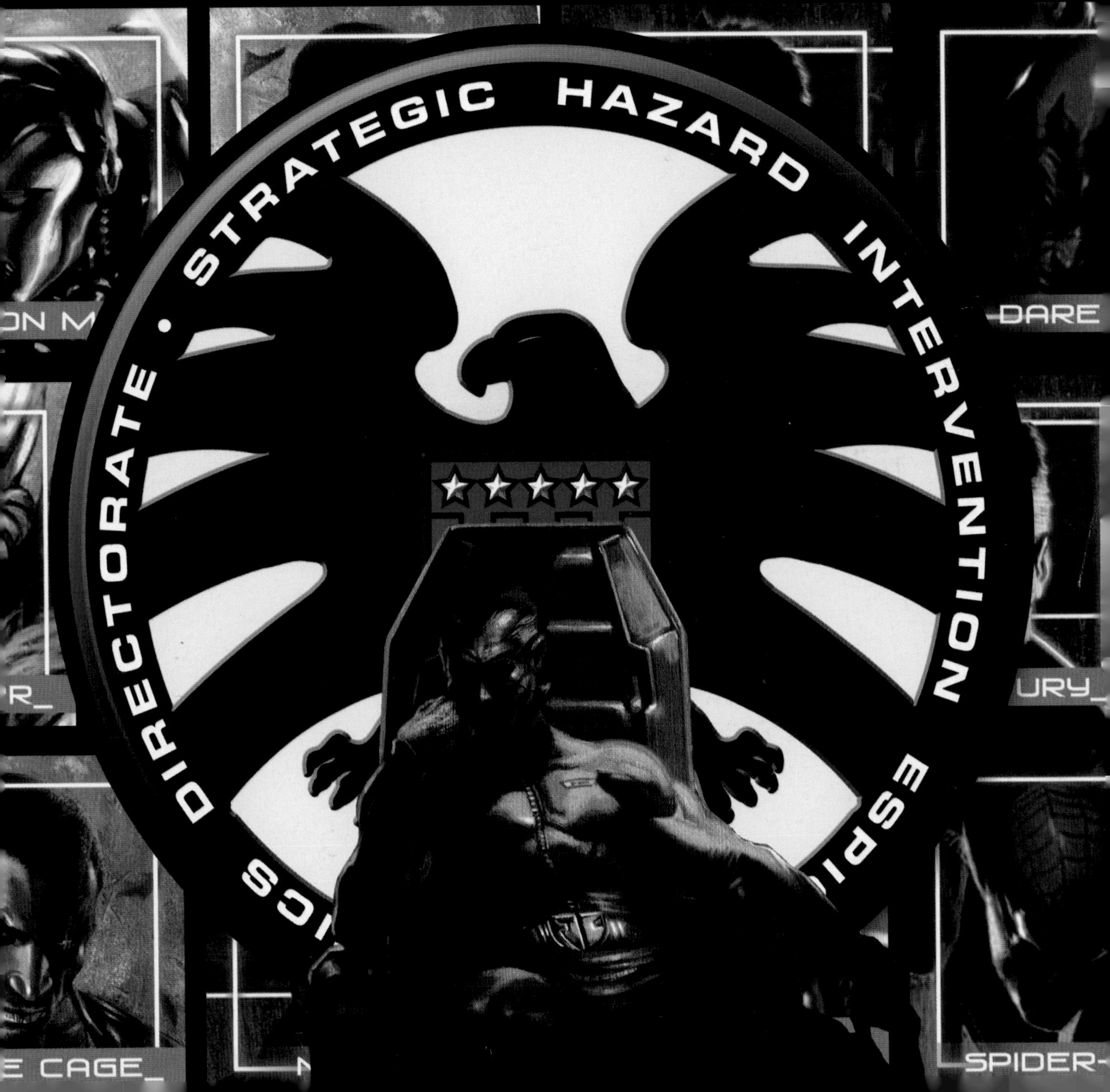
DIRECTORATE • STRATEGIC HAZARD INTERVENTION ESPI
ICS
ON M
DARE
R_
URY_
E CAGE_
SPIDER-

STAN LEE PRESENTS

THOR
IRON MAN
LUKE CAGE
NICK FURY
DAREDEVIL
CAPTAIN AMERICA

A MARVEL COMICS PRODUCTION

SECRET WAR

MIKE RAICHT
WRITER

GABRIELE DELL'OTTO
PAINTER

BRIAN MICHAEL BENDIS
INSPIRATION

JEFF CHRISTIANSEN
STUART VANDAL
MICHAEL HOSKIN
MARK O'ENGLISH
RONALD BYRD
SEAN MCQUAID
AGENTS OF S.H.I.E.L.D. (LEVEL 1)

JENNIFER GRÜNWALD
ASSISTANT EDITOR

JEFF YOUNGQUIST
EDITOR

DAVID GABRIEL
DIRECTOR OF SALES

TOM BREVOORT & ANDY SCHMIDT
CONSULTING EDITORS

CARRIE BEADLE
BOOK DESIGNER

PATRICK MCGRATH
COVER & S.H.I.E.L.D. DATABASE DESIGNER

TOM MARVELLI
CREATIVE DIRECTOR

JOE QUESADA
EDITOR IN CHIEF

DAN BUCKLEY
PUBLISHER

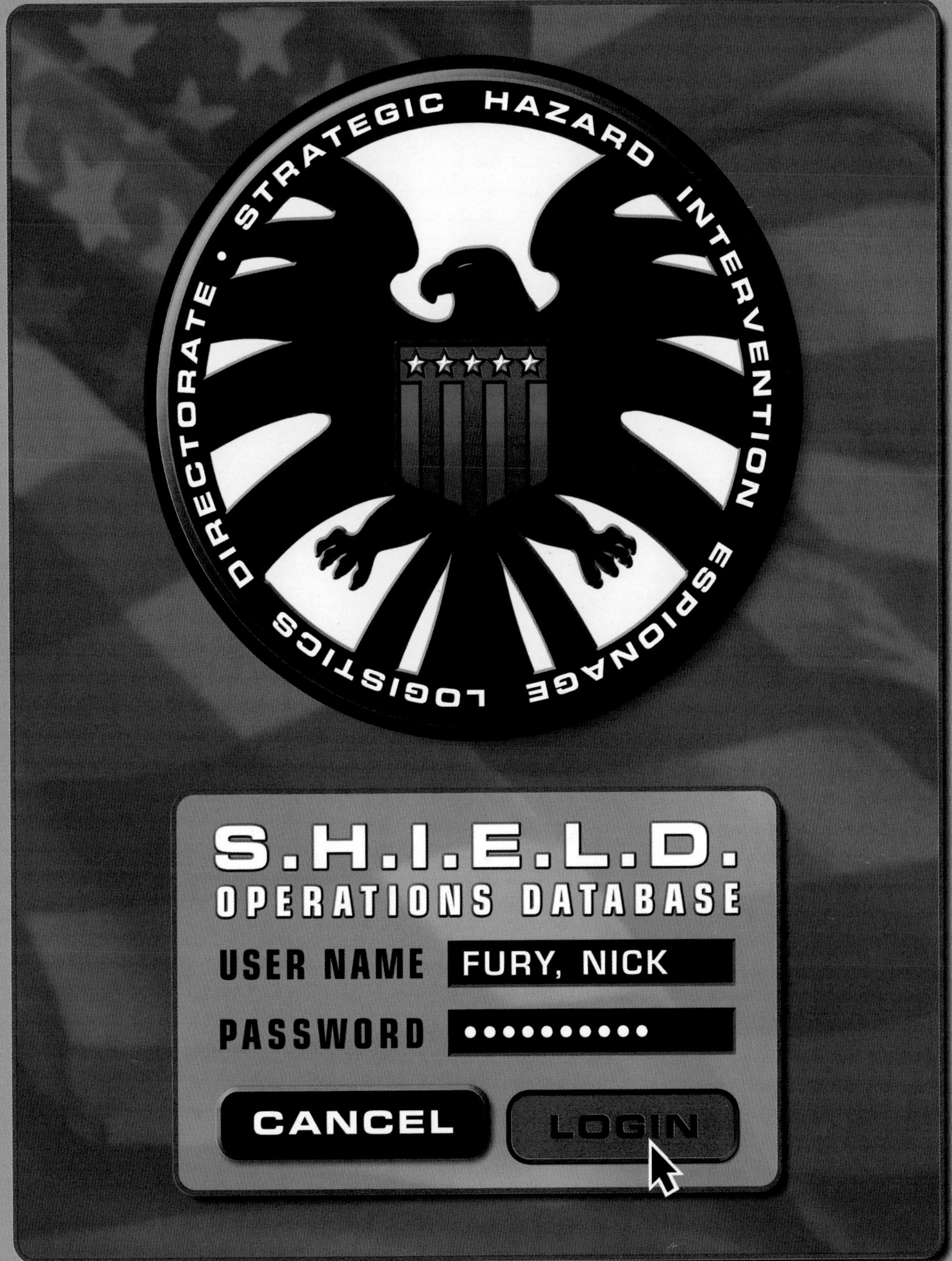
STRATEGIC HAZARD INTERVENTION ESPIONAGE LOGISTICS DIRECTORATE
S.H.I.E.L.D.
OPERATIONS DATABASE
USER NAME
FURY, NICK
PASSWORD
••••••••••
CANCEL
LOGIN

S.H.I.E.L.D. OPERATIONS DATABASE

HOME | ADVANCED SEARCH | DATABASES | LOG OUT

S.H.I.E.L.D. FILE >> MEMO TO UNITED STATES SECURITY COUNSEL
DOCUMENT >> 439991-972RF >> S.H.I.E.L.D. OPERATION REQUEST FORM
CODENAME: CIRCUIT

LEVEL 10 — REQUEST MADE BY S.H.I.E.L.D. DIRECTOR NICK FURY
SECONDARY LEVEL 9 — REQUEST MADE BY S.H.I.E.L.D. DEPUTY DIRECTOR VALENTINA ALLEGRO DE FONTAINE

OPERATION DESCRIPTION:

It has recently come to S.H.I.E.L.D.'s attention that various technologically advanced villains (TAVs) have been dealing exclusively with the Tinkerer (see attached Phineas Mason file 6305021-03TNK) when in need of upgrades and repairs. These repairs are above and beyond the monetary resources available to TAVs and it is obvious the Tinkerer is trading his services for favors from these villains. According to recorded interrogation testimony (see attached), the Tinkerer is apparently working for a mysterious backer. Recently, the Tinkerer was spotted in Latveria meeting with Prime Minister Lucia von Bardas. S.H.I.E.L.D. requests the resources necessary to investigate Bardas and Latveria, and prevent any offensive actions against the United States or the rest of the world.

Colonel Nick Fury
Director of S.H.I.E.L.D.

REQUEST DENIED:
PURSUE DIPLOMATIC CHANNELS

NICK FURY NOTE **— If that's how it has to be, then that's how it has to be. No S.H.I.E.L.D. No Avengers. We do this the hard way.**

PHILADELPHIA ENQUIRER ARTICLE
By Nancy Buczak
MAN ELECTROCUTED BY ALIENS IN DOWNTOWN PHILLY
— FLYING MEN SPOTTED ON SCENE

Eyewitnesses described "men and women with rocket packs" flying onto the scene after a man was seemingly electrocuted on the front steps of a local apartment building. This is similar to an event that occurred in early 2001 one block over. The man, described only as a white male in his early 30s, was whisked away by the aliens before anyone could come to his aid. "They had flying cars and were dressed in human suits," said Jason Sitwell, who was in a local bar when the incident occurred. "They were taller than normal humans. I didn't hear them talking."

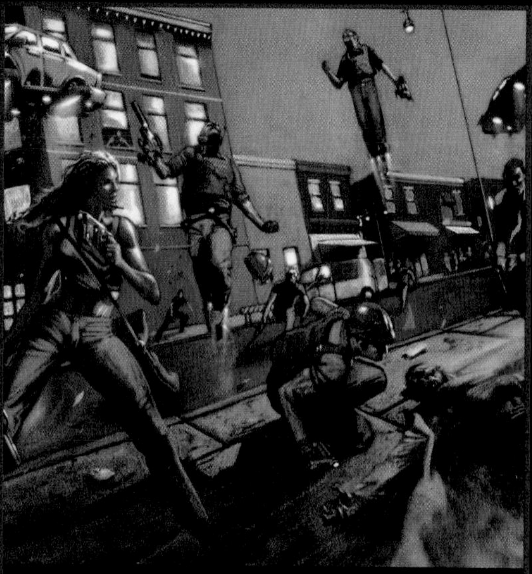

NICK FURY NOTE **— Thank former Special Agent Johnny Rogers, Philly Enquirer Editor, for covering for us. He was always the best at media control. Speak with Woo and Sitwell about the handling of this operation. Not good. Maybe they should stay in the interrogation room? Jasper Sitwell needs to keep his quotes shorter. He has a little too much fun with this at times. Make sure from now on he doesn't just change his first name. Sloppy.**

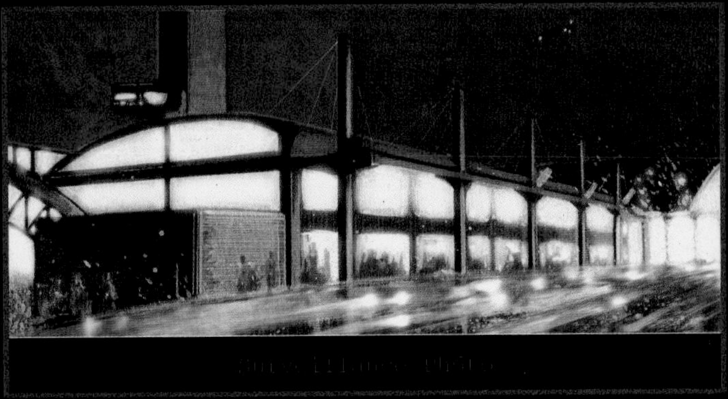

DAILY BUGLE ARTICLE

By Julie Slott

UNDER THE CAPES — SUPER HERO BEAT

It's been a busy week for mutant media mongrels so, without further ado…

Alison Blaire, the one-time mutant superstar known better as the Dazzler, was seen at Club M. Did she leave with a certain local cop who works the streets of Mutant Town? Are they an item? Or was this strictly a business call?

Steve Rogers, Mr. Captain America himself, was seen boarding a plane early Friday morning. The plane was on its way to Latveria. An unnamed source from the airlines revealed resident Hero for Hire and Harlem bruiser Luke Cage was also on board. What type of vacation could they possibly be on in Latveria?

What tiny super hero was seen with her ex-husband at the grand opening of a super-chic restaurant? We'll only give you one Giant guess to figure out the answer to this stinging question…

NICK FURY NOTE **— "Under the Capes"? Their @$$es are under the capes! Not the best choice of titles…under the masks, maybe…**

And an email from Kat Farrell to Robbie Robertson…

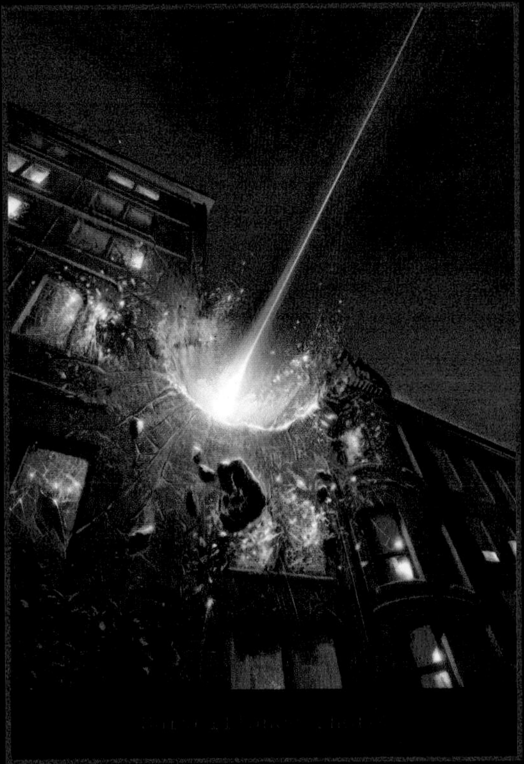

-----Original Message-----

From:	**Farrell, Kat**
Sent:	**Thursday, February 12, 2004 5:17 PM**
To:	**Robertson, Joseph**
Cc:	**Urich, Ben**
Subject:	**Bring on the Bad Guys?**

Robbie,

Working on this for tomorrow? I know it's too late for the morning edition but maybe an Extra later in the day?

1ST DRAFT
VILLAINS RAGE ACROSS CITY
HEROES INJURED IN ATTACK

Local super hero and former Hero for Hire Luke Cage was injured in an explosion at his Harlem home according to neighbors. At approximately the same time, Steve Rogers, Captain America, was attacked as well. Are these two attacks connected?

Explosions were reported at Matt Murdock's apartment, too. Some eyewitnesses report seeing Spider-Man and Daredevil moments later fighting with two unidentified villains at approximately the same time. Do we want to include this? With the litigation currently going on between Murdock and our distinguished competition, do we want to make a claim that would imply a similar belief on our part?

— Kat

S.H.I.E.L.D. FILE >> NYPD DISPATCHER RECORDING ...

SGT. GREG WIMMER

Ted? Are you getting reports of a disturbance at Mt. Sinai Hospital and the piers out that way? I can see smoke and I—

DISPATCH OFFICER TED LING

Yeah. We've got quite a few calls. I think you're the third officer but, yeah... calls are coming in pretty heavy, civilian and blue, right now.

SGT. GREG WIMMER

Well, Katie and I are en route. Any suggestions before we get there?

OFFICER TED LING

No. We don't have much information at this time. Just be careful out there. Super heroes are involved.

SGT. GREG WIMMER

Well, hopefully they'll have things figured out before we-- WHOA! (rumble heard in the background)

OFFICER TED LING

Greg! You okay?

SGT. GREG WIMMER

Yeah, we're okay. Um, I think Iron Man just flew over.

OFFICER KATIE LAYTON (BARELY AUDIBLE)

Yeah. It was Iron Man. I've seen him over Avengers Mansion —

SGT. GREG WIMMER

We better get over there. It looks —

OFFICER TED LING

Greg, hold up. We're being told to stand down. The situation has gone to hell over there. Just act as crowd control. Keep people away from the docks and get anyone who can't lift a building at least 10 blocks away from what's going on.

SGT. GREG WIMMER

Okay. No problem. Sounds like a good idea. (explosion heard in background) Jeez... I think we'll make it 15 blocks.

OFFICER TED LING

Sounds like a plan. Check in soon.

SGT. GREG WIMMER

Will do.

END OF DISPATCH

SEARCH DATABASE

OPERATIVES, SECRET WAR | **SEARCH**

ICK FURY'S PRIVATE JOURNAL
VEL 1 0— CLEARANCE (Fury Only)
SER NAME: FURY, NICK
ASSWORD: ———

Who can I trust?

It's not an easy question to answer. I've worked with so many heroes. So many men and women who have powers far beyond those of us "normals". And most of them noble beyond words. For the most part. How do you decide which ones are the best for a particular mission? Do I go with pure power? Leadership? Do I chance using some of our super S.H.I.E.L.D. agents? And what would happen to their careers if we're found out?

Do I chance calling in a favor from one of my wildcard agents? Logan is one of the best but are his antics worth the results? And how will the rest of the team respond to him? How will I if he goes too far? Is this even a mission where "too far" is a factor? And what about someone like Parker? He's been a loner for so long, will he be able to adjust to working with a team?

On top of everything, this mission is something different. Something I need to keep quiet… secret. A Secret War against whatever the Tinkerer and Latveria have going on. Who would have thought a man like the Tinkerer, or a Latveria minus Doom for that matter, would cause me this much trouble. And who would think the United States would choose to turn its head the other way and allow something like this… and a possible terrorist action… to go unchecked. The more things change the more they remain the same.

My first choice is obviously Rogers. All the heroes will follow his lead. He's an inspiration to most of them. But from there, where do I turn? And will they all be willing to carry this type of mission to its conclusion? And can I trust them to stay quiet afterwards?

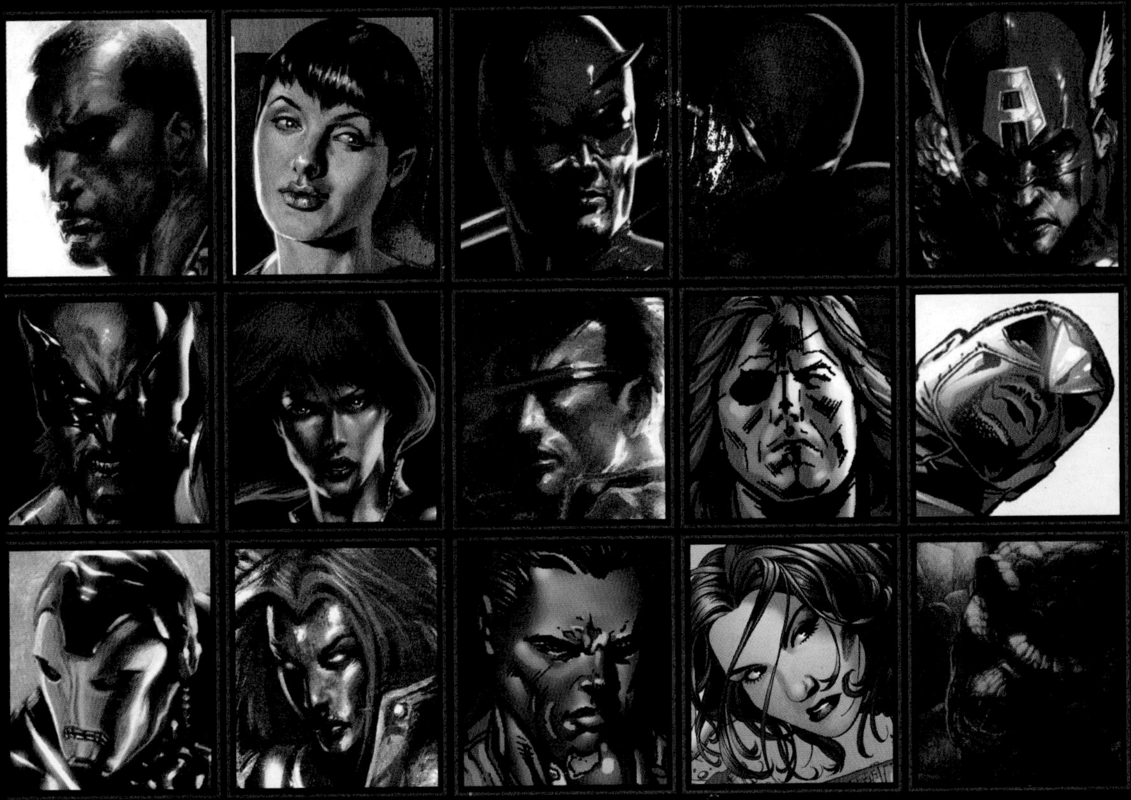

S.H.I.E.L.D.
OPERATIONS DATABASE

HOME | ADVANCED SEARCH | DATABASES | LOG OUT

S.H.I.E.L.D. FILE NUMBER 4545587-34LKC

REAL NAME: Carl Lucas, legally changed to Luke Cage

ALIASES: Hero for Hire (former) Power Man, Mark Lucas, Ace of Spades, others

IDENTITY STATUS: Public

MARITAL STATUS: Single

RELATIVES: James Leonard Lucas (father), Esther Lucas (mother, deceased), James Lucas, Jr. (Coldfire, brother, deceased), unborn child

BASE OF OPERATIONS: Harlem, New York City; (former) Chicago, Illinois; Seagate Prison

PLACE OF BIRTH: New York City

LEGAL STATUS: American citizen acquitted of criminal charges

OCCUPATION: Hero for hire; (former) Bar owner, theater owner, private investigator, various odd jobs

AFFILIATIONS: Heroes for Hire Inc.; (former) Daredevil's unnamed team; Secret Defenders, Nightwing Restorations, Fantastic Four, Defenders, Bloods

ENEMIES: Diamondback (Willis Stryker, deceased), Gideon Mace, Master Khan, Constrictor, Bushmaster / Powermaster, Hardcore, Purple Man, Shades & Comanche

HEIGHT: 6 ' 6" **WEIGHT:** 425 lbs. **EYES:** Brown **HAIR:** Black

POWERS/WEAPONS: Power level 8. Superhuman strength, dense muscle and bone tissue. Steel-hard skin.

NICK FURY NOTE: Cage will take money from anyone on the planet except me for services rendered, but he has an intense sense of patriotism and duty that can easily be manipulated. But only for the right kind of mission. He has a tendency to do interviews.

LEVEL 10 - EXTENDED NOTES

This man has pulled himself up by his bootstraps and made something of himself. Luke Cage spent time in prison for a crime he was framed for. He could have become a criminal but he didn't. During his time in prison, Cage volunteered for a questionable scientific test—based on the process that empowered Mitchell Tanner--that gave him incredible abilities. This test has been attempted on subsequent subjects, occasionally yielding similar results.

Cage was eventually cleared and pardoned. Instead of leaving his Harlem community behind – a community that most heroes would leave to the law – he has become a hero there. I respect that. Does he use questionable methods? Yes. Does he get results? Yes. I like that and it is the exact reason he is a man to go to when I need someone who doesn't mind getting a little dirty. Despite his numerous run-ins with the law as a youth, he respects those who are trying to truly make a difference. But he can not stand those who are trying to work an angle. It's best to give him the straight deal from the beginning because if he finds out he's been played... well, he will lose it. And he holds a grudge. A man with Cage's strength and ability is not someone you want to see lose it.

But will he play well with others? Can he be a team player? I say yes. He teamed with Danny Rand as a Hero For Hire, a little ridiculous but they were effective. Eventually their partnership ended. I truly believe he wants to prove himself and play with the big boys. I trust him to come through in the clutch... if only to prove everyone wrong.

NOTE: Recently Cage has renewed a romance with Jessica Jones, and she is pregnant with his child. Where this leads remains to be seen. Keep both of them under surveillance.

SEARCH DATABASE OPERATIVES, SECRET WAR SEARCH

S.H.I.E.L.D. FILE NUMBER 9283112-89DJ

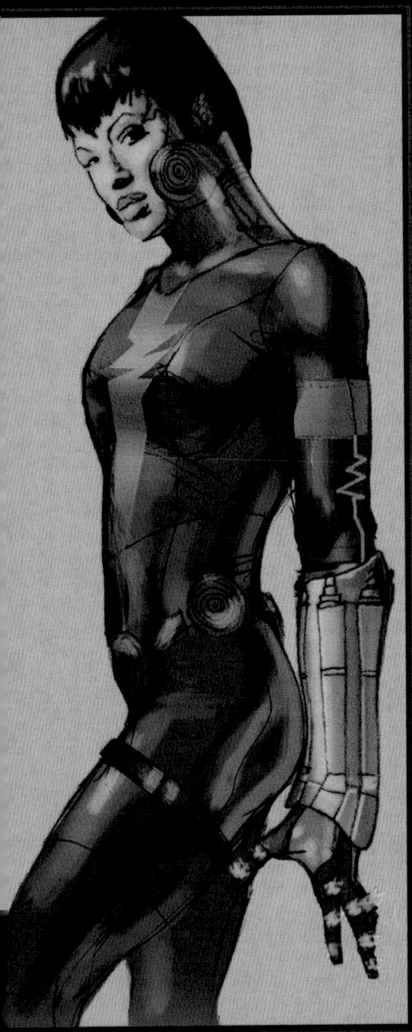

REAL NAME: Daisy Johnson

ALIASES: Cory Sutter (adoptive parents renamed her)

IDENTITY STATUS: Classified

MARITAL STATUS: Single

RELATIVES: Jennifer Johnson (mother), Calvin Zabo (Mister Hyde, father), Gregory and Janet Sutter (adoptive parents)

BASE OF OPERATIONS: S.H.I.E.L.D.

PLACE OF BIRTH: New Orleans, Louisiana

LEGAL STATUS: American citizen with no criminal record

OCCUPATION: S.H.I.E.L.D. Agent

AFFILIATIONS: S.H.I.E.L.D.

ENEMIES: D-Generation, Yi Yang, Arnim Zola

HEIGHT: 5' 9" WEIGHT: 135 lbs. EYES: Blue HAIR: Black

POWERS/WEAPONS: Power level 7, mutant with seismic powers, able to create earthquakes on a large scale

NICK FURY NOTE: Daisy has been an ideal operative since her recruitment. I usually wouldn't turn to a raw recruit like this for something so important but the girl has talent. And she's been itching for a chance to use her abilities. I hate to admit I've been grooming her for something like this but it's true. Eventually in secret ops work you even have to keep the operation secret from the guys in charge. I just hope she's ready for this.

LEVEL 10 - EXTENDED NOTES

S.H.I.E.L.D. Agent Daisy Johnson had quite a life sprung on her. And I did the springing. Looking back over the transcripts I feel a little bad about the way things went down. I could have used a little more tact but that's never been my strong suit. It was clear from the situation she was in when I picked her up that she needed a reality check. Shoplifting. Failing out of school. An IQ off the charts. If getting arrested wasn't going to shake her out of her situation then being interrogated by the head of S.H.I.E.L.D. was going to, I guess.

Johnson took to her training well. She showed a real aptitude for it. Especially the black ops angle. The girl would have finished at the top of her class even without her extra talent for seismic disruption. I'm glad we found her first because she had some serious pent up anger inside of her and who knows how she could have ended up. As far as our super-powered agents go she's one of the best.

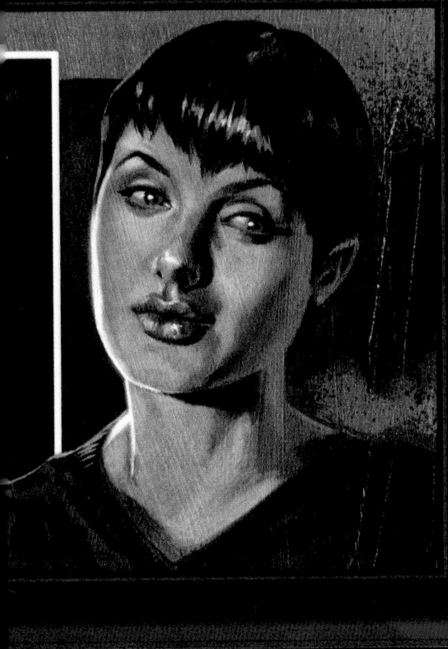

She's strong mentally. Regardless of her father's background it doesn't appear as if any of his baggage traveled down the genetic tree. Something did though, and it's an awesome power (Apparently Zabo had been experimenting on himself for years before facing Thor). An earthquake could really come in handy during some of our more intense missions. Imagine the surprise a mark will feel when he's not only being overrun by S.H.I.E.L.D. but the attack follows an earthquake. You can't create that kind of weapon... well, maybe someone like von Doom could, but you get me.

I do admit I feel a little guilt about involving a girl so young in our operations. But if I didn't scoop her up someone else would have. And it's better she work on our side than anyone else's. Let's just hope I don't live to regret it.

S.H.I.E.L.D. OPERATIONS DATABASE

HOME | ADVANCED SEARCH | DATABASES | LOG OUT

S.H.I.E.L.D. FILE NUMBER 535345-566DD

REAL NAME: Matthew Michael Murdock

ALIASES: Daredevil, Man without Fear, Kingpin; (former) Laurent LeVasseur, Jack Batlin, Nameless One, Red Man, Mike Murdock, several others

IDENTITY STATUS: Publicly Disputed

MARITAL STATUS: Marriage disputed

RELATIVES: Jonathan "Battlin' Jack" Murdock (father, deceased), Margaret Grace Murdock (mother), Milla Donovan (wife, disputed)

BASE OF OPERATIONS: Hell's Kitchen, New York City; (former) San Francisco, California

PLACE OF BIRTH: Hell's Kitchen, New York City

LEGAL STATUS: Citizen of the United States. No criminal record

OCCUPATION: Lawyer

AFFILIATIONS: Natasha Romanoff aka Black Widow; (former) led unnamed team

ENEMIES: Kingpin, Owl, Purple Man, Mister Fear (all incarnations), Stilt Man, Gladiator (Melvin Potter & his successor), Bullseye, Typhoid Mary

HEIGHT: 6' WEIGHT: 200 lbs. EYES: Blue HAIR: Red

POWERS/WEAPONS: Power level 7. Superhuman senses. All senses register at a high level. Acute radar sense. Olympic athlete and gymnast. Ninja, martial arts training. Highly effective in combat with his customized billy-club.

NICK FURY NOTE: Murdock straddles the line between enforcing the law and upholding justice. Perfect for certain types of covert ops. Black Widow has him wrapped around her finger; important to note for future.

LEVEL 10 - EXTENDED NOTES

Murdock has run into a bit of bad luck recently. Actually, if I'm being truthful while looking over his entire file, his whole life has been a run of bad luck. Murdock lost his eyesight when he was a child in a freak accident. His father, a professiona boxer, and girlfriend Karen Page were both murdered, and an earlier girlfrienc committed suicide after he broke up with her. All years apart, but how much tragedy can one man endure?

Now The Daily Globe has "outed" Murdock as the super hero named Daredevil. He's denying it and I don't blame him. The general public doesn't need to know his business and you'd think being blind for most of your life would be a pretty convincing disguise. We traced the information leak to FBI agent Henry Dobbs who has since vanished, but Murdock has been forced to continue the public denial of his dual existence.

The one thing you learn about Murdock by looking over his past is that he perseveres. Anyone else might have let the loss of their eyesight stop them from becoming more. Now, granted, Murdock's senses have adjusted to a superhuman level, but that didn't make him a lawyer or a super hero. And, just like Luke Cage, he's returned to his roots. He could have relocated anywhere as a super hero but he chose to take his skills as a lawyer and a hero to the streets of Hell's Kitchen. Not a place where it is easy to tell the good guys from the bac guys most days. And he does it everyday. Without fail. That's the type of guy I want by my side behind enemy lines.

Murdock has worked with S.H.I.E.L.D. against Wilson Fisk a.k.a. the Kingpin in the past. Murdock's record with Fisk is well documented and his anger towards him has clouded his judgment in the past. He has, at times, taken drastic steps to make changes in Hell's Kitchen and to usurp the Kingpin's rule. Hopefully, he'll have the strength to not succumb to that temptation in the future.

S.H.I.E.L.D. FILE NUMBER 69678-616SPI

REAL NAME: Peter Benjamin Parker (Classified)

ALIASES: Spider-Man; (former) Captain Universe, Mr. Cartwright, Dusk, Hornet, Mr. Jameson, Mad Dog 336, Man-Spider, Prodigy, Ricochet, Mr. Simmons, Spider-Hulk, Spider-Lizard, Spider-Morphosis, others

IDENTITY STATUS: Secret

MARITAL STATUS: Married

RELATIVES: Richard and Mary Parker (parents, deceased), Mary Jane Watson-Parker (wife), Ben Parker (uncle, deceased), May Parker (aunt), May (daughter, presumed deceased), Will Fitzpatrick (maternal grandfather), Horace Reilly (great uncle), Harold and Roger Reilly (cousins)

BASE OF OPERATIONS: New York City; (former) Portland, Oregon

PLACE OF BIRTH: Queens, New York City

LEGAL STATUS: American citizen with no criminal record

OCCUPATION: Freelance photographer, teacher

AFFILIATIONS: Avengers; (former) Secret Defenders, alternate Fantastic Four, Outlaws, Black Cat partner

ENEMIES: Green Goblin (Norman & Harry Osborn), Dr. Octopus (Otto Octavius), Electro (Max Dillon), Sandman (William Baker), Vulture (Adrian Toomes), Mysterio (Quentin Beck, Dan Berkhart), Kraven (Sergei & Alyosha Kravinoff), Chameleon, Venom

HEIGHT: 5' 10"   **WEIGHT:** 165 lbs.   **EYES:** Hazel   **HAIR:** Brown

POWERS/WEAPONS: Power level 8. Subject was bitten by a spider that was involved in radioactive experiments. The irradiated spider venom gave him his powers: strength, speed, agility, and the ability to stick to walls. Spider-sense -- a built-in radar that warns him of immediate personal danger. Homemade web-shooters: Twin wrist spinneret mechanisms that shoot thin strands of a special "web fluid." The web fluid is a sheer-thinning liquid that turns solid on contact.

NICK FURY NOTE: Parker feeds off a staggering guilt that propels him to basically do anything you tell him he has to do. The public perception of him is a big negative. Keep a distance unless absolutely necessary.

LEVEL 10 - EXTENDED NOTES

Another one of our super hero trouble children. For some reason, despite the staggering amount of good he has done in the world, Spider-Man is perceived as public enemy number one by the Daily Bugle. I know J. Jonah Jameson is a bit of a nut but the rest of the world seems not to notice. And if you print something enough, people will believe it. So, in a way, despite the whole masked vigilante thing, I feel sorry for the kid.

His origin is a bit of a mystery. We know he was bitten by a radioactive spider and given crazy abilities, which sounds crazy enough to me... but what forced him to put on the costume? Guilt is our best guess. It appears his uncle, Ben Parker, was murdered in a robbery attempt. Parker, for some reason, feels responsible for this crime. Our Level 9 IRT (Incident Recreation Team) has suggested Peter Parker may have been filming a TV show at the same place and time the robbery took place. What he had to do with the robbery is unclear but I'm convinced he was not party to it. What could have happened that night?

Since then, Parker has taken care of May Parker, his aunt, and seemed to have been able to conceal his identity from her for some time. He spent some time as a photographer for the Bugle. Mostly selling pictures of himself in action as Spider-Man, which were then used as fodder for Jameson's tirades on page one. Does this guy ever catch a break? Recently, Parker has taken on a job as a school science teacher.

We have some recent surveillance which suggests his aunt has uncovered his secret. I'd like the transcript of that one. From what I've discovered about May Parker she's quite the pistol. Either way, Parker has grown up. He's been through so much I wouldn't blame him for giving up the costume and turning his back on New York City. Or at the very least becoming a complete criminal, but he's done none of those things. Of course, he is married to supermodel and actress Mary Jane so his life is not a complete wash, right?

S.H.I.E.L.D. OPERATIONS DATABASE

HOME | ADVANCED SEARCH | DATABASES | LOG OUT

S.H.I.E.L.D. FILE NUMBER 00008643-34CAP

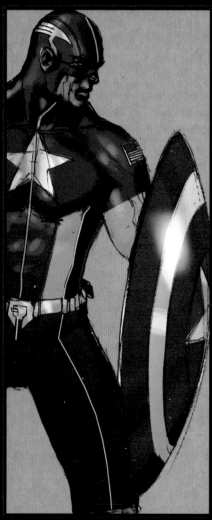

REAL NAME: Steve Rogers

ALIASES: Captain America; (former) Nomad, the Captain; Steven Grant Rogers, Roger Stevens

IDENTITY STATUS: Public

MARITAL STATUS: Single

RELATIVES: Joseph & Sarah Rogers (parents, deceased), grandfather (presumed deceased), Steven Rogers (ancestor, deceased)

BASE OF OPERATIONS: New York City, mobile; (former) European Theater of War; Camp Lehigh, Virginia

PLACE OF BIRTH: New York City

LEGAL STATUS: Citizen of the United States with no criminal record

OCCUPATION: Crimefighter, (former) freelance artist, special S.H.I.E.L.D operative, police officer, teacher, soldier, WPA artist

AFFILIATIONS: Avengers, (former) Redeemers, Secret Defenders, Captain's unnamed unit, S.H.I.E.L.D., Invaders; partner to Bucky (deceased), Nomad, the Falcon, Rick Jones

ENEMIES: Red Skull (Johann Shmidt), Batroc, Baron Zemo (Heinrich & Helmut) M.O.D.O.K., Hydra

HEIGHT: 6' 2" **WEIGHT:** 220 lbs. **EYES:** Blue **HAIR:** Blond

POWERS/WEAPONS: Power level 8: Steve is the product of a military experiment, super soldier Operation: Rebirth, in which he was given the Super Soldier Serum and bombarded with Vita-Rays (wavelengths of radiation). Peak human agility, strength, speed, endurance. Master of the martial arts, boxing judo. Virtually indestructible alloy shield.

NICK FURY NOTE: Cap is the most and least efficient agent. His public persona has become a large problem for stealth work, but for certain types of missions it's the perfect decoy. His patriotism is skewed and out of date. He rarely deals with his anger issues.

LEVEL 10 - EXTENDED NOTES

Imagine being a 100-pound weakling with your country at war. You might not even be able to lift a rifle much less fire it, but you want to make a difference. Would you do anything to pitch in? Maybe take an experimental drug that is supposed to make you the country's greatest soldier? That's what Steve Rogers did. And he fought for his country during its greatest and darkest time. He inspired people when inspiration was needed and then we lost him.

Now imagine waking up one day and finding out you've been asleep for over half a century. You can't. It's impossible. Things change so fast in this world there's no way you could imagine all the changes that may occur in the next few years let alone fifty. That's what Steve Rogers has had to endure and he's persevered the only way he knows how: by being a hero.

He represents everything great about this country at the same time he represents some of its flaws. We live in a country where freedom is fought and died for on a daily basis. And Steve Rogers will fight for what is right. But is he willing to do anything for his country? Should he be?

Steve would argue he wouldn't do anything for his country because anything is not always the right thing. I wish I could have his optimism. I'm not allowed the luxury of always doing the right thing. My world isn't that simple. But I have to say I sleep better at night knowing a person like Steve Rogers is out there. This all sounds like a bunch of "mom and apple pie" type talk but its how I feel. I'm afraid to admit this but sometimes I worry about letting him down. But then I realize I have a job to do and that it's not always a pretty one. I'm not Captain America. That's a blessing and a curse only one man can bear.

SEARCH DATABASE **OPERATIVES, SECRET WAR** SEARCH

S.H.I.E.L.D. FILE NUMBER 3445-765WO

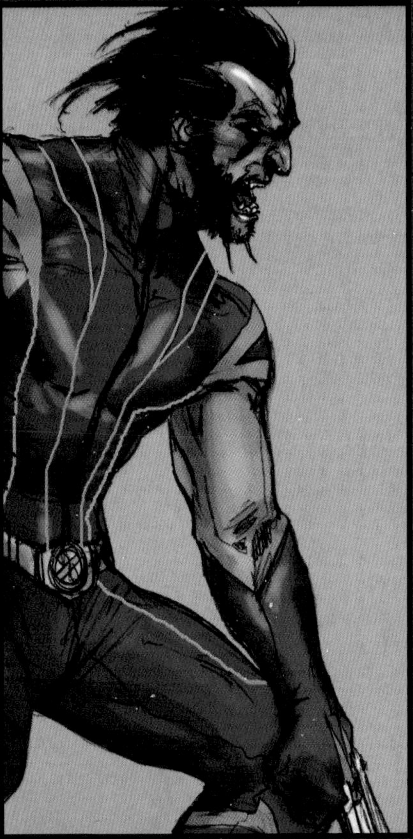

REAL NAME: Unknown

ALIASES: Wolverine, Logan; (former) Weapon X, Patch, Agent Ten, Weapon Ten, Death, Mutate #9601, Jim Logan, Emilio Garra, Weapon Chi, Experiment X, Canada, Peter Richards, otherwise CLASSIFIED

IDENTITY STATUS: Secret

MARITAL STATUS: Divorced

RELATIVES: : Erista (son), Amiko Kobayashi (foster daughter), Viper (ex-wife)

BASE OF OPERATIONS: Xavier Institute for Higher Learning, Westchester, NY; Madripoor, mobile; (former) Canada's Weapon X program and Department H; the Clan Yashida compound in Japan; Reaver's base in Australian Outback

PLACE OF BIRTH: Unknown

LEGAL STATUS: Canadian Citizen

OCCUPATION: Adventurer, member of the X-Men, instructor, spy for several agencies, former C.I.A. operative, bartender, bouncer, mercenary, soldier, otherwise unconfirmed

AFFILIATIONS: X-Men, (former) Horsemen of Apocalypse, Secret Defenders, alternate Fantastic Four, Clan Yashida, Department H, Department K, Weapon X, The Flight, Team X, Devil's Brigade, otherwise unconfirmed

ENEMIES: Sabretooth, Magneto, Lady Deathstrike, Silver Samurai, Cyber (deceased), Ogun, the Hand, Omega Red, the Reavers, Matsu'o Tsurayaba

HEIGHT: 5' 3" WEIGHT: 300 lbs. EYES: Blue HAIR: Black

POWERS/WEAPONS: Power level 9. Mutant. Regenerates damaged or destroyed areas of his body and internal organs. Resistant to poisons and alcohol. Superhumanly acute senses. Adamantium bonded to his entire skeleton. Three 1-foot-long Adamantium claws on each hand which he can "sheathe." Adamantium skeleton result of a top secret Canadian project named Weapon X. Everything concerning Logan's origin is a mystery.

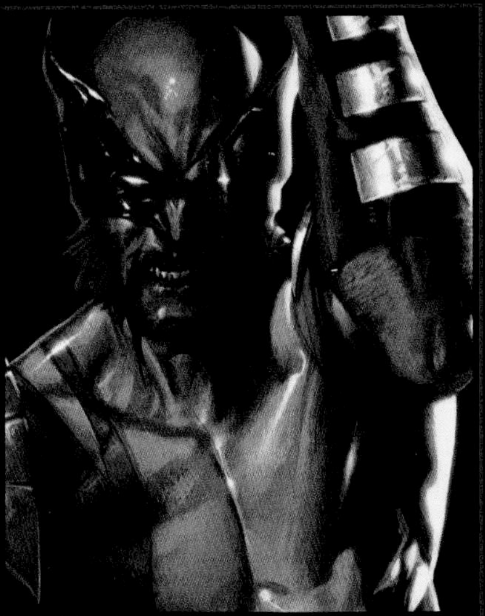

NICK FURY NOTE: Logan is my secret weapon. He owes me his life five times over. His entire persona makes for the perfect ruthless stealth agent. In a perfect world, he would be a level ten S.H.I.E.L.D. Agent.

LEVEL 10 - EXTENDED NOTES

Logan is the biggest mystery in the mutant gene pool. How old is he? Where did he come from? His history is sketchy at best.

The most disappointing thing is he could be by my side as a part of S.H.I.E.L.D. doing more for the world in 24 hours than he does now running around playing hero for the X-Men… That's unnecessarily harsh. The X-Men have saved the day time and time again. I know that. It would just make my job a lot easier knowing which side he was on… not worrying about having to deal with him if, and when, he snaps. Maybe I just want to be the one keeping an eye on him, making sure he doesn't lose it at the wrong moment.

Why is he a potential "rogue" risk? First of all, it appears as if Logan is older than dirt. Even older than me, if you can believe that. And he hasn't aged a day since his run-in with Captain America during World War II. Shortly after the war he disappeared. He eventually resurfaced in the Weapon X program -- a group which tore him down and rebuilt him to be the perfect weapon. They also bonded Adamantium onto his bones. The process drove him insane. Weapon X eventually lost control of him and Logan, driven mad by the experiments he underwent, escaped into the Canadian wilderness. He was then captured by Department H and "reintegrated" into society. He then left them and joined Xavier and his X-troop. See what I'm getting at? He's been all over the map. Who knows how many times his mind has been messed with.

My biggest fear is that he's a bomb… a secret weapon waiting to be cut loose by any number of organizations for their own evil purposes. And it makes me wonder. If he's been messed with so much who knows if Logan's real mind even exists anymore. And if that's the case, why shouldn't S.H.I.E.L.D. get into the game?

S.H.I.E.L.D.
OPERATIONS DATABASE

HOME | ADVANCED SEARCH | DATABASES | LOG OUT

S.H.I.E.L.D. FILE NUMBER 5665656-678W

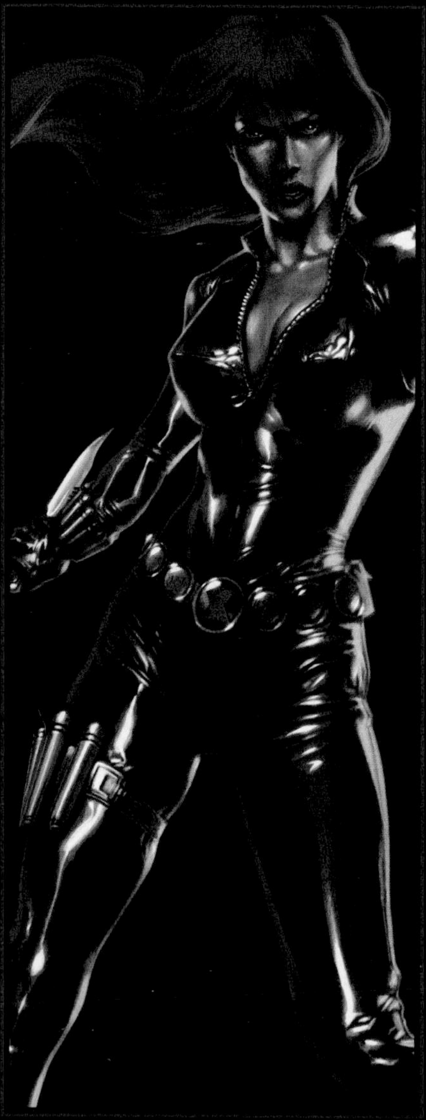

REAL NAME: Natalia Alianovna Romanova

ALIASES: Black Widow, Natasha Romanoff, Nadine Roman, Natalia Shostakova, Nancy Rushman, Laura Matthers, Oktober, Ebon Flame, otherwise CLASSIFIED

IDENTITY STATUS: CLASSIFIED

MARITAL STATUS: Separated

RELATIVES: Alexi Shostakov (Red Guardian, husband), Vindiktor (brother, real name classified); others CLASSIFIED

BASE OF OPERATIONS: Mobile

PLACE OF BIRTH: CLASSIFIED

LEGAL STATUS: CLASSIFIED

OCCUPATION: Spy

AFFILIATIONS: Avengers, S.H.I.E.L.D.; (former) Daredevil's unnamed unit, Champions of Los Angeles, Lady Liberators, partner of Daredevil, Hawkeye, Crimson Dynamo (Boris Turgenov); affiliations of past decades CLASSIFIED

ENEMIES: Bullseye, Damon Dran, Red Guardian; enemies of past decades CLASSIFIED

HEIGHT: 5' 6" **WEIGHT:** 125 lbs. **EYES:** Brown **HAIR:** Red

POWERS/WEAPONS: CLASSIFIED

NICK FURY NOTE: CLASSIFIED

LOG IN
Clearance Code: Fury, Nick
Password: ----------

POWERS/WEAPONS: Level 10 Operative. Power Level 7. Peak physical condition, bracelets which fire "widow's bite," expert in various forms of martial arts, weaponry, and sabotage

LEVEL 10 - EXTENDED NOTES

Professionalism. You'd be surprised how many of the younger agents out there have no idea what I'm talking about when I say that one word. Natasha Romanoff remembers what that word means. But she was around in the old days.

But like all things good and bad, the Cold War ended. At that point, Natasha became a free agent working for the highest bidder. Usually she ended up working on the side of the angels, but nobody's perfect. She even saved my life once. We've all made mistakes, right?

Eventually, Natasha went from being one of the best operatives in the business to a super hero. She held her own as a part of the Avengers for years, even leading them for a time. But she doesn't belong with the super-hero set. She should be behind the scenes with the rest of us spooks. Running in the shadows is what she was born to do. Wearing bright spandex, even though from what I remember she normally wore black, and jumping from building to building was never the best way for her to make a difference. And really, isn't that what the best of us are in this business to do? Make a difference. Right a wrong. Save the world. And then go out on the town in Paris or London. Just thinking of how it used to be gets me misty. Us versus them. Now you can't tell who's working for whom or... I'm getting off track.

Bottom line is the Black Widow is one of the best -- an operative who will get any job done regardless of the difficulty.

NOTE: Natasha has dated a lot of the super-hero set over the years, but Daredevil seems to be the man she was closest to. She even worked as his partner for a time. But like I said, I'm not sure if working as a super hero has ever suited her. This relationship, however, could be used to coerce both of them should the time come when they are needed.

SEARCH DATABASE

OPERATIVES, SECRET WAR — **SEARCH**

S.H.I.E.L.D. FILE NUMBER 6303012-36CX

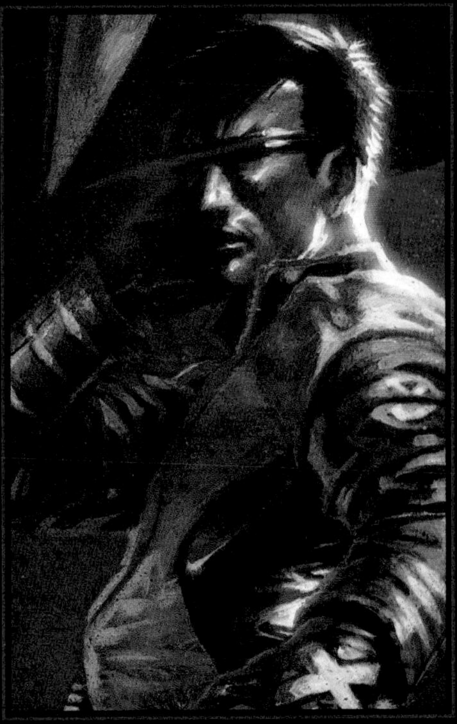

REAL NAME: Scott Summers

ABILITIES: Powel Level 7. Projects a beam of heatless, ruby-colored concussive force from his eyes

HEIGHT: 6' 3" WEIGHT: 195 lbs.

EYES: Brown, glowing red when using his powers HAIR: Brown

NICK FURY NOTE:

Summers is a natural born leader and a master strategist, especially in the heat of the moment. Oddly enough, the less time he has to think and allow doubt to creep in, the better. But he lacks a certain killer instinct this mission may require. Something the Canadian obviously has in spades. Summers is also a bit too reliant on his team. He counts on them as much as they do him. Summers is currently the co-headmaster of the Xavier Institute. His role as leader of the X-Men and the shaper of a new generation of mutant children may be the limit to what he can handle. Plus, according to reports, he is involved with Emma Frost. Who knows what kind of mind games she's been playing in there. We can't chance it. The Frost situation warrants further observation. Having her involved with children again, especially mutant children, is a disaster waiting to happen.

REJECT

S.H.I.E.L.D. FILE NUMBER 7107141-54DS

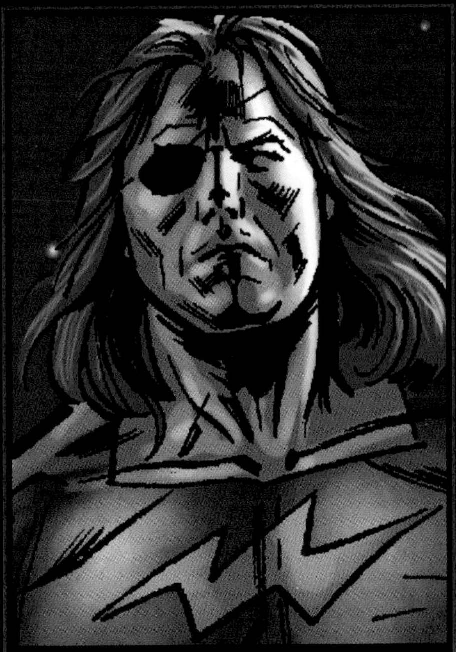

REAL NAME: Leonard Samson

ABILITIES: Power Level 8. Superhuman strength, stamina, and durability

HEIGHT: 6' 6" WEIGHT: 380 lbs.

EYES: Green HAIR: Green

NICK FURY NOTE:

He's not the Hulk but he could be the next best thing. He also follows orders for the most part. He would understand what we are doing. Who knows what version of the Hulk we would be dealing with even if we could somehow bring him along in his Banner guise. I realize a 6'6" guy with bright green hair isn't always the easiest guy to conceal, but he's gone covert before in tracking down the Hulk. His green hair is easily dyed. The one thing I worry about with Samson is his ability to come through. He wants to be a super hero and his career has been... well, a little bit less than distinguished. I think he could help but how would he respond in the clutch, when his teammates' lives are on the line? This is not the mission I can afford to find out the answer to that question.

REJECT

S.H.I.E.L.D.
OPERATIONS DATABASE

HOME | ADVANCED SEARCH | DATABASES | LOG OU

S.H.I.E.L.D. FILE NUMBER 2311703-07FLC

REAL NAME: Samuel Thomas Wilson (formerly alias "Snap")

ABILITIES: Power Level 6. Supreme world class athlete, flight, telepathic communication with birds

HEIGHT: 6' 2" WEIGHT: 240 lbs.

EYES: Brown HAIR: Black

NICK FURY NOTE:

Captain America trusts Sam Wilson and usually that's enough for me. But this mission feels different. Something feels off about it... more intense. And I have a feeling we're going to need someone with a little more power on this mission. The Falcon is a great hero. He's worked beside S.H.I.E.L.D. and the Avengers and proven his worth time and time again but this one may be a little over his head. I'd trust Falcon to do the right thing but I'm not sure if it would be enough. Best to leave him behind on this one.

REJECT

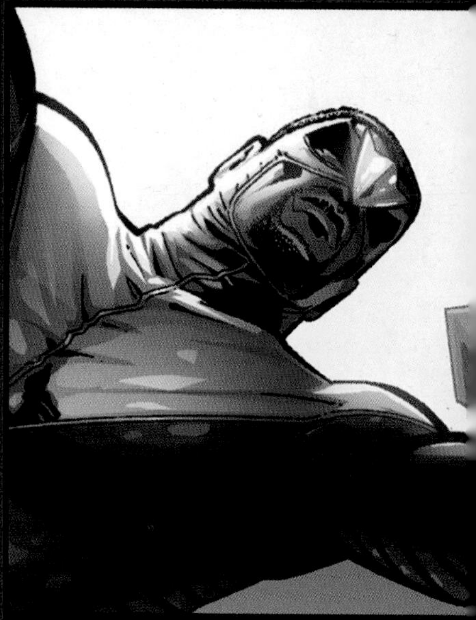

S.H.I.E.L.D. FILE NUMBER 6339584-21IM

REAL NAME: Anthony Edward "Tony" Stark

ABILITIES: Power Level 9. Wearer of hi-tech Iron Man armor, offensive and defensive capabilities constantly upgraded, basic powers include flight, superhuman class strength and multiple forms of energy blasts

HEIGHT: 6' 1" WEIGHT: 225 lbs.

EYES: Blue HAIR: Black

NICK FURY NOTE:

Stark is a good man. And a genius. His Iron Man armor is the most sophisticated weapon on the planet. A one-man army. A piece of weaponry I know would be a definite asset to S.H.I.E.L.D. but, to be honest, it might be more than our operatives should be in possession of. I'm getting off track. Stark would be an ideal warrior against a technological threat like the one we may be facing. Or, if the Tinkerer is involved, he could be the last agent I'd want involved in something like this. Without his armor he is just a man and the Tinkerer may have something which could take him off the board. And a man with a widely reported health condition, no matter how "well" he claims he is, would be useless without his armor. But the problem runs a little deeper. Of all the Avengers, he is often the one who asks the most questions. The bottom line is he needs answers too often. He is not a soldier and this situation needs one.

REJECT

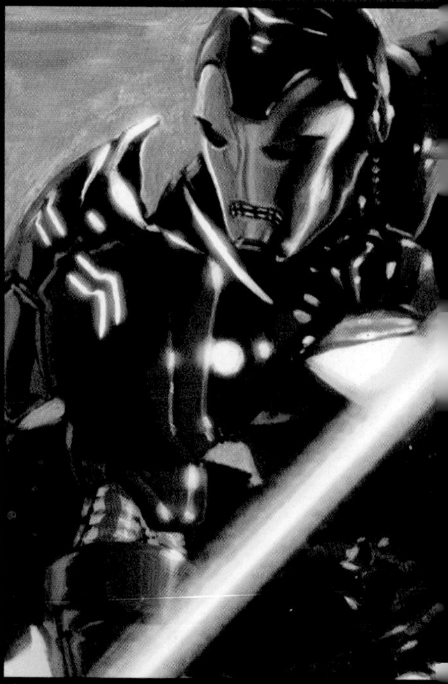

SEARCH DATABASE **OPERATIVES, SECRET WAR** **SEARCH**

S.H.I.E.L.D. FILE NUMBER 7816042-11MY

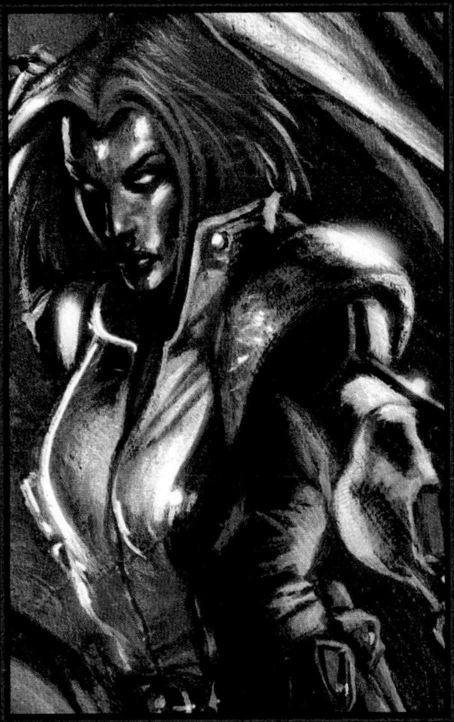

REAL NAME: Classified; aliases include Raven Darkhölme, Raven Wagner, Ronnie Lake, Holt Adler, Mallory Brickman (along with who knows how many others)

ABILITIES: Power Level 8. Shape-changer

HEIGHT: 5' 10" (variable) WEIGHT: 120 lbs. (she can adjust her volume, but not her mass)

EYES: Yellow with no pupils (variable) HAIR: Red (variable)

NICK FURY NOTE:

This woman is part of the reason people are afraid of mutants. A woman who can become anyone and chooses to become a mutant rights terrorist. Not the best way to calm the public. But if we're going on a covert mission, this is one woman who could really be an asset in bringing it off. She's worked with the government before as a part of Freedom Force and X-Factor. Unfortunately, both of those operations were colossal mistakes. Raven is currently working undercover for Xavier. I wonder how that's going to turn out. Not good, I'd wager. I doubt Xavier truly believes it will either. But she is talented and the temptation to bring her in is great. Imagine what she could do for our side... imagine the damage she could do to it. Val Cooper called her "the most dangerous operative in the world" and I'd have to agree with her assessment. But she also told me her mind is so manic from her "identities" that it's difficult to tell which side she'll end up on at any given moment. When this secret operation is over, I am making her a PRIME priority. But there's no way I can have her in on this. I don't feel like worrying about someone on my own side slitting my throat.

REJECT

S.H.I.E.L.D. FILE NUMBER 6408049-72PM

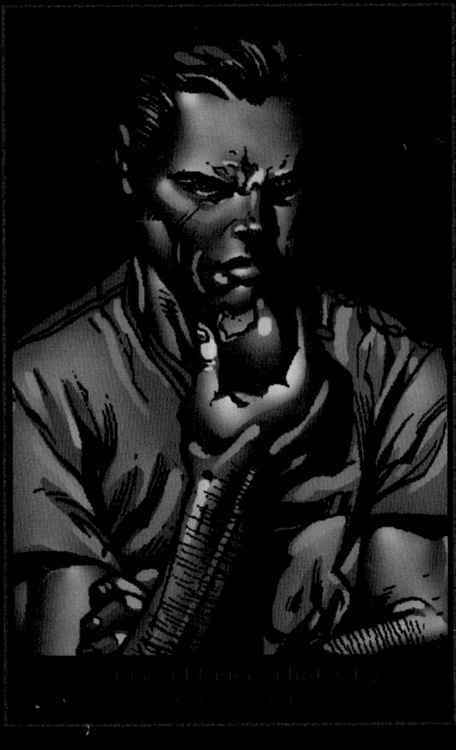

REAL NAME: Zebediah Killgrave

ABILITIES: Power Level 10, Superhuman power to command by the power of suggestion

HEIGHT: 5' 11" WEIGHT: 165 lbs.

EYES: Purple HAIR: Purple

NICK FURY NOTE:

I'm desperate... but am I crazy? I'm trying to figure out a way to take over a foreign government without bloodshed. Is that even possible? It could be with the help of the Purple Man. With all the different superhumans out there why is the most accessible one with ultra mass mind control abilities a serial killer? Without his powers he's harmless. A joke, actually. We've had to separate him from the other prisoners on the Raft. It seems some of the other detainees have a grudge against the guy since he used a couple of them in his "Mad God" schemes. And with what I've read about his time controlling Jessica Jones, sometimes I'm tempted to let the other prisoners have their way with him. Bottom line is I plan to keep him locked up there forever. There's no way I can release this man. Even though he would be the answer to my prayers... and the only operatives I would be forced to put into danger on this secret op would be myself and the Purple Man. But how would I control him? How would I get him to do what I want? And what if something happened to me? If he ever got loose I would never forgive myself and neither would the world. Like I said, I'm desperate... but I'm definitely not crazy.

REJECT

S.H.I.E.L.D.
OPERATIONS DATABASE

HOME | ADVANCED SEARCH | DATABASES | LOG OUT

S.H.I.E.L.D. FILE NUMBER 8001129-90SP

REAL NAME: Katherine "Kitty" Pryde
ABILITIES: Power Level 7. Ability to phase through matter and become ghostlike (this form can cause a disruption of tech equipment)
HEIGHT: 5' 6" WEIGHT: 110 lbs.
EYES: Hazel HAIR: Brown

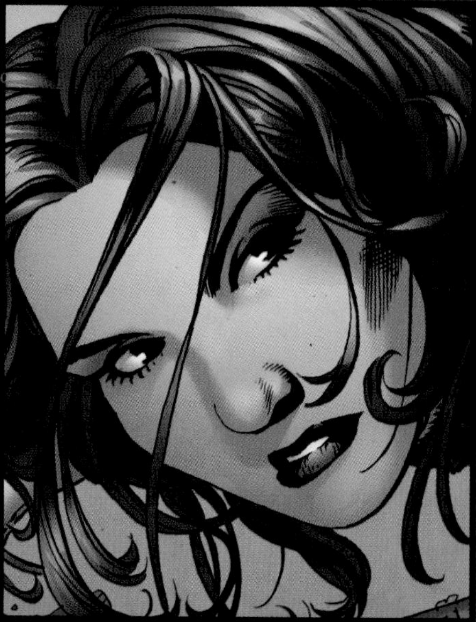

NICK FURY NOTE:

Pryde did some work for S.H.I.E.L.D. in the past, but looking back I think that may have been a mistake. She is a little idealistic for our crew. But her powers lend themselves to this type of work. Who knows what type of tech the Tinkerer has constructed and, for the most part, Kitty's phasing powers seem to short out the tech. But with the nature of the mission... what we may have to do in Latveria... asking her along may be a deal breaker for Logan. And we need him. I have a feeling I may regret this but I think she's a no-go.

REJECT

S.H.I.E.L.D. FILE NUMBER 1161017-12TH

REAL NAME: Benjamin Jacob Grimm
ABILITIES: Power Level 8. Superhuman strength, rocky skin
HEIGHT: 6' WEIGHT: 500 lbs.
EYES: Blue HAIR: None

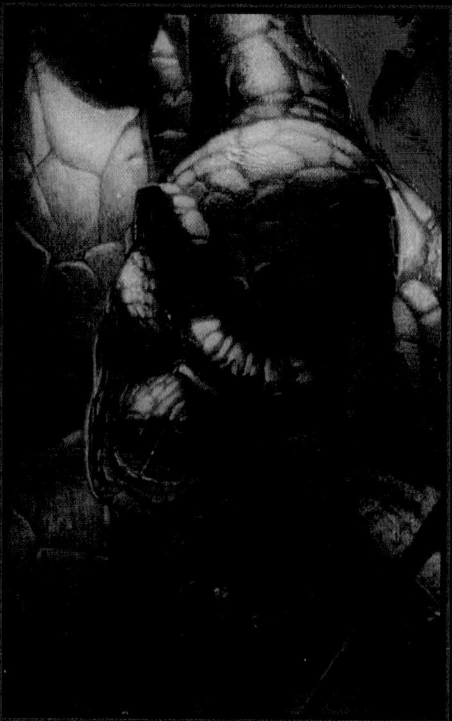

NICK FURY NOTE:

Grimm has a military background. He is one of the most honorable men I know. He has the heart of a lion. He would fight until he dropped or his enemy did. And he has saved the planet countless times alongside the Fantastic Four. But he is also one of the most recognized and beloved heroes on this planet. He is a man who makes us see the goodness inside of every man, regardless of appearance. Corny as that sounds, it is true. He's the genuine article. A man who has every reason to be a villain, but wants to be a hero. Unfortunately, he would be difficult to sneak into Latveria unnoticed... especially with his background in Doom's old stomping ground and of course the fact that he's five hundred pounds and covered in orange rocks. He might even be my choice over Cage but it wouldn't work. If I asked him, Ben Grimm would follow me into Hell. But we're not going to Hell, we're heading into Latveria. And, tragic as it usually is, his appearance is the one thing holding him back.

REJECT

SEARCH DATABASE | OPERATIVES, SECRET WAR | SEARCH

S.H.I.E.L.D. FILE

PRIME DIRECTIVE >> SECRET WAR >> CIRCUIT PROTOCOLS

LEVEL 10 — EYES ONLY

MARKED FOR CONTESSA VALENTINA ALLEGRO DE FONTAINE ON ASSUMPTION OF COMMAND OF S.H.I.E.L.D. OPERATIONS.

Val,

If you are receiving this message, then I have been off the reservation for over 72 hours. Things must have gone terribly wrong on many different levels but, to keep this short, I'll cut through the bull.

I secretly smuggled a band of agents into Latveria to discover what Prime Minister Lucia von Bardas was hiding. There was too much evidence and the danger was too high to let it slide any longer. I did not use S.H.I.E.L.D. agents but instead some of the most powerful superhumans on the planet. If you are receiving this letter, my infiltration unit was insufficient to prevent von Bardas' plans and the United States, and possibly the world, is in grave danger.

As the new acting director of S.H.I.E.L.D., you may choose to ignore this directive. I have no authority left in this matter. Especially from where I am now. But you know me, and you know how seriously I take the place of S.H.I.E.L.D. in this world. Would I have gone rogue without proper provocation? As you know from our discussion outside the White House, I could not stand by and allow innocents to die as fat men in suits argued over treaties that no one pays attention to but us.

I have a secondary plan. A more radical solution than my failed attempt. I prepared a small list of Omega Agents for you to send into Latveria on a Scorched Earth operation. A drastic measure, I know. And one I'm sure you will not take lightly. I wouldn't have. But if whatever is going on in Latveria was enough to stop the operatives I assembled, then things will escalate quickly and people will die. This team is not a scalpel. I didn't pick them to be a precise instrument. They are meant to tear the country down. It's a drastic measure but one that will save millions of lives.

Don't get caught up in the politics, Val. You're the protector of the world. Sometimes, in order to save the patient, you have to remove a limb.

Good luck.
Nick Fury

MARKED FOR **DELETION** FROM FILES BY NICK FURY

S.H.I.E.L.D. OPERATIONS DATABASE

HOME | ADVANCED SEARCH | DATABASES | LOG OUT

S.H.I.E.L.D. FILE NUMBER 5708545-04HE

REAL NAME: Clint Francis Barton

ALIASES: Hawkeye, Goliath, Golden Archer

IDENTITY STATUS: Known to S.H.I.E.L.D.

MARITAL STATUS: Widowed

RELATIVES: Barbara Morse (Mockingbird, wife, deceased), Harold Barton (father, deceased), Edith Barton (mother, deceased), Charles Bernard "Barney" Barton (brother, deceased)

BASE OF OPERATIONS: Avengers Mansion, New York City; (former) Avengers Compound, Los Angeles; Mt. Charteris, Colorado; Cross Technological Enterprises, New York City;

PLACE OF BIRTH: Waverly, Iowa

LEGAL STATUS: American citizen pardoned of criminal charges

OCCUPATION: Avenger

AFFILIATIONS: Avengers; (former) Thunderbolts, Defenders, Great Lakes Avengers, Swordsman, Trickshot, briefly served as agent of S.H.I.E.L.D. and operative of Silver Sable

ENEMIES: Crossfire, Death Throws, Egghead, Masters of Evil, Crimson Cowl

HEIGHT: 6' 3" WEIGHT: 230 lbs. EYES: Blue HAIR: Blond

POWERS/WEAPONS: Power Level 4, Master archer with a variety of special arrows. With Pym Particles: Power Level 7, super strength, increased size to 100 feet tall.

NICK FURY NOTE: Hawkeye is not your average soldier. He asks a lot of questions. He hates authority. He takes chances. But at the end of the day Clint is a hero and someone who realizes, almost more than Captain America does, that in order to get things done you sometimes have to bend the rules and fight dirty. He's also worked undercover for S.H.I.E.L.D. before so I trust him. Barton's a good man.

Now when you approach him with this mission he's going to ask a lot of questions. Particularly, why he wasn't on the first mission. Some of these questions may come out a little obnoxious, but after he finishes, just tell him I was holding him back in case something did go wrong. At that point the jerk will probably smile and say if he was with us the first time, the mission would have gone off without a hitch.

Another thing I need you to hold off on, no matter what you know, is the condition of my first team. If we are off the board and not just captured... if we're all dead... you can't tell Clint that. As much as he disagrees with Cap on a lot of things, the man looks up to Cap. Not that most people don't but... Hawkeye's emotions need to be in check. He is the best marksman in the world, but when his blood gets hot he can be a little off the mark.

Now, I know what you're thinking, Val. He has arrows. And he's just a man. Both of those things are true. But when times are tough, Barton's a leader who can make the tough decisions. And before this horrible mission is over we may need a little humanity to bring us through.

Also, and now that you're in charge you need to know this: We have a small amount of Pym Particles available to him if he wants it. It's sealed in an unmarked bottle of Whiskey on the shelf in my office. (As a matter of fact make sure all of the liquor in my office is sealed up tight. I'll leave a different memo regarding all of the bottles.) He's been Goliath before and by the end of this mission he may need to become Goliath again. Arrows can only keep you alive so long. No matter how great a marksman you are.

SEARCH DATABASE OPERATIVES, SECRET WAR **SEARCH**

S.H.I.E.L.D. FILE NUMBER 6204019-44HK

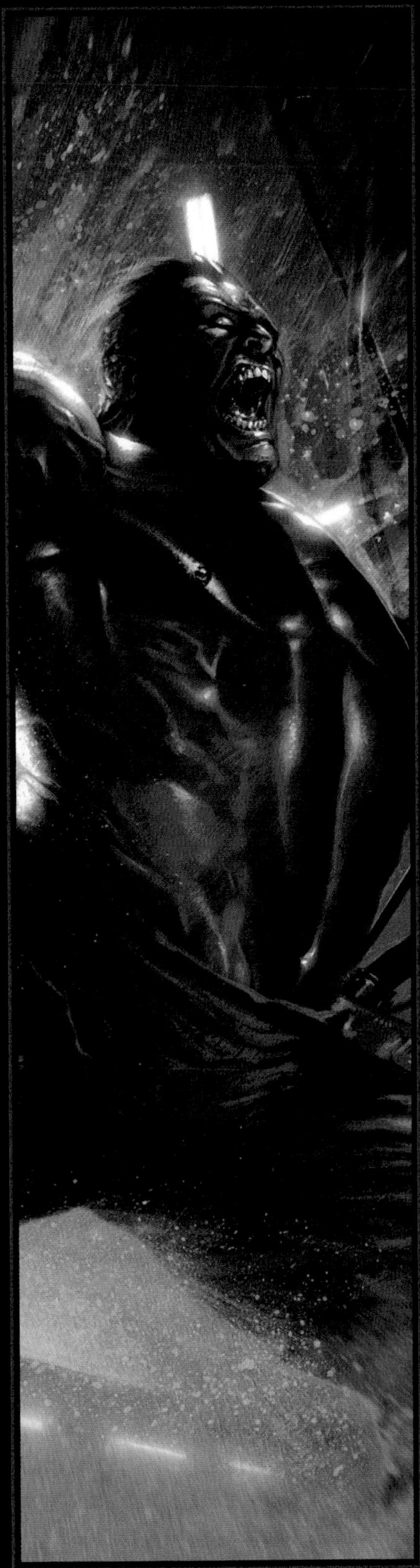

REAL NAME: Dr. Robert Bruce Banner

ALIASES: Hulk, Fixit/Mr. Fixit, War, Captain Universe, Mechano, Bruce Bancroft, David Banner, David Bixby, numerous others adopted while on the run

IDENTITY STATUS: Public

MARITAL STATUS: Married

RELATIVES: Elizabeth "Betty" Ross Talbot Banner (wife), Brian Banner (father, deceased), Rebecca Banner (mother, deceased), Susan Banner (formerly Susan Drake, aunt), Morris Walters (uncle), Elaine Banner Walters (aunt, deceased), Jennifer Walters (She-Hulk, cousin), Thaddeus E. "Thunderbolt" Ross (father-in-law), Cassandra Walters Pike (Brain, aunt), David Pike (Brawn, cousin)

BASE OF OPERATIONS: Mobile; formerly Las Vegas, Nevada; New Mexico; the Mount, Colorado

PLACE OF BIRTH: Dayton, Ohio

LEGAL STATUS: American citizen with criminal record, previously pardoned

OCCUPATION: Former nuclear physicist, construction worker, enforcer, janitor

AFFILIATIONS: Defenders; (former) Order, Secret Defenders, Pantheon, alternate Fantastic Four, Hulkbusters, Avengers, others

ENEMIES: Abomination, Absorbing Man, the Leader, Rhino, Wendigo, Zzzax

HEIGHT: 8' WEIGHT: 1300 lbs. EYES: Green HAIR: Green

POWERS/WEAPONS: Power level 10+, immensely superhuman strength, dense skin, highly advanced recuperative capabilities

NICK FURY NOTE: The Hulk will be difficult to bring in. He always is. If he wasn't, we would have put him down by now. A hard fact for a hard world, Val. It's an attitude you're going to have to get used to as the head of S.H.I.E.L.D. Surprisingly, the Hulk's human form is more difficult to capture. Banner's intellect is on a par with Reed Richards and Tony Stark but he has none of their confidence. Especially after the idiotic accident which caused his condition in the first place.

I have attached a tentative plan for you to follow based on protocols Dr. Banner himself developed during one of his calmer moments as part of the Hulkbusters. (See BANNER PROTOCOLS.) Embarrassing name, but the solution he provides is feasible. It hasn't worked yet so, if it fails, use his former wife Betty Ross, who was recently resurrected, as bait.

I obviously could not use Banner in our initial mission because not only did it call for stealth, but Banner is unpredictable in human and monster form. The Hulk is an uncontrollable force of nature, something I would never consider unless the situation was at its most dire. If you are able to secure him, I would suggest dropping him in Latveria prior to the arrival of the rest of the team to stir things up. It will make it simpler for our main team to reach its objective and will also weaken the Latverian military machine. Most people around the world will believe the Hulk just wandered there and began to wreck things. Not the most advanced plan for deniability but it has happened before and it allows S.H.I.E.L.D. to continue to deny their involvement.

This is not a decision to make lightly. I considered Doc Samson and She-Hulk because they are both controllable to a certain extent. But if things have gone Black in Latveria we have no choice.

And God help us... who would ever believe we would purposely unleash a monster like this on the world?

S.H.I.E.L.D.
OPERATIONS DATABASE

HOME | ADVANCED SEARCH | DATABASES | LOG OUT

S.H.I.E.L.D. FILE NUMBER 1290274-50PN

REAL NAME: Frank Castle

ALIASES: Punisher, Charles Fort, Frank Rook, Johnny Tower (numerous others)

IDENTITY STATUS: Publicly Known

MARITAL STATUS: Widowed

RELATIVES: Maria Elizabeth Castle (wife, deceased), Lisa Barbara Castle (daughter, deceased), Frank David Castle (son, deceased), Mario Lorenzo Castiglione (father, deceased), Louisa Castiglione (mother, deceased), Fredo and Rocco Castiglione (paternal uncles, deceased)

BASE OF OPERATIONS: Mobile, normally New York City

PLACE OF BIRTH: Queens, New York

LEGAL STATUS: United States citizen with criminal record

OCCUPATION: Vigilante

AFFILIATIONS: (Former) Daredevil's unnamed team, Secret Defenders, Green Berets, Marine Corps, Microchip partner

ENEMIES: Jigsaw, Russian, Saracen; most of the criminal underground considers Frank Castle a bigger threat to them than the law.

HEIGHT: 6' 1" **WEIGHT:** 200 lbs. **EYES:** Blue **HAIR:** Black

POWERS/WEAPONS: Though he has no powers, his fighting skills, destructive weaponry, and use of lethal force make him equivalent to a power level 6 or greater. Highly conditioned athlete, combat expert in multiple forms of armed and unarmed combat, psychotically high pain threshold

NICK FURY NOTE: Castle and I have a bit of history which I'd rather not get into. Too messy. Just realize this, Val, I wouldn't be suggesting him if he wasn't absolutely necessary.

The bottom line is Castle is a criminal... a cold-blooded killer. But he's one of the best soldiers I've ever seen. And after what happened to his family... I don't know. It's tough to make sense of. What would anyone do if their family was killed in front of them? If they had the ability and will power to actually do something about it?

I do know he would deliver what we're looking for in the SCORCHED EARTH initiative: Total annihilation of the enemy. He could probably single-handedly disrupt the infrastructure of Latveria for weeks with his Special Forces training. He did it before in countless other military initiatives. Initiatives only a handful of others beside myself know about.

But... there's always a "but" on a mission like this, isn't there? Is a man like Castle able to work with others? He seems to have a major aversion to the super-powered set. What am I supposed to make of a criminal who only goes after criminals? And who's to say as soon as I actually put this mission into motion that I'm not a criminal as well? I've been asked to back off by the President of the United States... but I can't. The stakes are too high. The question is, are they high enough to bring in a killer like Castle? A man who kills so recklessly? Or is that the exact reason I should bring him along? Because this mission could become something not even the heroes I gather for it are ready for. Something Castle has experienced firsthand: War. This man was a highly decorated soldier -- a man I might have fought side by side with in a different world.

On the initial mission I said no. But if that mission failed, we have no choice. Let loose the dogs of war. Drop Castle on the opposite side of Latveria as you did the Hulk, and see who gets to the middle first.

S.H.I.E.L.D. FILE NUMBER 7911801-03IM

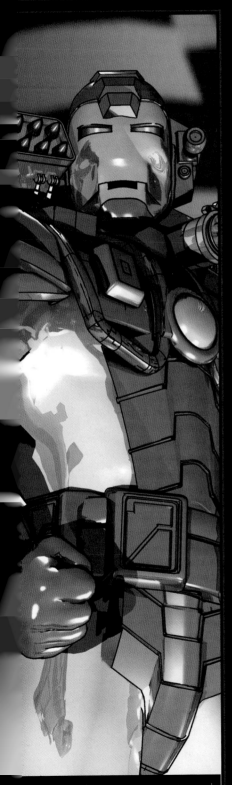

REAL NAME: James Rupert "Rhodey" Rhodes
ALIASES: Iron Man, War Machine
IDENTITY STATUS: Known to S.H.I.E.L.D.
MARITAL STATUS: Single
RELATIVES: David and Roberta Rhodes (parents), Jeanette Rhodes (sister, deceased), Josh (uncle), alleged son
BASE OF OPERATIONS: Oakland, California
PLACE OF BIRTH: Philadelphia, Pennsylvania
LEGAL STATUS: US Citizen
OCCUPATION: Adventurer; (former) bodyguard, salvager, political activist, CEO of Stark Enterprises, pilot, aviation engineer
AFFILIATIONS: (Former) Secret Defenders, Avengers, Worldwatch, US Marines; partner of Josiah X, Danny Vincent, and White Tiger (Kevin Cole)
ENEMIES: Advisor, 66 Bridges, Hate-Monger / Animus, Sons of the Serpent
HEIGHT: 6' 1"   **WEIGHT:** 210 lbs.   **EYES:** Brown   **HAIR:** Brown
POWERS/WEAPONS: Power Level 8 in War Machine armor; Power Level 7 in Mandroid X armor (See MANDROID X FILE, LEVEL 10 ONLY)

NICK FURY NOTE: Val, unlike my initial mission, this will be a military action, not covert. Obviously, it won't be a S.H.I.E.L.D.-sanctioned action but the purpose of this mission is to disable the Latverian military. Aggressively.

I want to fit Rhodes with our most advanced Mandroid X. Now, I know this is an armor that, until today and your new Level 10 clearance, you didn't realize existed, but it's out there. I've included the basic design for the suit in this file. It's not fully realized because we've been working on it secretly. Its operation system is based off of Tony Stark's Iron Man armor. So, besides Stark, Rhodes would be our resident expert. Unlike Stark, however, Rhodes is willing to be aggressive. Overly in some cases, especially during his War Machine days, but this is a military action, not a super-hero mission, and we're going to need a certain amount of aggression.

Rhodes will be part of the air support for our other superhuman operatives. The Mandroid X armor is fully prepared for air-to-air combat and should hold its own against anything von Doom may have prepared for his air defense. I want you to make sure Rhodes understands the Tinkerer is involved. This means Rhodes needs to stay in the sky and not come into contact with any jamming devices. Easier said than done I'm sure, but it is why I am only using one tech operative. I'm especially concerned the Tinkerer may be developing a device that allows him to take over others' armors and control them. Or some variation of that plan. If the Mandroid armor is taken over, I suggest you scuttle the armor. Not something that is easy to do but it would be for the safety of everyone involved.

Why Rhodes and not one of our own? Rhodes has more experience in the armor than any other man on the planet save Stark. At the same time, he has opposed S.H.I.E.L.D. and refused to join us in the past. However, Rhodes was a marine; he has a background with the Avengers and some of the heroes I have suggested you gather for this operation; and, to be honest, he has spent time as a bodyguard. He knows how to watch people and place his life on the line for others. If he knows the stakes are extreme, and I believe they will be, Rhodes will be willing to make the ultimate sacrifice for this team. Hopefully, that won't be necessary.

S.H.I.E.L.D.
OPERATIONS DATABASE

HOME | ADVANCED SEARCH | DATABASES | LOG OUT

S.H.I.E.L.D. FILE NUMBER 501000-005E

REAL NAME: Robert "Bob" Reynolds

ALIASES: Sentry

IDENTITY STATUS: Known to S.H.I.E.L.D., but most of the world is unaware of the Sentry's existence and adventures

MARITAL STATUS: Widowed

RELATIVES: Lindy Reynolds (wife)

BASE OF OPERATIONS: Formerly the Watchtower, currently in S.H.I.E.L.D. custody on the Raft

PLACE OF BIRTH: Presumed to be New York, New York. Birth records are being searched

LEGAL STATUS: American citizen currently being investigated following the disappearance of his wife and his claim that he murdered her

OCCUPATION: Currently incarcerated on the Raft

AFFILIATIONS: Former ally of Fantastic Four, X-Men, Avengers, Hulk, Spider-Man; former sidekick Scout (NOTE: apparently only Reed Richards remembers the Sentry's existence)

ENEMIES: The Void

HEIGHT: 6' **WEIGHT:** 194 lbs. **EYES:** Blue **HAIR:** Blond

POWERS/WEAPONS: Power Level 10+, Superhuman strength, durability, intelligence, flight, energy field, absorbs potentially limitless power from solar energy, Sentient computer CLOC, high-tech Watchtower HQ, Watchwagon transportation

---

NICK FURY NOTE: We deal with some weird things, Val. And this one... well, I know everything about this situation is overwhelming but try to follow me on this one. This man, Robert Reynolds, is a man we have no files on up until a few months ago. I have no recollection of ever meeting the man, but apparently I have. According to Reed Richards, one of the most brilliant men on the face of the Earth, Sentry is one of the greatest heroes our world has ever known. And not one of us can remember him. He has been removed from our memories. Every. Single. Person. In. The. World. What a bunch of mumbo jumbo, right?

Well, when it comes to mumbo jumbo, Reed Richards is one man you have to believe. So, if the Latveria situation has reached critical, we have to use every card in our deck... including the wild card.

We are currently holding Reynolds in the Maximum Security wing of the Super-Maximum Security prison on the Raft. He claims to have murdered his wife, although we have been unable to verify his story. We are holding him on the Raft as a favor to Reed Richards. Currently, Reynolds is basically allowing us to hold him. If he wanted out, he could get out. He has not tried to escape so far, so I'm inclined to believe he is a genuinely good man. And at this point, I realize that's not the best reason to rest the fate of the planet on his shoulders, but it's all we got.

Therefore, you will contact Jessica Drew, current Super Powered S.H.I.E.L.D. Agent overseeing the Raft. Use the code-words UNICORN and SUNSHINE and she'll know what to do with Reynolds. If he can be used, Drew will let you know within the hour.

It is unsure if Sentry would be willing to join our task force but use the psychics if necessary. Not sure if they will do much good but if he's the hero Richards says he is, he will see how badly we need him in this situation. And if our initial mission failed, we're going to need him on our side to take care of Latveria.

Reed Richards mentioned a dark side to this man, a side which could be released if Sentry becomes too powerful. Give Jessica Drew the BRUTUS Protocol as well and hope if she needs to carry it out she can.

SEARCH DATABASE

OPERATIVES, SECRET WAR SEARCH

S.H.I.E.L.D. FILE NUMBER 3202778-10AR

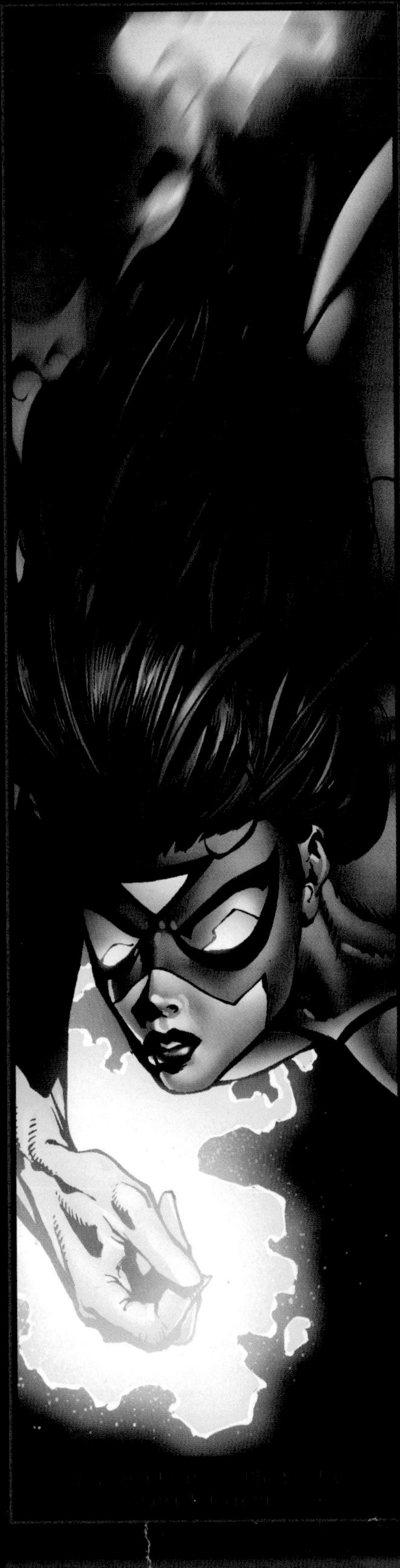

REAL NAME: Jessica Drew

ALIASES: Spider-Woman, Arachne

IDENTITY STATUS: Known to S.H.I.E.L.D.

MARITAL STATUS: Single

RELATIVES: Jonathan Drew (father, deceased), Merriem Drew (mother, deceased)

BASE OF OPERATIONS: The Raft, S.H.I.E.L.D. Headquarters; (former) Madripoor; Los Angeles, San Francisco, California; London, England; Mt. Wundagore, Transia

PLACE OF BIRTH: London, England

LEGAL STATUS: UK citizen acquitted of criminal charges; naturalized US citizen

OCCUPATION: S.H.I.E.L.D. Operative, formerly a Private Investigator and bounty hunter

AFFILIATIONS: S.H.I.E.L.D., Avengers ally, (former) Hydra, Drew & McCabe, partner of Scotty McDowell

ENEMIES: Hydra, Void-Eater, Morgan Le Fay, Viper

HEIGHT: 5' 10" WEIGHT: 130 lbs. EYES: Green HAIR: Brown; dyed Black

POWERS/WEAPONS: Power Level 8. Superhuman strength, endurance, and speed; bioelectric blasts; adhere to any surface, immunity to all poisons and drugs, pheromones (attracts men & repels women)

NICK FURY NOTE: I trust Jessica. I hate to put her into a position like this. I had considered her for the original team but I wanted to... well, I wanted to keep her safe. She's been through enough, hasn't she? She was locked away for years by her father to save her from uranium poisoning. She spent decades in nearly suspended animation and then grew to adulthood alongside animal men. She accidentally killed her first boyfriend. Lost her powers more times than I can keep track of. She's been brainwashed. And had her spirit lost on the Astral Plane. God help her, that's more than most people could even handle without being locked away in some loony bin. And what assignment do we give her? We place her as a super-powered liaison to the Raft. Nice.

But now we need her. And not just because of her powers as Spider-Woman. Jessica can persevere. She sees the big picture. And most importantly, she owes me. Her recent S.H.I.E.L.D. training makes her an ideal candidate for this type of covert mission. I almost chose her over the Johnson girl. But, like I said, Jessica has been through enough and Daisy has a bit more power. I usually go with my gut... but I didn't this time. And it may have cost us on the mission if you're gathering this new team, so now we have to use her.

Jessica is trained to deal with any super-powered situation our team may encounter. But more importantly she's trained to take down super-powered agents like herself. To keep things under control. Basically, I want her to keep an eye on Sentry and the Hulk, if they cross paths, and keep them in some semblance of control. This is a SCORCHED EARTH operation but it needs to be handled with some care.

She has been trained by the best at "superhuman observation" and that's why she has been stationed as a superhuman S.H.I.E.L.D. agent in the most dangerous prison in the world. And make sure you tell her to lay off the perfume for this mission. Her pheromones may be the only thing to keep some of our more uncertain agents in line. We also need every advantage we can get taking down whatever is going on in Latveria. If she can enamor herself of a few men on her way so be it. It just may save her life... and the rest of the world as well.

S.H.I.E.L.D.
OPERATIONS DATABASE

HOME | ADVANCED SEARCH | DATABASES | LOG OUT

S.H.I.E.L.D. FILE NUMBER 2136703-26MM

Surveillance Photo by

REAL NAME: Carol Susan Jane Danvers

ALIASES: Warbird, Binary, Ms. Marvel, Ace, others

IDENTITY STATUS: Secret but known to S.H.I.E.L.D.

MARITAL STATUS: Single

RELATIVES: Joseph Danvers (father), Marie Danvers (mother), Steve Danvers (brother, deceased), Joseph Danvers, Jr. (brother)

BASE OF OPERATIONS: Office of Homeland Security; (former) Avengers Mansion; Starjammer ship, mobile in Shi'ar galaxy; Xavier's School, Westchester, New York; Limbo dimension; New York City; CIA headquarters, Langley, Virginia; Cape Canaveral, Florida; Boston, Massachusetts

PLACE OF BIRTH: Boston, Massachusetts

LEGAL STATUS: United States citizen with no criminal record

OCCUPATION: Chief field leader and super-hero liaison for U.S. Homeland Security Agency, former NASA security chief and intelligence officer, writer/editor

AFFILIATIONS: Avengers, X-Men ally; (former) Starjammers

ENEMIES: Kang, Immortus, Mystique

HEIGHT: 5' 11" WEIGHT: 124 lbs. EYES: Blue HAIR: Blonde

POWERS/WEAPONS: Power Level 8. Superhuman strength, durability, flight, able to absorb and rechannel energy

NICK FURY NOTE: Danvers is the most qualified agent for this mission. As you know, she is currently the chief field leader for Homeland Security. And whatever is happening in Latveria right now is a security threat to America and probably the world. From the numerous field reports I've read from her since she joined Homeland Security, it's clear she is in favor of a more proactive stance on terrorism. And this mission is about as proactive as you can get.

With her extensive military and super-hero background Danvers would have been an ideal addition to my initial team as well. But I was hesitant. If we were discovered it would have jeopardized her current position. And she's needed there. It's the same reason I held back information about my Secret War from you, Val. Even if I was successful, I wanted you to have deniability so you would be in place to carry on. But, if my team failed, there's no way we can continue to play it safe. I trust you to take care of things now that I'm gone. Danvers has been briefed before on possible SCORCHED EARTH scenarios in Latveria. I think she even helped prepare a few of them based on her access to files with the Avengers, so I'm confident she knows what needs to be done to take down the Latverian military and infrastructure.

I'm sure you have some reservations about her leading the mission. Don't. Danvers is a natural leader when she trusts her own instincts. Will she be able to handle a cutthroat mission like this one? Yes. You'll probably also see she has had her difficulties with alcohol. Everyone has personal demons to deal with and those days seem to be behind her. I know the woman and believe in her. You should as well.

Danvers has the respect of her peers. Most of her teammates on this mission know her military background. Barton may ask to be in charge just because he believes in himself so unquestionably -- like any marksman would have to -- but a mission like this needs military direction. This is not a super-hero mission. It's a military action with different rules. The others will most likely have heard her record and trust her. And the Hulk and Punisher are inconsequential since they will be working solo as diversions. Either way, she's the best choice as your field leader. I trust she's up to it. And so are you.

S.H.I.E.L.D. FILE NUMBER 546-MANX3

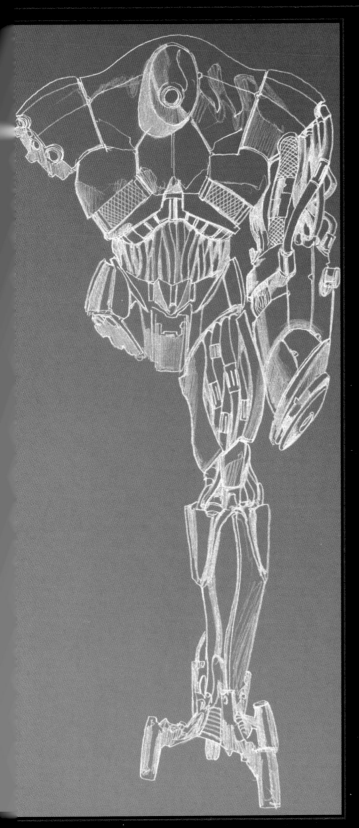

MANDROID X ARMOR
LEVEL 10 — ONLY
PROTOYPE 3

I know you haven't seen this before, Val, but it's a strong program. It's not the same group of guys who just ripped off Stark's designs a couple years ago. We've got our best tech guys on it. But it's been a tough road. Prototypes 1 and 2 had critical malfunctions and were destroyed. This is the last of the Prototypes. And it appears to be the best. We've kept this armor secret from all of S.H.I.E.L.D. because of previous malfunctions and missteps. The last time we unveiled the Mandroid armor, Tony Stark was… well, he became very upset our scientists used some of his designs and tech. And while Stark has been unstable from time to time, I don't blame him. This newest design was developed using different tech. It's probably the reason we ran into so much trouble with the first two prototypes. It's all new stuff. The one thing we did take from Stark was his operation mechanism for the suit. The man is a genius, so why mess with perfection. That's why we want to use Rhodes. He might be the most knowledgeable person other than Stark himself on the operation of this type of armor. Using Rhodes in the armor could leave us open to Stark discovering us again, but with the ever changing nature of their relationship, and the seriousness of the threat in Latveria, it's a chance you should be willing to take.

The armor has a Titanium coating that can withstand high-impact shells, high heat, and radiation levels.

Super-strength
Flight
CLOAKING ABILITIES — Can run "dark" for up to 6 minutes at a time before reappearing on radar
SENSOR ARRAY >> Infrared >> Radar >> Night
LIFE SUPPORT >> An air supply capable of supporting the wearer for up to 24 hours
FOOT BLASTERS >> Rocket boosters
Laser Eye
Ice and Heat Wrist Blasters
Punch Blasters

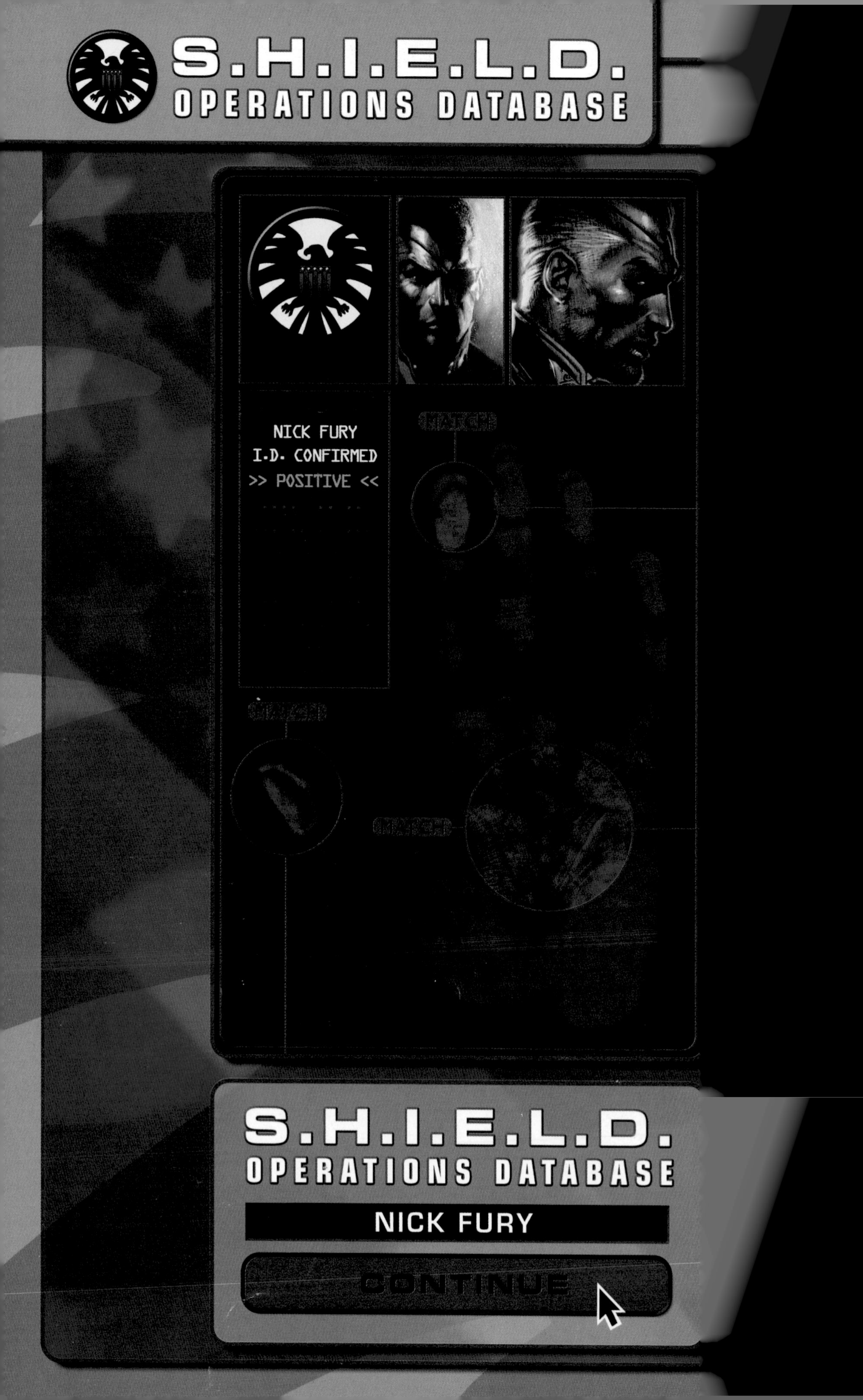

S.H.I.E.L.D.
OPERATIONS DATABASE

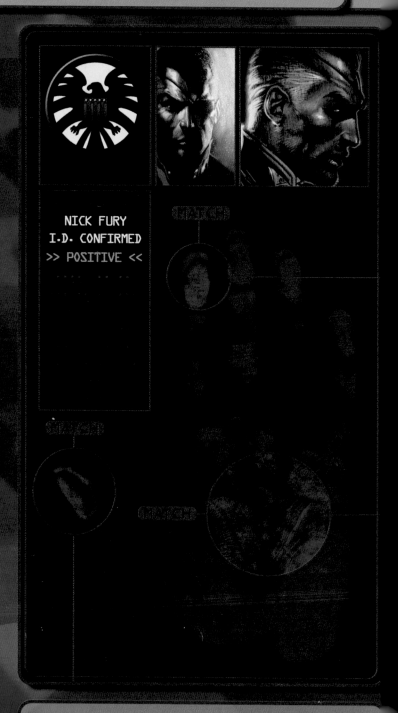

NICK FURY
I.D. CONFIRMED
>> POSITIVE <<

S.H.I.E.L.D.
OPERATIONS DATABASE

NICK FURY

CONTINUE

S.H.I.E.L.D. FILE NUMBER 1446605-27SIT

REAL NAME: Jasper Sitwell
ALIASES: Jason Stillwell
IDENTITY STATUS: S.H.I.E.L.D. Agent
MARITAL STATUS: Married
RELATIVES: Collin Sitwell (father), Sally Sitwell (mother), Gregory Sitwell (brother), Jason Sitwell (grandfather, deceased)
BASE OF OPERATIONS: S.H.I.E.L.D. Headquarters
PLACE OF BIRTH: Salt Lake City, Utah
LEGAL STATUS: American citizen with no criminal record
OCCUPATION: S.H.I.E.L.D. Agent; former SHIELD liaison to Tony Stark
AFFILIATIONS: S.H.I.E.L.D., Tony Stark
ENEMIES: AIM, Baron Strucker, Grey Gargoyle, Hydra, Mordecai Midas, THEM, Ultimo
HEIGHT: 5' 11"   **WEIGHT:** 190 lbs.   **EYES:** Blue   **HAIR:** Blond
POWERS/WEAPONS: Power Level 2 (normal human, no PSI or advanced abilities), Level 5 Interrogator

NICK FURY NOTE: Jasper is a talented man. He graduated top of his class in airborne and underwater maneuvers. He's one of our best shots. One of our earliest agents, he quickly impressed me, and I had him sit in as interim director a couple of times while I was in the field. He's smarter than most give him credit for; when he was trapped in a cave-in caused by the Grey Gargoyle, Sitwell deliberately touched the villain to temporarily turn himself into stone and increase his survival chances. National security concerns saw me assign him to Stark International. Stark wasn't too happy about that to begin with, but things improved after Sitwell saved his life. He even romanced one of Stark's flames, Whitney Frost (Madame Masque). Jealousy strained things between him and Stark, but they've gotten over it. When Obadiah Stane took over Stark International, Jasper was the man I trusted to retrieve the Iron Man armors for S.H.I.E.L.D. – one of the few times he's failed.

Like most of the old S.H.I.E.L.D. top echelons, he was replaced by a Deltite LMD to facilitate taking over the agency (hey, who among us hasn't been replaced by an LMD?). I thought he'd died, but even though he initially came back a brainwashed Hydra agent, I was still glad to see him.

Jasper subsequently became an interrogator. Our best. People really like Jasper. They want to trust him, to laugh with him. Surprisingly, even criminals want friends and Jasper has been able to convince murderers and terrorists that he's on their side. After Jasper fell into a slump, I decided to pair him with Woo. Their chemistry is... strange. They seem to both be directing their anger at their interrogation subjects but it seems as if Woo has adopted some of Jasper's humor into his style. It's like they are competing for attention. A combination which is dangerous and often fatal in combat... but surprisingly amusing and effective in the interrogation room.

Their interrogation tapes are the most logged out by S.H.I.E.L.D. Agents. And it's not for their educational value. Agents are watching these tapes for fun. It appears they have a way of... speaking with the subjects... that entertains their fellow agents. It's like a Saturday Night Live skit that's actually funny.

The two of them have helped crack more subjects than I thought possible. And to be honest, I've cracked a smile on more than one occasion. Regardless, Jasper has refound his groove and is the best again. The man just seems to find a way to be on top. All the best S.H.I.E.L.D. Agents do.

S.H.I.E.L.D.
OPERATIONS DATABASE

HOME | ADVANCED SEARCH | DATABASES | LOG OUT

S.H.I.E.L.D. FILE NUMBER 1101965-56JW

REAL NAME: James "Jimmy" Woo

ALIASES: None

IDENTITY STATUS: S.H.I.E.L.D. Agent

MARITAL STATUS: Divorced

RELATIVES: Kim Woo (father, deceased), Margaret Woo (mother)

BASE OF OPERATIONS: S.H.I.E.L.D. Headquarters

PLACE OF BIRTH: Cheverly, Maryland

LEGAL STATUS: American citizen with no criminal record

OCCUPATION: S.H.I.E.L.D. Agent

AFFILIATIONS: S.H.I.E.L.D., FBI, U.S. State Department

ENEMIES: The Claw, Centurius, Damon Dran

HEIGHT: 5' 8" **WEIGHT:** 170 lbs. **EYES:** Brown **HAIR:** Black

POWERS/WEAPONS: Power Level 2 (normal human, no Psi or advanced abilities), standard S.H.I.E.L.D. agent, Level 3 Interrogator

NICK FURY NOTE: The first thing everyone notices when they check out Woo's full file is his D.O.B. My advice? Ignore it. It's no one's business in this game if a guy proves to be a little older than they look. Woo came to us through the FBI. At the top of his class in the academy, he worked with a number of heroes to stop Soviet spies and other threats before he joined us. I invited him to join S.H.I.E.L.D. as a field agent after he assisted me during what at the time seemed to be a plot by one of his old enemies, the Claw (see S.H.I.E.L.D. file number 1101965-55YC).

He was part of Dugan's Godzilla Squad taskforce on the Behemoth Helicarrier a few years back, and he worked with the Widow to stop Damon Dran's mad schemes. Like too many agents, he was temporarily replaced by a Deltite LMD, and brainwashed by Hydra, but we got him back eventually.

Woo has become one of the best interrogators S.H.I.E.L.D. has ever seen. Never say a little anger and personal strife doesn't help an agent. Woo has been an invaluable asset to us on the Tinkerer case. Alongside Agent Sitwell, Woo has proved himself to be an elite interrogator, as good as there is minus Psi abilities. And we know how unreliable the Psis can be under certain conditions. So far, we have not seen that unreliability in Woo. An amazing 98 percent success rate. (No one can crack the Purple Man.) His interrogations of Hobgoblin, Grizzly, and Killer Shrike were the reason I began to see the connections between the Tinkerer and Latveria in the first place.

S.H.I.E.L.D. FILE NUMBER 7412139-53GRZ

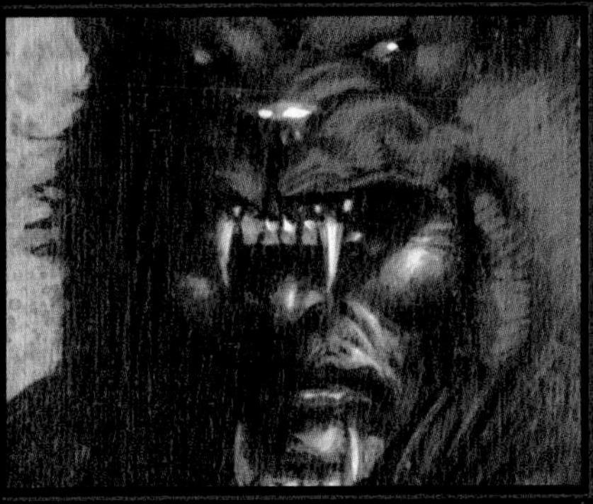

REAL NAME: Maxwell Markham
ALIASES: Grizzly
IDENTITY STATUS: Known to Professional Wrestling fans; otherwise secret
MARITAL STATUS: Single
RELATIVES: None known
AFFILIATIONS: Spider-Man Revenge Squad (also see: Legion of Losers in S.H.I.E.L.D. file)
ENEMIES: Spider-Man Revenge Squad (minus the Gibbon); (former) Spider-Man, Jonah Jameson
HEIGHT: 6' 9" WEIGHT: 290 lbs. EYES: Brown HAIR: Brown
POWERS: Bear suit exoskeleton that enhances his strength levels to superhuman proportions, body armor, claws
RELATED DOCUMENTS: 69678-616SPI, 0001220-12GIB, 1992110-19 JAC

NICK FURY NOTE:

Who would have believed it? The Grizzly was the first lead in this case. A man that was so unimportant on the list that I wasn't even present for his interrogation. Unbeknownst to many of the S.H.I.E.L.D. Agents, including interrogators Woo and Sitwell, Markham was attempting to turn over a new leaf. It was a failed attempt. He usually caused more problems than he prevented but he did eventually deliver some information that started me down this road… down the road to my Secret War. It was our first inkling that the Tinkerer was up to something. I had no idea how deeply the conspiracy went but it was a start. Sometimes even the lowest rungs on the ladder are important. Even if they don't realize it.

S.H.I.E.L.D. FILE NUMBER 696369-34930 THK
CRIMINAL DATABASE >> OPERATIONS DOCUMENT >> INTERROGATIONS
SECRET CODE: WHITE

Interrogation Transcript
Subject: Maxwell Markham
A.K.A.: Grizzly

Interrogation conducted by: S.H.I.E.L.D. Agent Jasper Sitwell – Level 8 and S.H.I.E.L.D. Agent James Woo – Level 8
Interrogation Observed by Contessa Allegro De Fontaine – S.H.I.E.L.D. Deputy Director – Agent Security level 9
Recording date: 1/7/2003

S.H.I.E.L.D. AGENT JAMES WOO
Hello, Mr. Markham—
S.H.I.E.L.D. AGENT JASPER SITWELL
Or would you prefer to be called Grizzly… or Mr. Grizzly?
S.H.I.E.L.D. AGENT JAMES WOO
Seriously, did you really think that name was going to strike fear into anyone?
S.H.I.E.L.D. AGENT JASPER SITWELL
Aren't grizzlies close to being extinct? Or is that the black bear? I haven't had a chance to watch the Nature Channel lately with all the tech guys we're bringing in.
S.H.I.E.L.D. AGENT JAMES WOO
I would have never guessed a guy like the Grizzly was a tech guy, would you? I mean, why go to all that trouble to make a tech suit that looks like a grizzly?
S.H.I.E.L.D. AGENT JASPER SITWELL
You guys sure do make it easy for us, don't you?
MAXWELL MARKHAM
Listen, I wasn't—

S.H.I.E.L.D.
OPERATIONS DATABASE

| HOME | ADVANCED SEARCH | DATABASES | LOG OUT |

CRIMINAL DATABASE → S.H.I.E.L.D. DOCUMENT 096369-34930 THK (Cont.)

S.H.I.E.L.D. AGENT JASPER SITWELL

Hold that thought for a second there, Grizz. Let's have some fun with this. Just pretend we're some sparring partners from your old wrestling days. You can do that, can't you? Or was that fake? I could never tell when I was a kid.

S.H.I.E.L.D. AGENT JAMES WOO

Oh, I'd say those fights were pretty fake. This guy was one of the best back then, though. I had his action figure. And the Action Wrestling Ring. He had the belt. Oh man, were you a monster. I remember one time he threw The Iron Curtain into the crowd and—

MAXWELL MARKHAM

The Steel Curtain.

S.H.I.E.L.D. AGENT JAMES WOO

Really? The Steel Curtain? Are you sure?

S.H.I.E.L.D. AGENT JASPER SITWELL

You're doubting the man's memory? He lived it.

S.H.I.E.L.D. AGENT JAMES WOO

True. But, he has been beaten up quite a bit since then... You know, our guy here, he even had a write-up in the Bugle about how vicious he was. I think he got thrown out of the sport for the negative publicity that caused. Imagine that kind of publicity now. He'd have a movie career.

S.H.I.E.L.D. AGENT JASPER SITWELL

Man, back then the Bugle had a beef with everyone, didn't it? So you don't think this guy was in one of those real wrestling leagues?

S.H.I.E.L.D. AGENT JAMES WOO

Have you seen this guy's record? I think Power Pack would be tough for this guy to handle.

S.H.I.E.L.D. AGENT JASPER SITWELL

Well, that's a little harsh.

S.H.I.E.L.D. AGENT JAMES WOO

Grizz did organize a little team to take on Spider-Man which he then turned on. You and the Gibbon—

S.H.I.E.L.D. AGENT JASPER SITWELL

The Gibbon?

S.H.I.E.L.D. AGENT JAMES WOO

Read your files, man. I can't believe you came in here without finishing the notes.

S.H.I.E.L.D. AGENT JASPER SITWELL

I finished the notes. I skimmed some of them but I finished them.

S.H.I.E.L.D. AGENT JAMES WOO

Anyway, you and the Gibbon made quite a name for yourselves by pulling that little maneuver. I mean, really... gathering a team and then turning on them when you face off against your arch enemy. Might have wanted to think that one through a little better.

MAXWELL MARKHAM

I realized this--

S.H.I.E.L.D. AGENT JASPER SITWELL

Hold that thou--

MAXWELL MARKHAM

No, you guys have to understand. I was trying to stop the robbery. I've changed. Ask Spider-Man. I helped him out against the White Rabbit. He--

CRIMINAL DATABASE >> S.H.I.E.L.D. DOCUMENT 696369-34930 THK (Cont.)

S.H.I.E.L.D. AGENT JAMES WOO

The White Rabbit. Was he in a big white rabbit suit?

MAXWELL MARKHAM

I got the bag of cash at the bank but SHE got away.

S.H.I.E.L.D. AGENT JAMES WOO

Of course she did. That would explain why you were holding the bank's marked bills when the police arrived, right?

(30 second pause)

MAXWELL MARKHAM

Yes.

DEPUTY DIRECTOR VALENTINA ALLEGRO DE FONTAINE (FROM OBSERVATION BOOTH)

Agent Woo? Can I see you for a second?

S.H.I.E.L.D. AGENT JAMES WOO

Sure. Keep him company, Jasper.

S.H.I.E.L.D. AGENT JASPER SITWELL

Sure. Now where were we?

MAXWELL MARKHAM

I caught the girl and grabbed the bag of cash. That's not a crime, is it? A guy's got to have time to return the cash after he saves the day.

S.H.I.E.L.D. AGENT JASPER SITWELL

So you weren't after the cash. How do you make money then? How do you keep that suit of yours running? Because from the records I've seen, your track record as a super-villain—

MAXWELL MARKHAM

I'm not a villain. That was a long time ago.

S.H.I.E.L.D. AGENT JASPER SITWELL

Fine. Your record as a super... guy, then, is less than positive. You don't really seem like the tech type so--

MAXWELL MARKHAM

There's a guy. He keeps the suit in shape. He usually asks me... I used to do jobs for him. But now I...

S.H.I.E.L.D. AGENT JASPER SITWELL

Look. The condition of your suit when we brought you in was less than perfect. It's going to be tough to convince us you weren't trying to get the cash to fix it... so tell me a little about this guy.

MAXWELL MARKHAM

He's old. White hair. Long nose. I don't know his name. He never told me. I just heard where he was going to be and--

S.H.I.E.L.D. AGENT JASPER SITWELL

Old guy. White hair. Long nose. Great.

MAXWELL MARKHAM

The Rhino suggested him to me. Never gave him my name and he never gave me his. He said he could fix the suit for a price. He never really dealt in cash; he always dealt in favors. Usually, someone would have to steal some stuff for him. Tech, mostly, so he could tinker with stuff I assume. Maybe give him a cut of their take. He wanted me to leave the suit so he could study it. He said he wanted to study the design.

S.H.I.E.L.D. AGENT JASPER SITWELL

So you let him take it to reproduce—

MAXWELL MARKHAM

No. I'd feel awful if my suit was used for anything bad again. The guy would normally just fix my exoskeleton while it was on me. I didn't want to leave the suit with him to copy it. Like I said, I'm trying to change things.

S.H.I.E.L.D. AGENT JASPER SITWELL

Well... you did say that, didn't you? And from the look of your suit, nobody has been fixing anything on it.

S.H.I.E.L.D.
OPERATIONS DATABASE

HOME   ADVANCED SEARCH   DATABASES   LOG OUT

CRIMINAL DATABASE >> S.H.I.E.L.D. DOCUMENT 636369-34930 THK (Cont.)

MAXWELL MARKHAM

No. But a lot of other guys seem to be taking the deal.

S.H.I.E.L.D. AGENT JASPER SITWELL

Really? You guys talk a lot?

MAXWELL MARKHAM

The guys who still talk to me... none of the big names. I'm not tight with the Trapster or Boomerang or anyone. They're not real nice. The ones giving their stuff away are just guys with wrist shooters or rocket boots. There's one guy with two extra legs. That guy never really made sense to me. They all handed over their tech for some cash. I was thinking about it but I have things to make up for.

S.H.I.E.L.D. AGENT JAMES WOO (FROM OBSERVATION BOOTH)

Hey, Sitwell. It looks like our guy's telling the truth. Bank cam has him chasing the robbers. Not very impressively but he was doing a good deed.

S.H.I.E.L.D. AGENT JASPER SITWELL

No kidding? A man with a change of heart? Woo, have you been listening? It sounds like we have some black market tech being run here. Could you describe the guy better than old, white hair and long nose? That could be my father-in-law for all I know! Where did you meet him?

MAXWELL MARKHAM

It was always a different place. Maybe, I... The guy's always had a different look. Beard. Shades. Moustache. I could try to—

S.H.I.E.L.D. AGENT JAMES WOO (REENTERING ROOM)

Jasper, let's get him down to the records room and get cracking on this.

MAXWELL MARKHAM

Am I going to get my suit back?

S.H.I.E.L.D. AGENT JASPER SITWELL

Let's not rush things...

RECORDING DEVICE SWITCHED OFF AT 10:12:34.
SUBJECT MOVED TO RECORDS ROOM
TRANSCRIPT REVIEWED AND EDITED BY COLONEL NICK FURY FOR SECURITY CLEARANCE.
542-773

SEARCH DATABASE **ADVERSARIES, SECRET WAR** SEARCH

S.H.I.E.L.D. FILE NUMBER 6305021-03TNK

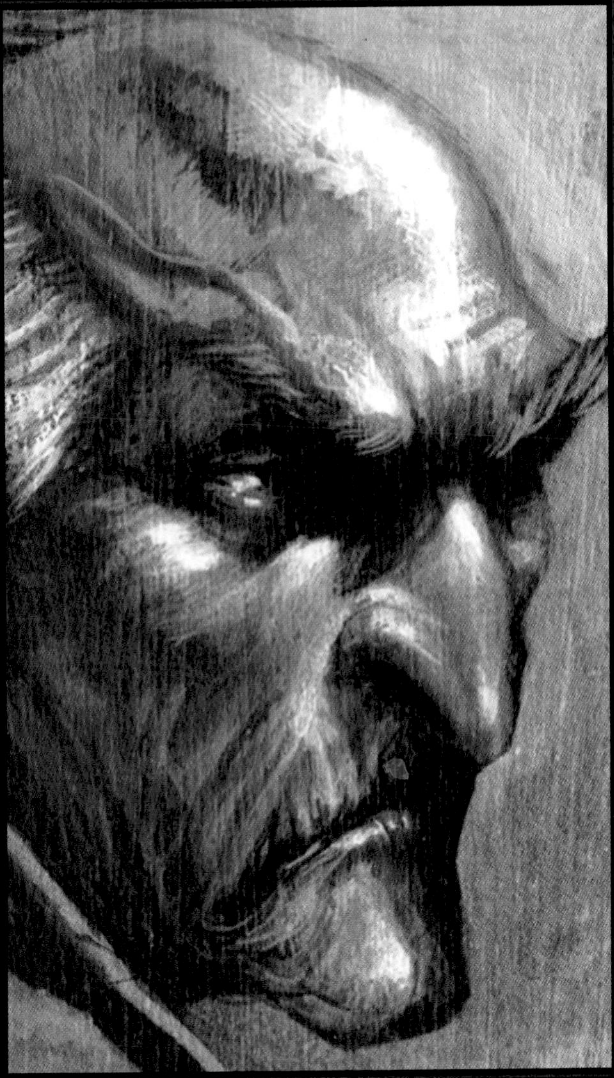

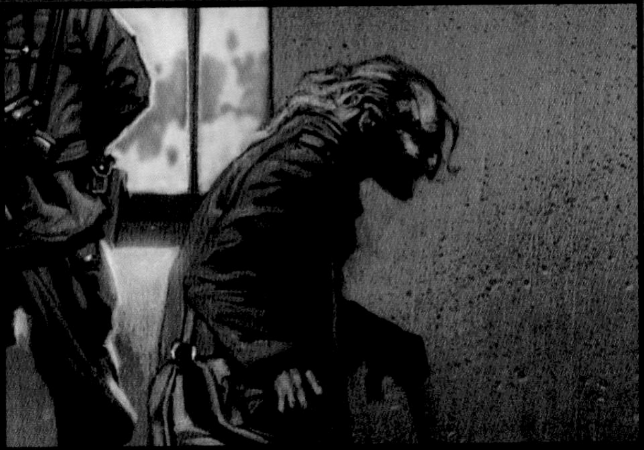

REAL NAME: Phineas T. Mason

ALIASES: The Tinkerer

IDENTITY STATUS: Known to S.H.I.E.L.D.

MARITAL STATUS: Widowed

RELATIVES: Rick Mason (Agent, son, deceased), Deborah Watts Mason (wife, deceased)

BASE OF OPERATIONS: New York City, NY; Philadelphia, PA; also spotted in Latveria

PLACE OF BIRTH: Lac du Flambeau, Wisconsin

LEGAL STATUS: American citizen with criminal record

OCCUPATION: Genius inventor, professional criminal

AFFILIATIONS: Lucia von Bardas (former prime minister of Latveria), Toy; various tech criminals including Goldbug, the Grim Reaper, Jack O'Lantern, Killer Shrike, Mysterio, Scorpion, Warrant; (former) Hawkeye, Judge

ENEMIES: Corporation, Spider-Man

HEIGHT: 5'8" WEIGHT: 175 lbs. EYES: Grey HAIR: White

POWERS: Mason is a genius with tech and electronics. He serves as the underground dealer and fixer of various technological villains' armor. Proceed with caution when attempting to apprehend Mason. He has been known to booby-trap his lairs.

NICK FURY NOTE: Who would think an old eccentric inventor could cause so much trouble? I know I didn't. But now, after discovering his plans include Latveria and the super-tech black market, I'm more than concerned. What does he have to do with Latveria? What is his connection to Lucia von Bardas? I'm going to find out and put this guy down for good. Mason's been treated like a second-class villain for too long. His latest moves have put him at the top of the list. And I have a feeling a guy like Phineas is not going to like that too much.

LEVEL 10 - EXTENDED NOTES

I don't have much to say about the man known as the Tinkerer. He's been around for awhile. But he was never much of a concern for S.H.I.E.L.D. Though his son was an international mercenary and a personal ally, the Tinkerer was just not a major player. Just a cog in the machine. He eventually became more a myth than a reality, able to appear and than disappear into thin air. With all the other maniacs out there I wasn't losing any sleep over it.

S.H.I.E.L.D. FILE NUMBER 6305021-03TNK (Cont.)

But recently, that all changed. Following the death of his son, Mason's methods changed. He briefly worked with the supernatural Judge in a mission of justice, but his anger over his son's death drove him to new depths. The Tinkerer's name began to come up more and more frequently in our interrogation rooms. Especially with our tech villains. And it was there, during interrogation sessions with Woo and Sitwell, that we had some breakthroughs into the Latverian situation. We started to find out the locations of old safe houses. Usually booby-trapped in some manner but we were finally getting someplace.

Woo and Sitwell hit the jackpot in interrogation sessions with Grizzly, Killer Shrike and Jack O'Lantern. Mason was collecting tech and studying it as a fee for his services. It made us anxious. Separately, these tech villains aren't much of a threat, but combined they would be quite a force. And it sounds like Mason has been collecting tech... maybe even tinkering with their tech without them knowing it. Who knows what he's doing.

One thing is for sure, no man should have his hands on that much power. Even if he's just tinkering with it.

S.H.I.E.L.D. FILE NUMBER 31570803-12914882949T7 EVIDFILE
EVIDENCE FILE >> OBTAINED FROM SAFE HOUSE OF PHINEAS MASON A.K.A. >> THE TINKERER
Reviewed and tagged by — level 10 clearance by — S.H.I.E.L.D.
CODE CLEARANCE: WHITE

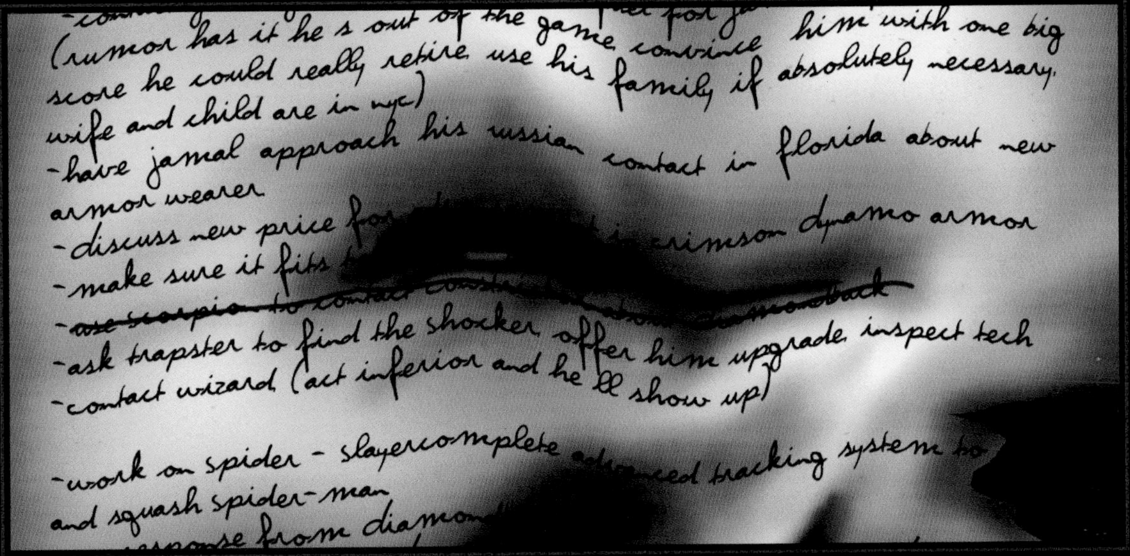

(rumor has it he's out of the game ... for ... him with one big
score he could really retire. use his family if absolutely necessary.
wife and child are in nyc)
-have jamal approach his russian contact in florida about new
armor wearer
-discuss new price for ... crimson dynamo armor
-make sure it fits
-ask scorpion to contact cousin ... diamondback
-ask trapster to find the shocker offer him upgrade inspect tech
-contact wizard (act inferior and he ll show up)

-work on spider - slayer complete advanced tracking system to
and squash spider-man
... response from diamo...

FURY EVIDENCE NOTE -

You would think a tech genius like the Tinkerer would be able to remember names but apparently he couldn't. It's actually a common problem among "genius" types. It could be that he simply didn't care or he truly can't remember them but this partially burned list recovered from his safe house (discovered during the Killer Shrike debacle. Perhaps the field is not always the best place for those two) gave us a bunch of leads. Some I couldn't decipher at the time but they are now becoming clearer in the aftermath of their attack. It has led us to discover the identity of the new Diamondback (see Debbie Bertrand). And eventually it may lead us down some other paths as well.

The amazing thing about the Tinkerer is he seems to work in a never ending string of favors that lead to some unknown goal. Each "customer" he works with gets a task that leads to another "customer". It's like he's working on the barter system. And all for the benefit of his backer, Lucia von Bardas. Or so it seems. Is there a way to exploit this system? It's obvious they would eventually squeal on him, wouldn't they? Or do they worry about losing their supplier? Is this tech their drug? It appears so. But unlike most addicts they seem unwilling to give up their supplier.

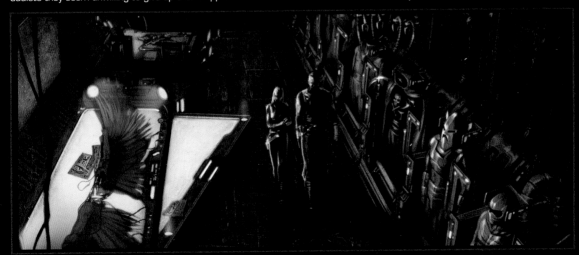

S.H.I.E.L.D. FILE NUMBER 58733647-33281 RISTY

Observation Transcript
Marked for puege: Commander Nicholas Fury (Level 10)
CODE CLEARANCE: BLACK (Fury only)

Observed conversation between unidentified woman and two former S.H.I.E.L.D. Agents, Mike Johnson and Chris Nolan, following the deboarding of Flight 456 from New York to Latveria.

FORMER SPECIAL FIELD AGENT MIKE JOHNSON
The packages are delivered, sir.
UNIDENTIFIED WOMAN
You don't have to call me sir, Mike. This was a favor and I appreciated it.
FORMER SPECIAL FIELD AGENT CHRIS NOLAN
It was no problem, sir.
UNIDENTIFIED WOMAN
Neither of you need to call me "sir" -- you are both private citizens now.
FORMER SPECIAL FIELD AGENT MIKE JOHNSON
Yes... um... ma'am.

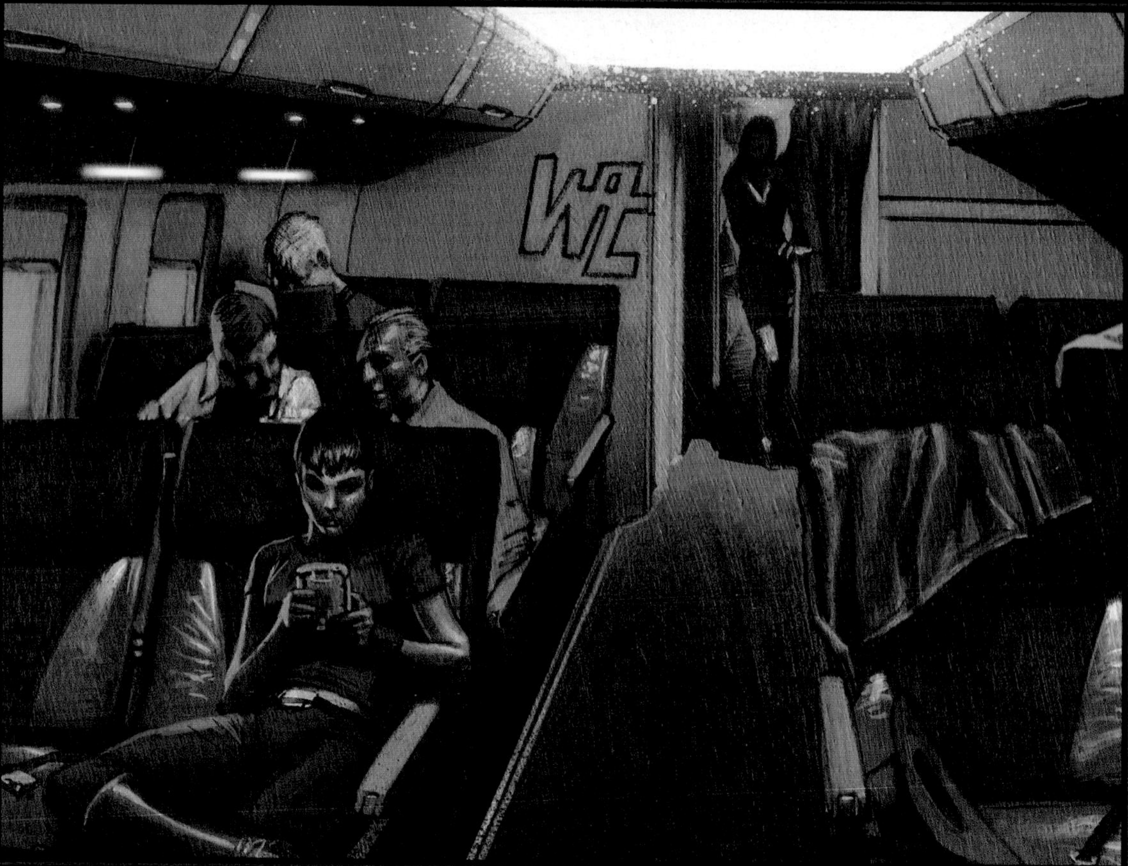
WL

SEARCH DATABASE **TRANSCRIPTS, SECRET WAR** SEARCH

CRIMINAL DATABASE >> S.H.I.E.L.D. DOCUMENT 98733647-33281 RISTY (Cont.)

UNIDENTIFIED WOMAN

Don't get smart. How was the flight?

FORMER SPECIAL FIELD AGENT CHRIS NOLAN

Well... it was fine. Fine.

UNIDENTIFIED WOMAN

Would there be any reason anyone would think the packages are here for a reason other than what we claimed?

FORMER SPECIAL FIELD AGENT CHRIS NOLAN

Well... we had to calm one of them, sir.

FORMER SPECIAL FIELD AGENT MIKE JOHNSON

You could call it that. The guy was crazy. He put away close to—

UNIDENTIFIED WOMAN

The Canadian? What did he do?

FORMER SPECIAL FIELD AGENT MIKE JOHNSON

Well, they threatened to turn the plane around, number one.

FORMER SPECIAL FIELD AGENT CHRIS NOLAN

I would have turned the plane around. The verbal abuse alone was—

FORMER SPECIAL FIELD AGENT MIKE JOHNSON

Stars and Stripes got up to take care of it when it looked as if there was going to be an altercation.

UNIDENTIFIED WOMAN

Altercation?

FORMER SPECIAL FIELD AGENT CHRIS NOLAN

Yessir... um... he, the Canadian, and the teacher began to argue about a woman on a magazine cover. The Canadian made some comments about... um... the model turned actress... that he wished he—

FORMER SPECIAL FIELD AGENT MIKE JOHNSON

You know the redhead, Mary Kate or something like—

UNIDENTIFIED WOMAN

Oh lord... It's Jane. Mary Jane. What did he say?

FORMER SPECIAL FIELD AGENT MIKE JOHNSON

I'd prefer not to go into specifics but it ended with the Canadian calling her a "hot momma."

UNIDENTIFIED WOMAN

"Hot momma"? Seriously?

FORMER SPECIAL FIELD AGENT CHRIS NOLAN

I couldn't make this up. Not in all our years as delivery boys had I seen anything like this

UNIDENTIFIED WOMAN

I know you two are retired... but I needed my best. And most discreet.

FORMER SPECIAL FIELD AGENT CHRIS NOLAN

Well, this was the craziest thing I've seen. Even in '92 when we had the Eagle following his ascension...

UNIDENTIFIED WOMAN

I know you love your stories, Chris, but we're on a time frame. How did you settle the situation?

FORMER SPECIAL FIELD AGENT MIKE JOHNSON

Like I was saying, Stars and Stripes got up to calm them down. The teacher calmed down immediately. Looked like he'd been caught talking in the back of the room.

FORMER SPECIAL FIELD AGENT CHRIS NOLAN (LAUGHING)

Yeah. That one seemed like a nice enough kid. Reminds me of my son. Did you know—?

HOME   ADVANCED SEARCH   DATABASES   LOG OUT

CRIMINAL DATABASE → S.H.I.E.L.D. DOCUMENT 987-53647-33281-8iKTY (Cont.)

UNIDENTIFIED WOMAN
Timeframe, Chris. We'll catch up at the next reunion.
FORMER SPECIAL FIELD AGENT CHRIS NOLAN
Right... Sure. So the Canadian stood up and told Stars and Stripes to mind his own business.
FORMER SPECIAL FIELD AGENT MIKE JOHNSON
"Why don't you mind your own business, bub."
UNIDENTIFIED WOMAN
He said "bub"?
FORMER SPECIAL FIELD AGENT CHRIS NOLAN
Yeah. Bub.
UNIDENTIFIED WOMAN
Oh, boy.
FORMER SPECIAL FIELD AGENT MIKE JOHNSON
So it looked as if the two were going to tussle. We used maneuver twenty-three... "the friendly patrons" and tranqued him with the special stuff you gave us.
UNIDENTIFIED WOMAN
Did anyone—?
FORMER SPECIAL FIELD AGENT CHRIS NOLAN
No sir. Things were quite heated at that point— I don't think anyone saw. Although the large—um— Mr. Cage smiled at us.
UNIDENTIFIED WOMAN
Smiled? Really?
FORMER SPECIAL FIELD AGENT CHRIS NOLAN
Is that bad?
UNIDENTIFIED WOMAN
No. I just have never seen him smile. At least not before beating someone within an inch of his life
FORMER SPECIAL FIELD AGENT MIKE JOHNSON
Um... The stuff we used on the Canadian. The stuff you told us we might need for him. It was the "elephant paralyzer"?
UNIDENTIFIED WOMAN
That's right.
FORMER SPECIAL FIELD AGENT MIKE JOHNSON
Twenty minutes. We used enough to knock him out for three days, sir...
FORMER SPECIAL FIELD AGENT CHRIS NOLAN
What the hell did you get us into?
UNIDENTIFIED WOMAN
Nothing you guys couldn't handle. You guys were the best babysitters in the business. That's why I called you in.
FORMER SPECIAL FIELD AGENT CHRIS NOLAN
Yeah. Those were the days, huh?
UNIDENTIFIED WOMAN
Yes they were...
FORMER SPECIAL FIELD AGENT MIKE JOHNSON
This a big deal, sir?

CRIMINAL DATABASE >> S.H.I.E.L.D. DOCUMENT 98733647-33281 RISTY (Cont.)

UNIDENTIFIED WOMAN
The biggest... So what happened when he woke up?

FORMER SPECIAL FIELD AGENT CHRIS NOLAN
He seemed to forget the whole thing.

UNIDENTIFIED WOMAN
Yeah. He tends to do that. He's been toyed with a bit upstairs.

FORMER SPECIAL FIELD AGENT MIKE JOHNSON
Then he asked the teacher how his wife was.

UNIDENTIFIED WOMAN
Oh lord.

FORMER SPECIAL FIELD AGENT CHRIS NOLAN
But the kid just pretended to be asleep.

UNIDENTIFIED WOMAN
He's a good boy...

FORMER SPECIAL FIELD AGENT CHRIS NOLAN
He sure reminded me of my son.

UNIDENTIFIED WOMAN
I'd like to meet him soon, Chris. Maybe after all of this is over.

FORMER SPECIAL FIELD AGENT CHRIS NOLAN
Yessir. That would be nice.

FORMER SPECIAL FIELD AGENT MIKE JOHNSON
Do you need our help, sir? We're rusty but ready.

UNIDENTIFIED WOMAN
No. You two have done enough. Now go catch your connecting flight. And enjoy the rest of your vacation.

FORMER SPECIAL FIELD AGENT CHRIS NOLAN
Hell of a way to get to Hawaii.

FORMER SPECIAL FIELD AGENT MIKE JOHNSON
Take care.

UNIDENTIFIED WOMAN
You too, boys. You too. And next time you see me, don't call me sir.

Former Field Agents Johnson and Nolan then boarded flight 325 bound for Hawaii. The unidentified woman slipped into the ladies' room and was never seen again. Marked for possible entry into rogue-agent log on Fury's approval.

END OF TAPE
TRANSCRIPT MARKED FOR DELETION BY FURY
NO LOG ENTRY NECESSARY

S.H.I.E.L.D.
OPERATIONS DATABASE

HOME | **ADVANCED SEARCH** | DATABASES | **LOG OUT**

RECORDED IN ROOM 274
CLEARANCE – BLACK
LEVEL 10 EYES ONLY
AGENTS IN ROOM
NICK FURY [Level 10] and STEVE ROGERS [a.k.a. Captain America]

NICK FURY

Say what's on your mind, Steve. You don't have to worry. No one can hear us in here.

CAPTAIN AMERICA

You know why I'm here, Nick. We have to tell them. They need to know what happened if only so they can protect themselves against—

NICK FURY

No. We've covered this. This was not an Avengers mission that was going to pop up in the Bugle on Monday morning. This was bigger than that.

CAPTAIN AMERICA

I know that, Nick. I'm talking about the others. The ones who fought for you. Luke, Parker, Matt – even Logan – they deserve to know what they were a part of.

NICK FURY

It's not that simple, Steve. Not everything is black and white. I thought you'd been unthawed long enough to know that...

1 minute and 24 seconds of silence...

NICK FURY

I'm sorry, Steve. That was unfair. Keeping this secret and quiet... It's for their own—

CAPTAIN AMERICA

If you say safety, you're crazy. How does keeping them in the dark make them safe? These are grown men and women. They need to know.

NICK FURY

No one can know what happened. End of story, Steve. You know how bad it was. What we did... what we had to do. It needed to be secret. It needed to get done. Bottom line.

CAPTAIN AMERICA

It's wrong, Nick. If something were to happen. If—

NICK FURY

What could happen? It's been six months. And nothing has happened. It was a war. You fight it like any war and if there are repercussions, so be it. The mission ended the day we went our separate ways. Nothing more. Nothing less.

SEARCH DATABASE **TRANSCRIPTS, SECRET WAR** SEARCH

CAPTAIN AMERICA

You don't really believe that, do you? We may be able to handle the repercussions but Cage... Parker... Murdock... all of them... they trusted you. Calling revenge against men who trusted you and were willing to give their lives for your war... to call that repercussions? That's something those fat guys in suits you're so fond of mocking would say.

NICK FURY

Now it's my turn to be silent, huh?

CAPTAIN AMERICA

I didn't come here to fight with you, Nick—

NICK FURY

Could have fooled me, Steve. What did you come for then?

CAPTAIN AMERICA

Because I want you to do the right thing. Need you to. This country is great because of men like you. I trust you. You trusted us to go. To help. Trusted these men to know what they were a part of, if for nothing more than to give them a chance to defend themselves. Retribution, Nick. It will come.

NICK FURY

It's bigger than that, Steve. And if it does come, these guys are grown men. They can handle themselves.

CAPTAIN AMERICA

I hope you're right, Nick.

NICK FURY

Steve?

CAPTAIN AMERICA

What?

NICK FURY

Why don't you just tell them?

CAPTAIN AMERICA

It's not my place. It was your war. You had your reasons for running it the way you did. I was a soldier in a war before and.... Soldiers don't make policy. I'm just telling you, there will come a reckoning. And they should be prepared for it.

(Door opens. Captain America leaves room.)

Tape runs silent for 22 minutes and 43 seconds.

(Nick Fury departs room)

END OF RECORDING
ERASED BY NICK FURY (LEVEL 10)

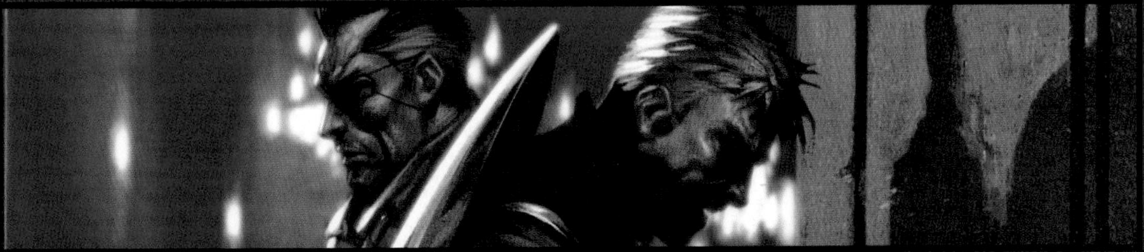

S.H.I.E.L.D.
OPERATIONS DATABASE

HOME | ADVANCED SEARCH | DATABASES | LOG OUT

S.H.I.E.L.D. FILE NUMBER 5353557-72SCO ADD
PROJECT DATABASE -> PROJECT: 9083728-1245 SWR_AFT

LETTER FOUND IN APARTMENT OF KALI HUDAK
EX-WIFE OF JAMAL HUDAK (SCORCHER – FILE 5353557-72SCO)
DISCOVERED 6/14/05 BY S.H.I.E.L.D. AGENT SIMONSON

POSTMARKED 6/09/05. MAILED FROM NYC ADDRESS.
RETRIEVED FROM TRASH ALONG WITH $380 CASH (3 $50'S, 7 $20'S, 1 $10)

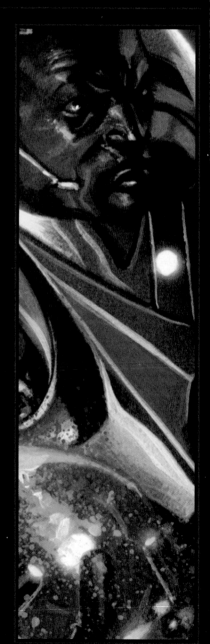

Dear Kali,

Here's some money. I know it's not much. I've been busy taking care of things. You know how it is. I've been in a bit of a rut. You lived it for eleven years so you should know what I'm talking about. And I'm still sorry about it. Neither of you deserved what we were going through.

How is Lucas? Is he still getting good grades? He got your book smarts, didn't he? Tell him I miss him. And that I'm thinking of him. Does he know who I am? Does he remember me? Do you tell him about me? I don't blame you if you don't. A lot of things didn't really go as planned, did they?

I need you to do something for me. I know you don't want to listen but if you won't do it for me, do it for Lucas. I need you to leave town for a week or so. I can't explain it. I won't ask you to trust me. I guess I know better than to do that. Just use the money to get a nice hotel room in Jersey or go visit your mom in Cleveland. Please get out of the city.

Something big is happening. I've been called in for a thing which I'm not really sure about but it involves a lot of my colleagues who are in a similar line of work. Other technicians. The guy who fixes my hardware called in a marker and we're all doing a job together. Not a normal thing. It's going down in New York in the next couple of days and I'm worried about you and Lucas. So, even though I know you hate my life and what I've done with it, please listen.

I swear I'm thinking about giving up the life. Things have gotten scary. I can't get much more into it than that but I'm worried. I got into this to get rich. Not to hurt people. Just make sure you leave the same day you get this.

Maybe after this is all over we can try again. I would really like to be a part of my son's life. I'll send another letter after this is over. Just stay clear of the city.

Love,
Jamal

S.H.I.E.L.D. FILE NUMBER 9205013-55DB(UPDATED)

REAL NAME: Debbie Bertrand
ALIASES: Diamondback
IDENTITY STATUS: Known to S.H.I.E.L.D.
MARITAL STATUS: Single
RELATIVES: David Bertrand (father), Kirsty Bertrand (mother)
BASE OF OPERATIONS: Mobile
PLACE OF BIRTH: Greenville, North Carolina
LEGAL STATUS: American citizen with no previous criminal record
OCCUPATION: College student, University of North Carolina; All-American Olympic athlete, possible mercenary, (former) waitress
AFFILIATIONS: Lucia von Bardas (former president of Latvaria); Tinkerer; Scorcher
ENEMIES: Unknown
HEIGHT: 5' 6" **WEIGHT:** 125 lbs. **EYES:** Blue **HAIR:** Formerly blonde, now dyed red
POWERS/WEAPONS: Olympic-level athlete excelling in gymnastics. Accomplished hand-to-hand combatant, expert knife thrower, numerous 4-inch elongated diamond-shaped throwing spikes. Carries "diamonds," needle-sharp, occasionally filled with various substances.

NICK FURY NOTE: This new Diamondback is going to have a problem when the real deal finds out someone has taken her shtick. Rachel is going to flat out kick this girl's butt. Debbie here seems new to the game, her actions and attitude suggest she's a first timer and is extremely paranoid that she'll get caught—that's exactly why it'll be so easy. She'll overplan and doesn't seem to adapt well.

LEVEL 5 - EXTENDED NOTES

Extended Notes provided by Special Agent Jasper Sitwell

Why? Why can't these losers figure out their own name? I mean is Diamondback so desirable a villain name that we needed, what, three of them now? Was there such a legacy provided by the former Diamondback as a part of the Serpent Society that Debbie Bertrand had to choose that name? Or did she think it would get her some time with Captain America? The previous Diamondback and Cap were involved for a time. At least she didn't pattern herself after Cage's old foe, Willis Stryker, who was killed by his own exploding knife!

Either way, whenever one of these villains appears using an old name I get sent to deal with it. How come Woo is never called in? Or Special Agent Drew? Jessica's in charge of the RAFT and all the crazies we put there. You'd think it would be a good idea for a super-powered agent to deal with these freaks.

Instead, once we've pieced together what small bits of information we can about these crazies from small pieces of paper -- name, hometown, relatives, schooling -- I'm left scouring Middle America for the reason these people lose it. My daddy ignored me. My boyfriend left me. My mommy didn't love me enough. I heard voices. I wish just once I met up with the parents and they said, "Well, Debbie seemed to be the daughter of Satan from the moment she was born. There was not a good bone in that girl's body. We hope you arrest her soon." But it doesn't work that way. Most parents say it couldn't be their son or daughter. Our son/daughter was an angel.

Debbie Bertrand was no different. A twist of fate here or there and she would have lived a normal life. Instead she receives the heading 9205013-55DB in a S.H.I.E.L.D. file. And it's just my luck I end up having to fill that file. I'm sure Woo is having a great vacation. Maybe when he gets back I can take one.

S.H.I.E.L.D.
OPERATIONS DATABASE

HOME | ADVANCED SEARCH | DATABASES | LOG OUT

S.H.I.E.L.D. FILE NUMBER 77822190-01276 HJFBK
CRIMINAL DATABASE > OPERATIONS DOCUMENT > INTERVIEW
SECRET CODE: WHITE
INTERVIEW TRANSCRIPT
SUBJECT: DAVID AND KIRSTY BERTRAND, PARENTS OF DEBBIE BERTRAND A.K.A. DIAMONDBACK
Interview conducted by S.H.I.E.L.D. Agent Jasper Sitwell (Level 8)
CODE CLEARANCE: WHITE.
INTERVIEW OBSERVED BY S.H.I.E.L.D. AGENT CLAY QUARTERMAIN (LEVEL 5)
Recording Date: 4/17/05
Place: S.H.I.E.L.D. Compound, Raleigh, North Carolina

S.H.I.E.L.D. AGENT JASPER SITWELL

Hello, Mr. and Mrs. Bertrand, my name is Jasper Sitwell. As you probably realize, I'm a S.H.I.E.L.D. Agent. I hope your trip was all right. Just so you know, we will be recording this conversation and it is being observed by one of my immediate superiors.

MRS. BERTRAND

Recorded?

S.H.I.E.L.D. AGENT JASPER SITWELL

Yes. Standard procedure. Protects you and us and keeps everything –

MR. BERTRAND

Why are we here, Agent Sitwell?

S.H.I.E.L.D. AGENT JASPER SITWELL

We've asked you here to tell us a bit about your daughter—

MRS. BERTRAND

Is Debbie okay? Is she dead? Ohmigod. What's happened to—

MR. BERTRAND

Let the man talk, Kirsty. If Debbie's in trouble, let's not make it worse by upsetting a man trying to do his job... Is she dead?

S.H.I.E.L.D. AGENT JASPER SITWELL

No. She's not dead, Mr. Bertrand. But I can understand your concern and I apologize for the secrecy in calling you here. As crazy as this sounds, Debbie has taken on the guise of Diamondback and engaged in multiple criminal acts.

MR. BERTRAND

What?

MRS. BERTRAND

You have to be wrong. She is working as a waitress in Charleston for the summer. She even told me she had an interview with one of her seminar professors from freshmen year. She—

S.H.I.E.L.D. AGENT JASPER SITWELL

She hasn't been to her job at Chimichuchu's in over two months. According to her shift manager... um, Chip, she showed up for her paycheck one Friday and just never came back.

MR. BERTRAND

Agent Sitwell, are you sure it's her? Maybe—

S.H.I.E.L.D. AGENT JASPER SITWELL

It's her, sir.

MR. BERTRAND

Okay... okay. What can we do to help? Do we need lawyers?

S.H.I.E.L.D. AGENT JASPER SITWELL

No lawyers unless you feel uncomfortable with what's happening here. You're not in any trouble. We just need to find out a few things and try to trace the series of events. How did she get involved? Why did she get involved?

MRS. BERTRAND

So you want us to help you catch our daughter? I don't believe any of this but we're not going to help you put our daughter in jail. I won't allow—

MR. BERTRAND

Kirsty... please. Could you give us a minute, Agent Sitwell?

S.H.I.E.L.D. AGENT JASPER SITWELL

Sure. No problem. I'll shut down the recording device so you can have some privacy. Just knock on the door and I'll come back in.

MR. BERTRAND

Thank you.

Recording halted for 4 minutes and 38 seconds...

S.H.I.E.L.D. AGENT JASPER SITWELL

Is everything okay?

MR. BERTRAND

Yes. We'll answer your questions. Just promise us you'll try your best to help our daughter.

S.H.I.E.L.D. AGENT JASPER SITWELL

I'll do my best, Mr. Bertrand... OK. Let's start with the easy one. Was your daughter ever involved with any of these people?

MRS. BERTRAND

(Sitwell provides a series of photos including the Tinkerer, Scorcher, and Lucia von Bardas)

Debbie would never associate with men like this. How old is... waitaminute. Why is Dr. Bardas in this file? She took me to one of her seminars on Parents Weekend. We even went to lunch together. Lucia -- she told me to call her by her first name -- said Debbie had such potential. That was who her job interview was with. We were so proud when Debbie told us Dr. Bardas was elected Prime Minister of Luxemburg. Debbie was so --

S.H.I.E.L.D. AGENT JASPER SITWELL

Latveria... Bardas was elected Prime Minister of Latveria

MRS. BERTRAND

What did I say? I said Latveria, didn't I?

MR. BERTRAND

No, hon. Latveria is Doctor Doom's country. Isn't that right, Agent Sitwell?

S.H.I.E.L.D. AGENT JASPER SITWELL

Yes. It used to be. Quartermain? Did you get that?

S.H.I.E.L.D. AGENT CLAY QUARTERMAIN

Already contacted the big man. Fury is on his way.

S.H.I.E.L.D. AGENT JASPER SITWELL

Folks, you're going to have to sit tight for a bit. I'm sorry about this.

MR. BERTRAND

Will this help us help our daughter?

S.H.I.E.L.D. AGENT JASPER SITWELL

I hope so, sir.

MR. BERTRAND

Then stop apologizing. You're just doing your job. It's not your fault Debbie ended up the way she did.

S.H.I.E.L.D. AGENT JASPER SITWELL

Yes sir.

End Recording

S.H.I.E.L.D. FILE NUMBER 74054491982746378 DATABASE
PROJECT DATABASE → PROJECT 9083726-1948 SWF → LOGISTICS
→ FIELD REPORT & DOCS → COMMUNICATION
TRANSCRIPTS
SECRET CODE: WHITE
Recording Date 8/11/05 9:32 P.M.
Call Origin: S.H.I.E.L.D. Operations
Call Recipient: Jackson Research
Phone Location: Subject Unknown
Broadcast Secured: Pooled and processed at op site 7 code black

S.H.I.E.L.D. OPERATOR

Deputy Director?

CONTESSA VALENTINA ALLEGRO DE FONTAINE

Yes. I'm here. Is this a secure line?

S.H.I.E.L.D. OPERATOR

Of course, Contessa.

CONTESSA VALENTINA ALLEGRO DE FONTAINE

What do you have for me, Operator? I'm dealing with a bit of a situation here so let's keep it brief.

S.H.I.E.L.D. OPERATOR

Um, I've been monitoring the Jones woman's phone like you asked and coordinating any agent discussions in the field.

CONTESSA VALENTINA ALLEGRO DE FONTAINE

(mumbling heard off-line) Well, find him. How do you lose track of…? Anyway… Yes, Operator. I'm listening. Go ahead.

S.H.I.E.L.D. OPERATOR

She has called many subjects involved in Fury's altercation including Matt Murdock's law firm and Luke Cage. She also contacted Misty Knight and Danny Rand. Rand was seen at the hospital with Cage and Jones earlier, but this is the first contact we have with Knight. Not sure how she ties in—

CONTESSA VALENTINA ALLEGRO DE FONTAINE

Cage is Jones' boyfriend. She worked for Murdock. Knight worked with Rand and Cage. You boys need to study a bit better before an Op. If the photos of Cage and Rand aren't enough to keep you interested in the file, nothing will be.

S.H.I.E.L.D. OPERATOR

I'm just an operator, ma'am. I don't see a lot of the files. I'm not a field agent yet.

CONTESSA VALENTINA ALLEGRO DE FONTAINE

I know that. But if you want to get ahead you… just forget it. Is that all?

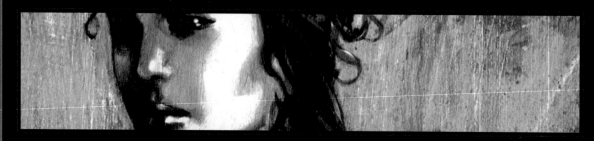

S.H.I.E.L.D. OPERATOR

No, ma'am... um, Contessa. It appears Murdock's home was attacked last night as well. Both he and Spider-Man were seen together. He... well, his Daredevil persona and Spider-Man were seen alongside Fury before...

CONTESSA VALENTINA ALLEGRO DE FONTAINE

Murdock's home as well? (yelling off phone) Why am I just getting this information? Let's start connecting the dots, people. This is not the way S.H.I.E.L.D. works. Is there anything else?

S.H.I.E.L.D. OPERATOR

Are you talking to me, ma'am?

CONTESSA VALENTINA ALLEGRO DE FONTAINE

Yes. Yes. Go on.

S.H.I.E.L.D. OPERATOR

We also know the Jones woman attempted to contact Special Agent Aspen.

CONTESSA VALENTINA ALLEGRO DE FONTAINE

Aspen? He's been off the board for over... well, it's apparent Jones is panicking a bit. And she seems to think her ex may have had some information. I thought Fury was there with her... all right. OK. Can we bring Jones in for some questioning? All of our agents are still in contact with her, right? Maybe we can try to calm her down a bit. According to Captain America she's pregnant so she shouldn't be running all over the city playing detective regardless of what's going on.

S.H.I.E.L.D. OPERATOR

I was about to get to that. There's been an incident. Following the disturbance last night and the disappearance of many of our principals we, uh, I've been informed we have lost contact with Jessica Jones. We still have the man she was with under surveillance... a Mr. Ben Urich. Reporter for the Daily Bugle and current co-worker.

CONTESSA VALENTINA ALLEGRO DE FONTAINE

You lost contact with a pregnant woman?

S.H.I.E.L.D. OPERATOR

Well, I wasn't... From what I can tell, our operatives were not aware she was a superhuman... or pregnant... and they lost her.

CONTESSA VALENTINA ALLEGRO DE FONTAINE

Not aware... do we work up these files for no reason?... (Talking off phone) We've lost Jones. I want a sweep to make sure she's not taking a catnap in her apartment or having a coffee at the Daily Bugle. Operator?

S.H.I.E.L.D. OPERATOR

I'm here, ma'am.

CONTESSA VALENTINA ALLEGRO DE FONTAINE

This situation has gone ROANOKE. Please delete this conversation as per protocols. Can you connect me with Special Agent Jessica Drew?

S.H.I.E.L.D. OPERATOR

Just a moment.

CONTESSA VALENTINA ALLEGRO DE FONTAINE

And one other thing. When you reach Field status, make sure you read the files. It will help your career last a little longer.

S.H.I.E.L.D. OPERATOR

... of course I will, Countess.

CONTESSA VALENTINA ALLEGRO DE FONTAINE

I'm sorry. It's not your fault Operator. It's been a trying 24 hours. You've been very helpful. I want a Level 9 line. My ears only.

LINE DISCONNECTED
IMMEDIATELY DELETED ACCORDING TO ROANOKE GUIDELINES.

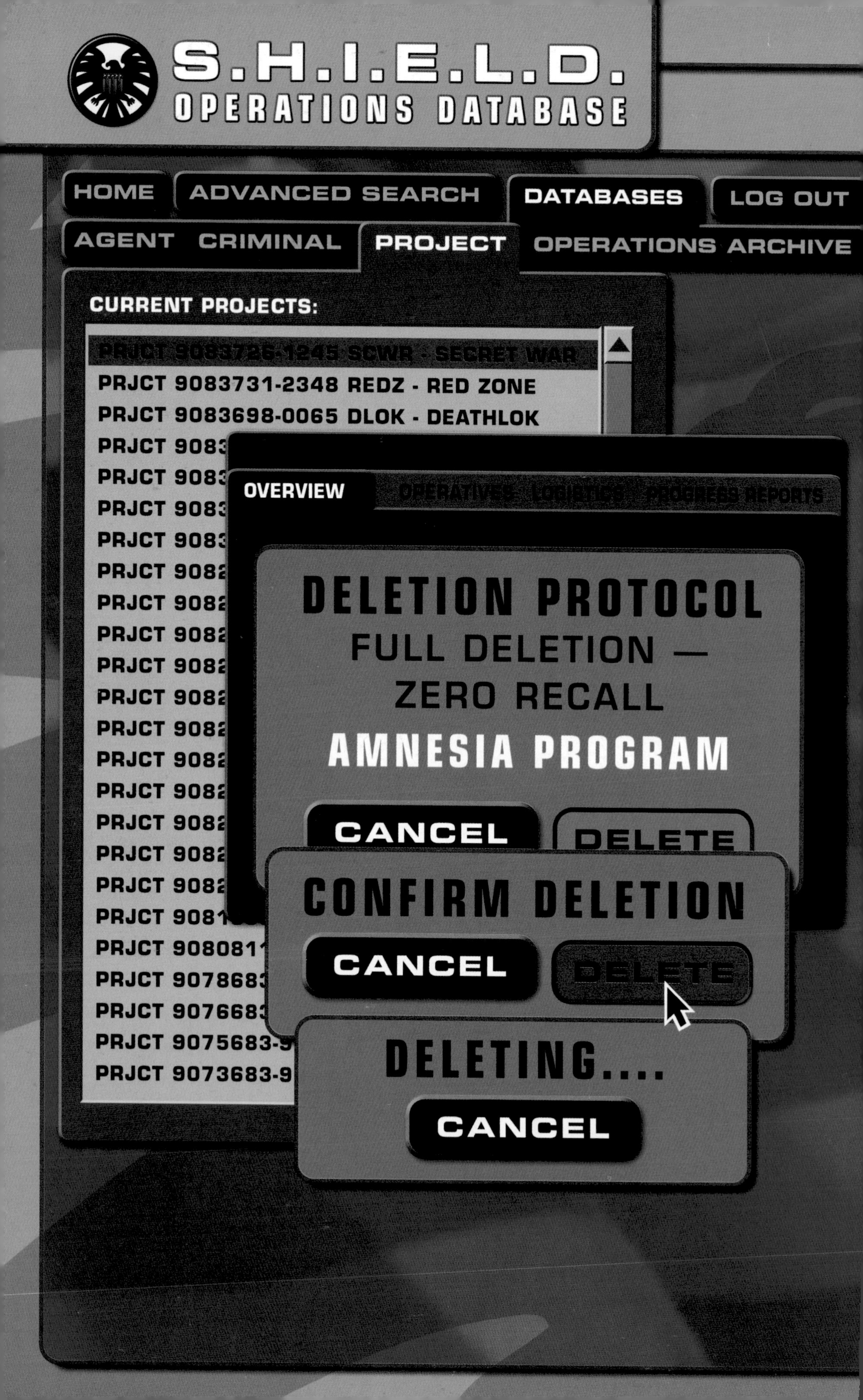

S.H.I.E.L.D.
OPERATIONS DATABASE

HOME | ADVANCED SEARCH | DATABASES | LOG OUT

AGENT | CRIMINAL | PROJECT | OPERATIONS ARCHIVE

CURRENT PROJECTS:

PRJCT 9083726-1245 SCWR - SECRET WAR
PRJCT 9083731-2348 REDZ - RED ZONE
PRJCT 9083698-0065 DLOK - DEATHLOK
PRJCT 9083
PRJCT 9083
PRJCT 9083
PRJCT 9083
PRJCT 9083
PRJCT 9082
PRJCT 9082
PRJCT 9082
PRJCT 9082
PRJCT 9082
PRJCT 9082
PRJCT 9082
PRJCT 9082
PRJCT 9082
PRJCT 9082
PRJCT 9082
PRJCT 9081
PRJCT 908081
PRJCT 9078683
PRJCT 9076683
PRJCT 9075683-9
PRJCT 9073683-9

OVERVIEW | OPERATIVES | LOGISTICS | PROGRESS REPORTS

DELETION PROTOCOL
FULL DELETION —
ZERO RECALL
AMNESIA PROGRAM

CANCEL | DELETE

CONFIRM DELETION

CANCEL | DELETE

DELETING....

CANCEL

SECRET WAR QUICK SYNOPSIS
BY BRIAN MICHAEL BENDIS

To all reading this—because of the unique nature of the scheduling format of the book, and how the story is unfolded, it in very important to me that this info not leak to the internet.

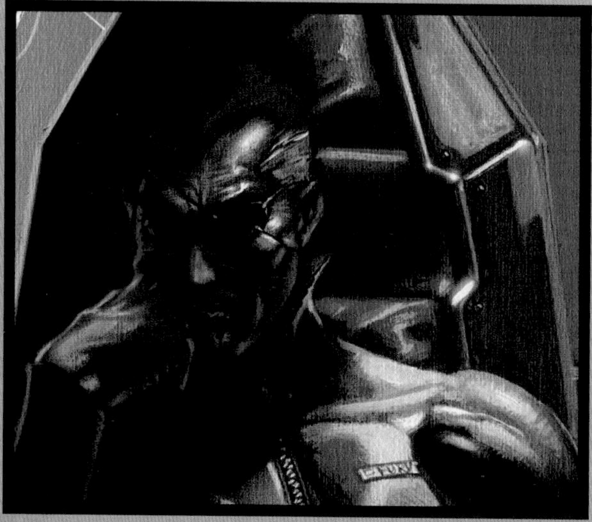

Nick Fury, director of S.H.I.E.L.D., Discovers the alarming fact that dozens of lower tier, technology based super criminals are being secretly funded by what America thinks is a new ally... The new prime minister of Latveria.

When Fury tells the president this alarming news, that these criminals are now technically foreign funded terrorists, he is dismissed in the name of world politics.

Fury, in a panic, knowing that something bad is brewing, something nightmarish, vows to do something to stop this even if his government won't.

Fury gathers some of the world's most colorful and misunderstood heroes, all people that owe him favors: Wolverine, Daredevil, Spider-man, Captain America, Black Widow, and Luke Cage for a covert trip to Latveria.

When they get there, Fury tells them the plan: that they are going to overthrow the Latverian government.

The mission is a failure. That was a year ago.

But now the secret war has come back to haunt Fury and his crew of superheroes. First Luke Cage, then Daredevil and Spider-man are attacked by an increasing large number of name Marvel tech villains as revenge on something they don't even remember doing.

What happened on that mission is a mystery to everyone involved because Nick Fury 'mind wiped' them for their own safety and security

Fury confesses that he mind wiped them without their knowledge- never realizing that Latveria would be so bold as to take revenge in such a manner.

The hero versus Villain battle takes to the streets and escalates to a level never before seen in New York city. Every superhero: the Avengers, Defenders, FF, and some of the X-men are called in to fight a large number of tech Marvel villains on the docks and piers of New York.

The president is forced to go to war with Latveria. The day is won.

All the heroes are very angry at Nick Fury at how he violated their lives. But he did it to save lives, and save lives he did. And with that Nick Fury hangs it up. He quits.

(Only to make a big comeback soon after, I am sure.)

Notes- In the mix of the battle we are introducing a couple of new heroes, and one villain will change sides, becoming a new Marvel hero with a lot to answer for.

Also, the fight scenes will resemble 'Black Hawk Down', dark and gritty battles versus the cosmic, big, Marvelly stuff that people might expect.

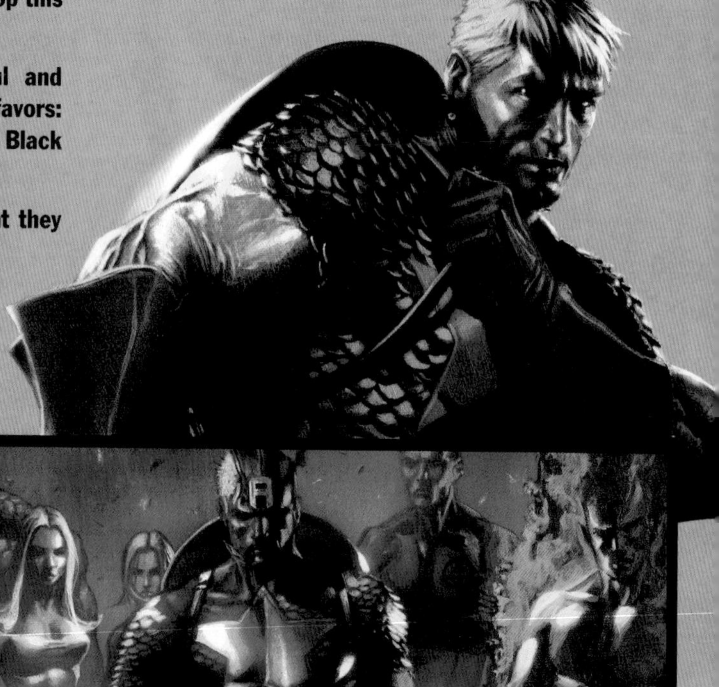

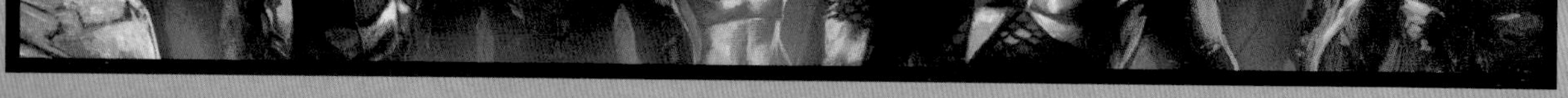

PAGE LAYOUTS BY BRAIN MICHAEL BENDIS

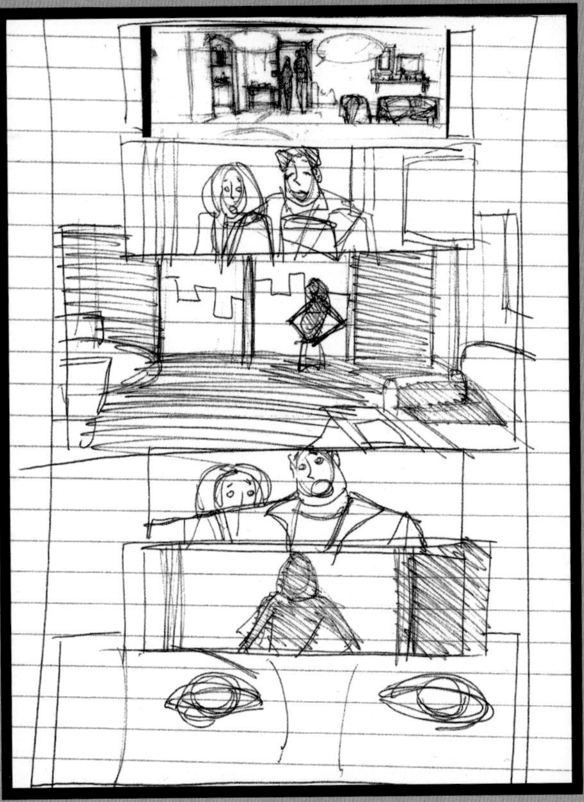

ISSUE #1, PAGE 2

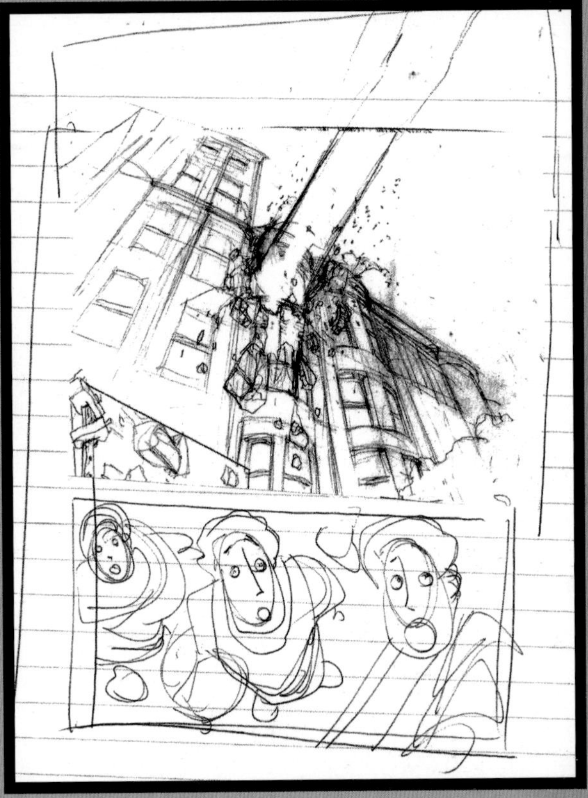

ISSUE #1, PAGE 3

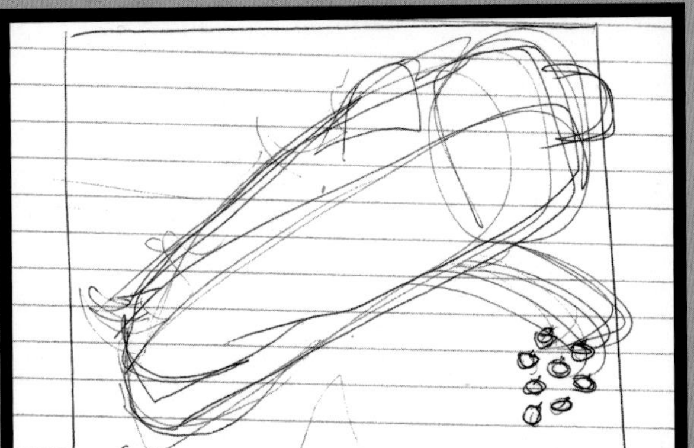

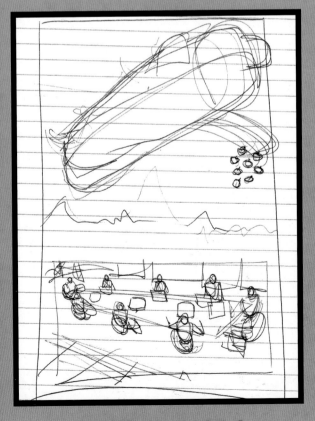

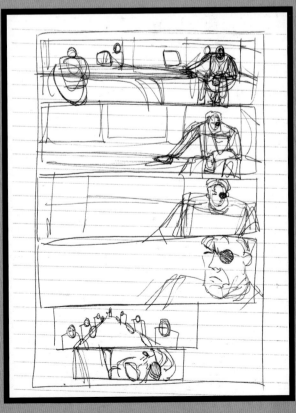

ISSUE #1, PAGE 4

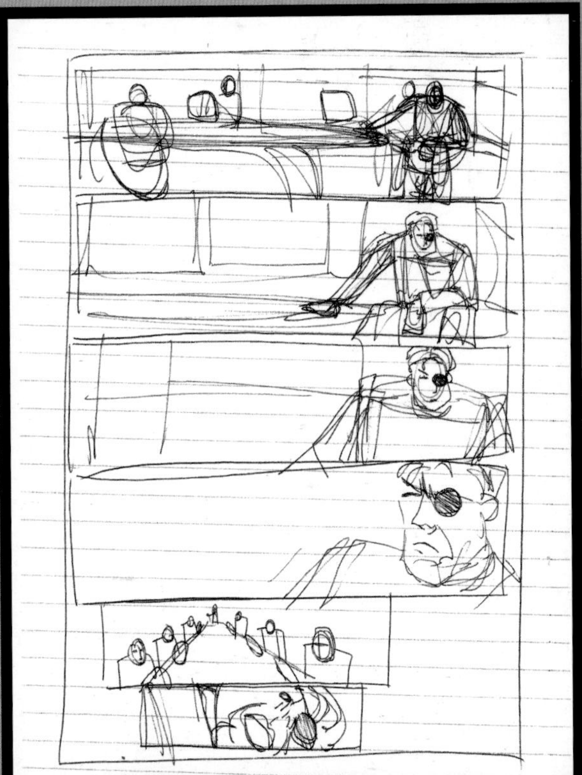

ISSUE #1, PAGE 5

PAGE LAYOUTS

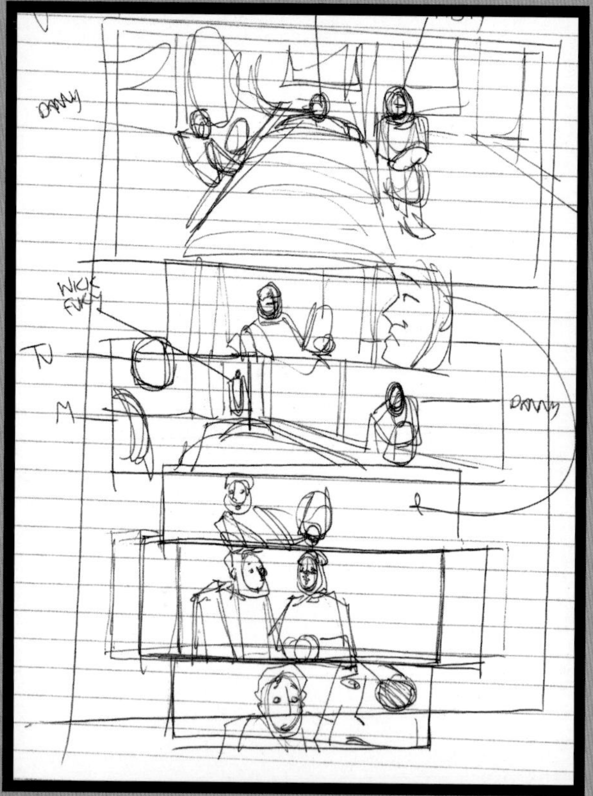
DANNY
NICK FURY
TV
M
DANNY

ISSUE #1, PAGE 6

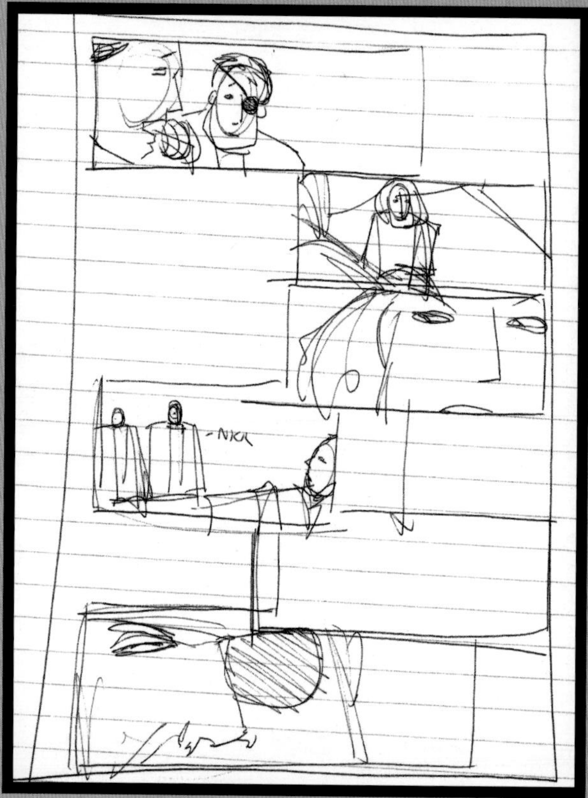
NICK

ISSUE #1, PAGE 7

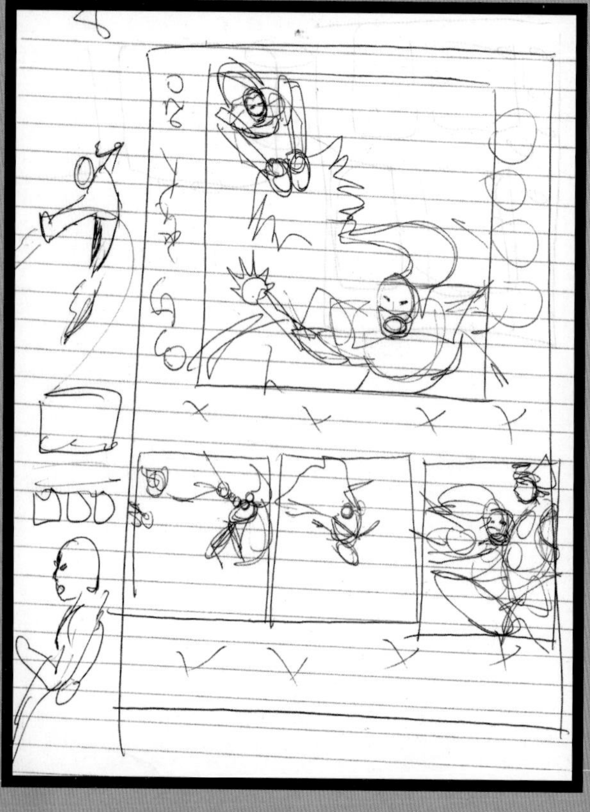

ISSUE #1, PAGE 8

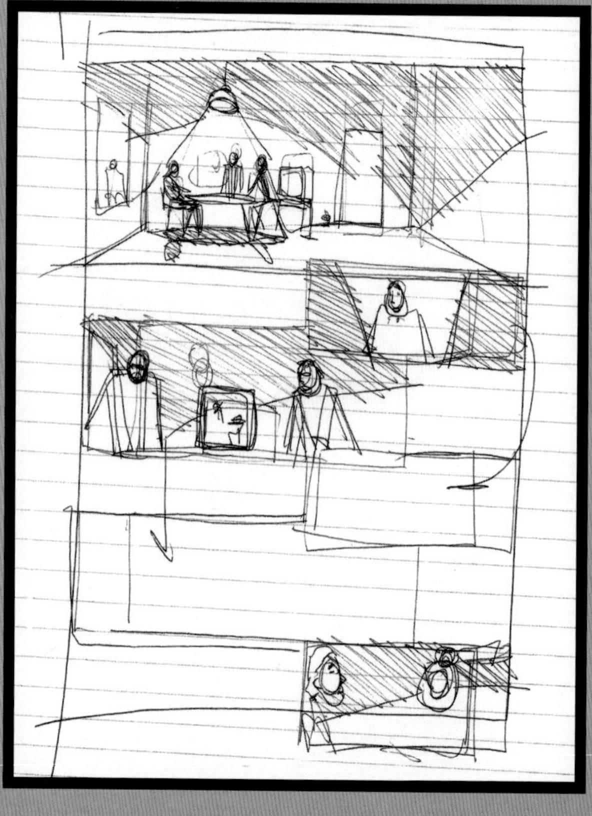

ISSUE #1, PAGE 9

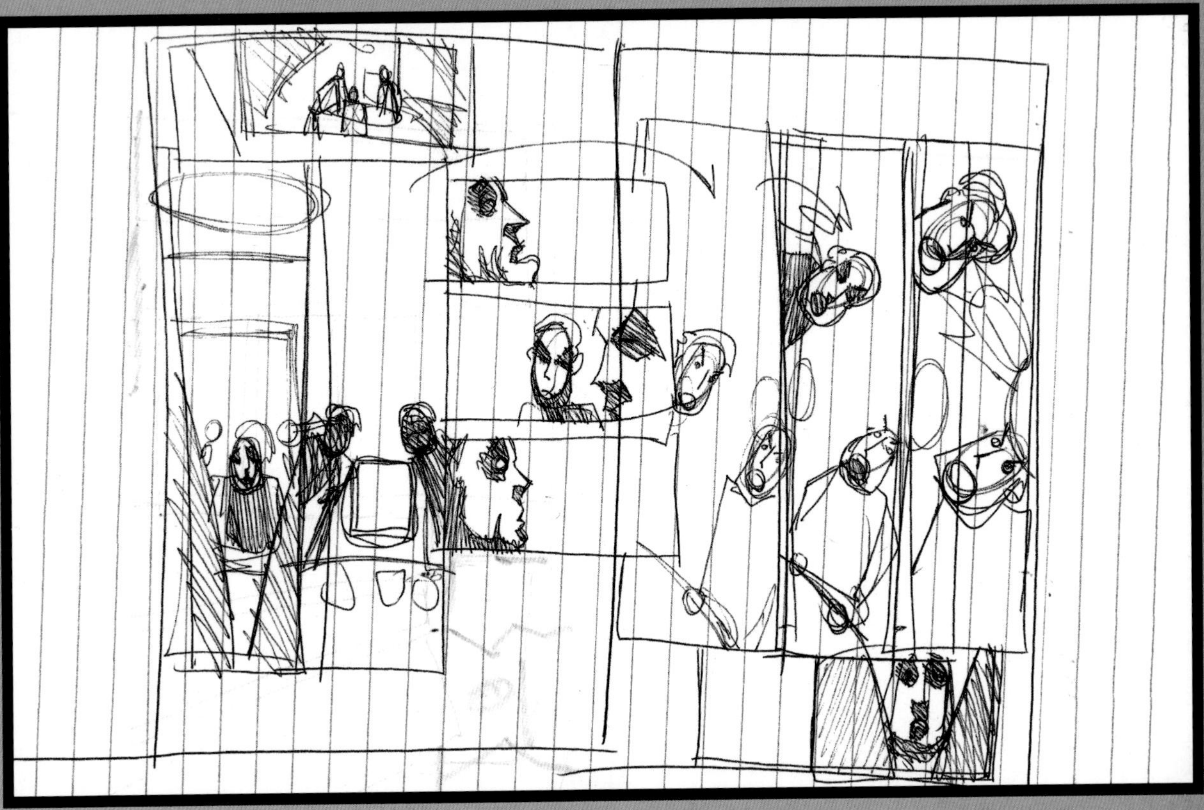

ISSUE #1, PAGE 10 & 11

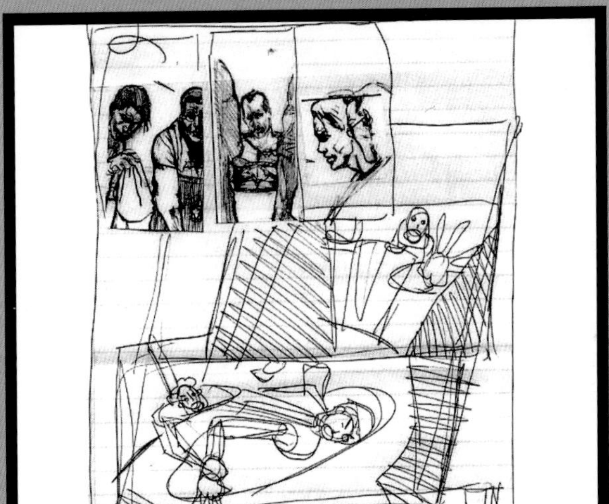

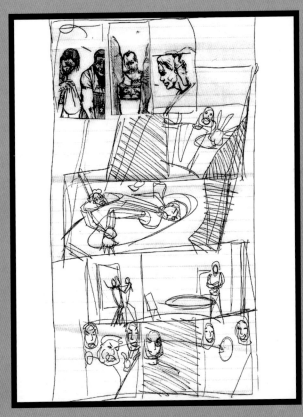

ISSUE #1, PAGE 12

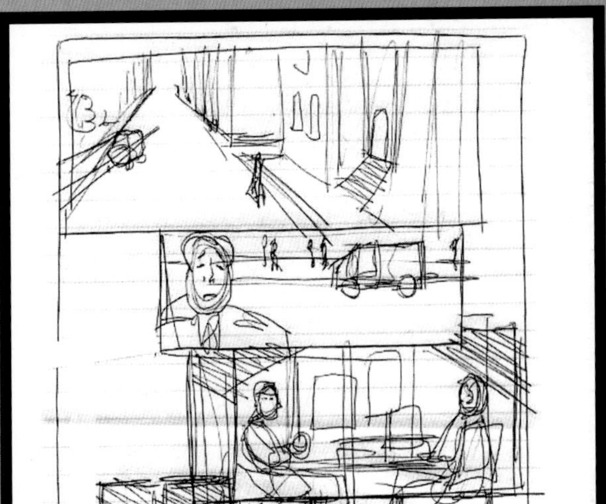

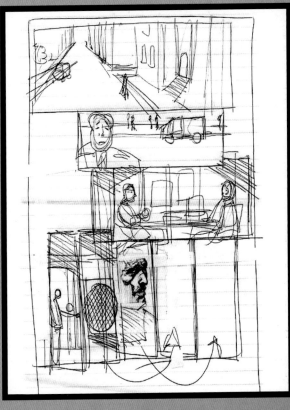

ISSUE #1, PAGE 13

PAGE LAYOUTS

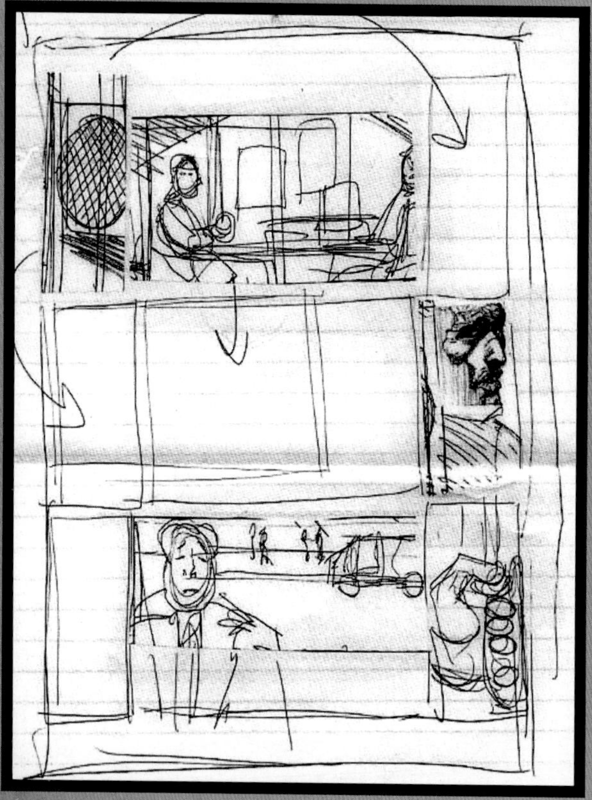

ISSUE #1, PAGE 14

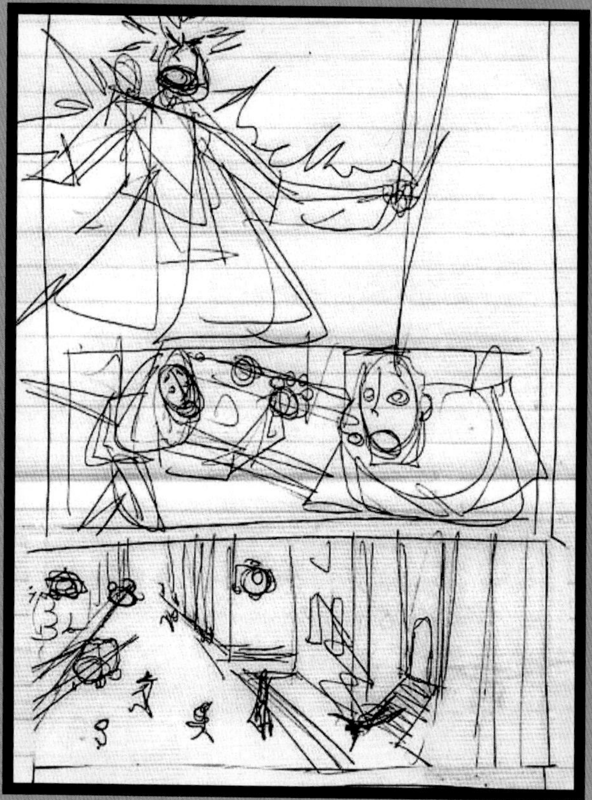

ISSUE #1, PAGE 15

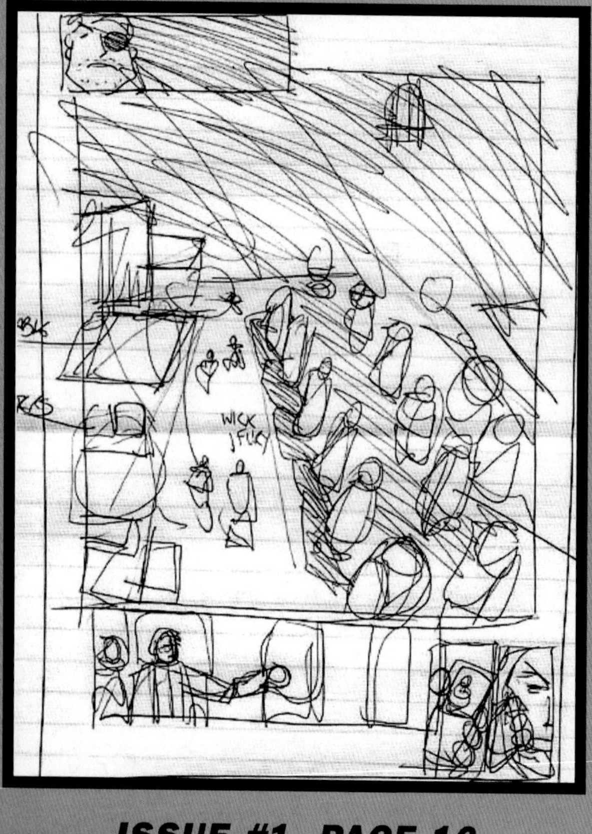

ISSUE #1, PAGE 16

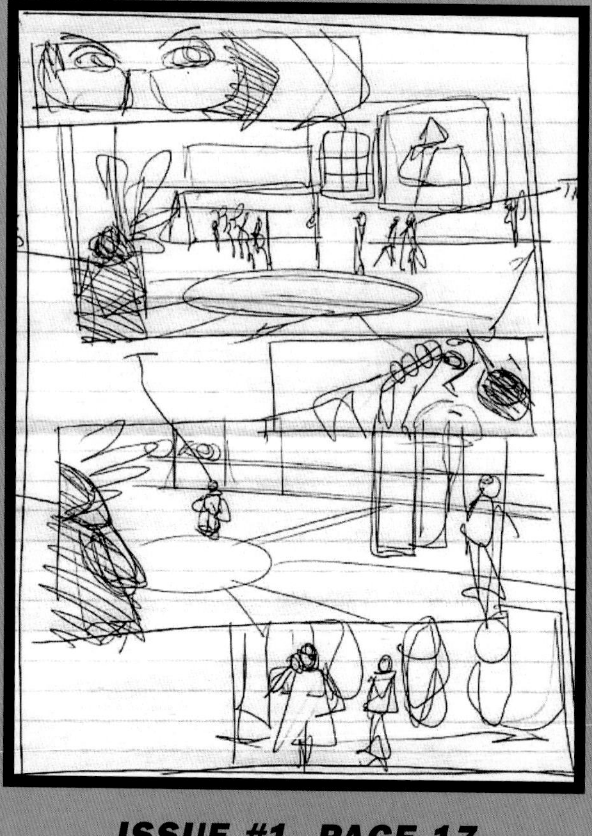

ISSUE #1, PAGE 17

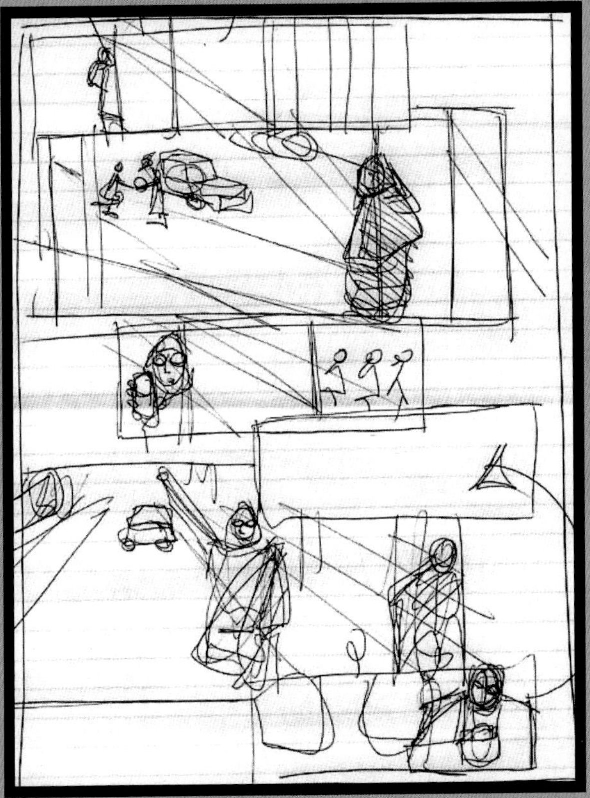

ISSUE #1, PAGE 18

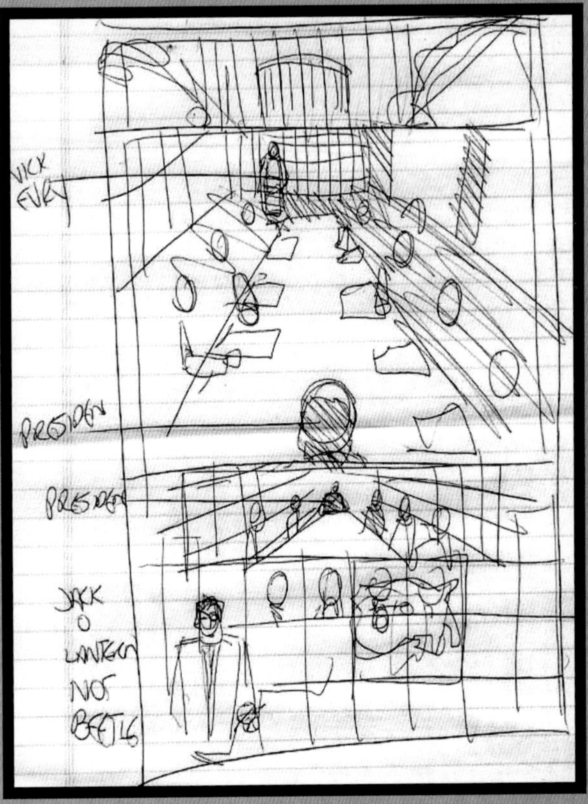
NICK FURY
PRESIDENT
PRESIDENT
JACK O LANTERN NOT BEETLE

ISSUE #1, PAGE 19

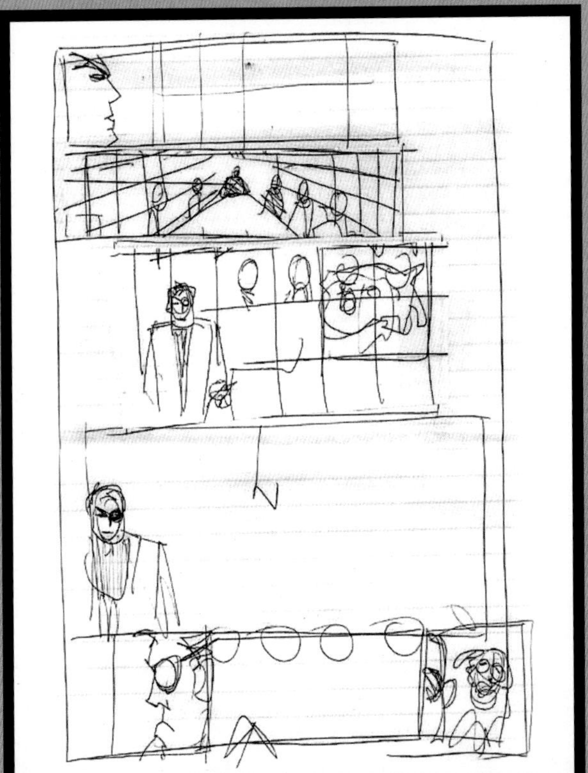

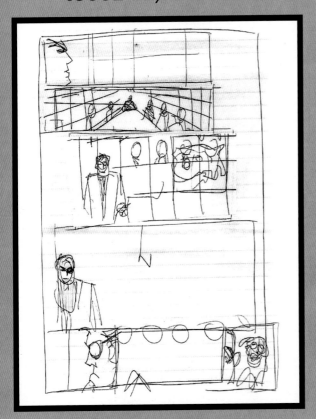

ISSUE #1, PAGE 20

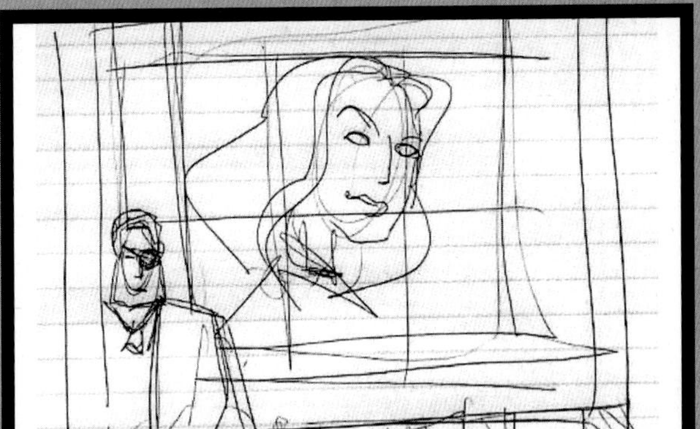

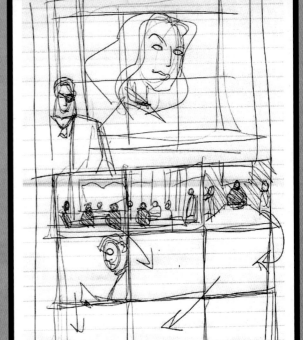

ISSUE #1, PAGE 21

PAGE LAYOUTS

ISSUE #1, PAGE 22

ISSUE #1, PAGE 23

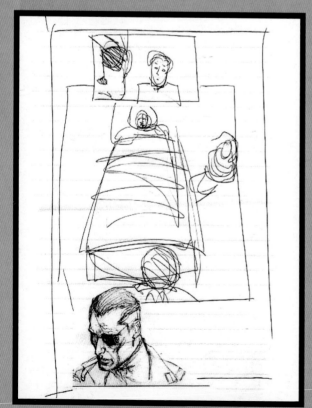

ISSUE #1, PAGE 24

COVER TO WIZARD #149 — BY DAVID FINCH

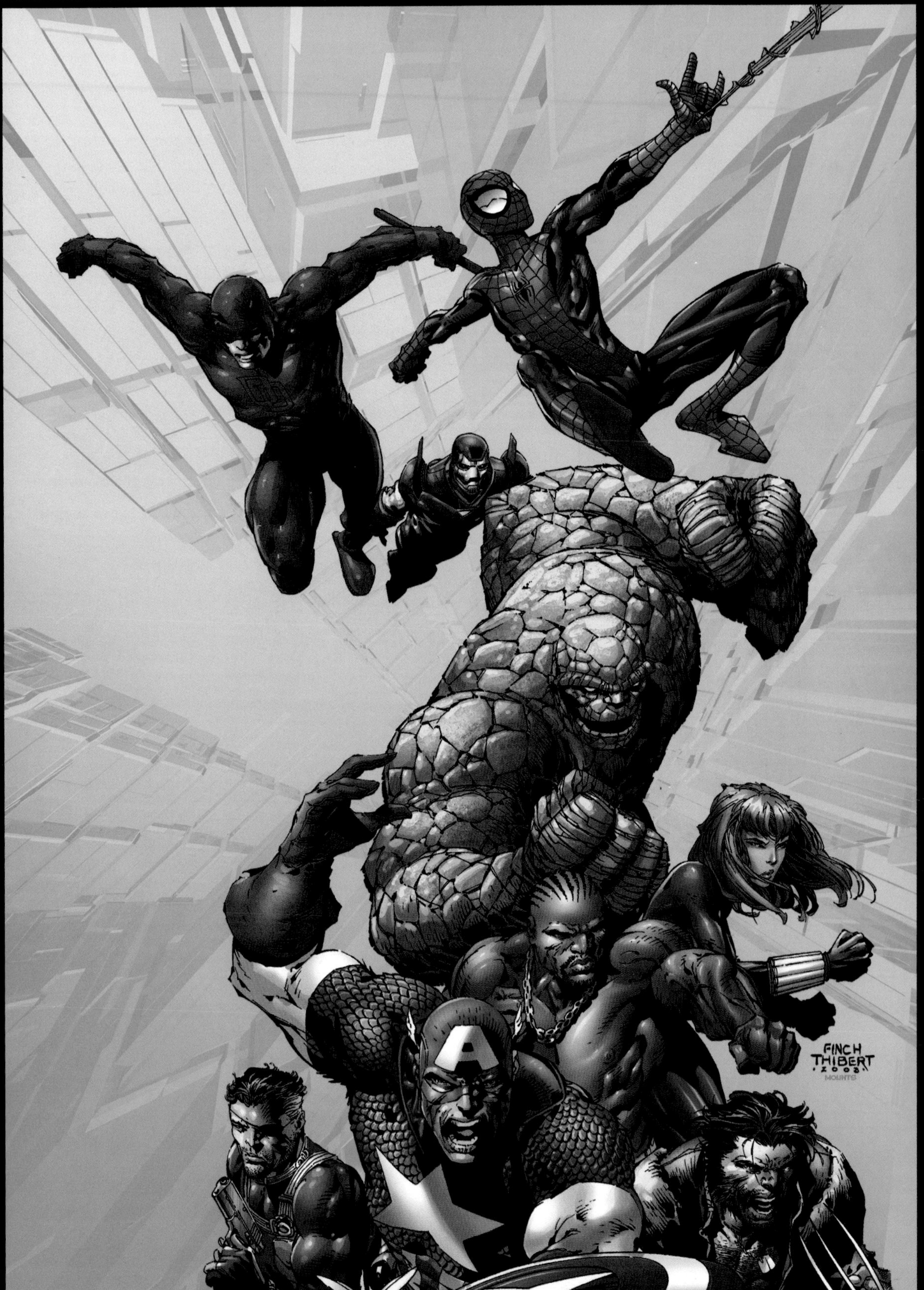

FINCH
THIBERT

THE COVERS

MARVEL
SECRET WAR
DIRECT EDITI

ISSUE #2 COVER SKETCH

MARVEL
SECRET WAR
DIRECT EDITION

ISSUE #3 COVER SKETCH

MARVEL
SECRET WAR
DIRECT EDITION

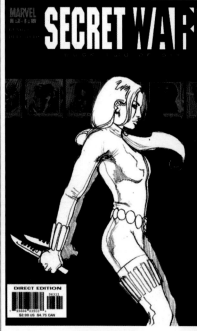

ISSUE #4 COVER SKETCH

INTRODUCTION

By Andy Schmidt

It's good to know talented people.

When Joe Quesada handed me SECRET WAR as a project early last year, I was absolutely terrified. I knew this was my opportunity to shine and I didn't want to mess up. However, had I known then what I know now about the people with whom I'd be working, I wouldn't have dropped a single bead of sweat.

What you're about to discover is the culmination of working with some of the most talented people in the industry. Before I introduce you to Adam Cichowski, our cover designer, let me walk you through what led to his involvement...

When I came on board, not a single page had been painted. I wish I could take credit for hiring Gab to paint the book, but Joe and Brian had already invited Gab into the fold. Man, what an inspired choice he was! This guy's enthusiasm for comics in general is staggering—his level of excitement for this project in particular is nothing less than intoxicating. Gab does far more than paint SECRET WAR; he is the driving inspirational force behind it.

Gab was so hot to start painting covers, he turned in sketches I hadn't asked for! Now, you've got to understand that Gab loves the splashy images—and as you're beginning to see in the series, he excels at them. He turned in an early (what we call "storytelling") cover (look to your right for it). It depicted a scene from the first issue, but this is a "secret" war and we didn't want to tip off what was happening in the book.

I went to Tom Brevoort and Joe to discuss the possibilities for cover designs. We all agreed on striking, single-figure images immediately. I went back to Gab with that, and it was time to do the covers, BIG and BOLD. As you've seen, Gab nailed them!

Simultaneously, I also went to Tom Marvelli (no, he doesn't own the company) and Adam Cichowski and said to them, "Here's the deal: I'll ask Gab for single figures, and it's up to you to make them look EVEN cooler." And because he's good at what he does, Adam made the images striking even without seeing any of Gab's sketches. As you'll see in the pages beyond, Adam took my very professional-sounding demand and helped cook up the most striking covers on the stands today.

So, I didn't design them or paint them. I did ask the right people to knock your socks off. And in typical Marvel style...they delivered. So to Gab and Adam, thanks for making my job easy—it's VERY good to know talented people!

I'll turn this over to Adam now to walk you through the design of the covers. Enjoy...

—Andy Schmidt
Editor

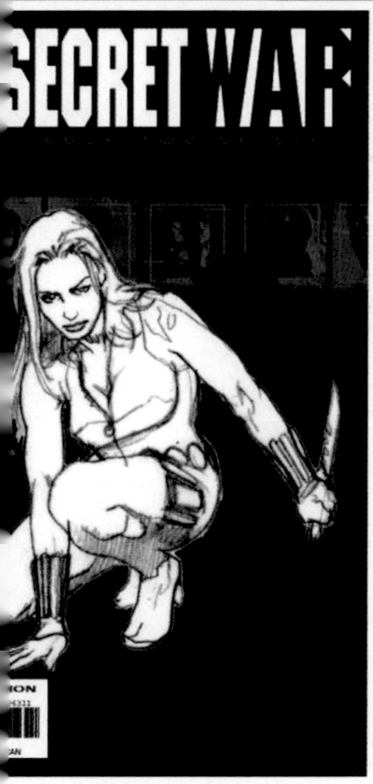
SECRET WAR

ISSUE #4 COVER SKETCH

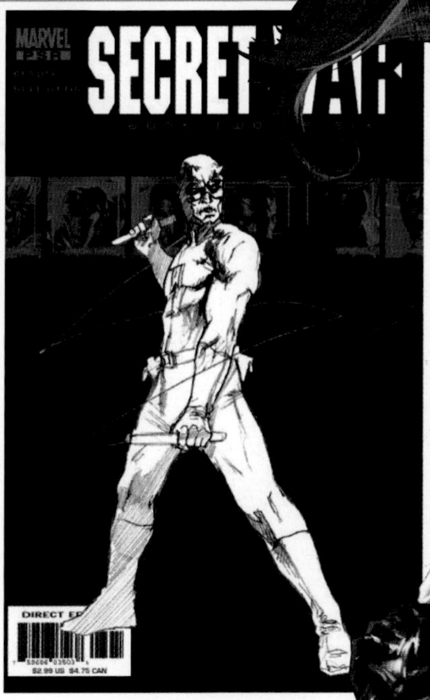
MARVEL
SECRET WAR
$2.99 US $4.75 CAN

ISSUE #5 COVER SKETCH

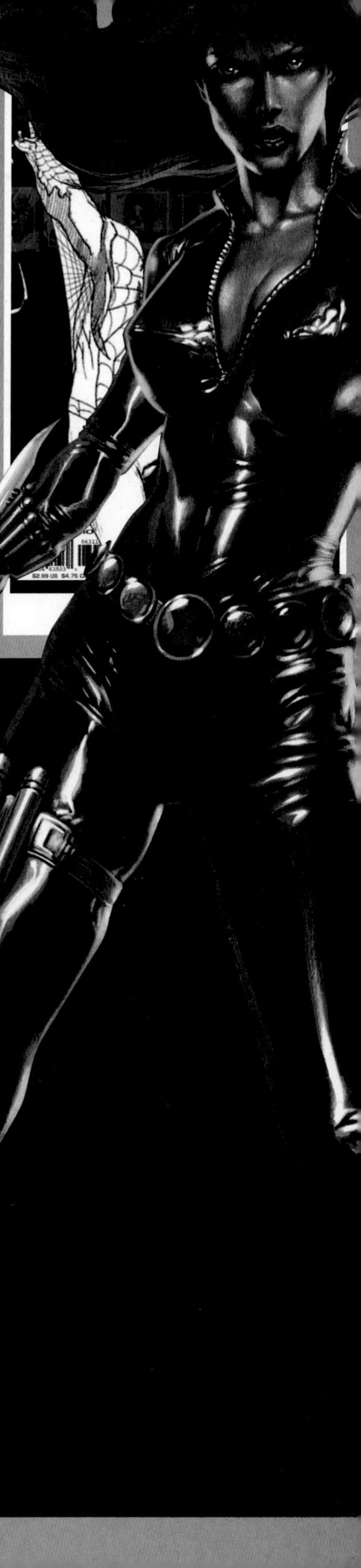

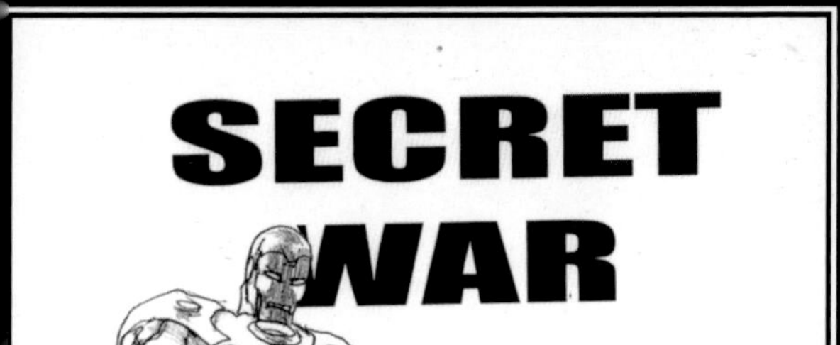
SECRET
WAR

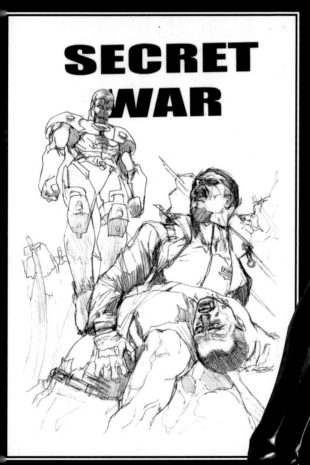

GABRIELE'S ORIGINAL COVER SKETCH FOR ISSUE #1

COVER MOCK-UP DESIGN'S

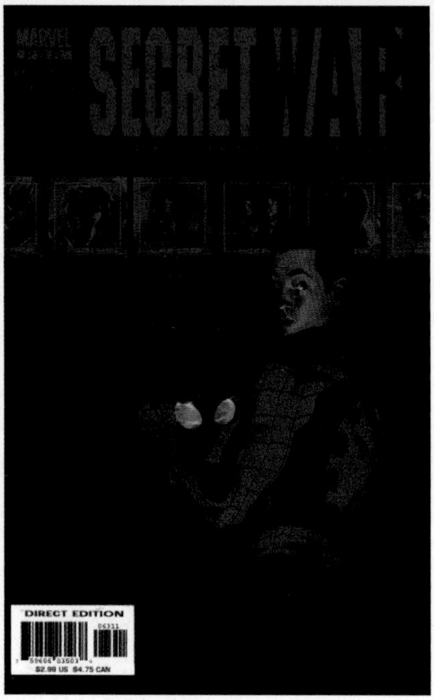
SECRET WAR
DIRECT EDITION
$2.99 US $4.75 CAN

FIGURE BY KAARE ANDREWS

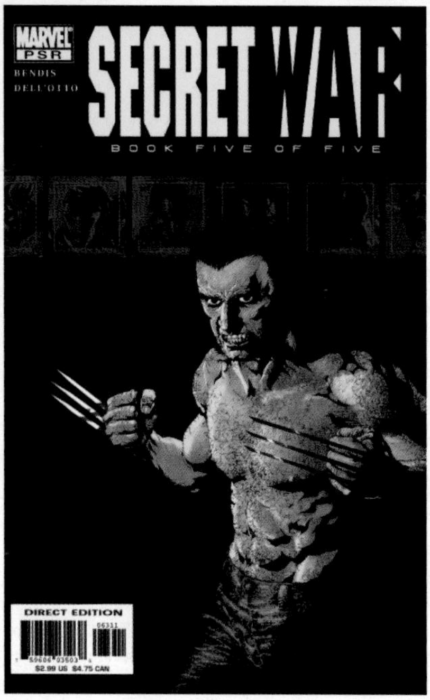
MARVEL
PSR
SECRET WAR
BENDIS
DELL'OTTO
BOOK FIVE OF FIVE
DIRECT EDITION
$2.99 US $4.75 CAN

FIGURE BY J. H. WILLIAMS

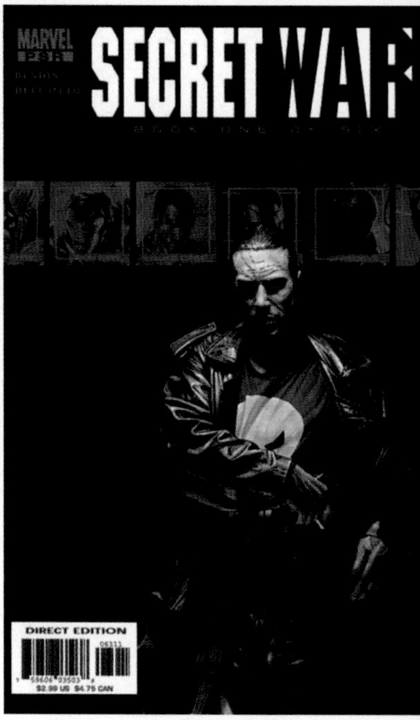
MARVEL
PSR
SECRET WAR
DIRECT EDITION
$2.99 US $4.75 CAN

FIGURE BY TIM BRADSTREET

DESIGNING THE SECRET WAR COVERS

By Adam Cichowski

I was asked to give a little behind-the-scenes account of how the covers to this series were created.

It started by meeting with the editors of the book. We decided that we wanted the covers to be iconic and serve as a template that could easily work for each issue's cover with only minor changes made. We felt that one cool image of a character per cover would be a simple strong design. Using the Punisher (who isn't used in the book, but it didn't matter, it was just to help convey the design), Spider-Man, Wolverine, Daredevil, Black Widow, and Captain America, I placed each figure on the cover around where we'd use the foil.

The first thing I did after getting the assignment was to review any artwork and scripts that were completed. I read the script to issue one and reviewed the artwork to parts one and two.

Then I tackled the logo. I knew that S.H.I.E.L.D. was involved, so I figured I should use a bold, blocky, strong, military-type font. Playing around with different ideas, I hit upon the notion that the "war" is a "secret." From there, I made the word "Secret" stand out and the word "War" inverted, somewhat hidden.

After finishing the logo, I went on to the cover design. I started by going through Marvel's massive digital archive, looking for the coolest images of the characters I mentioned earlier. These would not be used on the actual covers but act as placeholders for the artist to paint his own version of each character in the designated space. I silhouetted each character image and placed it on my cover file. I decided a black background would be nice and simple and allow each character to pop off the page. Something was still missing from the cover though...

SECRET WAR

After seeing that a ton of Marvel characters appear in the comics, I figured there should be a way to incorporate that into each cover. There was a page that had Nick Fury looking at a wall of computer screens filled with characters. So I used that computer

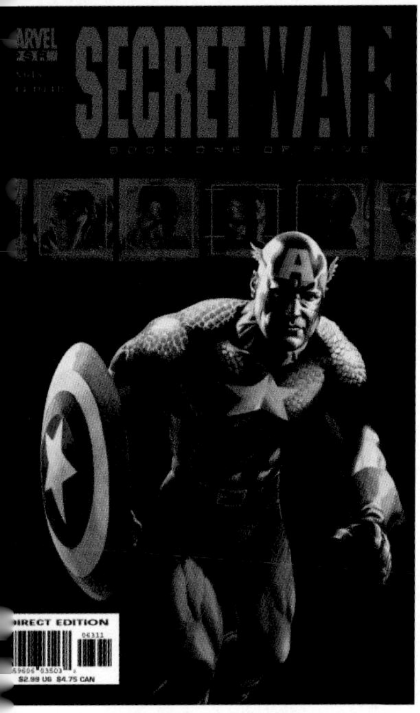
MARVEL
SECRET WAR
DIRECT EDITION
$2.99 US $4.75 CAN

FIGURE BY J. G. JONES

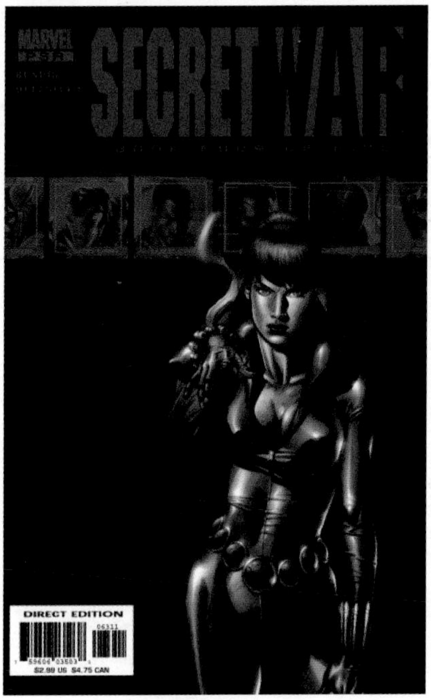
MARVEL
SECRET WAR
DIRECT EDITION
$2.99 US $4.75 CAN

FIGURE BY J. G. JONES

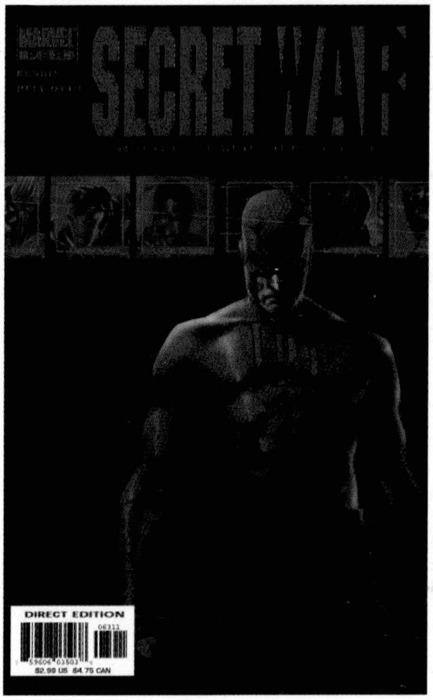
SECRET WAR
DIRECT EDITION
$2.99 US $4.75 CAN

FIGURE BY ALEX MALEEV

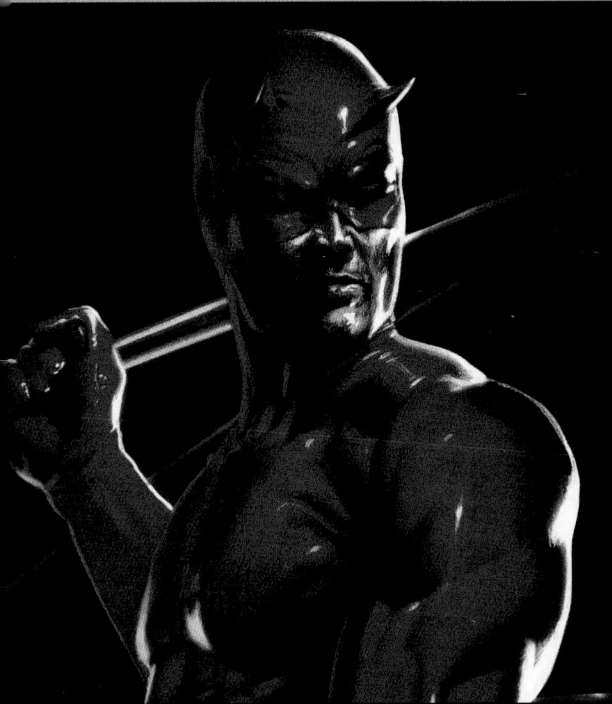

interface idea on the background of each cover, with the characters on the screen changing for each cover.

The final part of the cover was deciding what was going to be foil and what foil colors to use. Some colors were easy to pick: Daredevil—Red, Wolverine—Gold, but other characters were a little more complicated. Black Widow, for example, couldn't be black or gold to match her costume or armbands, since the background was black and Wolverine would be gold. Purple was decided on, based on the fact that we would have the artist paint Black Widow with purple highlights on her black costume. After trying different elements with foil, we decided that only the logos and text would be foiled.

So there you have it, a little behind-the-scenes of how the covers were designed. Hope you enjoyed it.

—Adam Cichowski
Cover Designer

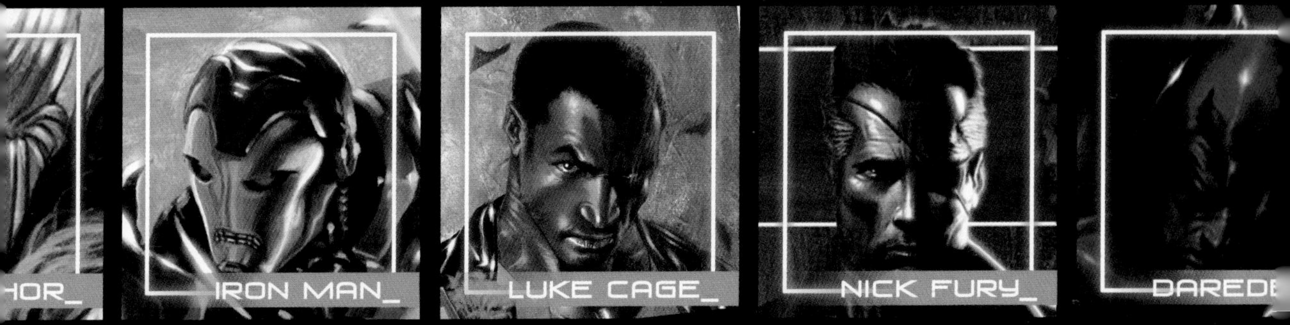
HOR_
IRON MAN_
LUKE CAGE_
NICK FURY_
DAREDE

BEHIND THE SCENES

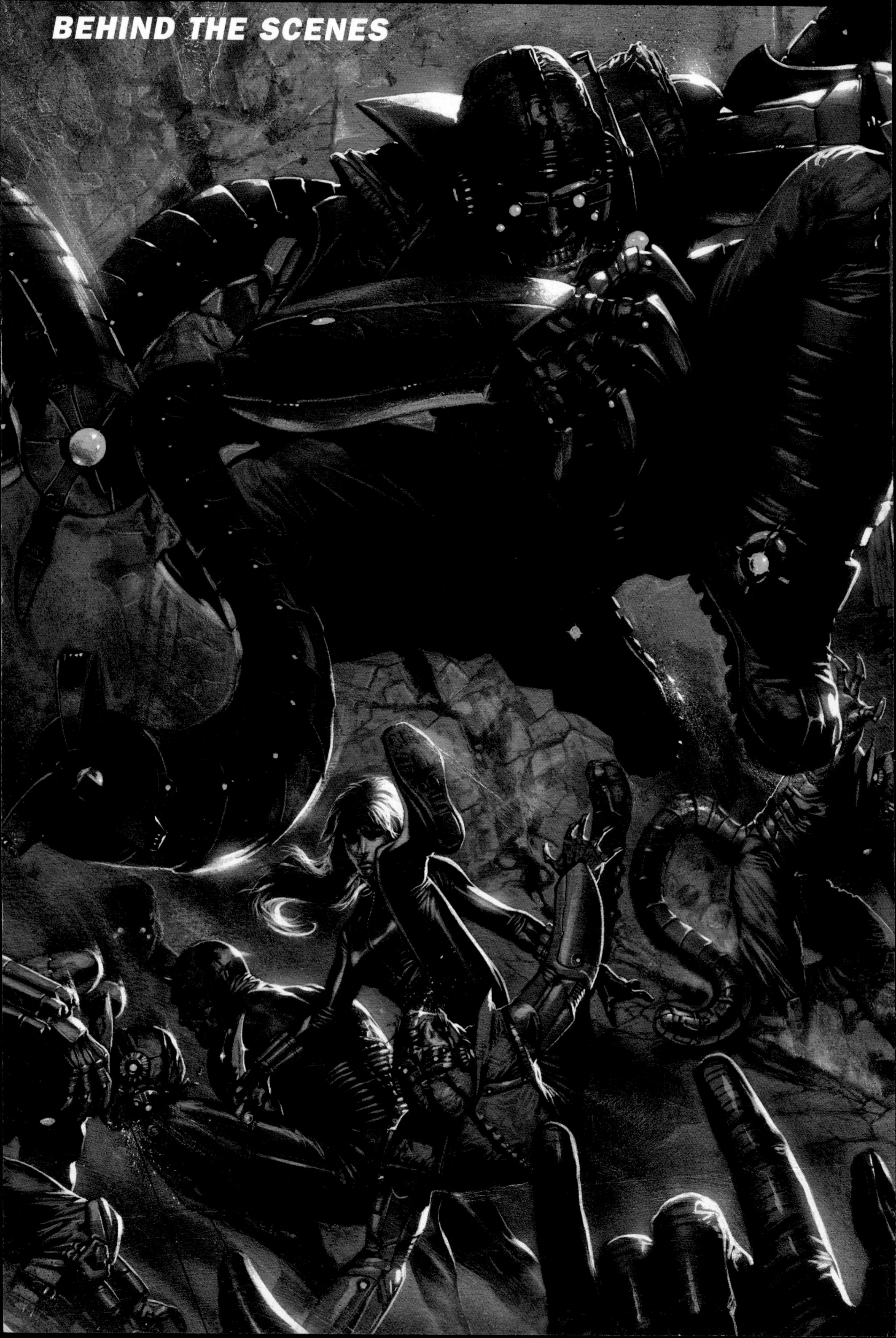

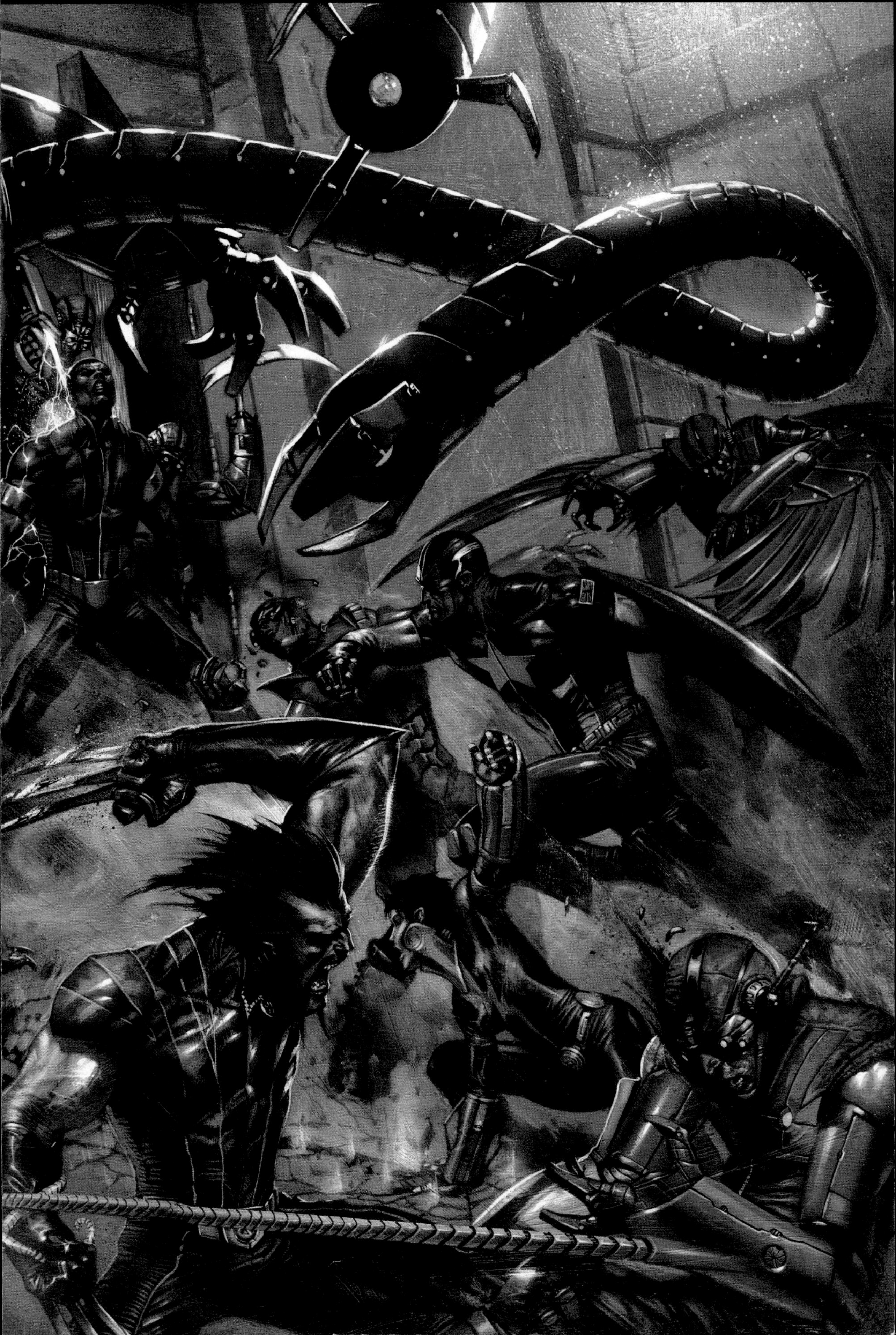

CHARACTER DESIGNS

The original idea was that the heroes would be disguised at some point in SECRET WAR. But, it was noted early on, that if they're disguised, no one, including the readers, would recognize them. What were we supposed to do with Captain America's shield--paint it black? Spider-Man's web-shooters? Wolverine's claws? How does one hide these things?

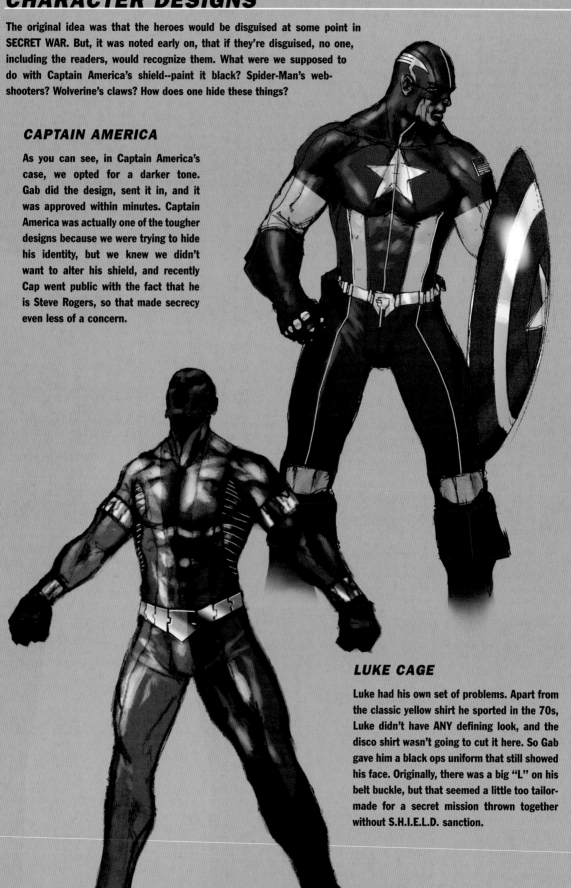

CAPTAIN AMERICA

As you can see, in Captain America's case, we opted for a darker tone. Gab did the design, sent it in, and it was approved within minutes. Captain America was actually one of the tougher designs because we were trying to hide his identity, but we knew we didn't want to alter his shield, and recently Cap went public with the fact that he is Steve Rogers, so that made secrecy even less of a concern.

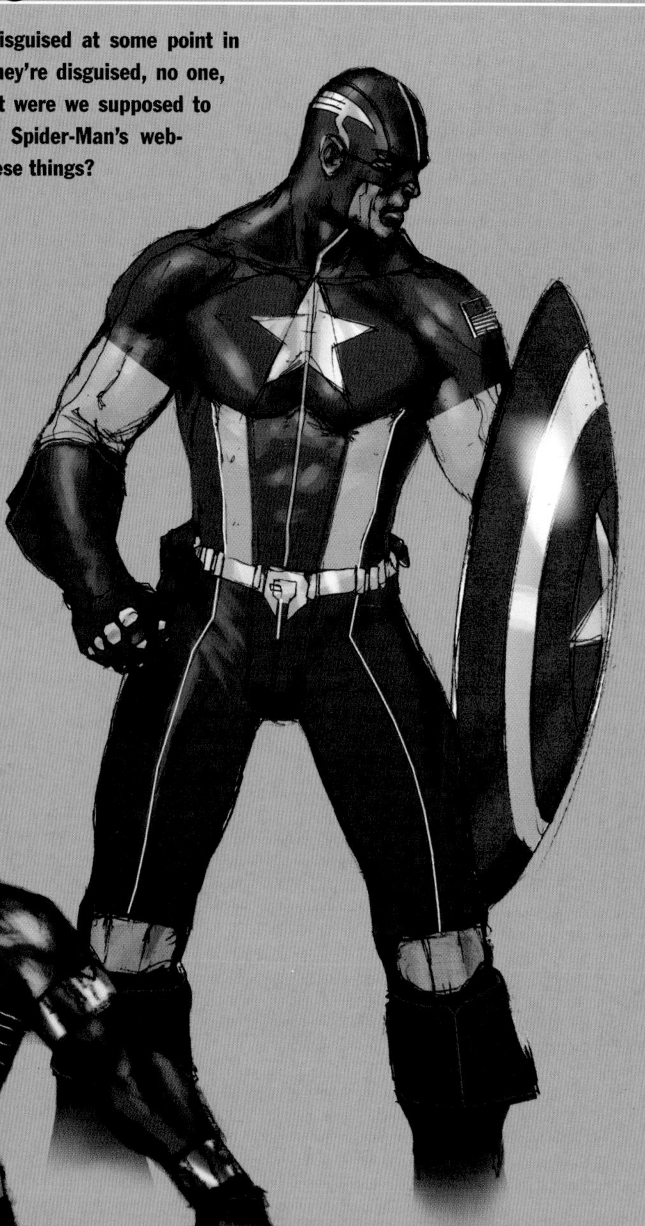

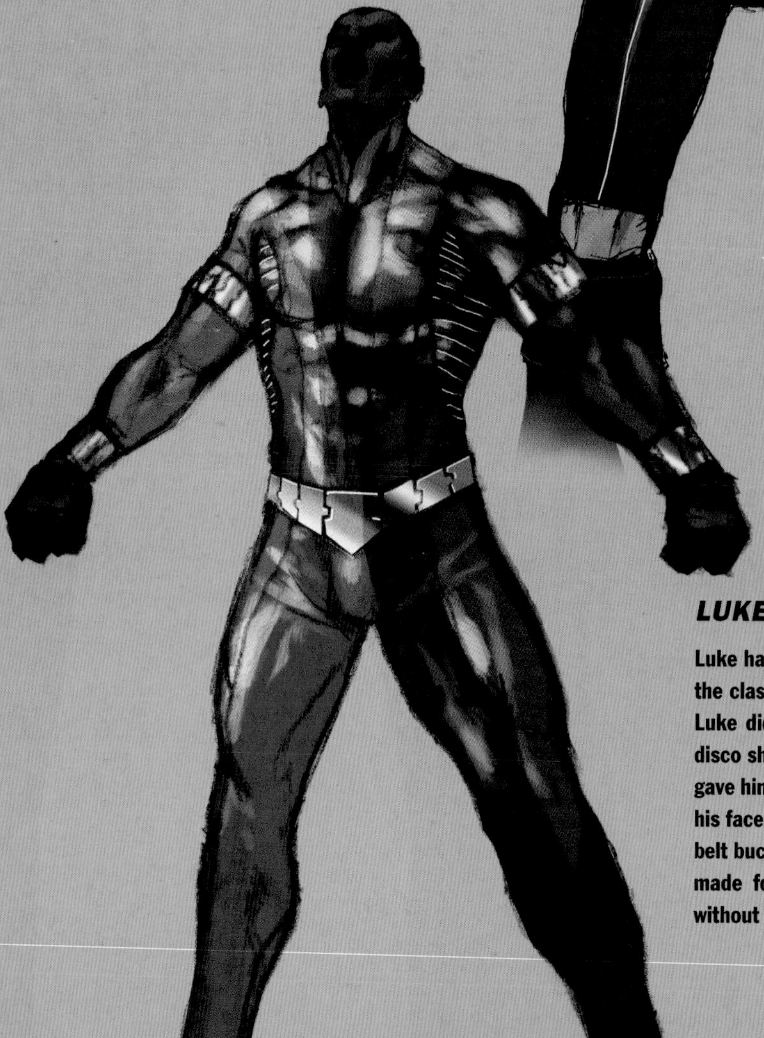

LUKE CAGE

Luke had his own set of problems. Apart from the classic yellow shirt he sported in the 70s, Luke didn't have ANY defining look, and the disco shirt wasn't going to cut it here. So Gab gave him a black ops uniform that still showed his face. Originally, there was a big "L" on his belt buckle, but that seemed a little too tailor-made for a secret mission thrown together without S.H.I.E.L.D. sanction.

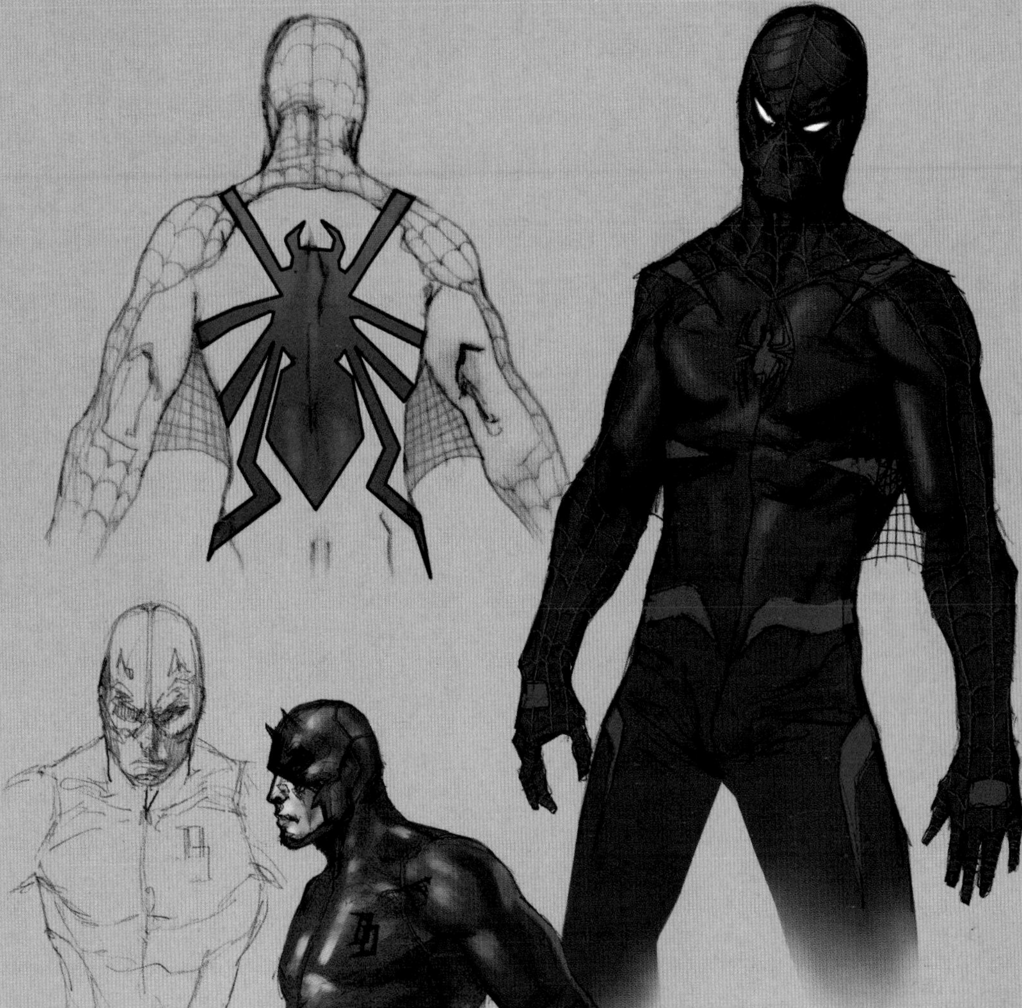

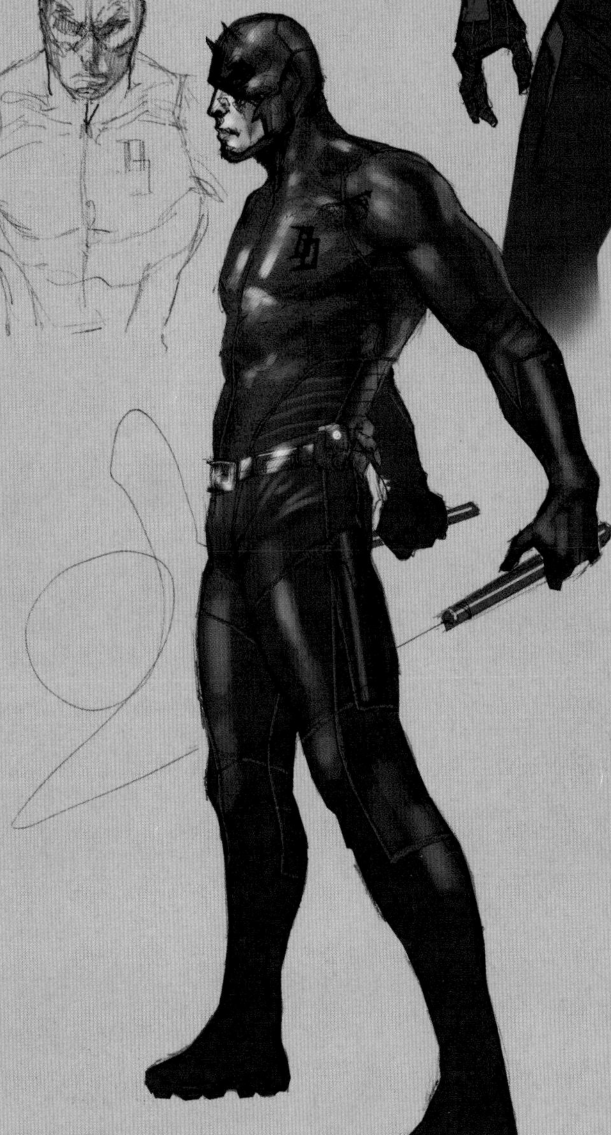

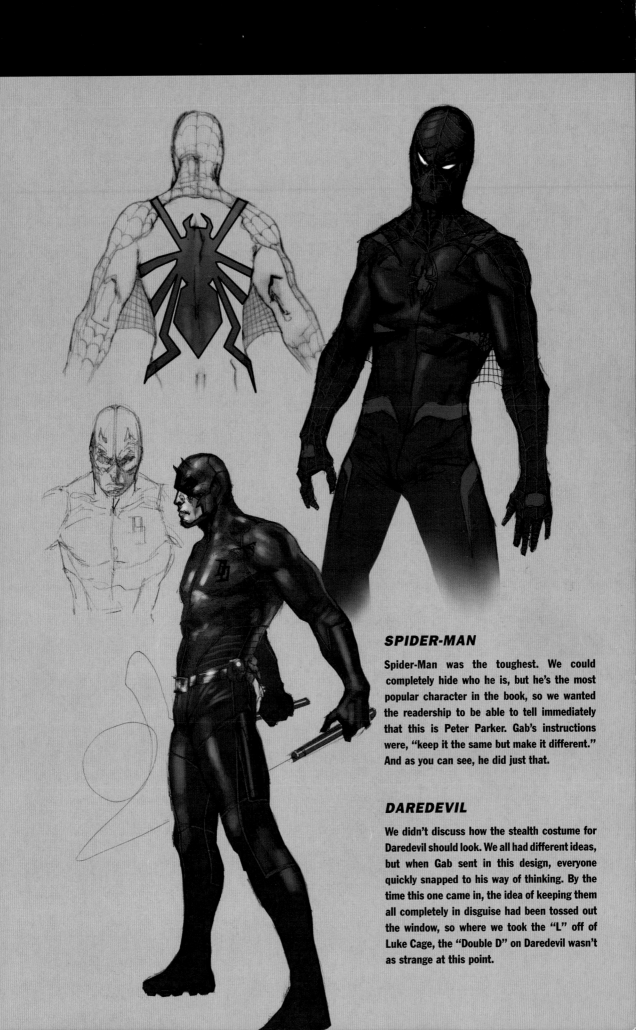

SPIDER-MAN

Spider-Man was the toughest. We could completely hide who he is, but he's the most popular character in the book, so we wanted the readership to be able to tell immediately that this is Peter Parker. Gab's instructions were, "keep it the same but make it different." And as you can see, he did just that.

DAREDEVIL

We didn't discuss how the stealth costume for Daredevil should look. We all had different ideas, but when Gab sent in this design, everyone quickly snapped to his way of thinking. By the time this one came in, the idea of keeping them all completely in disguise had been tossed out the window, so where we took the "L" off of Luke Cage, the "Double D" on Daredevil wasn't as strange at this point.

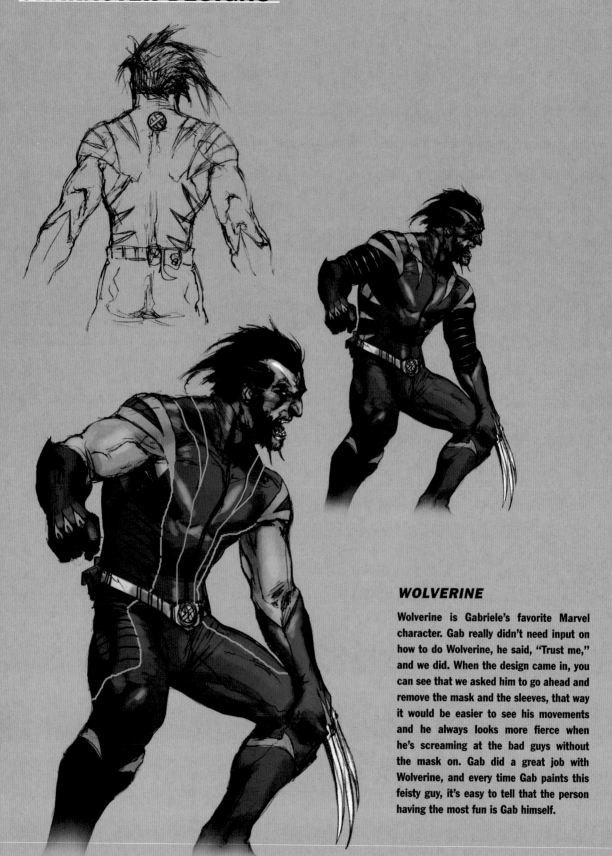

WOLVERINE

Wolverine is Gabriele's favorite Marvel character. Gab really didn't need input on how to do Wolverine, he said, "Trust me," and we did. When the design came in, you can see that we asked him to go ahead and remove the mask and the sleeves, that way it would be easier to see his movements and he always looks more fierce when he's screaming at the bad guys without the mask on. Gab did a great job with Wolverine, and every time Gab paints this feisty guy, it's easy to tell that the person having the most fun is Gab himself.

DAISY JOHNSON

Given that Brian created Daisy specifically for SECRET WAR, we let Gab know that other than her age, she was all Gab's to design. Gab picked up on Daisy's cocky attitude and gave her the short hair and sharp look that makes her charming. For the battle suit, Gab went with the color scheme he used with Luke Cage to help give the stealth costumes a more unified look.

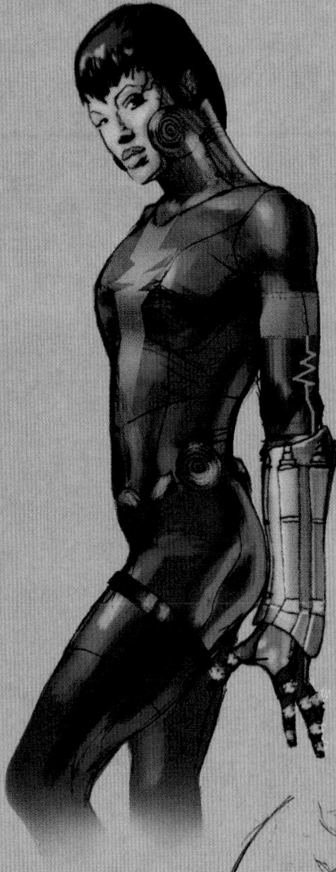

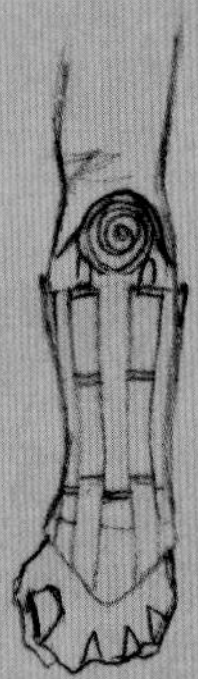

TECH WARRIOR

Gab also did drafts on several of the tech-themed villains making appearances, and here is one of his first soldier designs.

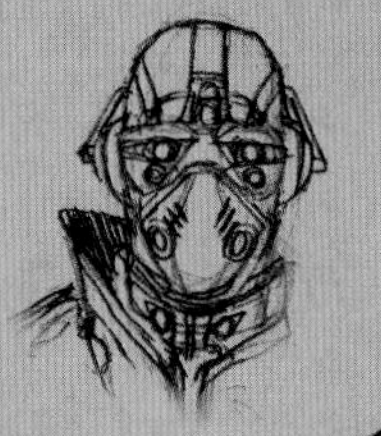

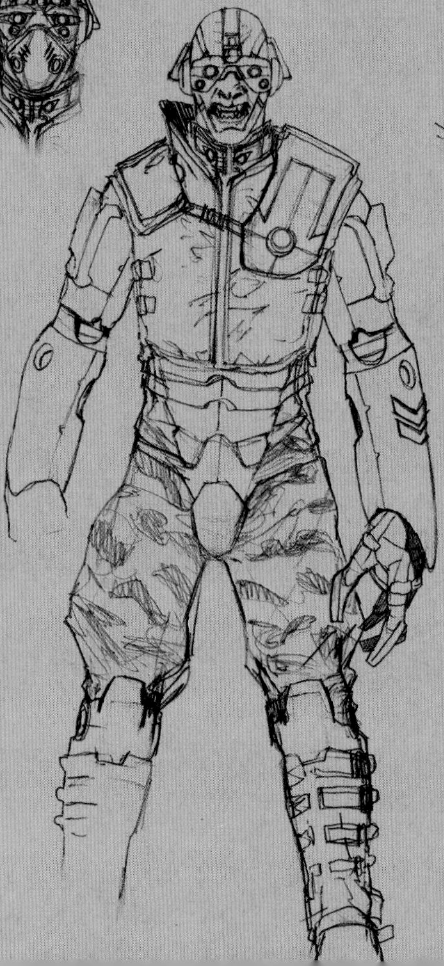

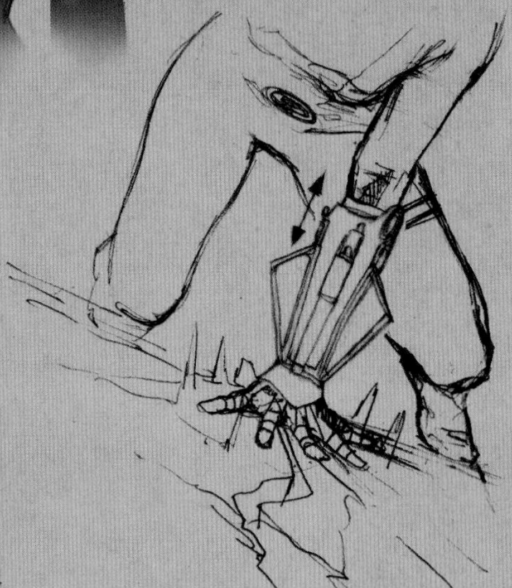

EPILOGUE

While the designs are now out in the open, the real question isn't what the heroes looked like, or even why they needed the different costumes; the question is: what was their mission, and did they succeed or fail?

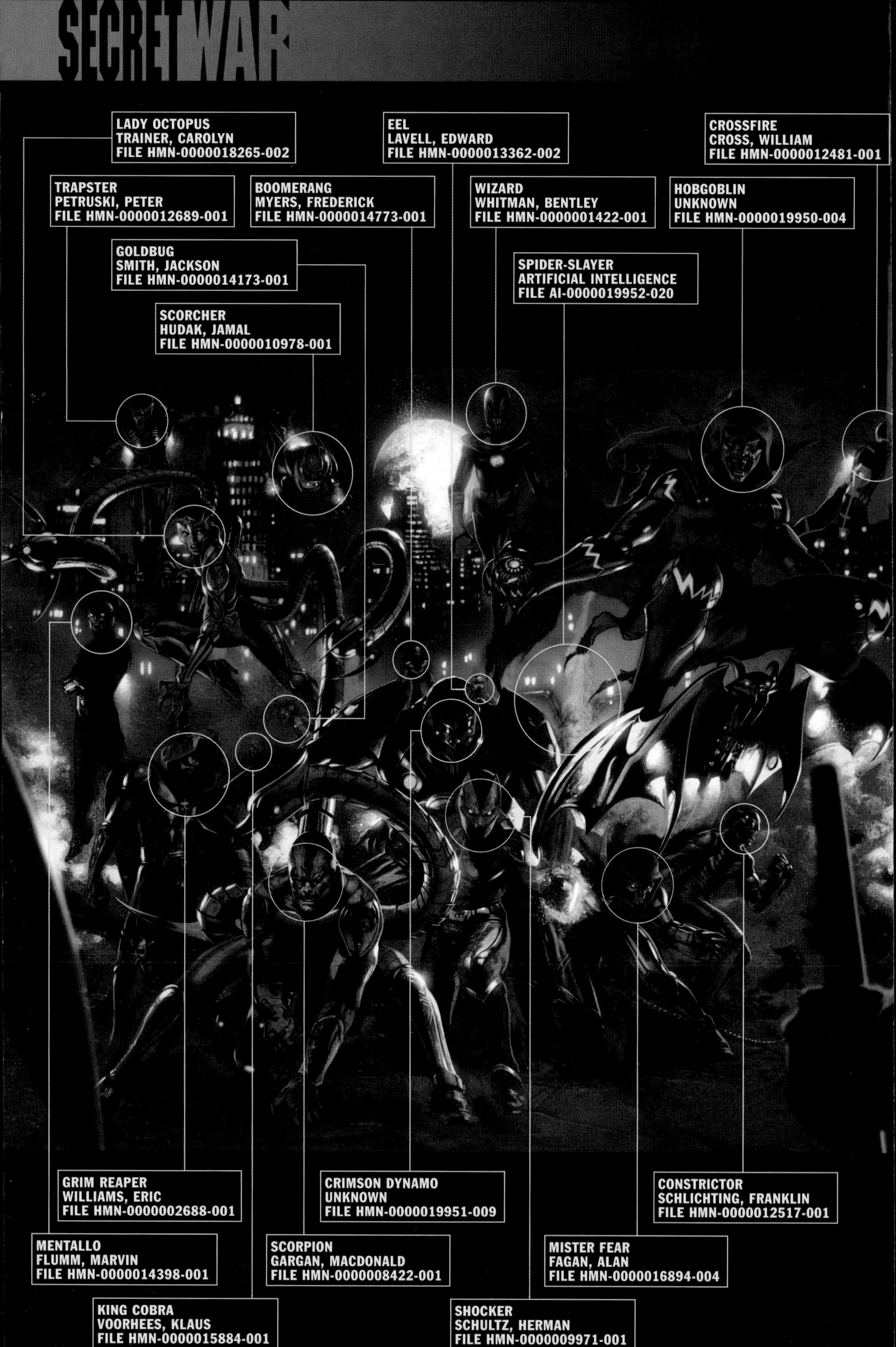
SECRET WAR
LADY OCTOPUS
TRAINER, CAROLYN
FILE HMN-0000018265-002
EEL
LAVELL, EDWARD
FILE HMN-0000013362-002
CROSSFIRE
CROSS, WILLIAM
FILE HMN-0000012481-001
TRAPSTER
PETRUSKI, PETER
FILE HMN-0000012689-001
BOOMERANG
MYERS, FREDERICK
FILE HMN-0000014773-001
WIZARD
WHITMAN, BENTLEY
FILE HMN-0000001422-001
HOBGOBLIN
UNKNOWN
FILE HMN-0000019950-004
GOLDBUG
SMITH, JACKSON
FILE HMN-0000014173-001
SPIDER-SLAYER
ARTIFICIAL INTELLIGENCE
FILE AI-0000019952-020
SCORCHER
HUDAK, JAMAL
FILE HMN-0000010978-001
GRIM REAPER
WILLIAMS, ERIC
FILE HMN-0000002688-001
CRIMSON DYNAMO
UNKNOWN
FILE HMN-0000019951-009
CONSTRICTOR
SCHLICHTING, FRANKLIN
FILE HMN-0000012517-001
MENTALLO
FLUMM, MARVIN
FILE HMN-0000014398-001
SCORPION
GARGAN, MACDONALD
FILE HMN-0000008422-001
MISTER FEAR
FAGAN, ALAN
FILE HMN-0000016894-004
KING COBRA
VOORHEES, KLAUS
FILE HMN-0000015884-001
SHOCKER
SCHULTZ, HERMAN
FILE HMN-0000009971-001

PENCILS OF GABRIELE DELL'OTTO'S FAVORITE PAGES
PAGE 5, ISSUE #1

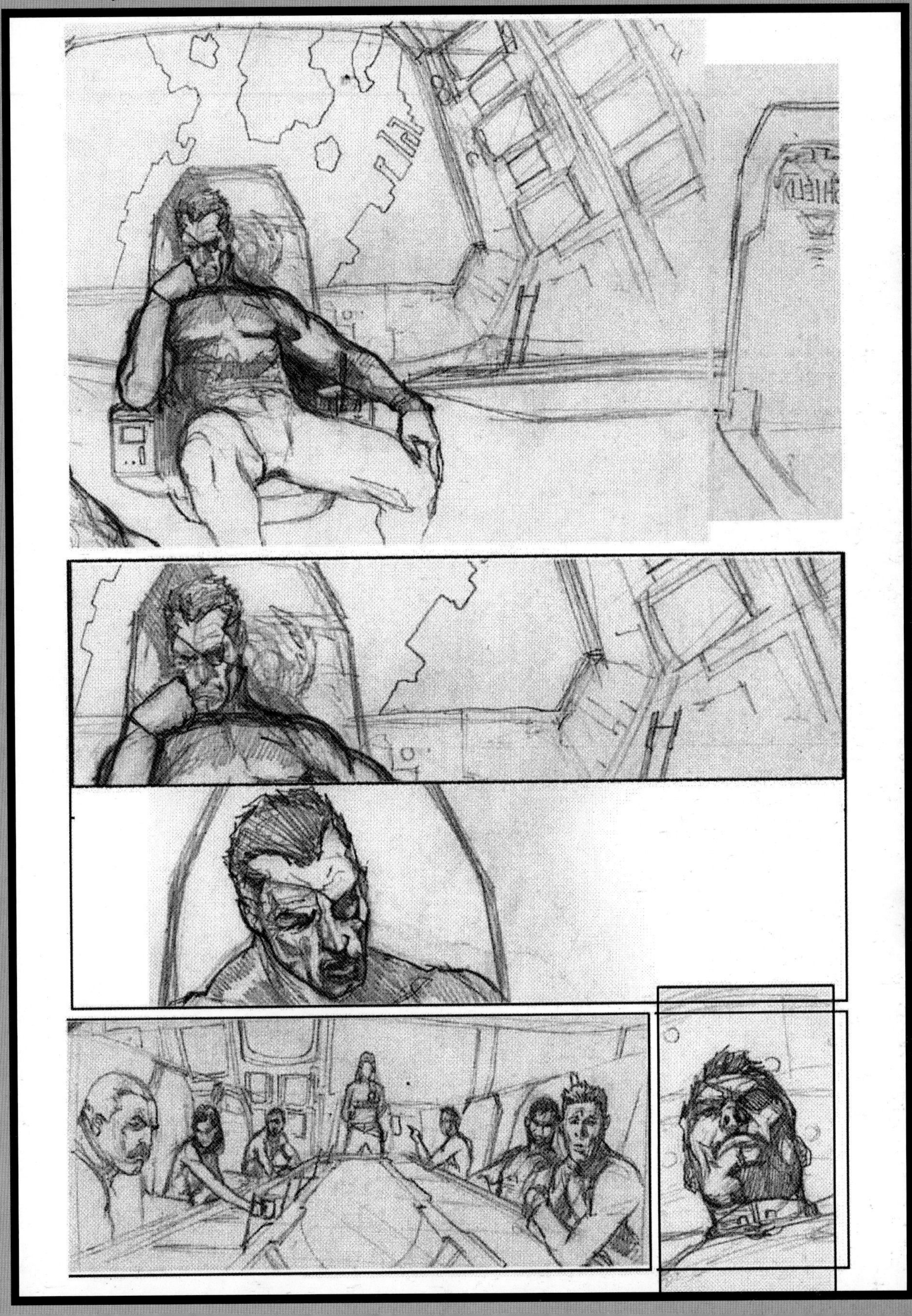

PAGE 2, ISSUE #2

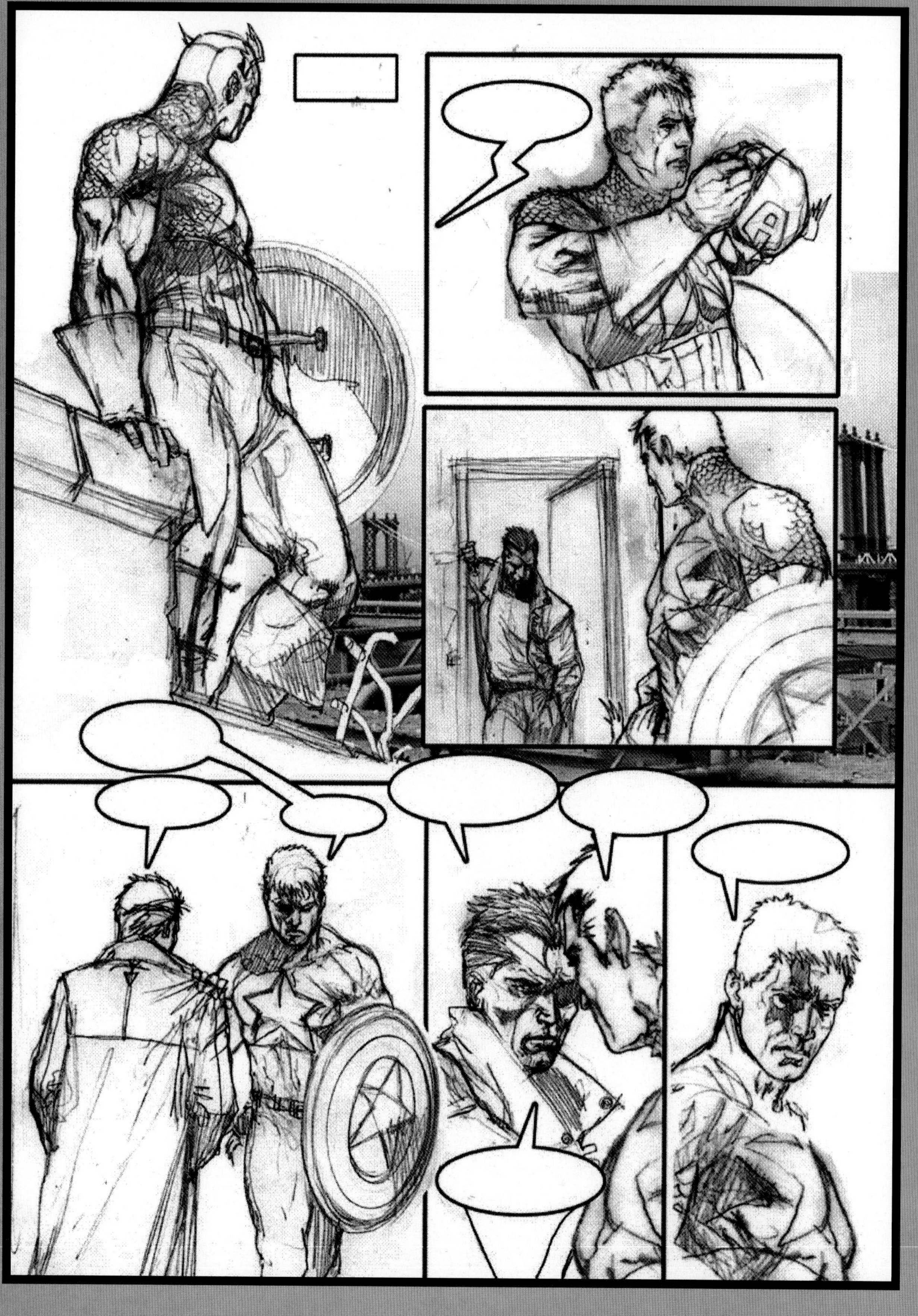

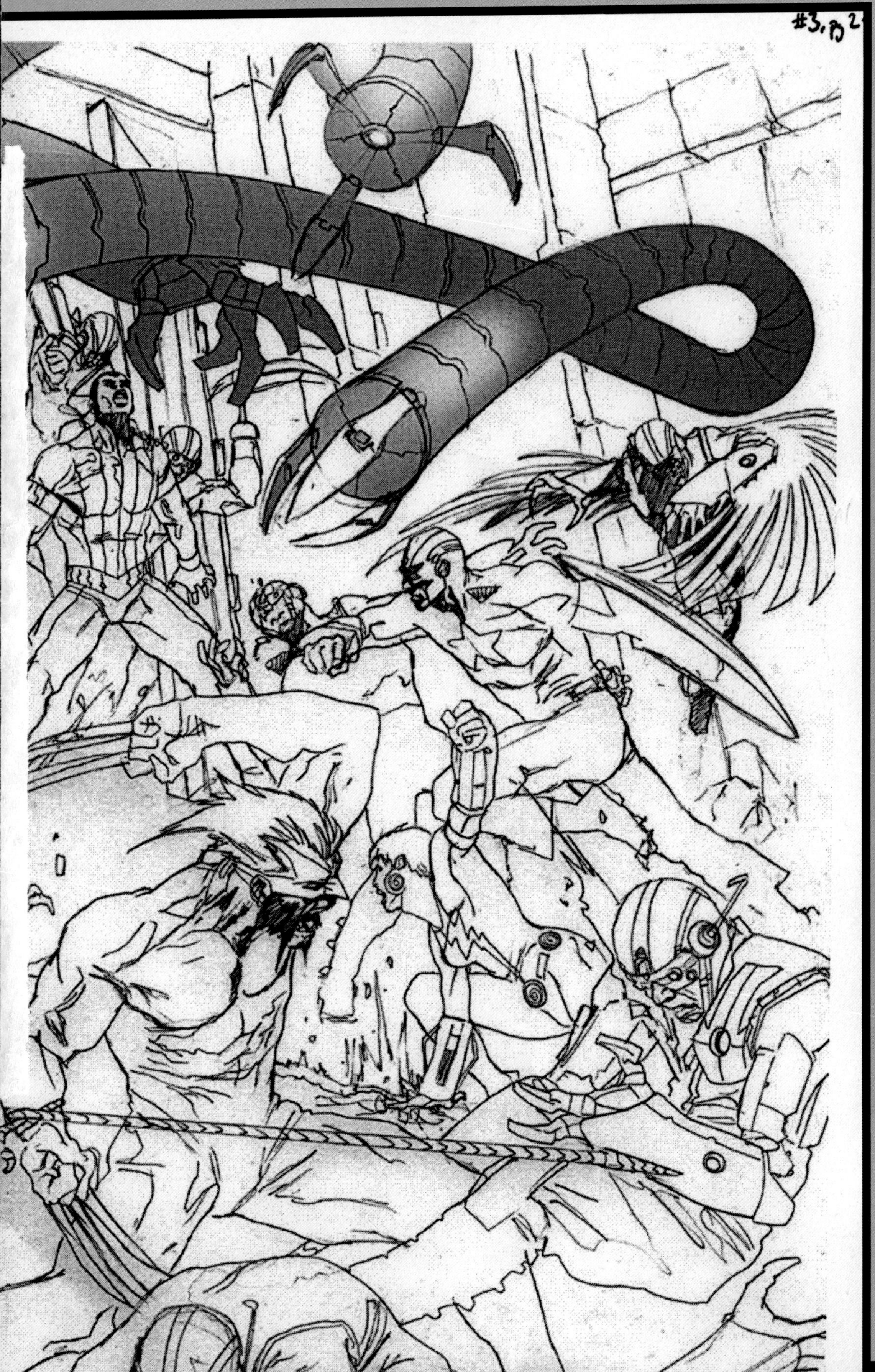
#3, pg 2.

SECRET WAR PIN-UP

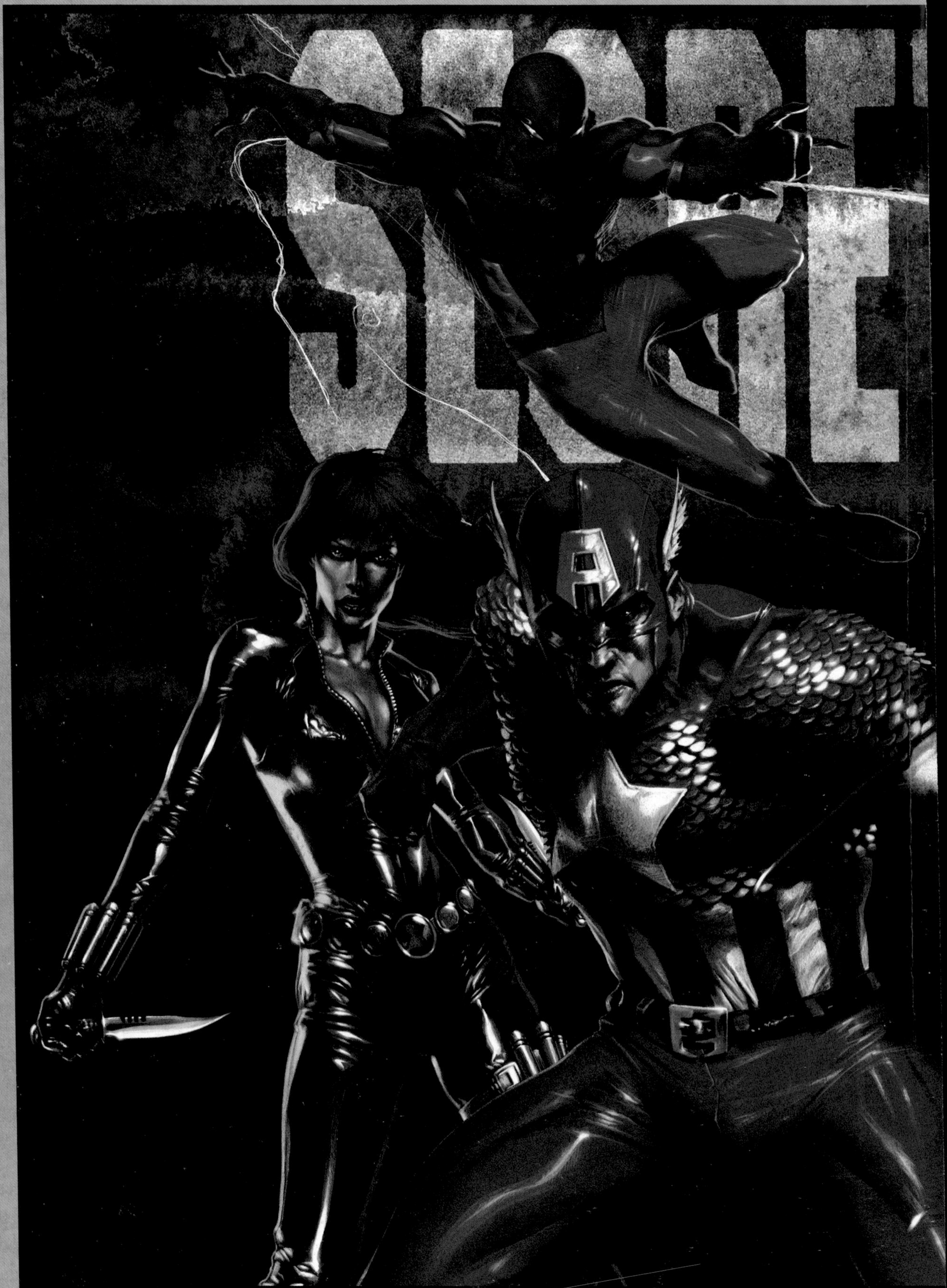

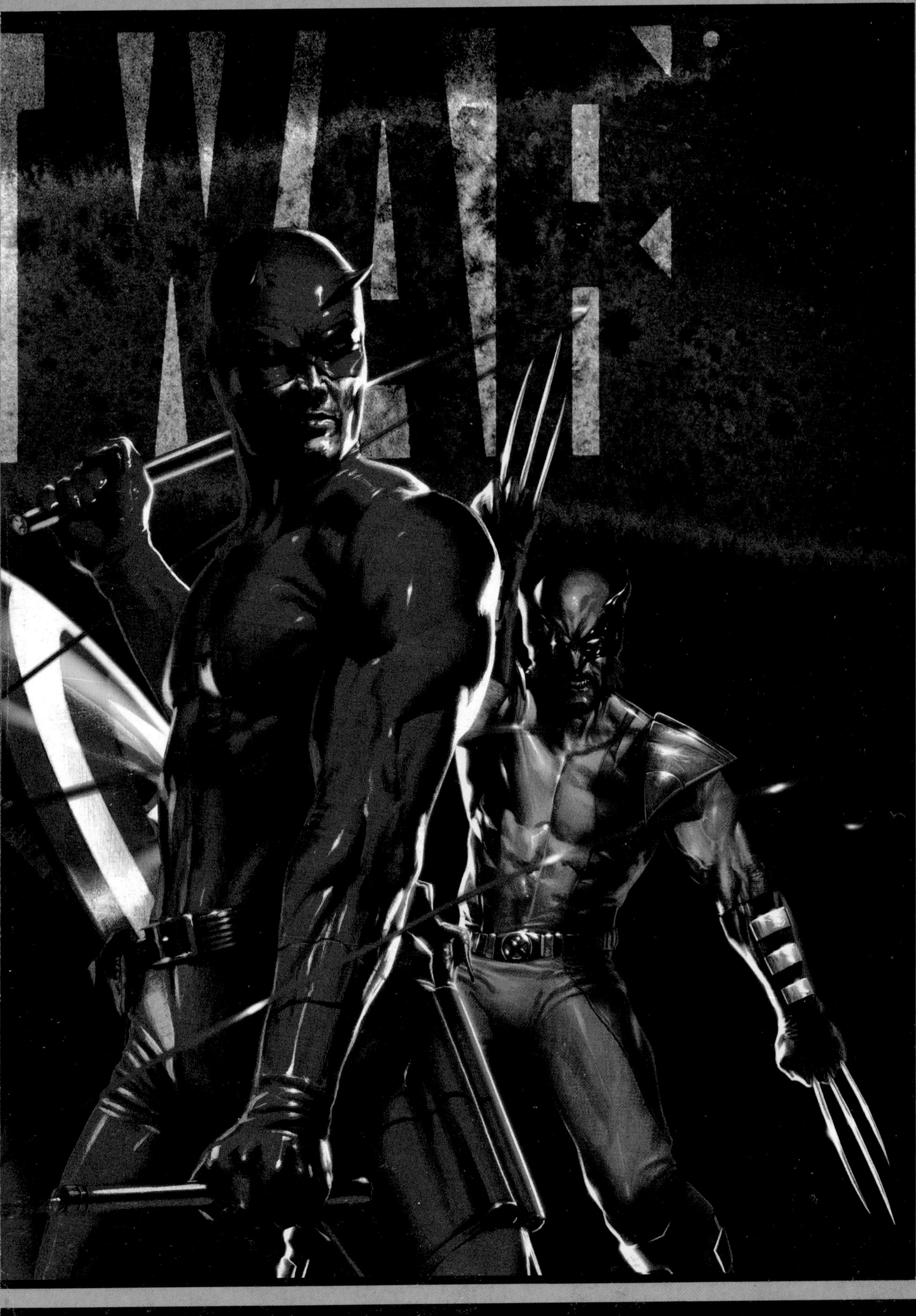

SECRET WAR

UNUSED COVER WITH SKETCH
BY GABRIELE DELL'OTTO